Genue 2024.

nE

So
LEAH

by
Geoffrey
Hellborg Moorhouse
Smiles

'BEST WISHES',

'Cosmic Smiles'

Geoffrey Hellborg Smiles

Scott
X

IN MEMORIAM

Clare Moorhouse
Norma Smiles
Winnifred Bailey
Sandie Edgeworth
Andrew Protheroe
Patricia Lumbroso
Christine Bunting
Hannah Timmings
Lyndsay Cruickshank
Jim Mcdevitt, Bernie, Oscar
Martyn Werreitt, Terry Dobney
Vic, Steve, Jeff Coull
Sebastian Blair
Mitch Skye
Howard Piper
Ashley Craven
Crispin Hackett
Tim Sebastian
Dave & Luke Hawkes
Keith 'Skinny' Prosser
Terence Septimus Brown
Peter Morss
Michael Tandy
Neil Grimmitt
Pixie, Angel, Seren
Pete Brown
Ron Coltman

These people and no doubt some others, I was
privileged to meet as I lived this book.
They touched my heart dearly.

WITH THANKS

To you, my reader.

To Saffron.

To my dear friends.
In particular Michael Bunting,
who has been my neighbour
for nearly 40 years now, even
though we live 127 miles apart.

Finally, a special thank you to
Amelia and Pippa, my grand
daughters by Elizabeth, who I hope
will grow up in a World where Peace &
good Conversation have not been lost.
Their unconditional love & laughter
is so precious to me.

'nEXt' by Geoffrey H Smiles is an imprint of
Windsong Press. Available as a Paperback and
Ebook. Copyright G.H. Smiles 2024
For further information contact the author at
geoffsmiles@icloud.com or search the web.
Cosmic Smiles music is also available on
the usual platforms, Spotify, Youtube, iTunes etc.

The right of Geoffrey Hellborg Smiles to be identified asa the
Author of this work has been asserted by him in accordance
with the Copyright, Designs and Patents Act. 1988.
Cover design G Smiles. Photos Arillas, Unearthed Festival '23
A CIP catalogue record of this book is available from the
British Library.

PROLOGUE

I am a 'Word' junkie first and foremost, any printed type on a scrap of paper draws me to it like an iron filing to a hungry magnet. I have other addictions, to which I have dedicated fifty years of my life; they are past now and I candidly offer the wisdom of those experiences within these paper walls. Like a trip up the Amazon such journeys are not for the foolhardy or the weak at heart. I also count numbers now and then, sheep or shovels, but words are my dearest love. They live in my imagination, conjuring voices from their guttural vowels and neighing consonants.

My role as a writer is to make life, beauty and art from these whimsical syllables, to tempt the eye of my reader with an entree; hoping it might entice the tongue to want more, melting on these warm lips.

The era this memoir spans laments the last hurrah of an unique species of Word, which used to roam in its millions over the plains of our civilisation but now is sadly threatened with ultimate mass extinction, 'Conversation.'

Conversation was once a beautiful but often unruly child, whose babble filled every human endeavour and yet has been slowly strangled in our own hands by mobile phones. The global cacophony of voices, loud and soft, old and young, fast and slow, being replaced by the 'Tap tap tap' of fingertips, loud and soft, old and young, fast and slow.

Stout walking shoes are recommended for reading this book and a good appetite for hunger.

OMEGA

In every end is a beginning…

"Veuve Clicquot?" The African Princess smiled at me, repeating the word Clicquot softly, then silently. The words dived onto the licked velvet cushions of her lips, the tongue, flicked forwards, cruised round the edge of her smile like a motorboat in a hot day in Paradise Bay.

She was neither African, nor a Princess, but I was undeniably willing to overlook both those points; if only she would let me dive, breathless, between the two sighs trying to escape from her lace bodice.

The problem was my fiancee, a petite red head, was still at the wedding and it wouldn't be long before she noticed the betrayal of my absence. There's a reason dynamite comes with 'Danger,' stamped on it in blood red and why the strongest pills are always the smallest.

"That would be lovely," I replied and before I could stop it, my tongue added, "Have you ever seen such a beautiful thatched cricket pavilion?"

The lawns of Stanway House drifted off westwards, through the dappled shade of trees, to reveal a cricket pitch on the far side of the road. The pavilion rested on saddle stones and seemed suspended in mid air; which is where my fiancee would want me if she knew what I was thinking. However, it was only a snapshot of impossible desires, a daydream many imaginations entertain, hoisted aloft on Champagne bubbles and cocktail sticks.

For one moment we both turned and contemplated the idyllic scene. She imagined my broad shoulders, shadowing the sunlight twinkling through the thatch, I envisioned her semi naked body, caressed against the pavilion wall, her skirt pushed up, her knickers pushed down, her legs open and the tremble of my fingers opening the Lotus.

She drew a slow deep breath in reply, her breasts blushing with the rush of emotions that ran through her body. Those impeccable lips parted and a word fell onto her tongue, rolling round her pouting smile like a ball on a Roulette wheel. Red. black, red black. But before she could speak, the ball tumbled on the white zero.

A voice shouted across the lawn. "Darling. Darling! Darling?"

As we turned, her breasts brushed against my arm, the smallest of untouchable touches. She smiled but her nose wrinkled at the sight of Oliver, the Groom, puffing across the grass to where we stood. Behind him pranced a gangly tall chap waving dramatically, as if he had sighted land after months at sea. There was a look of relief and consternation on his face.

As the African Princess turned round to them, she beamed a huge radiant smile, while quietly mouthing the word, 'Boyfriend.' Yet her face turned sideways to me for a moment and the briefest of winks caught my eye. She began a step towards them, while, with the perfection of a ventriloquist, she added, "Prick." Then, much louder, "What a view…Darling."

A bottle of Clicquot appeared in her hand, my glass wasn't empty but I let her fill it anyway. She blew a kiss at the bubbles as they spilled down the side of the bottle. Then she strolled away, forever, into the embrace of her lover. Olly glanced over his shoulder as they crossed the drive to the hall. He smiled, he was having the Wedding of a lifetime, which is what it should be.

I followed behind them, dragging my feet, stopping to sip the champagne. By the time I had circled the lake they were gone. 'Jesus,' I whispered to myself, 'What was all that about?' The girl had been flirting coyly with me, it was her suggestion that we took a stroll for some fresh air. Which wasn't a bad idea as she had that breathless beauty.

I rearranged the thumping drumbeat in my trousers and entered the Great Hall. The table, where rows of Veuve Clicquot bottles had stood earlier was now spread with every delight and delicacy. Waitresses circled with bottle after bottle of bubbles and more bubbles.

A brief scan of the room didn't reveal my girlfriend and I presumed she was on the lawns at the back of the house that ran up to the fountain, probably looking for me, a regular occupation of hers. I never wander off purposely, I just seem to get involved in some conversation or passing event; I go out for a pint of milk it could be hours before I return; it's just my way of walking through life. I am a wanderer.

At the other end of the room I saw a huge pink couch and decided the best ploy would be to sit it out there and await her return.

To be honest whatever small dent I had made in the twenty grand's worth of champagne was starting to pay off and I figured five minutes lining my stomach with a few Vol au Vents would recharge me.

I was the world's worst drinker at that time, though with regular practise I have become slightly better at it. I unsteadily propped myself against the armrest on the couch with a plate of pastries and my glass. However, I spent an unlucky half hour pushing them round the plate as some blond was giving me the Cosmopolitan, 'Five questions to ask a man to find out if he's filthy rich or fuckable.' It was the late'ish Eighties, an era of prosperity and aspiration.

As she ticked off the first three: salary, house owner and job, she began to get quite excited. So I added a resume of the joys of smoking Cannabis just to calm her gold rush.

Foolishly, something I'm surprisingly good at, I got so enamoured of my topic I added with great gusto and an inappropriate hand gesture, "It also makes sex fabulously intense!" just as my girlfriend's head appeared behind her. I always had impeccable bad timing, when it came to screwing up.

"Hi darling." That was enough to convince the blond it was Game Over. I call her the 'Blond' as I only really saw the side of her head. She sauntered off and quarried the next 'Cosmo' survey.

A girl like that had been packed off to her friend's wedding in the Cotswolds, at Lord So and So's, with strict instructions from her girlfriend's not to come back without a Duke or Prince. Every girl dreamed of being Diana in those days, or her best friend.

"Don't fucking 'darling' me. Take me home now!" Her leg red hair was flicking flames at me while her green eyes bored through my soul. She was right about my dreams of infidelity, but wrong about their infatuation. Where the hell had that African Princess gone?

"But babe, it's Rosie and Olly's wedding, come on, what's the matter?"

"You know fucking well what's the matter. Take me home. Now." She hadn't liked the blond's intentions either, yet had presumed I was the instigator.

"But honey I've been drinking."

"Not my problem, take me home." She turned and began walking towards the other end of the room. The beautifully carved archway led through to the huge front door.

'Shit.' I got up and followed. Two minutes later we were in my car. The three litre engine tore the stones off the drive as I took her back. In less than another two minutes we were at my cottage, 'Windsong.' The passenger door slammed and I headed back. It was pointless hanging about to be assassinated. Anyway my good friends were depending on their guests to pay their parts with gusto! Lines of 'Coke,' were animating the conversation and somewhere an African princess may be waiting, wondering where that tall man with the long blond hair had gone.

Sadly, she had gone, whisked off by a disgruntled beau before midnight to the hotel. I plundered the remains of cake and champagne in the hall while meeting endlessly beautiful people. The lawns at the back were bathed in the half light of summer nights as yellow flames danced like figurines on candles within the stained glass windows.

I would run through the grounds regularly, it was one of my routes, giving old Lordy a wave as I shot past his study and headed up the landscaped lawns.

Stanway House was made of butterscotch and honey stone with layers of cream between. Two gently sloping banks brought you up to the lake, where ducks and swans pottered about like gentry, nonchalantly. In the centre a small metal nozzle would emit, on Tuesdays and Thursdays, the highest gravity powered fountain in Europe, I believe. It delighted any audience, young or old, rich or poor, famous or infamous.

I circumambulated the long thin strip of silver water, somewhat erratically, sqiffy as all that champagne and Vol au Vent of emotion hit me. It couldn't be described as walking, I was drifting. Half way up the rise that led to the Folly with its perfectly round pond I turned back and surveyed my universe.

You really just cannot write a book like mine, you have to live it, as painful and ecstatic as the process is, there is no other way to do it. I was blessed and cursed as a growing boy to have the girl forced out or into me. That cunning intuition, that self serving protection failsafe, if all other brain cells fail. I knew the woman I had loved, so truly once upon a time, was unfortunately a beautiful portrait on a canvas with such a dark heart.

The centre of my soul was pretty messy too, normally awash with chemical residues and toxic waste. I just couldn't put the needle away, forever. I knew too, I couldn't do 'Forever' with her. I was slowly learning that a person's inner spirit was vital to the deal of life for me. How the hell was I going to sort this mess out?

I was in no hurry to return to the glowing lights below. All day I had listened to smiling faces go, 'You'll be next...' I thought, 'like fuck I will.' I had discovered my gorgeous babe was a tiger with a viper necklace, all five foot, one flipping inch of her. I'm sure she's mellowed out now but boy she could blow a woman out of a shopping mall at fifty feet with just one look. I learnt way too much about women from her.

My eyes followed the rooftops of the manor house, across the tops of ancient trees, past the beautiful thatched pavilion and the cricket pitch. They picked up the line of the old steam railway, over the viaduct, to where Windsong waited. A small cottage, the middle of three, slap bang in the middle of paradise. No wonder it entranced others as it did me.

The bell of Stanton church called out one sonorous gong, or was it two or three, along the north escarpment of the Cotswold Hills. I climbed the last bit of the slope and sat on the wall of the folly. 'Ah well, something will happen.' It usually did.

I suddenly remembered the Genesis gig at Knebworth the following day. Andy, best man to Olly, a great jeweller and drummer had a spare ticket. As his musical buddy I had got it. Perhaps that's what had pissed madam off, it was all a bit last minute. Departure was due at stupid o'clock in the morning, single figures, so I decided it was time to split.

I made my way back down to the house. I went in the side door, up past Lordy's study, down the corridor to the library. The ashtrays were full, that was about it. The drawing room on the way back to the hall had a couple draped on each sofa. The hall itself was silent the huge stained glass window was melting honey down moonlit tapestries. I closed the front door and sauntered over the gravel and down the drive. The lake looked like a scene from a fairy tale. I wondered how the African Princess was getting on, whether she might possibly be African and even, maybe, a princess?

Way too early the next day a small silver sports car came flying round the corner at the back of the cottage coming to a dusty stop. I guessed Andy had probably had as little sleep as me, though for different reasons. He was a natural night Owl whereas I was a born Lark. I waved through the kitchen window at the shadow in the driver's seat, finished my coffee and quickly dashed into the bathroom. Splashing the cold water on my face helped to wake me up. As I opened the back door I thought about shouting, 'See you babe,' up the stairs, but I didn't. No point in waking an unhappy woman, that much I knew; or if I did, it better be with croissants and roses. I had neither of these, nor the inclination.

I discovered after a gig that summer the darkness and unkindness that dwelt within her heart. I had experienced one of those moments when she said something and I could have just opened the car door and walked away right then and there.

Despite the traffic! However, the car was a Toyota Supra, in metallic blue, so I endured the jam out of Wembley, but it was one of those blunt sign posts, 'Dead End.' It was only a matter of time before we split up. Youth can be that strong or self sufficient, or was it heart felt or heartless?

"Hey dude. You ok?" One look at Andy was enough to convince me to shut the car door quietly. Poor bugger looked worn out; perhaps his Best Man duties had left him adrift on the good ship Clicquot too.

"Sure, can't wait. We'll stop for coffee and breakfast in a while. Bit knackered but hey it's rock and roll. Isn't it?"

"Fab. Well done mate. You had much sleep?"

"Few hours."

"Me too. You want me to drive?"

His brow frowned for a millisecond. "Nah, I'm fine. You catch a nap if you want." He flicked a switch on the steering wheel and Genesis began to hum through the speakers.

I thought about protesting more to drive, I like to do my bit, especially if the team Is flagging. But I could feel one of those lead weights the size of a yacht descending over me. I leant my head against the seatbelt and fell asleep.

The events of that day, the Hob Nob trick and the moment my eyes caught sight of Tania's are all detailed in my previous memoir, so I won't re run that tape. But I needed to start back at that point, like an old radio serial, picking up the story where it left off, because it was one of those days that changed my destiny.

We often consider the big decisions of our lives are pondered for weeks, pros and cons carefully weighed up and then, hey presto, we move forward in the direction chosen. I prefer the John Lennon view that 'Life's what happens while making plans to do something else.' I learnt the biggest decisions we make are often borne out of the smallest and most insignificant choices.'

My career as a Teacher was due to a five word advert in a Bristol Newspaper, 'Part Time Sports Teacher needed.' Had I not bought a paper that day, had I not been walking up Whiteladies Road, I wouldn't have seen the shop, had I caught the bus instead? Such is life in my view.

Returning home from Knebworth with Tania's phone number etched in the 'Do not forget this you pillock,' part of my brain was going to change the future forever. Had I not committed this monumental cock up with Fate's help, I may just have found myself on an inescapable route being married. As nice as that normally sounds, it would have been a disaster for any woman with me. It's not a melodrama, it is just I knew my limits then…There were few.

Also, life with a musician was like sharing a twin heart, as well as the drugs and the lack of drugs. However, I had figured getting 'engaged' was, contrary to popular beliefs not one step to the altar but a statement of intent and belief. I know, wrong again! I thought it was a cool idea.

But in the end the biggest decision in my life at that time came down to Andy's girlfriend not using the ticket and a packet of biscuits. So many 'What If's?'

This is the the way life has a habit of turning corners while I thought I was going straight ahead. Thus I soon gave up trying to fashion my future out of my present dilemmas. I turned my energy towards riding the roller coaster than was, 'Today... Right here right now. This pile of dogshit.'

I didn't really fathom it out at the time, I was too enthralled with the chase and the smell of fresh perfume to wonder why I was suddenly entering the world of youth, with its first throes of passion, about fifteen years late. But that one day at Knebworth, led to Cambridge then Oxford, those mysterious ancient places of learning and of course debauchery.

Gaz opened the drawer of his desk and said, "I guess you'll be needing these." He pointed to a pack of condoms hidden amongst the other paraphernalia of his intellectual pursuits. On top of the desk several sheets of paper covered in small Spanish writing were becoming his latest letter to his girlfriend in Madrid.

"Nah man, this lot are a bunch of kids, fuck they're hardly out of High School and Rose got me the gig so I better be on my best behaviour." I did have a second's pause and wondered, 'Nah, it would be too easy buddy, not fair, not my style at all. I'm going to play my guitar, entertain the troops and fuck off. I should be back by one or two."

"Ok gringo," Gaz drawled in his best spaniola, "You know best. Here's my spare key. Don't lose it!"

"Ahh, thanks man, you're a real pal. Hey guess what I'm getting paid too. Fifty quid or something. God Rose is a star."

It would have been easy, as an older wiser fox with a free ticket to the 'Chicken Ball', to have planned a campaign designed to disrobe some poor pissed maiden at three in the morning. I'd been raped by three men and there was no way that pile of shit was going any further than my body, my brain, my soul. The 'Fuck' stops here. That was why young people have always known I was okay, I wasn't about to destroy their innocence, I wanted them to preserve their dreams. I was cool. Like the kids I taught, they indisputably knew I was on their side and they were safe with me. Most of us knew the look in the eyes of those other men, the way they preyed on easy meat. The Collectors, the Scavengers, the Spikers, the Bullshitters and the Dirty Old Men brigade. Never a shortage of those bastards.

"What time you playing?"

'I dunno, Rose said to get there for eight and she'd show me the set up. I think I'm entertaining at the main gate and then in the JCR. Who knows man, play it by ear.'

"Usual gig then…" Gaz smiled. He knew how hard it was to make anything different happen outside of exams, mundane reality and career jobs. Wherever we had laid our hats in life someone was soon over to tell us we couldn't leave them there. He knew like me I didn't stand a dog's chance in a minefield of making it big time with my music.

But Gaz knew music and musicians, He sure had enough proof I was one. As he was officially the other half of my first band The Intergalactic Garbage Corporation, he had prior knowledge of my commitment, honest barre shoplifting commitment. Yeah, I should have been committed.

We had played our one and only official gig at the Bridgewater Arts Centre many years before. Some of that audience probably never recovered! We sure made an impact. Like some flashing lights, if you didn't have epilepsy you sure would have in five minutes or so.

He went off to make a coffee and I tuned my guitar before putting it in the battered case. "Jesus Gaz, if this guitar case could talk we'd all be locked up!"

About an hour later I set off down the Cowley Road towards Magdalene Bridge and St Hilda's where the Ball was happening. I dawdled slowly past the two main music shops, one big and glassy, full of new this and newer that, the other, 'The Music Box,' was a haven for guitarists like me, a place you could always cut a deal with Keith or his side kick Gary, an awesome Tenor Sax player. This was the shop you spent hours in, prayed in to the great gods, Gibson, Fender and Marshall. This was where you met other guys, either by chance or through the hundred or so little sticky adverts scribbled on corners of paper. 'Bass Player needed. Must have transport. Gigging band.' Or maybe, 'Drummer wanted, must be able to keep time.' Gosh they wanted it all. I stopped for a minute or so trying to peer through the grill on the door to see if anything else had come in since the three hours ago when I was last there. There wasn't.

I strolled on towards Magdalene Bridge past a couple of new Vegetarian cafes. Seemed like everybody was finally catching on to the healthy trend. Browns was the Green Mecca at the time, but way over the other side of those vaulted spires.

I was early for once, so I strolled down to the bridge and stared at the shallow murky water, where droves of idiot lemmings in tucker and bib dived into history or A&E at dawn with annual devotion. Students were crossing the bridge as they had for centuries. Some, like me, wandering through the Botanical Gardens, a magical haven from the hustle of the pavements and the bustle of traffic.

No doubt one or two of these young men and their fair maidens stared somewhat incredulously at the man with a guitar case, oversize flares, Ocelot print shoes, a furry florescent mauve coat and a top hat. I was never known for understatement when it came to clothing attire. I would pout, 'If you're gonna knock them over, better knock them right over.' I had purchased the hat at a basement stall in Kensington Market years ago, it had seen a few gigs, several Druid ceremonies and many hippy festivals go by. A scarf flowed down my back, mingling its colours with a waterfall of blond hair.

Although it was just a few steps that separated me from these students, I knew I was on the other side of an impassable abyss, one carved in time by one deed almost two decades and one too many deaths ago. There was no going back to fill that chasm, the pieces were buried on hallowed ground, it was the best I could do. I had accepted the lead in my heart and by now I was so used to carrying it I felt hardly anything. I was thirty seven, I had been up and down that valley road from Shitsville to Paradise and back so many times I could do it blind. I never thought I would have the chance to walk back into a story I had left behind one night at boarding school.

However, there was one other factor about that top hat I should mention, it was a Magic hat. Despite a wry smile, I would never jest about such Arts, I know their sinuous tentacles. That hat had attended many spiritual gatherings at Rollright Stones, Avebury and Stonehenge, I think it had been quietly stashing away Spells, for it worked a miracle that night.

Had I not absconded from boarding school for one late night party at the end of term I should have arrived on Magdalene Bridge, or its equivalent in Cambridge in 1977, not the mid Nineties. I was fully aware that I could have walked in those footsteps, if only I had towed the 'Straight and Narrow,' as my House Master Mr Knott drummed into me. But that was never me, a wanderer follows a wandering path.

I can only describe that path of life as having some magical properties, from beginning to end really. However I regret those fallen from grief, the losses and scars of those who stood beside me, loving me, watching me destroy myself and their dreams. It must have been almost as bad as loosing a child, to know I was out there, somewhere on those streets playing with the devil.

I learnt also that almighty journeys usually began from a few small moments upon a bridge, between Here and There. A career, a love affair, can start with a few words on a piece of paper, a phrase, a line of Life Poetry.

However, despite the amazing journey some days I felt I'd come so far to reach Nowhere in Particular. If just one of my plans in life got a bit of stardust luck, a break, a showcase. I hate to admit it but by the time I'd been slapped in the face by a Kipper three times I started to hate the mere mention of them. I got fried and battered way too much.

Lack of faith in future plans led me to prefer to go with the roll of the dice on the day. I make it up as I watch the world heading towards me. In my twenties and thirties, free from but also without the guidance of elders, I was still a big step behind the game, expending lots of energy into thin air to make almost zero. Everything I did pretty much was, 'If you can afford Free, book me.' It was idealistic, but perhaps hardly realistic. I've not changed much.

I felt in my pocket for a coin and found a silver five pence. I flicked it into the water below and wished, 'Make tonight a good one.' I picked up my guitar case and left the rush of Magdalene Bridge. Round the corner, the sprawling mass of the Prep School building was spread out twenty feet below me, the grounds ran down to the river bank. Through leaded windows I could hear slices of chatter, high pitched animated voices. I knew those conversations, the rooms they came from, the huge radiators, the dark panelled walls, the rules and the silence of well worn floors; the photos on the walls, the teams, the lists, the names, the dates, the competitions and prizes; faded echos of mind photos.

I made my way down the side street towards the gates of St Hilda's. It wasn't far. There were lights and balloons in bunches attached to the railings, shapes fluttered about like butterflies in a gas light.

I wandered through the open gates, usually locked and past the Porter's Lodge, into the heady scent of perfume promenading from the corridors.

I found Rose, bless her, she had got me the gig, if you could call it that. The plan was for me to sing and entertain the queue as the students turned up for the ball. I figured that was fairly easy enough as I'd busked a few hundred pavements in my time. Then there was to be a sort of music 'Free for all' in the JCR, Junior Common Room, which had a piano and a makeshift stage in one corner. More lights and more bunches of balloons bouncing off ceilings.

Girls were rushing back and forth. It was a college for young women only in those days. But the mood felt like a girl's teenage birthday, bursting with joy and excitement from every orifice.

I nodded, concluding my assessment of the night at Gaz's had been right, a bunch of kids at play, the brightest buttons of the lot were here trying to get seriously tarnished, la creme de la creme about to curdle the night away.

I smiled, "Looks like it's going to be a great night. Thanks Rose."

"We'll sort the cash out tomorrow, I'll pick up yours. Do you need any money tonight?" Rose knew me too well.

"No, I'm good, I may have a pint later. I've got that." I didn't do drinking much then and especially not before gigging, I had my guitar to look after.

I milled about for awhile until the first guests began arriving. The weather was threatening to be wet but just kept holding off long enough for me to play. I seemed to be making the punters laugh, either at me or with me, I didn't care. It must have been an odd sight, a Hippie, flown in from the Seventies, to entertain Oxford's intelligentsia. Rose returned a bit later and smiled. I was in full flood, entertaining. She was happy.

The boys in the Tuxedos, the girls in their evening gowns were just stunning, the most beautiful visions I could imagine, arriving in pairs, triples and groups.

Gosh what a world, I'd never seen this lot busking outside Woolworths. I wondered, if only I had played it safer, but it was too late for a Wonderer now.

There was a sprinkling of rain but I carried on, the hat kept me dry and the guitar had weathered worse storms. The queue wasn't slackening much and as a small bundle fed past the ticket table a voice called out with an Irish lilt, "I like your Top Hat."

I looked closer at the queue to see who it was. The voice belonged to a red lipsticked smile, surrounded by a mass of dark curls, wrapped in a black feather 'Boa.'

"I like your Boa."

The figure laughed, "Maybe we can do a swop later." That was it. She disappeared, a flash of red dress caught my eye and vanished on long legs.

"Sure," I shouted after her, more for polite banter than any curiosity. After all 'Magic' hats were hard to come by and I wasn't sure what the hell to do with a Boa, feathers or not! I didn't even like snakes.

The light rain eventually moved me under a tent serving drinks where I carried on playing. At last the queue ended, except for sporadic taxis disgorging semi drunk bucks, draped over or under beautiful women. Tonight the odds were stacked in the boy's favour. What wealth they plundered or squandered?

"Hi Geoff," Rose handed me a glass of champagne, "Well done, they loved you." Her friends on the Ball Committee had approved apparently and she was hoping to impress, as everyone was, at Oxford. "Have a break and then come to the JCR." She was lovely, an all round sound trooper. If Rose was on a team, winning seemed assured.

The music was memorable that night as the sound system broke down almost immediately and I had to fill in with acoustic guitar until a young woman turned up and started singing along next to the piano. The poor bloke on the ivories was as relieved as I was when her voice filled the room.

Years later Rebecca would be a singer in my band. One night she mentioned a gig in Oxford where the sound had gone wrong and she had sung with a guy on piano and some bloke on guitar. "That'll be me."

I also remember a German Frau' who seemed to be hitting on me, but I dismissed her gently thinking she would surely regret it the next day. I wouldn't. But it was too easy, not my style. Besides, it would just be my luck she had a brother studying Law and Rugby, who happened to be visiting her this weekend. Help!

On the pretext of going to the bar I disappeared into the crowd. I loitered near the throng waiting at the heaving counter, trying to decide if I was going to even bother having another drink or wander back to Gaz's. He would still be up.

Just then an arm slid round my waist. I looked to my left and got a face full of black Boa. "Getting a drink?" She smiled and pressed her warm body closer to mine. As the Boa parted it revealed the flawless white skin of her cleavage, squeezed tightly into a red dress.

"Sure." All thoughts of Gaz vanished, "What would you like?"

"Ah, I suggested it, come on, what's your's?" She had a lovely voice that sang the words, a London accent but unmistakably Irish in origin. It reminded me of a voice from the past.

"Guinness. Thanks, that's very sweet."

"Ahh, you've entertained us all and I like your Top Hat." She laughed, an innocent girl's laugh, throwing her head back, a flash of white, a Swan's neck above the black feathers of her boa. Her lips were Cherry Red, of course, her arm tightened round my waist and we blended the curves of our bodies. Her free arm appeared and suddenly we were at the bar.

I looked in the mirror behind the row of Spirits and caught sight of her mass of curls and those dancing eyes. She smiled. She looked happy. I smiled at the guy in the mirror, his long hair falling on the furry coat, his face glistening with the sweat of singing for hours and the crush of a hundred teenage Sirens.

Much like the previous girl I had no intentions and even less expectations that this encounter would lead to more than fifteen minutes banter on the dance floor. I was on best behaviour after all. Simple as that. I decided to be as playful and pleasant as possible, if I could make her laugh and give her a story to tell her mates, then all's good.

We retreated from the bar with our glasses and pitched up against one of the pillars in the corner. She took out a pack of Marlboro and offered me one. I shook my head. Her long fingers delicately brought a cigarette to her lips. The ends of her thin fingers tapered like ballet dancer's legs. I smiled, "No, strictly Cannabis, I'm a Health Freak!"

She didn't flinch at the mention of dope, she burst out laughing, like a melody, "Oh some of the boys smoke, everybody does it these days. Which college are you at?"

"The University of Life honey pie, though I did study at Bristol and Manchester. I was doing a gig here for Rose. She's a friend here studying Meds, plus I have mates up the road at Brooks." I remembered Gaz long enough to think he'll never believe this and promptly forgot him. "I love Oxford."

"Where do you live?"

"In the Cotswolds, not far away, about an hour. I have a little cottage. I was teaching but got made redundant so I'm writing a book and I have a band I am recording with. They're a great bunch, one lives here in Oxford, one in Worcester, one in Bath. It's a lot of fun." She was listening, that was good, she didn't seem to want to fight her way out of there. I continued, "How about you?"

"I'm from Harrow in London, do you know it?"

"Oh yes, I've played rugby against Harrow when I was at Public School, it's half way up a hill isn't it and the pitches are miles away I think."

"I walked up that hill to school for years, carrying my bag of books. There's a graveyard at the top and a place I like to sit. Did you know Byron's tomb is up there at St Mary's Church?"

"Gosh, I'd love to see that one day." I suddenly realised that might have sounded a bit forthcoming but she just smiled.

"It's truly beautiful, I love the view. I'm at St Hugh's doing PPE."

"Doing PPE?" I looked at her quizzically.

"Philosophy, Politics and Economics. I'm not sure it's really what I want to do," her face flickered a brief sigh, "I feel some days like I'm not sure I should be here, like I didn't deserve it. Does that sound mad to you?"

"You must have passed the Entrance Exam, Jesus you need brains to do that, plus A level results."

"I got five straight 'A's, but I still feel an imposter some days, as if at any moment someone will come along and say, 'Oh sorry, it was all a mistake.' But I love it so so much!" She laughed. That song again.

"I guess a lot of people doubt themselves; I never really wanted to be a teacher, but it came along and I loved it. However, the last school I was at cocked up the finances and somebody had to go. As I didn't have kids living with me like the other teachers I jumped." I instantly realised what I'd said and added, "I've also got two children, though they live with their mother in Somerset." I never hid the fact of being a Dad from prospective girlfriends, I had no qualms about that, but to be fair I didn't always bring them up five minutes into chatting with a beautiful lady.

She didn't bat an eyelid, "Do you see them often?"

"At least once a month and they have holidays with me. The boy's nineteen…"

"What!" Her eyes were shocked, "How old are you?"

"I'm thirty seven."

"You're joking me."

"No serious, I was born in fifty eight," I paused, "In Chile."

"Where? Chile? But you don't look that old, you don't even look like twenty seven."

"Gee, thanks, you can come again!" I gave her a cheeky smile and she burst out into that song of laughter again. I was amazed she didn't beat a hasty retreat, considering I'd pretty much scored zero on all three counts of, previous drug use, previous baby production and previously too blinking long on the planet. "I was never married though," I said, as if it made some difference, "It's a long story." I figured I may as well fill the bucket to the brim if I was going to knock it over.

"I'll have to listen to it one day." She smiled taking a puff on her cigarette.

Just then Stevie Wonder's song 'Superstition' came on the disco "Fancy a dance?" I grinned.

Her arm grabbed me again by the waist and off we went. "My Mum raised me on Stevie Wonder.'

"Your Mum's got taste. Let's go."

We danced in a crush of bodies, beautifully scented blushed cheeks, sweating with sheer exuberance. These were the high fliers finding their wings.

It was intense, moving, chaotic and yet supremely choreographed. Less drunk than them and wise to the cruel world I knew beyond these hallowed walls, I observed their innocence like Blake.

Several songs later a haze of smoke and breathless bodies finally drew us to the fresh air outside. She lit another cigarette.

"Where's your friends?" I presumed she had come with the group I'd seen at the gate.

"Ahh Lulu and Shisha have gone. The boys are still here I think. I'm walking back."

"Being a gentleman I'd hate to see you stranded or walking the streets on your own. I'm only too happy to escort you. No funny business…You know I'm not like that. Is it far, do you need a taxi?"

"Be Jesus no!" She howled in a broad Irish brogue, "These legs are made for walking." Her arm linked in mine and we strolled past the Porter's Lodge into the soft rainy mist that enveloped the amber spotlights illuminating the ancient stone walls of the college. They had waited centuries and I had waited twenty years, ex communicated outside, but now this young girl was leading me by the hand into a world only the privileged few ever entered.

She tugged at my daydreaming expression, "Come on, it's not far if we cut through by the Bodleian."

It was miles! But I didn't mind walking this gorgeous girl home, that was enough to make me feel like the luckiest man on Planet Earth; which is how Love should feel.

At some point the mist became rain and we sheltered under one of the huge trees opposite the rear gardens of Trinity College. I held her close to keep the drips from falling on her face, her arms tightened around my waist, she looked up as I looked down and our lips met. By the time we stopped kissing it was raining hard.

We paused at several more trees up Park's Road before the main Banbury Road. As soon as we turned into St Margarets Road a magical hush left the late night hum of Oxford behind us.

We entered the gates of St Hugh's, "I'll have to sign you in." The Porter smiled at me. He was an old man with a friendly face. Suddenly, she looked at me and half smiling, half in shock, she chocked in a whisper, "Jesus mother, I don't know what your name is."

'Geoff,' I added, 'Smiles. It is my real name.

As we left the lodge she laughed, "Maud is mine."

"Ah, that's unusual and beautiful." I smiled.

She sang that song of laughter again.

As we walked through the entrance hall I marvelled at the grandeur of it all. We made it to the second floor, at the end of the corridor a left turn led to two doors. Her's was at the end.

The small room was typical of any student of the female variety; a desk with books, files, pens, A4, ashtray and empty chocolate wrappers; a radiator with knickers and socks, a single bed with Teddies, a coffee table with a cassette player on it.

"I'll put on some music. What do you like. I haven't got much." She pulled out a shoe box with tapes in.

"Play what you like best. I'd like to hear what you enjoy listening to."

"How about some John Lennon."

"Wow, yeah, The Beatles are my all time favourite, the first band I really got into. I love Lennon and 'Give Peace a Chance.' I've always been into that."

I don't know how long the tape was, a C90 I guess, an hour and a half. We kissed and cuddled and eventually all our clothes came off. I told her there was no way we were having full sex, "It wouldn't be right." Not my style.

"I haven't got any condoms anyway." She smiled.

Her reply intimated that she wasn't shocked or horrified at the idea. Suddenly I was regretting not taking Gaz up on his offer. But I honestly didn't want this lovely girl to wake up and feel a fox had been through her chicken coup. I knew how it felt to be taken advantage of, especially by men. I wasn't going to pass that experience on to anyone. We played 'Body Chess,' until she finally fell asleep in my arms.

I moved the blankets over her and listened to the tape that was still playing. I was exhausted but my brain was on such a high it wasn't going to shut down yet. One song ended and 'Imagine' began. I listened with tears in the corners of my tired eyes, watching the rise and fall of her naked breath.

I looked at the ceiling mumbling to myself, 'Jesus Geoff, what are you doing in bed with a Roman Catholic schoolgirl for fuck's sake?' Then realising I had blasphemed I hurriedly added, 'Sorry God.'

Just then the song came to an end. I waited. The tape made a funny whirring sound and then clicked as it stopped. The hiss from the speaker cut out and left a gap of silence. My breath stopped. I hung like a marionette from the momentary pause. Then the Church Bell in North Parade began to toll. One. Two. Three.

In those seconds I knew without a shadow of a doubt, the timing of it all was impeccable, the choice of song and singer far too memorable for this to be anything other than pure magic. I knew this girl and I were destined to be together.

It was perfect. 'Falling in Love.'

Naturally in the hungover light of the next day I figured she may see things differently. But somehow I knew as terrified and horrified and everything else 'fied as she was going to be, we had a connection. Those three bells had been rung by Eros, loud and clear.

I remember she woke up that morning for awhile and we chatted, then she went back to sleep again. So I wrote her a note to say how much I enjoyed meeting her and having promised to meet her again I had left my Top Hat with her, That way she knew I'd definitely be back, I wouldn't break the promise.

If it wasn't for the Top Hat she may have forgotten me or refused to see me again. But I had to pick that hat up and I had to see her again, face to face.

I always reckoned first meetings were great but the second was a clear indicator as to whether things were going to work out, or basically die on the spot. If the second evening was great too, it boded well, If the soup was cold the chips soggy and the band forgot to turn up. Forget it.

I closed the door quietly behind me and made my way back through the college to the Porter's Lodge. I poked my head in. 'Do I have to sign out?' I was used to this from my boarding school days.

"Thank you Sir. That would be lovely."

"Oh you don't have to 'Sir' me chap."

"Oh, but we do, Sir." He smiled. "Have a good day."

I waved goodbye. "I am already chap, another fine day in Paradise."

CHI

I drove back to the cottage in a dream. My mind was full of this girl, the song of her laugh, her brazen energy and the curves of her gorgeous body. I was entranced and yet somewhat confused as to why a girl so innocent, so untouched by the hand of man or boy should fall into my embrace. We couldn't have come from more opposite worlds and yet I knew our paths in life had collided and I guess I would just have to wait and see what happened next, if anything.

Any experienced man will agree that no matter how stunning the first night might have been with a new lover, there is always the doubt that come the next day or so the call will come, or the letter in those days, saying how much she loved the loving, but right now she either, didn't want a relationship, was already in a relationship, was out of a relationship but not ready for the next one. The list is endless and I must have heard most of them.

So I resigned myself to wait until the next weekend and then retrieve my magic hat, maybe Saturday afternoon when there would be no pressure on her, I figured we could meet in Browns and she could just drop it off, give me the embarrassed blush and the gentle brush off. Ahh well, it was a fab night anyway.

I presumed the weekend would be the next available opportunity, foolishly thinking these Oxford students would be hard at their work. I would learn that every day of the week had the potential to be a

Friday or a Saturday in their rose scented lives. So I was surprised when I had a call from her inviting me up on the Thursday. 'Would you like to go and see a film at the Phoenix, in Jericho?'

'Crumbs,' I thought to myself as I heard her Irish lilt again, instantly bringing up the vision of her lips. I brushed that thought to one side and and laughed, 'Hey, I'd watch a paper bag get wet in the rain, if it means coming over to see you.'

From some call box in Oxford I heard the peal of that song and, "Jesus, Mary and Joseph, you're pure class," she paused, taking a puff on a cigarette and added, "at playing the fecking idiot!" Then that laugh again.

'Ah, fab, playing the Fool is my speciality, I'm so chuffed you've arranged something for us to do, that's really cool.' This girl had no problem calling the shots, I liked that, she wasn't a dough ball that needed kneading, first one way and then the other. 'What sort of time should I come over?'

"About five would be grand, we can walk down from college and meet some friends of mine for a drink before, if you like."

'Sounds awesome, shall I come to St Hugh's then?'

"Gand. Just sign in at the Porter's Lodge and come up. You remember which room? You can pick up your hat, I love it."

'Sure thanks, that'll be great, five o'clock.' I couldn't help digging a bit, 'Er, you enjoyed the other night?'

"To be sure! I was banjaxed all Sunday but it was a great craic." Her laugh began bubbling over again.

'Brilliant, I'm glad you enjoyed it, I certainly did.' I quickly decided I'd probed enough and added, 'Wow, look forward to tomorrow then, five o'clock.'

"To be sure." I heard an echo of that laugh as the phone went down and the sound of another girl saying something, then the dial tone cut in.

I looked out of the window, sitting on the stairs at 'Windsong.' Suddenly Lord Neidpath's fountain at Stanway House sprung up. Magically it adorned the tree tops and fields of the North Cotswold Escarpment with a white figure whose robes flew towards the south on the breeze, mesmerising my eyes. Magic timing, magic everywhere it seemed. I crossed my fingers for a moment hoping the second date was going to be alright. What would her friends make of me? Oh shit.

Then a second call came. I held my breath, I figured this was the panic reverse up the road and out of my life, but it was only to say let's meet at a Cinema, she had chosen a film for us to go and see. I was chuffed, relieved and didn't even bother to ask what it was. I liked the fact that she made a decision about what to do rather than leave it to me. I thought that was cool, she seemed to have a strong mind of her own. She was a character, I liked that.

I arrived at the Electric Cinema well before six and had a stroll round. A lively bunch of students were hanging about outside. I would discover that most of the gatherings I frequented around Oxford during those years had this same frenetic fervour in the conversation; a breathless, keen youth, unbroken and undimmed by those freaking vicissitudes of fate which had pummelled me many times, half to death and half back to life.

The bar inside was fairly full. I bought a Coke and waited at one of the high tables perched around a pillar in the middle of the small room. I wasn't there long before a voice came up behind me. "Hi Geoff."

I turned around and not one but four beautiful young ladies were there. Maud, Clarice, Xena and Lulu, all smiling. "Hi, great to see you and…"

Maud piped up with a big grin, "Ahh, these are my mates." We did the introductions and as they already had drinks we plunged straight into a chatter that didn't stop for two years. I asked what the film was, there was a choice I think and it hadn't occurred to me up to then. I'd have watched Bambi with this lot. A flicker of doubt ran across Maud's face, "Er, it's 'Train Spotting,' is that ok?" Before she could add, '…As I remember you saying you were a drug addict once,'

I hurriedly enthused, "Of course, sounds fab."

"Fab!" All of them laughed at my choice of a word from another era. These were Thatcher's children to a degree, far removed from the hippy kids I knew. But they were laughing, that was good.

I did keep glancing behind them occasionally, thinking any moment now the 'Boyfriends' would appear, but they didn't and eventually we finished the drinks and went in to see the film.

We shuffled in and sat down, I smiled at her next to me, "Thanks."

"What for?"

"Just for inviting me along and deciding what to do. Makes a change from 'Pub and Chips.'" The song of that laugh briefly filled the Cinema. You couldn't miss her in a crowd, nor me, I was beginning to like this girl a lot more.

'Trainspotting,' concerns some pretty hardcore Scottish Heroin addicts, trying to survive their life of crime and chaos. There are several pretty harrowing scenes where the hero is either getting an injection together or fucking up in some god awful tenement.

I took it all in, thinking I could have written this script, forgive the pun, wondering if she knew I had spent a few crazy years in those rooms, in a surreal teenage dream that just kept getting wilder and crazier the longer it went on.

Being a 'City Junkie' is different to the towns and villages scenes; the dealers are diamond hard, don't give a damn and take no prisoners. No one in the maze of streets is accountable; faces come and go without warning. Nobody really knows anybody; whereas in the country everybody knows who is on drugs, who is a junkie and who isn't.

During the movie our hands had met. I felt no panic, no fingers reaching for reverse. Cool. When we all came out it was still a warm summer evening. The oncoming darkness had already been filled in with neon orange blushers from the old street lights, every one a work of art, casting their shadows over the walls and pavements where many of the greatest minds an intellectual could ever aspire to meet had wandered with pissed impunity.

I was stunned on many levels, not least by the fact that I was now off to some bar with not one, but four beautiful young ladies. Listening to the excitement in their conversation, watching the lithe movements of their svelte bodies, literally brimming with youth and vitality was entrancing.

I might have felt awkward pitched into this mass of teenage ebullience, but to the casual onlooker I was unrecognisable as any different from them. I was of course much older, but not noticeably so. I didn't look out of place.

I was obviously not a first year student, but oddly enough, my eccentricities of dress and the long hair actually gave me something of an ageless quality. Such 'Timeless' or 'Out of Time' people were plentiful in Oxford, I was often asked what I was studying, to which I would reply smiling, 'For a BA in Life, plus an MA in Love.' Cheesy!

We were heading back to St Hugh's JCR, the student's bar. I had quietly noticed that no 'Top Hat' in a carrier bag had been produced after the cinema with a polite, "Well, great to see you, but..." I had heard that line more than once in my forays upon the battlefields of young love. So, it seemed this lovely young woman and her friends had decided I was at least worthy of taking back to the fort for further inspection.

I was of course quietly dancing with every footstep down the pavement. It wasn't just the attraction, every where I had looked that night the creme de la creme of unspoilt youth were in attendance, casually tossed from the ramparts of the Bourgeoisie to melt in the enormous Fondu of university life. These kids had class, 'Upper class,' written over every thread they wore. I recognised the colours of distant halls and playing fields that were once my domain, before I was exiled.

"Ex Public School boys, they're the worst!" One of the girls had mentioned this adding hurriedly, "Though 'You' don't quite seem typical of the boys we've met here."

Jesus I thought, I'm about as untypical as you're ever going to meet. "To be honest the thing is, it depends quite a lot on whether they've been a Boarder and if it was a single sex school." I tried to put up some defence for the old chaps, but the girls, no doubt, had personal experience to draw on.

I was still waiting for their boyfriends to show up but none materialised out of the shadows; perhaps they were elsewhere on a Boy's night out.

I pondered that I could well have been one of those petulant Public School Boys, had I stayed the course at Sherborne, 'On the straight and narrow.' I, for one, couldn't blame them for their ineptitude and I knew how being locked into a regime as tough and demanding as any, with no prospect of escape, then to be suddenly let loose on the world could be too much. Oxford could very easily become 'Too much' for some students.

My mind was tap dancing as fast as my feet, trying to keep up on these flights of conversation, pirouette and swirl, somersault and twirl. We crossed the road to Church Walk, leading past St Philip and St James Church towards North Parade; it was the bells of this church that marked the passing of the hours, the beginnings and endings of everything we did, that first night, to the very last.

Suddenly, as if it knew I was thinking about it, the bell chimed the hour. I squeezed her hand and she hugged her body into mine. He slender fingers slid around my back and pulled me closer, our footsteps became one. Ahead the chatter of the girl's filled the gaps of silent night with laughter, like flashes of winged colours, pirouetting Birds of Paradise caught in the flash of Fireflies.

I whispered in her ear, "One, two, three…" Our lips met and didn't part as we walked on. A voice suggested a quick drink at The Gardener's Arms, to which they was a general 'Hurrah.'

"Boom!" As the door swung open an explosion of smoky voices and tightly packed bodies warmed our faces and polished our smiles. The closer we got to the bar the more intimate it became. The girls insisted on buying my pint of Guinness and we ended up on a bench seat at the back. I reckoned this would be where the lads would show up. But it seemed most of the girls had other girl friends there and before long we were surrounded by…more girls. Everybody seemed to love Maud and were curious to meet her mystery man with the hat. I smiled and did my best to cling on to the coattails of sentences in the rising hubbub of voices; all the while, quietly stunned by that I was here at all.

This was another world, so far removed from some of the stranger ones I had once inhabited. These kids still had hopes and dreams. Gosh, what a new sensation that was, to sit amongst the hopeful. I had my aspirations also, but was only too aware that the 'Sell By' date on these had long since passed.

That night I met several of the other characters who would share the next few years of my life. In some bizarre way I would rewind my life to the point where I should have arrived from Sherborne in the late 70's. But now it was the early 90's. It felt as if I had strayed back through time. It was as if the chapters of my life were fifty two cards, plus a Joker!. The first fourteen had gone down pretty much in order, then some almighty vicissitude of Fate, in other words a bloody cock up, had thrown the lot into the air. They had then been picked up randomly by me ever since. This gilt edged, golden card now lay in the palm of my hand.

My companions could have no idea of what brought me to their world and the streets I had walked to get here. But I had arrived and it looked like I was here to stay, for awhile at least.

"Another pint?" One of the girls asked. I hadn't finished the first and was the 'World's worst drinker' at the time. Two pints of Guinness would be plenty, three and I would be heading for 'Dodgeville.'

"Ah thanks, but I'm driving…" I smiled in reply to her raised eyebrows. I never presumed anything, but I felt four thin fingers wrapped round mine and I knew I wasn't going anywhere. They all had another pint and the pitch of voices went up a notch or two. It was brilliant on every level. There is nothing as enticing to a man as beauty scented with a level of intelligence that was definitely 'Gifted.' it is simply enrapturing, for the eye is hooked and the mind reeled in, like a silver fish darting left and right, but hopelessly caught and ultimately netted. I enjoyed the cut and thrust of their views, the excitement they felt in everything.

There were other crucial factors that made this generation of students so special. It wasn't only me who realised that. Years later the Landlady and the Lodge Porter would both agree the undergraduates of those years were a unique 'Vintage.' St Hughs was one of the first colleges taking in a broader catchment of society, allowing students to apply from Grammar Schools. This new blood, lit the fire beneath the culture of debate. Those hallowed and harrowed views on furrowed brows were now cross bred with the breath of voices that had never felt the cloth of privilege, as indeed, oddly enough, I had.

Unleashed in Oxford, inspired perhaps by the role model for some in that era by Thatcher's story that any Shop Assistant can make it to the top. Some of these students had already fought many battles to get here and their energy wasn't dimmed in the slightest. They wanted more. We all laughed at 'Loadsamoney.' But just above their heads the ripe golden grapes of 'The City' awaited them as the Millennium approached.

It was their age also, from my perspective I could see the girls were ahead of the boys in maturity, they seemed to be eighteen going on twenty one years old, while the boys were nineteen going on sixteen. Bless them, eager pups prancing about, surrounded by endless bowls of gorgeous milk and honey.

With girls, I had realised there is a time that lasts one to two years when every young woman has their reign as a Princess. It's as if all those years spent planning the gardens of their imaginations and now they draw the curtains one morning and every Rose has blossomed. At such a time as this, they have such a beauty which is a mix of their youth and the coming possibilities of life. To watch the seasons of this beauty changing a girl into a woman is also enrapturing. At that time they have the power to command their universe.

Sadly, like many men they only realise the immensity of that power on the day it begins to dim. Boys by contrast rarely experience such a moment of utter glory, unless it's on the sport's field, for them it's spots, gangly legs and awkward moments trying to figure out what the hell is going on inside this woman's head. Does she like me, doesn't she? This can last a lifetime with some men never mind a few seasons.

There was one other element to this whole scene that inspired me to want to capture it and express it in this book. Something I didn't see was taking place and I feel changed the children, ultimately the adults, forever.

Perhaps it was inevitable; but like any parent you wish your child's innocence to last as long as possible, before their delight in life becomes burdened with Life. The sound I was listening to, the thrill and spill of animated conversation was perhaps in its final ecstasy, before being beaten to muted tones by the touchpad on a mobile phone.

As I looked around the room, filled with smoke and the clink of pints, laughter and voices barking orders at the Bar, I would have seen every head was raised to look towards the others, none were lowered to their laps, in bowed concentration on some distant flicker of an eyelid. Some snapshot of a Snapshot life, swapping snapshots of somebody else's Snapshot life. Silent. Stilled. Subjugated. Once the wrist is motionless, the body is handcuffed.

The babble of this and other pubs sounded on the street like hoards of excited teenagers opening their presents at Christmas, excitedly exclaiming, "Look what I've got!"…and 'Jesus, Joseph and Mary,' as Maud would say, they had it all by the bucket full. The glowing jewels of these minds would be those that unlocked the future of knowledge. They were the bridge to the 'Dot Com Bubble,' an unholy castle built on Silicon, known to the rest of us as 'Sand!'

Pints were finished, cigarettes stubbed out and our small group, one man, four girls, plus two I didn't know, made our way through the tightly packed chairs and tables. The pub was mainly full of students. A few bemused locals had their requisite tables, near the entrance. As I filtered through with this pride of lionesses, my eyes must have been on fire, I knew those seats by the door, I knew how it felt to watch from feet away this regal procession of privilege, knowing those few steps across the line may as well be across an endless crevasse. It was never going to happen and yet, here I was. Not a single soul guessed the man in multicolours was almost twenty years ahead of his peers, nor that his past had already filled one manuscript and was about to fill another.

As a youth I had read Jude The Obscure by Thomas Hardy. I had felt keenly his pain at not being able to get into University due to his social class, knowing too well I had thrown my chance away.

As we strolled out into the cooler air of the night I felt her arm slide round my waist again and the sweet lilt of that Irish brogue whispered in my ear, "We're heading back to the JCR for a drink. You be alright with that now?"

"Sure. Hey, anything. I'm loving the night."

"Ah, I'm glad. The girls think you're a right craic."

"Oh, great, I'm chuffed they think I'm okay, they're a lovely bunch too." That was the understatement of the year. I was batting so far out of my league I shouldn't even be near the pitch. My place was usually out back washing up and here I was scoring a century out there.

As our merry band sauntered through the main gates and past the Porter's lodge, his cheery face glanced towards me and smiled. He'd seen this Play, Act One, Scene Two, a thousand times before. He liked me, phew.

As a man who'd crossed one or two borders I was just happy not to get busted. I was almost waiting for a voice to come out of the holy panelled Oak walls and shout, "Hey you! Where the fuck do you think you're going? You can't go in there. You don't belong here!"

But I was in. No embarrassing questions, no hand on the collar, no, 'No stop or I shoot!' I combed my hair with my fingers and followed the howl of girl's laughter reverb'ing through the building as we burrowed down the ancient corridors to the JCR.

The bar ran the length of one wall as far as the back staircase. The room itself included a large dance area, marked out by several wide red pillars that supported the building above.

It was obviously my 'Round' by then. The girls acquiesced and gathered round as I ordered. The bar man was a young guy with long blond hair, a Postgrad student I think, but we both recognised the hair connection and he smiled brightly at me. I was thrilled, it looked like I had a mate on the inside!

"Hi dude, four Lagers and a Guinness." I was going to have to sip this one if I was going to keep my act together. The thought of buying a Half had crossed my mind, but sometimes in life, faced with what I call, 'A Keith Richards moment,' best forget every rule ever learnt, put a big smile on, try to remember enough to tell the story.

The next shock was the bill. A couple of quid, "You gotta be joking?"

"Nah, Student prices my friend," he smiled, "all the bars are subsidised."

"Jeee...sus." I'd already met the Professors and Dons in a previous lifetime, with their endless Sherry from lunchtime onwards, before the vintage wines and brandies came out. The Cambridge I had met as a teenager, via the Don of Oriental Studies at Kings, had been a different entry to those sacred walls, one tinged with the cheap scent of sin.

My dream then was that maybe one of these Dons might get me a back door entry to the hallowed halls. Though having met some of the students, I soon realised I was way out of my depth there. Had I been fluent in Ancient Persian, or a Math's genius, perhaps, but there were no available places for blind enthusiasm and a wild imagination.

These fresh faces, from far and wide had been given that chance. St Hugh, bless him had widened the cast of his net. Oddly enough it was a Hugh, my Sugar Daddy, who had driven me up to Cambridge in some Rolls Royce he'd begged, borrowed or hired that perhaps ignited the hope I could have, with my Poetry, maybe found a way through those walls. In the same way the Monk Dom Sylvester Houedard had promised to get me into the Poetry world.

As I returned to the table I wondered how these people would fare. I had seen the ordeal students of Medicine went through, this lot seemed to have a more relaxed attitude. As time went on I realised some Degrees took a lot more graft and hours in college than others.

I popped the drinks down and pulled my stool up to Maud's. Her wrists were thin, long, white, resting on the table next to her glass. She tapped the ash off her Marlboro and raised it delicately to her lips. The smoke glittered above us as she exhaled. Behind us some lights began to sparkle on the dance floor and the immortal kick of Stevie Wonder's 'Superstition' beat our bones into life.

We looked at each other and said simultaneously "You fancy a dance?"

"Yeah. Come on!" We both replied.

As we got up the girls rose too and we wandered onto the dance floor bejewelled with lasers. It's a good song, a great riff, I couldn't help but explode into energy, displaying to a bemused Maud I could dance, without being too over the top, well, maybe one or two twirls. I will admit I felt like it.

Before I could stop and slap myself awake the song died out and the humungous chords of Born Slippy dropped out of the sky.

It had been a theme in the film earlier, during one of the crazy scenes; suddenly I was circling the 'Dilly,' then I opened my eyes and she was there, smiling at me with her Cherry Red lips as he sang, 'You boy. She smiled at you boy.' I was entranced, I passed close to her and planted a delicate kiss on her cheek. She giggled and caught my waist. 'Babes and babes and babes,' I twirled around a dream world as the other girls on the dance floor chanted, 'Lager, lager, lager.'

Then the Hymn for the Nineties generation flooded the floor with feet. 'Unfinished Symphony.' After that we were both drenched in sweat and decided to take a break back at the table. An hour or so later I still had my first pint while the table was laden with several pint glasses in various states of drunkeness.

A couple of guys showed up who were friends of the girls. Every one a character bursting out of their persona. Tom, tall thin, pale, bleached blond with a friend who was the 'Belle of the Ball' wherever he went; a hilarious camp guy, black hair slicked back, eyeshadow and mascara. A floor length leather coat accentuated his outlandish gestures. His red satin shirt reminded me of the one I used to wear roaming the streets to score in London. Useful as it didn't show spots of blood from shooting up.

I kept having slices from that world diced through my thoughts. It was as if somehow I was forced to remember those years, to know that really this Student Bar was where I should have been, not out there hustling for Punters, freezing cold, looking for somewhere to crash and get smashed.

What were the Gods playing at? Every little part of my brain was switched to maximum. I really wanted this and yet I looked at the girl. A freaking Irish Catholic schoolgirl, who hadn't even felt the rush of a man's naked heart on her breasts.

Here I was, so tarnished as to be unrecognisable, so covered in scars they had made a new skin for me. Unless you got up really close you would never see the seams, the lines of crystal white glue that held them together. By the time I was the age of these people I had already spent seven of my nine lives.

"What are you studying?" A voice had asked from the next table.

"Life! A Masters in all that matters." I was a born natural at coming out with crap. To which I added, "Actually, I'm a Teacher, of boys with special needs, like me!" On it went...

I soon realised that I was generally mistaken for a student, probably Post Grad to be fair. But what the hell, I'd been taken for a fool plenty of times, I could live with that.

"You hungry?" She smiled.

I struggle to convey how the vibrancy that exuded from every pore of her perfect skin and the dance of those eager eyes was so entrancing. My heart was heading thumping, 'Warp Factor Eight.'

"Gosh. I'm having such a good time I'd forgotten I even had a stomach. Sounds fantabulous!" They all laughed.

"Come on then. We're all off to Ali's."

Before I could wonder who 'We' were a door at the end of the bar appeared and a group of us filed out.

It had already gone midnight. These girls obviously didn't keep office hours. Cool with my schedule, as I was temporarily out of regular work, for a year or so, at that time.

It turned out that Ali was a Moroccan selling Snack Food in his van. So I pulled, 'Shukran,' out of the bag. Ali laughed, "Oh, my friend, my friend, you were in Maroc."

"Oh yeah, Essaouira, Taghazout, Agadir and south."

"Beautiful, my friend, did you see the sunsets…"

"Best in the world." I smiled.

I think that got me an extra spoon of tuna. I was glad he didn't ask when I was there, 1976, which was pretty much when these lovelies were just being hatched. Life can seem a little crazy sometimes. Here I was, in this scene of innocence, while there I was, injecting Elixir Paregoric, in a scene that could have come from Dante's Inferno, with Gerard.

We gathered our baked potatoes in their burning hot cartons and headed back to St Hughs.

Somehow by the time we crossed the threshold of the gates it was just the two of us. She pulled me closer, "I better sign you in."

I kissed her, once, then twice. Her lips were hot with curry sauce. I listened to the voice of the Porter and the melody of her laugh. I looked up to the stars and wondered just how lucky one man could be?

We walked through the whispering corridors and up the stairs to a new life.

In her room she put on my top hat and wrapped her feather boa round my neck as she undressed.

PHI

Sex. The first ballet... The hushed auditorium. The silent, breathless, naked footsteps across the stage. The first tip of a finger touch, the first blush of a tender lip, the crush of a kiss on an undiscovered breast. The first trail of a thumbnail down an unmarked spine. The first steps of a girl towards the holy sepulchre.

The mingling and small talk of limbs meeting limbs for the first time. The thrill of knowing the serpent is lurking in the hiss and splutter of the lime lights, welded with shadow to the tip toe of fingerprints, tapped in braille on slowly mapped parchment skin.

She knows how it will all end and yet she takes each and every step, nearer, closer to the beast in his most unholy of holy sepulchres.

Button by button, her blouse parted, the sheen of breath warmed with kisses, breath spread like butter upon her skin, breath brushed with satin gloss over her surfaces, her edges, her centres. Every exhaled breath fell like a sleeping cat to the floor and curled round our tip toeing feet.

The clasp of her bra, clicked, one, two, three and the last hook and sinker, the penultimate, 'Do Not Cross' line. We leapt the chasm hand in hand. She was beautiful, poised, a ballerina caught in mid flight upon a fleeting moment. She had the perfect body, littered with curves upon which my lips would slide downhill, uphill, downwards upwards, onwards, towards the scent of Heaven. I could sense it.

Every pore exhaled her heat, her excitement, every message from every sinew and synapse, sinned and yet trapped, lovingly, inhaled willingly, relayed back and forth at the speed of sight.

Beyond the silhouettes of our silvered nakedness, reflected in the windows of night, the bells of North Parade chimed, 'Now is the hour.'

I paused for a moment, the outline of our bodies was one, but as I glanced away to run my fingers through her hair my eyes bounced off our reflection against the dark night of window pane, I noticed the young boy with blond hair and black eyes, staring through my blue eyes. I remembered the fourteen year old I once was, before my innocence was cut out, so full of hope and so undeterred by the gory addition and bloody subtraction of life, melded to my dreams with odes and sonnets, his long swan neck full of adjectives erupting like a volcano.

That boy should have been kissing this girl, not the man, so full of ragged life and drugged strife. It felt like a character from 'Trainspotting' had blundered off the screen and fallen into the audience, planting his cocky grin next to this pretty girl. But the boy was still inside me, still believing it must have been just a bad dream. One freakin' hell of a bad dream.

It was a waterfall of emotions flushed with sensation that sent the sweat skidding down my back, but it was too late now, I couldn't let my nightmares spoil this dream, I took my chance, I thanked my Gods and sank to my knees before the Goddess.

At some point the cassette player ran silent, moments later it clicked, the spool began to reverse.

The music began again.

Later it stopped and remained silent.

Even later the bells rang out, momentarily covering the purr of her breath. I studied the sleeping beauty, the unkept hair, the eye shadow slightly smudged, traces of lipstick on my chest.

As with other loves, younger than me, I wondered what had brought this new flower to me. Of all the varieties possible, one raised in the holy beds of Catholicism too. We couldn't be more different in many ways, or more wrong for each other and yet, I knew this was right, we had a future.

I had been lucky enough to fall in love before. I had watched and learnt how Eros played his cupid game with laughter and looks across a crowded room. I had felt his presence and I trusted his judgement to warrant a second encounter. I had come back to see her on that basis and to prove 'Will you still love me tomorrow,' was just a line in a song. I wasn't that kind of a man.

If, perhaps, maybe I had just seen the film that night, had a couple of drinks with her girlfriends, retrieved my Top Hat and disappeared into the night, that would have been fine with me. Every glimpse of paradise was gold dust in my eyes. I would have taken that away with me, happy, content.

But here I was, with this girl asleep taking up most of the single bed while I deftly fitted myself around her. The second date had been awesome, on many levels and I knew in the morning, late late morning, I would have a girl in my arms who had given me her most treasured gift and I hoped she might feel I was worthy and had returned the gesture with my heart.

I'm a natural Lark and a light sleeper, seven years of the seven o'clock bell at boarding school had left me with an indelible timeline in my mind. My ears gently surfaced through a sigh of dreams as the bells of North Parade rang out again. I counted each chime, interspersed with the gentle rise and fall of her breath next to me. She was fast asleep.

I considered a coffee but looking round the room I wasn't encouraged. A plastic kettle was perched next to a sandwich toaster which seemed to have various colours of something solidified on its sides, but no sign of the holy caffeine jar nearby. I lay back down in my warm crevice and listened, there were birds in the trees outside, some on the roof above, but no sound from within the building.

I wondered for a moment whether she might have a lecture or tutorial at nine, but decided she probably factored that in before going out last night. I had a lot to learn about student life. Apparently there was no pending tutorial disaster, no alarm sounded from deep beneath the bedclothes and she slept soundly, until around eleven. While she purred I had drifted in and out of my reveries.

On that morning I was still of the opinion that this affair had the possibility of running three days, three weeks or three months. I'd inhabited these heady emotions before. I was on a hiding to nothing, there was no way a relationship with such an age gap was destined for 'Forever.' My experience had taught me the wisdom of an older partner was a useful book of

'Life and Love,' for a younger person to ponder, but ultimately they had to write their own. Then there was the issue of having children, which would only loom larger as the years passed until one day that bubble would burst in a miserable haemorrhage of hormones.

My best case scenario was we would survive a few months together and then she would be whisked off by some adoring and adorable young chap. I was not going to stop that happening. I had no right. She deserved to live and love as I had, full on, flat out and as if today was the last day of life, everyday.

It's so easy to misjudge these relationships and indeed some of them do need judging, but ours was full of innocence. Everyone around us felt that joy, that aura of love which just exudes from a new couple. There was no way I wished to sully this first flight of the butterfly with shadows from my past or demands on her future.

I lingered over my musings, sandwiched between the slumbers of this gorgeous girl and the wall; the possibilities were endless. Christ! What would her parents say? To which thought I quickly added an humble, 'Jesus, Joseph and Mary.'

I had learnt that the highest accolade in education, that of studying at Oxford or Cambridge, could in fact be an utter nightmare for some students. This was made all the worse by the presumption that it was supposed to be the best time of their life, the 'Creme de la creme' of bloody everything. Part of the deal was to enter that castle of ivory towers and return with a prince, not a stoned pauper.

I tried to think how I was going to be cautious, not to leap in, how I wasn't going to give my heart away this time, like the other times; but something inside me, all these weird moments with the bells and stuff, just kept nagging me. "Pay attention for once you dumb hippy, this is special."

I nodded to the voice in my head and noticed the bundle of pillows and curls of hair were stirring.

"Ah." A short pause. "Morning," she murmured. As her eyes focused I could see seventeen emotions running across her face all in different directions as she recalled the night before, but they settled at last on a smile, "How's you? Jesus, my mouth's dry."

All my thoughts of caution blew out the window the moment she smiled at me. "Hang on." I sprang out of the bed and filled a cup with some cold water from the kettle and gave it to her. "Shall I make you a cup of Tea?"

"God, you're a fine fella." I wasn't sure if it was the offer of the tea or something else? After a yawn she added, "Are you hungry? I'm for eating a horse."

"Sure." I smiled back. I wasn't being kicked out.

"We'll go over to North Parade and get a baguette from the sandwich shop."

The kettle began to hiss and she handed back the empty mug. We kissed. We kissed some more then came up for air. "I'll make that tea for you. How do you like it?"

"Ah, I'd love a good strong cup of tea, two sugars. Jesus, I must look a state."

"Not at all, you're lovely. Bloody gorgeous!'

She looked surprised, as if no one had said that to her, in that way, before. "Thanks for last night. That was really special."

"Ahh, twas a great craic. There's a disco in the JCR tonight, if you're up for that?"

"Wow, that would be fab. Are you sure it's okay for me to come along? What about your buddies?"

She laughed again, that song, descending from the heights of angels. "Ah, the girls think you're class."

I had no idea what that meant, but it sounded better than 'Crap.' It looked like I wasn't going to get the brush off. She had no idea that I would gladly have watched the rain fill leaking buckets that night, if it meant hanging around with her.

"What's the plan? Have you got lectures today?"

"Nah, Friday's free. But I have some washing to do and stuff." Which I guess was code for I need to tidy up and go have a chat with my girlfriends.

"Cool. I'll go over and visit my mate Gaz up the Cowley road." I decided he could have an update on events, whether he wanted it or not. I was so thrilled, over the moon and back again, I needed to share it!

After tea we dressed and sauntered out across the immaculate lawns of the college, through the back gate of one of the houses which led onto Canterbury Road. With a few minutes stroll we arrived at the pretty mews of North Parade. We joined the queue in the sandwich shop. Nobody looked round as if an alien had landed. Most of the other customers were as dishevelled as us. I was accepted as just another student with his girlfriend. We ordered and took the baguettes back to her room. This would be our breakfast, brunch, or lunch on many occasions.

My eyes soaked up every impression until my mind was wringing wet. It felt great. I'd had relationships that kept you on your toes before, but this was sharpening my brain too. I really had to get up to speed. None of this lot were sitting around smashed mumbling, "Hey man, shall we go out and score some more Dope? Pizza? Ice cream?"

We talked as we ate. She told me of her initial tremor the first day, when she had seen the Top Hat. How she had run to the girl next door and howled, "Look at this, Jesus, Joseph and Mary!"

I asked her why she had picked me up in the first place, the Ball had been full of handsome young students. "Ah, they're mostly all feckin'ediots." Or something similar. She added that when she saw me singing with the hat, the hair and the flares she just thought, 'Gosh, I'll never meet a man like that.' Or something along those lines.

Perhaps I intrigued her? But sometimes old Cupid just fires his arrows and there's not much you can do about it. Either he'd missed or some other guy had ducked and I'd picked up the ricochet. I wasn't arguing, I just didn't want this to end in three days, three weeks, or three months.

There came a pause. I almost expected the church bells to ring. They didn't. "I guess I'm going to take a wander now for awhile, catch up with Gaz and see you later. When's good?"

"Anytime you like, if I'm not here I'll be in Shisha or Lulu's room." She gave me vague directions and mentioned the Porter would be fine with me coming and going. I knew it was time to leave for awhile. She would probably want to see her mates and have a good old Post Mortem on the night. She'd go in. They'd look at her. She'd giggle and by the time that laugh had descended from the ceiling they would all be in each other's arms.

They were a tight crew, they didn't bitch the way other women I'd met did. I'm sure they had their moments, but somehow their conversation never dropped to that level. They were bright enough to fill in all the gaps. By Jesus Joseph and Mary they were bright as diamond sparks.

I set off down Banbury road with wings on my heels only slowing down to cross where the tree stood we had first kissed under. I wanted to give it a hug but I took the first left towards the Pitt Rivers Museum. I swung into University Park and followed the line of flower beds strung like beads along the path. I headed down to the Cherwell river and watched it meander past. The ripples and the slender curves of the water's edge reminding me of her body.

I made my way back to the museum and headed for the walkway past the Bodleian Library. Every where I looked students were cycling past or walking with determined grips on serious satchels towards some hulking stone archway which swallowed them; or Professors padded by on Hush Puppy feet, with stiffened spines and rigid arms tucked into their comfortable lifestyles, black capes flowing behind flat legs, towards the next College Luncheon.

I wandered about for awhile, lost in thought in this land of ivory towers. I pondered what I'd do when her friends figured out I was older than I looked and years of my life had gone missing. 'Absent Without Leave.' I'd have to tell them, the truth, straight up, I always did.

At first it had been a kind of purge, an emotional blood letting that went on for years and years. 'Hey you motherfuckers! You never guess what happened to me on the way to school?'

However, now it was, 'Wise up young friends, learn from my experience, or rather mistakes. There's some evil bastards out there you really don't want to meet. Guess what? Most of it comes packaged as 'Male.' I know what it's like to be prey.

But all that was a long way off. For now I was just a new boyfriend in college with long blond hair who played guitar and owned a Top Hat. I would come back to St Hughs that evening and for many more, experiencing everything of that hallowed life I had missed the first time around. Except the exams!

I read the books, did the worrying and studying, ate the chocolate, watched 'Friends,' drank the coffee and waited outside the library for her to finish. Or sometimes we'd meet in there and I'd sit at the table with her in silence, marvelling at the studious faces around me and the rows of vellum tomes. Maud and her girlfriends allowed me into every part of their lives, I became an honorary member of this sisterhood, as they pursued their own love stories.

That evening, courtesy of my 'Poor man's Rolls Royce,' the Cortina, I drove Maud and a couple of her girlfriends out to The Trout Inn, a wonderful pub by a weir on the Thames. Peacocks roamed about freely on the banks and the endless rushing of water over the rapids gave any conversation some drama.

We drank a beer with the girls and then headed off by ourselves to the ruins of a monastery on the other side of the river. As we got there, light mist became rain then lightning flashed! The heavens opened and we kissed in raindrops, hugging tightly every time the rumble of thunder thrilled us, through our spines.

We didn't care as the rain began to lash down, soaking our entwined bodies. Her 'Superman' T-shirt clung to her breasts, I squeezed inside the soft collar of her coat and she hugged me breathless.

We giggled, "Come on. We better get back before the others think we've drowned." As we strolled, careless through the soaking wet grass, the lightning and thunder, flashed and roared around us. But every shudder of the sky was muted by the louder beating of our hearts.

When we got back, soaked to the skin, the girls just laughed and smiled at us. Their faces were beaming. Everybody loved Maud and everybody loved that Maud was in love. I sure did.

VAU

I crossed Magdalen Bridge and paused to stare at the Cherwell River as it mumbled between the old stone buttresses below, parting the long green grass flowing underwater, like student's spirits from the past tense; lying on their backs in the glory of a midsummer's morn, the College bells still ringing in echoes of ringlets, the choir singing on the turret of dawn. No doubt some of these long dead graduates were led by glory to the inglorious battlefields, where the joy of a heartbeat felt on such a moment as this would be their last memory.

Behind me the present tense was unfolding, with shrieks and laughter from bicycling graduates; their voices like fleeting, flapping Crows on the winds of poetry, the wings of Kipling, Sassoon, Owen and the feathers of dear Rupert. I knew so many Brookes that filled this red river, such handsome boys, their good looks carved out of granite, whilst ours were eroded from sandstone. The irony was their beauty, like some Rock Stars, never had the chance to grow ugly, captured in mid frame, mid flight, mid stride.

To the right of me leaves and branches from the Botanical Gardens were trying to escape the walls, seeking to build a raft and float away on the Isis; not knowing they were better off in there, before they shared the effluence of main stream life. They had no memory of the hands that captured them, each one held in awe once upon a time, by some dumb struck botanist.

A bus rumbled past, full of expectant faces, tourists and shoppers, clutching their carrier bags full of ready packaged Future tense from the shops.

But it only took a moment's diversion, a brief step through the archway of any college and the world was stilled, hushed, intimate again. Here the Present was left waiting at the Lodge, next to the bicycles, unnoticed except by the Porter, while the eagle eyes of those within pored over endless sentences saved from the Past.

This was Oxford for me, every footstep went back and forth in time. Everything was out of sync but somehow ran like a dream. Perhaps only I imagined this world, a poet's mind, a writer's insane curiosity, the musician's bravado and that look of a dog that's seen it all but still ravished by hunger. I thought of Burroughs, Ginsberg, Dylan and other distant heroes that had come to feed at this font of all things almost forgotten.

"Hi." Rose was coming out of Cowley Place. "How's you?" She slowed up on her bike and pulled in.

"Brilliant, great night on Saturday, thanks for the gig and yeah, I met a really lovely girl."

"Geoff! Honestly!" She laughed, "What college?"

"St Hugh's."

"Is she a medic? I might know her?"

"No, she's doing PPE, whatever that is, she's lovely and we hit it off. She has a great bunch of mates too. We're out again tonight. See how it goes ay."

"Great, be seeing more of you then. Drop in for tea soon." She was off, like the wind, as swift and as truly uncatchable, ever the dedicated student.

I headed up the Iffley Road and crossed over to The Music Box. Here time stood still too, but somewhere between 1965 and 1985, depending on where you looked. It was a fabulous shop for second hand musical instruments. It was the size of a poor man's kitchen or a rich man's en suite, run by Keith the owner and Gary who was his coffee making, Sax playing, ever smiling side kick.

From the floor to waistline were amplifiers and speakers, which acted as props for keyboards and pedals, but from the chest up hung the treasure of boyhood dreams. Second hand Lead and Acoustic guitars. Any musician that knows their stuff will tell you most instruments get better as they age and get played, except the queen of them all the piano, once her back begins to break, with metal spine fatigue, she can only be slowly detuned and laid out to pasture in small village halls where 'Concert Pitch' was lost long ago. But there wasn't room for a piano here.

I had bought a few guitars off Keith, but that wasn't why musicians went to the Music Box, buying anything was the last thing in our mind. First of all it was just the looking, the hoping and thinking that maybe if I had that amp and that pedal, with that guitar and strap, I could be a star. It had happened for guys who shopped here and up the road, guys who made it to the Head of the Radio; but they were few and far between. Really we came here to chat with Keith and Gary, about everything and nothing. I don't know why, but it's all part of the music trip. No Keith or Gary, no gear for the gig, no dreams.

Once they knew a loitering customer wasn't a complete tosser he or she may get offered a cup of tea, or worse still Gary's coffee. Then we felt part of the family. Keith was a big man and he encouraged lots of struggling musicians in the nicest way. "When are you going to be famous Smiles?" A few weeks later it would be, "Aren't you famous yet?"

God knows I was trying to find a niche somewhere, but I remember wandering round HMV record store at the time and realising they didn't even have a category that came close to Cosmic Smiles.

I had a call from Keith once, "I've got a guitar for you." He was right, he knew his customers that well, especially someone like me who was always in there dreaming. "A twelve string. You're going to love it. I thought of you because it's an old Washburn, in the Woodstock Festival series, it's called the Monterey." There was a pause, "You still there Smiles?"

"No motherfucker, I've already left. On my way. Give me about forty eight minutes and ten seconds."

As I opened the case my eyes nearly fell out of their sockets. I picked it up, held it to my heart and gave it one strum. Gorgeous. "How much?" He could of named the Moon and I'd have put it on my American Express in a flash. He mentioned a figure which I can't remember, that's the best kind of price. "Sold!"

That night I had slept on Gaz's floor with the case open next to me, waking up every now and then to strum the strings. Angels singing in octaves.

After a cuppa of Gary's finest I strolled upwards and onwards, to the topper most of the popper most, past the Curry House, took a right and wound round to Richmond Road where Gaz lived.

Gaz was one of my dearest comrades and one of the few people who had met my parents and knew my past. Indeed he'd watched the entire plot unfurl from the start and caught me on many a Comedown Sunday at sundown. We had tripped the psychedelic light fantastic on Westminster Bridge, even Highgate Cemetery, inside Stonehenge and beyond the endless boundaries of our brains.

Both Public School Boys, both rebels and both early finishers, mine compulsory, his voluntary. Hence, his return to education years later, after his retail career had floundered with his marriage. Such are the joys of 'Wife.'

"Hi man." I smiled

"Heeeyyy Gringo!" Gaz put on his best Cheech and Chong accent, though his Spanish was so good he really didn't need to try. He was still writing the letter I had seen the previous Saturday, to Teresa his lover in Madrid, except it was gaining in leaves of paper.

"Wow!" I said, glancing at the pile of paper, "How's the book going?"

He laughed into a big smile. He was a man who had already inherited the suave good looks of his Welsh ancestry, coupled with a beautiful heart that had been cruelly broken. This only made him the more handsome. He also had integrity. His parent's home with the Barn at the top of the garden was a haven, before, during and after my escape to London. I was always welcome, until the Datura Stramonium event. His folks banned me for three months over that.

"So man, zee wanderer returns?" He sat down at his desk and made some space among the sheaves of paper. He was studying Spanish too, so there were dictionaries and text books in various heaps.

"How did it go the other night? I noticed you didn't come back, the carpet wasn't slept on." He laughed. He knew I preferred the floor to a bed, 'Can't fall much further from here,' I used to say. He knew why too, he had seen the same underworld in London, well half of it, the bit where we scored and roamed the streets till dawn. I remember the first time I showed up at his folks covered in makeup, purple satin flares and a Musquash coat, a gift from my psychiatrist, who else? Yeah Gaz had seen it all. The fact he had known my mother meant a lot to me.

"Yeah, I met a lovely girl."

"Wait, don't tell me, she's the love of your life and this is the one and so on, just like the last one and the one before that." He did know me well.

"Nah, nah man, she was the one, they're all the one! I'm just a bit much sometimes, well most of the time and usually way too much for the parents. I mean, if I brought me home from a date, I'd throw myself out," We laughed

"You're not lying there; Jesus I wouldn't take you home to meet my hamster." We both howled. The friendship between men is truly special, though not without its dramas, one limb bruised by another.

I would often say, whenever I came across friends arguing, 'Remember the word 'Forgiveness' comes just before the word 'Friendship' in the 'Smiles Dictionary of Life.' To which I usually got a, 'Fuck off you tart, it's none of your f'ing business.' It probably wasn't, but I am programmed to pour oil on troubled waters, for I have witnessed how easily they lead to the wreckage of ships, especially at night.

"Well, we'll see how it goes." I grinned, "You know what the prediction is, weeks or months I guess then I'll get burnt. Then I'll get trashed for awhile. Fuck it's a roundabout. Anyway I really like her, she's cool and if we make it to the summer holidays that would be great."

"Where does she live?"

"She said Harrow at first 'cause people have heard of that, but actually it's just next to it, Wealdstone." Before he could ask I added, "No idea? But," I paused, "Well…" I paused again.

"Come on gringo gimme zee facts or I blow ze little brains to even more tiny pieces !" I explained about her Irish Catholic background while his eyes rolled.

I had my doubts too. One or two parents had sent me packing even before I even got to the drugs and kids bit, long hair was still an emblem that clearly stated an inability to toe the party line. This was a simple prejudice many folks clung to.

As it turned out her parents were lovely to me, though there was the inevitable twist of fate, or cosmic cock up; oddly playing with the Timeline of my life. The day would come at some point when Maud was in the kitchen and her mother asked the inevitable question, "So how old is this guy?"

After unclenching her teeth she had replied slowly, "Well Mum, he's thirty.." She only got that far.

"What? Thirty! Jesus, Joseph, Mary and all the Saints in Heaven." Or something along those lines. The poor girl seeing her mother's distress didn't have the heart to add 'Seven.' So for the next five or so years I had to lose seven years of my past somewhere. Not difficult! But what I found harder was remembering that I shouldn't know certain stuff, as I wouldn't have been born. Nearly screwed that up a few times. But she was worth it. I was blessed to have retained youthful looks, partly due to my long hair and I guess it was hard to believe anybody who played the fool like me could be as old as me.

Also, since my twenty first birthday I hadn't smoked tobacco or done a lot of drinking, even despite years of opiate use I had repaired most of the damage. However, closer inspection still revealed a dark shadow in the crook of my arm and the crude marks on my wrists. The left I could cover with a watch, the right I often forgot about until hanging on a bus or a Tube strap; then I'd realise somebody was staring, at the moment they hurriedly looked away.

How was I going to unfold all this dark history on somebody who was so far removed from such a life, attending church when it mattered and no doubt several times having the fear of God put in her about 'Consorting with the devil and them heathens you find drugged out of their minds or having children out of wedlock?' I expect the Sex Education in such schools went as far as one word, 'No!'

Indeed, even at college in Bristol in the Eighties a friend of mine was advised by the campus doctor on seeking the contraceptive pill, that, 'She had only to keep her knees firmly pressed together and such a problem would never arise.' Oh, for those naive and semi enlightened days of ignorance. Fortunately the next doctor looked at the lithe redhead in front of him and was more realistic.

"Coffee?" I nodded, Gaz lit a Marlboro and headed off to the kitchen.

"Ah yeah man! Now you're talking. I'm back over tonight, or well, later…ish. Something happening, I can't remember exactly? Man it's one long, non stop weekend for these students. She doesn't seem to have a lot of lectures and stuff, not as many as you."

Gaz cracked open one of his beautiful grins, "Ah, you know man, they're so brainy they don't need any of that lecture shit." We laughed again.

"Anyway, it's all great, her friends are like totally on natural brain amphetamines man. They got so many thoughts up there they can't get them out fast enough. I love it and I mean they actually debate stuff, they argue with me and say, 'Why?' I tell you it's like having to run your brain at top speed down the outside lane of a motorway. I just hope it keeps working out, see which way the wind blows ay man. How's yours going with the dancing Spaniola?"

"I got another letter from her yesterday and I'll be going out there in the summer holidays or maybe she'll come here. I dunno yet."

My turn to unwrap a fresh smile, "All happening man. Makes a change for Change to be knocking on our doors, it's usually the Cops." More laughter.

I took up his guitar and started plinking away at something or other. So it went on, as the afternoon blended into early evening. I figured it was best not to rush back, give her some time to catch her breath and chat with her best buddesses.

When I eventually got back to St Hughs they were all in Natasha's room, three of them still in pyjamas, in bed, watching 'Friends' on a small TV. Everyone was beaming. Maud was one of their dearest inner circle of mates, a character and a half and some! If the craic hadn't started when she walked in, it soon was about to.

"Love the flares," one of them said, as if I'd been there forever. I was hoping to stay for at least half that long. It wasn't about their age, or the college, or anything sexual, it was about enjoying their vitality, their conversation and bless them, they still had hope and aspirations. That's a heady mixture for any man to inhale, let alone a sniffer dog like me.

Their chatter was relentless, four songbirds in flow. There were no distractions other than the small TV, no small phones held in hot palms, checking into Ether Land or 'Anywhere else but where I am now.'

It was the last breath of Conversation, which would fade away slowly over the next ten years; to be replaced with another. The Fax would become a text or email. The Filo Fax a mobile phone. The hum and cadence of a million voices would be blanketed, only disturbed by random screams, laughs, or 'Oh my God! Look at this.' Snatches of music from a distant stratosphere. We were going to lose the 'Here and Now,' replaced with 'There and Somewhere Else.' If only we had known.

We had always expected Big Brother was out there and reckoned his means of detection and inspection could only get better. However, we never dreamed in our innocence that we would take him to our breast, into our bedrooms; even thrilled to pay a premium to have the latest version of his 'Ears and Eyes.' Still, I've got nothing to hide, no worries.

But the loss of those voices, the bending of heads downwards, towards the omnipotent tiny screen is truly a step backwards in so many ways for Man and Womankind. It should have been our tool, not our obsession, our addiction, enslaved from waking to sleeping to the 'Quick Finger Flick.'

For all the benefits and all the science it enables I wonder if it was really worth the cost of losing our children. Now they sit in the same house as their family, eat at the same table and yet are elsewhere, the chatter of infants overlaid with the soft blubber of contextual crap; new babies enshrined in the light of their green glow, bedrooms bathed in the semi darkness of small screen unreality.

Even then, during the early years it wasn't so bad. Phones were still phones. Then they became mobile discos, theatres, cinemas and mini computers; they founded their own label. 'Social Media,' a title which like many others is an utter misnomer. It should read 'Unsocial Media.'

Twenty five years later a generation of children live in their presence continually, in fear and awe of its unknown, unseen voices, faces looming out from the anonymous Internet shadows. Silent tables where they communicate with dancing fingertips rather than lips, tongues remain sealed in their fleshy box, bitten, chewed, released only to ingest.

Maud and I squeezed together on one chair and giggled at nothing in particular, behind us a 'Happy Monday's' poster cow moo'd. "I was wondering if you fancy a trip out to Woodstock, we could waltz round Blenheim Palace grounds and find a lovely pub. What do you reckon girls?"

"We'll get ready. Twenty minutes?"

"Perfecto Mundo!" I bleated. The harmony of their laughter sang out like a chorus of matinee angels.

It's hard to love an Artist, I should add, particularly one like me, as their hearts are already inscribed to the Muses of poetry, music or whatever art they bleed for. That is a love affair no physical form can ever compete with. Also, to be honest it is a love affair with oneself, searching to find that ethereal inner spot of beauty where creation begins. Trying to find what it is you have to say, or rather what you have to do with your life to find those words. It's a war between self and self to get there and somehow not to destroy one of those selves. To be the artist, the performer who gives all to the performance, the mind, body and soul must be yoked to the task. In the process of giving everything, for maybe six months or sixty years, often it seems there is nothing left for anybody else.

Two other major obstacles stand in anybody's way to reaching me. Between the cold sheets of the old school dormitory and the cold streets of the city I had learnt to become self sufficient in providing the love I wanted, the love any child craves, the comfort in a storm, a dry towel, a voice out there that cares. With my Mother's death, her suicide, after our last argument with those final twenty four words I spoke to her hammered like nails into my spine, I was truly alone, Exiled, Excommunicated in Exodus. Nobody cares the way a mother does for her child. This is why my biography has 'EX' in each title.

At that crucial time I had just discovered how to fix such wounds, with the ultimate form of self made sex, 'Fixing Up' drugs. The needle is a penis like no other, the junkie must subjugate themselves to its humiliation and yet it's worth it for that orgasm. Boy, what an orgasm. Which is what it comes down to in the end. Isn't it?

You can forgive and forget a lot in search of that moment of release, the brief sweet taste of Nirvana and the delicate afterglow of blood red butterflies fluttering in the dusk of every limb.

At first it was a safe place to head for, to play in, but as days and years passed it became a prison cell I only left in order to return, again, again and again. The loneliness of the long distance drug addict.

As we drove to Woodstock the girls had no idea that the guy driving might just as well have written 'Trainspotting.' They were all very bright and had no doubt spent the last few years studying flat out, they certainly hadn't been doing drugs in the back street toilets of 'Godawful Alley,' nor selling their bodies for cheap trinkets or a place to stay the night.

Their chatter in the back was full of such glorious enthusiasm, they had the world at their feet, if only they could toe the line another few years, the line I'd lost sight of twenty years before.

Like an explorer finding an isolated tribe for the first time, I wondered how much of the outside world I should pass on to these innocents. Should I share the ugly secrets and the black diamond backs that sweat over razor blades and burnt spoons.

I supposed they may have had their own shadows and harboured their own sinking memories in some god awful corner of a bedroom. Four beautiful girls. I remembered the title of a book I planned to write one day, 'Pity the Beautiful.'

As the daylight faded we drove into the ochre glow of Woodstock, the victorian street lamps gave it an 'Olde World' feeling, as if the houses were daubed with dimming candlelight. I turned the Cortina left and followed the road that led up to the side gates of Blenheim. I knew we'd never get through the main entrance at this hour. I parked up. There was a man in the lodge overseeing the driveway who gave us the once over and offered, "The house is shut now."

"It's ok we're just going to stroll down to the lake," and before he could point to the 'Grounds Closed' sign I shouted, "Thanks mate, we won't be long." He watched the four darling buds of early summer pass and couldn't help smiling at them. We were in!

I knew why I had brought them, I had experienced the frenetic pace of my own college years, I knew the joy of escaping the hubbub for a few hours into the country. I waited and watched as the beauty of the reflected trees in the lake, set off by the bridge at one end, worked its magic.

Birdsong replaced their word song as the grandeur fell about our velvet shoulders in capes of gold.

I wanted to give them that moment, an inhalation of breath, of beauty, of Mother Nature, an exhalation of relief, a piece of Peace. Maud's hand tightened in mine. It was like a pause in a symphony, a Rest beat between two breathless Minims.

I could make these girls laugh and sing, any fool could, but I wanted to show them more than that. I was a man to whom this mattered, these ripples on the surface of the silvered water, the descending sky and the fact that we had to break the rules to get in.

A Cuckoo called from somewhere on the other side of the lake. She leant closer to me and whispered on my shoulder, "Magic. It's so beautiful. I love it. Love you, er…" she panicked and added, "for bringing me here."

'It's ok,' I thought to myself as I whispered "I know how you feel."

As twilight beckoned we returned to the village, our man in his Lodge had gone and we stepped over his hanging chains. Entering a pub with four beautiful young women guarantees the local yokels, generally starved of such statuesque delights, will gawp and gander. They'll stop crunching for a moment on their Pork Scratchings, pints hang in mid flight to open mouths and a breathless lull pervades the smoke filled air while they analyse the incoming strangers. It wasn't until we sat down in a corner with our drinks that the tongues went back in and the background noise began again.

I smiled, "Phew. I thought for a moment there they'd seen me on Crime Watch UK last week! Whoops!" The howls of laughter from our table filled the saloon bar as a puff of smoke arose from their cigarettes.

We'd hardly just met each other but we all felt at ease and clicked together as old friends do. In fact we had somehow created our own 'Friends' show. Here we were on the first Series, nearly at the end of Episode One and I knew I had a hit on my hands.

The melody of Maud's laughter remained with me, to which she added a new catalogue of music. I was raised on the Beatles and Stones, 'My Generation,' the four pillars of Blues, Rock, Folk and Jazz had been on my stage. I hadn't taken much notice of the music coming out in the late Eighties and early Nineties. The 'Pretty Boy and Girl' bands had left me cold and I could never understand the thrill of Oasis. They summed up the worst aspect of the 'Pop Star' with their gnarly, ego laden stares. I found no deep message, no philosophy, no Peace and Love, just pissed off and shove off. As for their music, I'd heard all the riffs before, done a lot better.

However, the Maud and the girls were more in tune with 'Their Generation,' and Jamiroquai was one of the first fresh sounds they introduced to me. When he released 'Cosmic Girl' it was as if he'd written it for Maud and me personally. Then the anthems of Massive Attack, Underworld and REM, against the grey wastelands of Portishead, the sheer nihilistic energy of Nirvana, salted with Red Hot Chillis, Pulp, Blur and the New Radicals who wrote one of my most loved songs, 'You Get What You Give.'

In the car on the way back she slipped a cassette in the player. It was a 'Mix Tape' compilation she had made earlier that afternoon for me. If you've never heard a Cortina sing before…It sounds like two litres of magic on four wheels.

The following weekend I brought Maud back to my cottage Windsong, in Toddington, a village which nestles at the end of a gentle valley, below the hills forming the North Cotswold Escarpment. In those days it was the most beautiful, enchanting place any person could wish to visit, let alone live in. Our little patch of country had every aspect of traditional life, farms, village halls, old manor houses around every twisting lane and was littered with more millionaires than cows. For a London girl it was a baptism in the best of all the 'Shires' fonts.

Being a somewhat unusual chap, who has had an inordinately large amount of good and bad luck thrust his way, I was a man for whom money had never caused a bulge in his pants, a man who believed fervently that the things he wanted most to achieve were beyond purchase with mere coinage.

It was with some pleasure, as I had no proper job at the time, that Fate had also put the keys to a huge Revival Gothic castle in my hands, all seventy two bedrooms and one hundred acres. If anything really pissed the local wannabe Bourgeoisie off it was the hippy in the village getting those keys. Worse still, after allowing Dennis, a colourful local pub landlord to take Joan Collins round on a private visit, he had taken to calling me Lord Smiles. The faces of the tourists in the bar would be priceless if I wandered in, as they studied my tie-die flares or worse still if I was wearing my sawn off shotgun shorts, no doubt a flowery shirt, wearing enough rings to set up a pop up jewellery shop and the scent of my expensive Eau de Cannabis cologne following me.

Having shown any new guests my cottage, which was charming in its bijou form with its magnificent views. it was with some relish that I would take them for a casual stroll down the village lane to a spot that suddenly revealed Toddington Manor; then casually mention, "Fancy a look round? Come on then, I've got the key," which was a work of art in itself, two hundred years old, weighty and intricately formed. It was magical, from the first to the last. The Manor was like a massive Disney set filled with such beauty and power, which was reflected in both the good and the less good sense of magic.

But what is Magic? A five letter word people bandy about in reference to almost any topic, 'She was magic, he was magic, even 'It' was magic.' Any kid with half an imagination would be enthralled by the adverts of 'Magic Tricks to Learn at Home,' in the back of many comics, enticed to send off for the secret of 'How to be a Magician,' at four dollars, ninety nine cents. Alastair Crowley, Charles Manson, Druids, Magic Circles and Tommy Cooper pulling pissed off rabbits out of damp top hats were all part of Magic.

Although I roamed the grounds freely, it took me ten years to get into the Manor and I saw the whole deal as something of a spiritual quest. It had a guardian at the time I first moved into Windsong, old Charles, who looked after the grounds. He had promised on several occasions to let me inside one day.

Sandstone pillars supported the huge gates, with a blue sign on the curving walls either side, written in gold 'Toddington Manor.' Just inside there was a silent Gatehouse, curtains closed for years. Gently sloping banks lined either side of the long driveway, enormous ancient trees in every direction and a pair of bungalows, also deserted, were further down on the right.

Eventually the main drive turned to the right and disappeared into a small woodland, until it turned to reveal a dramatic view of the front of the building. Simply beautiful in every way, elegant, gothic revival architecture at its best. There were many similarities in its design to that of the Houses Of Parliament, due to the fact that the architect had apparently worked on plans for both buildings.

Charles Hanbury-Tracy began construction in 1805 and it was finished roughly thirty years later. Stone and glass panels from the previous sixteenth century Jacobean Manor were used, which had been sited closer to the Isbourne River, on lower ground which ultimately proved to be too damp. Next to the last standing arches of the old ruin a church had been built at great expense, with such perfect proportions the acoustics brought musicians from all over Britain to record there.

A crucial detail in the manor's legend is that an ancestor of Charles was reputed to be one of the four Knights who murdered the priest Thomas A Becket in Canterbury Cathedral. Thus by repute, all his descendants were cursed by the religious authorities of the Holy Roman Catholic Church.

This I can only speculate about as anybody can about such history; however Charles was not to be cowed, he gave the whole shenanigans a clear two finger salute by having a Monk at one side of the main entrance and a Knight with a raised sword at the other. Having been in and around that space for twenty years or more I saw that Evil had a foothold in that part of the village closest to the grounds; his playmates, Tragedy or Horror often visited the row of cottages, next to the church built. From Home Farm at the end of the lane to the church door a line of darkness seemed to emanate.

Magic comes in two flavours, 'Sweet White' and 'Bitter Black.' I had a natural curiosity to know about these forces, could they be a key to understanding Life. I'm sure even the most lugubrious butt brain on the dullest treadmill of existence must occasionally ponder his lot and the magic, or lack of it, in life?

In my search I had been initiated in the late Eighties as a Rosicrucian, the Rose Cross, a tributary of the Templar Knight tradition. I wasn't a fully fledged Rosicrucian, or a Zoroastrian as I stated on my Census, or even a Buddhist, but I was searching for something, a kind of magic. Even attempting to look is actually the key and over the years I found some understanding of the Mysteries I craved.

The Manor was part of that journey, which Is why I was content to have to wait until the Spirits opened that massive door for me, as was writing the book I called Baradour. I had no big flash of realisation that enlightened me, rather a trail of dim candles which led to the sun.

One thing which became very clear early on was the power of magic to corrupt a weak mind and it wasn't a subject to be played with or underestimated.

I left Maud at the entrance as I went round the side and turned the alarm off. I cut through the dark dank corridors of the kitchens and classroom areas in the annexed buildings. passIng the cellar door and cut through the chicane of rooms by the Rood Screen, to the stained glass windows of the inner corridors forming a quadrangle. They were bathed in rainbows of colour that drew shafts through the dusty air, my breath stopped, the emotion of this sight, the feeling of silence, stunned the lungs to stillness.

I padded with soundless leopard paws along the red carpet and turned left into the Atrium. The huge key turned the lock with a majestic creak, bolts burst back ceremoniously, suddenly daylight ventured into the dust laden air; though it felt unwelcome here, a long lost stranger.

Nobody could fail to be impressed, the inner quad of glass panels, depicting the life of such times, was even more beautiful by its imperfections. It was hardly noticeable that the wIndow of the Atrium had a softer hue than those in the corridors, as its glass was the only section remaining from the original. A previous owner experiencing hard times, had sold the entire quadrangle of stained glass on the basis that the Swiss buyer replace it, like for like, with a new but cheaper glass, obviously inferior.

The deal was duly completed and the craftsmen at Toddington found themselves with an almighty jigsaw of glass bits to conjure into their original designs. Everything was carefully planned and labelled, but this didn't prevent glass being left over and several gaps to fill. Thus the odd Knight's arm holds the turret of a castle aloft or a horse runs on wheels. Naturally, it only added to its charm and the song of Maud's laughter filled those quiet corridors.

Marble fireplaces, gold leaf ceilings and fine William Morris wallpaper adorned every main room, a statue stood at the foot of the stone staircase to the upper floor. Beyond were the attics and the roof, even then a high turret, with a ladder to climb up to the crow's nest. Every vista stretched out for miles to the north, south, east and west. Far beyond the ornamental gardens, swirls of Box hedging marked the paths encircling fountains and sculpture. It couldn't fail to stir any imagination.

Like a novice entering a monastery, at my first visit I was over awed with the majesty of it all; I saw and found only its beauty. As the years passed I realised these thick brocades of gold, filigree and stone covered long shadows.

Having toured the inside we returned with joy to the sunlight. At the centre of the west facing wall outside, a wide sandstone bench waited between the sturdy buttresses. It was warm, forgiving and enveloped us in its arms.

For a guy driving a beaten up Cortina, with irregular income, of dubious heritage, I surprised quite a few guests with my cottage in the Cotswolds annexed to this Gothic Manor. The village itself was still sleepy in those days, there was nothing to rudely awaken a dreamer like me, except for the smell of the chicken farm on the main road to Tewkesbury, but somehow that fowl breeze never blew my way.

"This is magical," She smiled.

"More magical than usual, because you're here." I pressed her palm, "Thanks for trusting me, not everyone would have left town with a new boyfriend. I appreciate that. You know you're safe with me."

"To be sure, you're a fine fella, no worries. It's great to be out of Oxford for a change and see what else is about. I've never been to this part of the country before, it's bloody gorgeous; we don't get a lot of this close to London, unless you drive out to Hatfield House."

"You like it there?"

"I've been once or twice," she bit her lip, "but Dad's busy with the building, you know the craic."

"Sure. Wait till you see Stanton and the pub. We'll shoot up there for a Sunset Pint. My favourite place on a nice evening. You'll love Colin and Lyn, she's like my second Mum, got a crisis ask her. She saved me from disaster once or twice."

"Gosh, what happened?"

I didn't say, 'I nearly screwed up and contemplated getting married to the wrong woman.' Lyn had advised me on that occasion, 'For some men she would be a dream, but not you. You're too much of a free spirit for her.' To which she had added, after rather too long a pause, 'Probably for anyone.' She was right. I smiled, "Ahh, I had girlfriend problems at the time and she put me straight. We'll go up around seven if you like, it's only a three minute drive."

"Fab, thanks for treating me, I feel like a queen."

"You are! Queen of my kingdom, honey pie." She squealed with laughter. We sauntered round the back of the Manor, past the old swimming pool, full of green water, home to a universe of wildlife, swimmers, dippers, gliders and sinkers of every size, design and colour.

We followed the huge crenelated wall of the second quadrangle which concealed a covered horse ride, the inside of which was once lined with leather to protect the riders. Past this was the long greenhouse with whitewashed shelves growing only spider webs and withered weeds now. Above were towering trees resplendent in their dappled shadows, looming like overgrown ancient adults.

When we got back to the cottage we made love in the silky late afternoon light. Then she bathed before we went up the pub. I could hear her singing in there. Life was sweet.

The night became the usual high jinks and malarkey at The Mount. Its regular clientele were either rich in character, life or pocket; there was no dead weight propping up this bar.

. The Till was a wooden drawer and 'Tabs' could be run up, as far as Colin felt; three figure sums were not a problem or uncommon.

We took our drinks outside and managed to get a pole position for the view. Thatched roofs above the melted, butterscotch, patch work of stone. The High Street meandered off below us, for The Mount was naturally perched on a mount from where any village fool could survey his realm, as I did mine.

Across the valley Dumbleton Hill was an eiderdown of quilted woods and fields threaded with woolly sheep, spread over its pregnant belly. Beyond this the Malverns slept soundly in Roman dusk.

Windsong was also visible at the end of my pointing finger, just past the old railway viaduct with its proud arches. It moved me, every time I surveyed it, with a beer in one hand, for nearly three decades.

We couldn't help but fall further in love with such surroundings as these. If it had been raining, if the car had broken down, 'If' so many things. We were lucky. It seemed the Gods and more importantly the Goddesses were on our side. The church bell in the village tolled midnight as we drove home, to plunder the warmth and breathless sighs of Windsong.

Sunday morning became midday. We went for a drive and parked the car opposite the thatched cricket pavilion at Stanway and slowly wandered up the hill, Stanway House to our right.

"Come on gorgeous, over this stile." We crossed into 'Lordy's' Manor, home of Jaimie Neidpath, now Earl Wemys, where I had dreamed of embarking on the African Princess in the pavilion. We skirted round the slim lake on the upper lawns. The fountain in the middle provided the highest, gravity powered, water spout in Europe. It wasn't on, normally a Tuesday or Thursday it would suddenly appear like a spirited Gandalf flying above the trees.

Further up, up, up the steep bank to the Needle Folly. Behind it the pearlescent round eye of the Shadow Pond stared upwards at the trees arching overhead its round mirror.

We turned back to look over the stone balustrade. I could see every detail of Lordy's Manor, the sloping roofs, outstretched fingers of chimneys scratching the cloudy back of the sky. In the distance the pavilion where I had hoped to board the African Queen, perched on its Staddle Stone knuckles, edged by the farm tracks I ran along every week.

"Would you like to see the Throne of Trees? It's not much further."

"Ahh, it's all just so perfect here, Jesus I didn't even know such places exist, let alone you could walk right into them. Christ in London the dogs would have had you by now." She put her arm round me.

"Well, not everybody can just stroll through, I know Lordy and he knows me." I smiled, "Anyway, I don't think he can't run as fast as me."

She laughed. "You're a joker for sure."

"Smiles by name, 'Smiles' by nature, and Jesus Joseph and Mary somebody's got to be happy!" I mimicked a priest's voice, "I feel it's my holy roman conjugational calling to be a semi professional twat on a part time basis!" Our laughter filled the Folly's echo to bursting.

We took a couple of steps along the grass bank and turned for one last look before we entered the small woodland. Suddenly the water spout shot up behind us. It was magical, pure magic, as only love and new lovers can create.

Good old Lordy. He'd probably seen the mad hippy with his 'Belle' trespassing up the hill from his library window and decided to entertain the renegades. He was that 'Kind' of a gentleman, Lord Neidpath, Earl Wemys, whatever his name, just a decent bloke.

As if she had read my thoughts I heard her whisper, "Jesus…That's so…Magical."

"That is Magic. You're magic." I purred.

Thus began our courtship in earnest.

Late on Sunday we headed back to Oxford. I took the scenic route of course, weaving in and out of the beautiful villages Broadway, Chipping Campden and Blockley. We were quiet together, which was always a good sign. It's good to fill the silence with nothing sometimes, to feel the silence.

As we drove through Woodstock our hands touched I said, "One, two, three…" I was watching the road but as she turned to look at me and I swiftly planted a kiss on her lips before she realised, "…four I'll be back for more."

She giggled, "God you'd get on well with some of my cousins in Dublin they're all feckin' nuts too." I think we laughed all the way back to St Hughs.

I wasn't sure what the plan was but it seemed I was staying over. "What about your Lectures tomorrow?"

"Oh, I've got a tutorial on Tuesday, that's about it."

"Gosh, it seems fairly relaxed here?"

"Ahh 'tis, until there's an essay due, then all hell breaks out for a few days."

The thing with so many students at Oxford is they were like professional athletes, they made it look so easy and yet years of training and natural brilliance had gone into that relaxed demeanour. I remember the first time I watched her work, reading and typing at a speed I couldn't even think at.

There was something 'To be sure' about this Irish lass. I found her so easy to get along with. We didn't seem to struggle to reach each other, to touch each other, to understand each other and we had music as an invisible bond between us. Music has always been as important as the blood in my body to me and that connection was a vital link.

What were her parents gong to think of me? I knew how disappointed they would be. After all, you pack your daughter off to the best university in the land and she comes home with a hippy, nearly twice her age with two kids in tow. I knew how hard that was going to bite into their dreams.

I couldn't blame them. After all, if I had come home with me in tow I would've chucked myself out!

The next day I left, promising to return on Friday. On Thursday she rang to ask if I wanted to come over to a party that night. "Sure 'bout an hour or so…?" Our weekends eventually ran from Thursday to Tuesday, sometimes right through the week. It was perfect.

The summer term progressed. The weather just got hotter, the parties better, the voices louder as they crescendoed to the 'First Year Examinations' climax.

My friendships grew with many of the girls and guys in Maud's circle, they seemed to enjoy the campus hippy hanging about. If the occasion ever presented itself I would try to offer what entertainment I could with my guitar and what wisdom I felt they may benefit from; fully knowing I wouldn't sway these fresh faces from their goals, good or bad.

We spent the late mornings making love as she was never up early, a natural Owl, whereas I am a Lark.

Ever since those school bells had woken me up at seven I had an inbuilt alarm and an ability to get up and run! Oddly enough, this small detail would prove to be the only flaw in our otherwise perfect life.

Depending on tutorials we often wandered down to the Cherwell Boat House in the afternoon, where we only had to sign out one of the college's punts to be let loose on the river. Here we met the boathouse cat, called 'Friendly.' Years later my own Friendly would rock up at three in the morning while I was trying to walk off an heroin overdose. Sadly, even with this extraordinary adventure unfolding, the lure of one sweet dance with the Devil would bring me back eventually to his knees in supplication.

Friendly was a black cat with a white bib and paws, of no great pedigree or distinction other than he reigned supreme at the boathouse and would survey his Catdom from the small port hole in the apex of the building which housed the punts. He was indeed friendly and once we got to know him he consented to leave his view point, to come down and fraternise with us. I think even he felt our love.

I have never had pets, though I've borrowed a few, including Mr Tabbs who lived next door with my neighbours the Buntings. Unbeknown to them he loved a smoke and when he smelt the hippy next door lighting up a reefer he would pop round and sit on my lap, soaking up the cannabis atmosphere to which he would add his deep sonorous purr.

What we didn't know until years later was that Friendly was called 'Lonely' during the winter when the punts were laid up while the two burly boatmen afforded them some repairs.

There was one punt that lay drunkenly sunken at the end of the row all year, I begged them to sell it to me. Sadly not, the following year it duly reappeared, refurbished and floating merrily on new boards.

The key issue with punting is using the pole as a rudder too. If no one is kind enough to inform you of this factor, much bedlam and free mirth can ensue. One afternoon we watched a Japanese man spend an hour or two desperately pushing and pulling as his entire family floated ten feet one way, eight feet back again and eventually into the overhanging trees on the opposite bank. It was the sort of unscheduled comedy of life that made tears of joy run down our cheeks.

Gong punting as a couple, it was De Rigueur to carry a portmanteau with two flutes, of the glass type, a bottle of Champagne and some treats. A carrier bag could easily suffice but punting brought out the gentleman in even the dullest boar.

We were blessed to spend hours floating on the ripple of reflections, capturing the stupendous lawns and playing fields of the colleges beyond. From time to time another punt would pass, each glancing at the other, exchanging laughter for smiles. Usually couples or foursomes, handsome and proud, elite in their poised limbs. Indeed, they had all earned this glory with studious labour and by dint of being blinking brainy. Unlike myself, a pretender to the throne whose brain had been splattered round the universe more than once and yet had been gifted an entrance pass, a scholarship so to speak.

The one thing I knew, which they couldn't, was the knowledge of how fortunate they were to wear this crown and how sadly, far too soon, it would all be over, passed on to the next group of eager Freshers. The grubby hands of Commerce and Industry were waiting for them to be ushered in for interview. The market place of deals and deceit, high stakes and winning bets would swallow these innocents. Their passionate minds would learn to taper their wick to business hours and bills, whilst propping up the high octane bars of the cocaine nights in The City pubs.

These few years at college would remain forever as golden memories, with friends here and maybe more there. Holidays, skiing trips, villas in the sun, usually belonging to 'Daddy,' but hey, why not? Daddy had probably worked his ass off too.

Luckily, around this time I would also be drawn to London working for a Performance Arts Magazine called 'Don't Tell It.' Wages were more in the form of 'Freebies' and VIP passes to great clubs. Also, my job was tasked with meeting simply amazing people. If they were not off the scales incredible then Jiro the Editor wouldn't have entertained writing about them. You had to be 'Out There,' nearly as far as Jiro was himself, to get an article commissioned.

As we walked back it was hard to know how much to share of the future, moreover how much to share of my past. Everything in those first heavenly weeks and months was tempered with the understanding on my part that this could be a brief fling for her, a one term wonder. I could accept that and had to be thankful for the small insight I had already had beyond those high stone walls that supported the 'Dreaming Spires' of Oxford. Moreover, during the summer holidays she was planning to go 'Inter Railing' with three of her friends.

Four gorgeous girls let loose in Europe. Christ, never mind Jesus Joseph and Mary, I didn't stand a chance if someone her age, no doubt good looking and a thousand miles away from the nearest 'Geoff' pounced on her. When that time came I suggested what I call 'The Russian Ballet Dancer Rule,' before we had a chance to get into those mucky waters.

As the weekends came and went I became closer to her friends and many of the other students at St Hughs. It was mainly more girls via the girls, but also Tom, Phil and Howie, amongst others appeared. It was fascinating to compare their First Year Fresher photos, taken as they arrived at college, with the bleached blond, outrageously dressed 'Fools' visible nine months later. It was noticeable that the boys began their metamorphosis in college, while the girls had already begun that process and certainly led the way in maturity. It was like watching twenty years of labour by parents and teachers that in a few short terms metamorphosed into something completely new, different, individual. It was marvellous to see, yet no doubt somewhat daunting for the parents, watching these strangers arrive back home after a year at college with seemingly only more piercings, more tattoos and dodgy rashes to show for it.

"Shall we go for a drink?"

The Eagle and Child, The Lamb and Flag, The Turf, The White Horse and my favourite The King's Arms, were just a few of the charming denizens of cultural interest in an area running down St Giles to Broad Street. So many others had different stories, but The King's was a quintessential experience of everything that was fabulous about Oxford, its historic heritage, blended with a beer fuelled hubbub of bright voices.

As we entered the rush of warm smoky air and the volume of noise warmed our cheeks. It was always busy but never crowded because the main bar led through to other rooms behind with leather couches squeezed between old armchairs, warmed in winter with real fires. Groups of students would be lolling about in college scarves, wrists aloft, pontificating in leisured debate, or crunched up to the tables, knees to chest, fingers drawing equations or sums on fag packets, edged with glasses and beermats made into every conceivable item except their original use. They were handy for phone numbers, addresses, long multiplication and proving mastery of Origami.

It was different to any other pubs. I jest not! The vibe in these rooms was infused with a heady scent of youthful vigour, sharpened by minds that could quite simply dance blindfolded on a silk tightrope.

I had met many 'bright cookies' on my road through life up to then, but to come to this from the building sites, the streets and drug dens, to be bathed in this luminous excitement was inspirational for me. With no disrespect intended to any other crowd in their local pub, no doubt as vibrant in their own way, yet nothing matched the voices that enthralled me here.

I would park up on a pew with my pint and wallow in the waters of this font. I felt like I had been jolted off the hard shoulder of thought onto the highway of fast thinkers. I really did have to get up to speed. I couldn't risk a sweeping statement or an expansive diatribe without expecting it to be picked apart. These kids still demanded, 'Why?'

My hair alone was enough to state I was not playing the game according to the rules and they wanted to know my reasons, my justifications for not serving the Gods of Normality, they didn't just agree limply, 'Yeah man, that's cool...'

They would be dressed in clothes I once owned, the Cricket blazers, school or House Rugby shirts, corduroys or old leather 'Hand Me Downs' from Harrods, still worth more than my entire wardrobe. Badges of honour, edges frayed, Matron's stitching finally undressed, the Tweeds and Scottish woollens casually flung over well groomed bodies. Their ability to look so moneyed in ragged clothes was inherent. Every gesture seemed drawn from some hallowed hall, filled with years of intense practice; thus it was effortless, the wrists and ankles of ballet dancers, limbs draped like socks or satins over a Chaise Longue.

As I sipped my Milk Stout, my flared jeans hanging like a damp flag from a 60's rock concert, I watched their faces keenly, I studied the eyes and lips, the assuredness of their expressions, the nonchalance. Yet, I also remembered those faces from long ago, my friends with the same look, which no doubt I wore too; until life kicked the shit out of me. I knew I might have worn those blazers, my Abbey House purple and black rugby shirt, adorned with my childhood badges of success.

I considered whether the learning experiences I had gathered, such as how to survive sleeping in a multi storey carpark in winter matched theirs in any way? That's a steep learning curve at three in the morning and guess what, nobody gives a fuck.

These dear innocents were still adored, much loved, marked, assessed, discussed, for Exams, further Exams and then Final Exams. Their careers would demand scrutiny by a Mr Somebody or Mrs Other, whether they cared or not. One thing I figured out was nobody was marking me, grading me or placing me, except myself. I could imagine the 'Fail' stamp on my papers, the 'Expelled' word at the bottom of my file.

Despite these odd moments when I drifted back and forth from 'Now' to 'Way Back Then' I generally felt comfortable; I knew the territory after all. They just didn't know I'd been booted off the land; a place once lost was virtually impossible to return to.

If my spirits ever sighed for the loss of that world and the damage it did to my parents I had only to look over the table at those beaming young people I shared those years with, to feel uplifted. For some reason or other I had been gifted another chance to enter those high walls, with an enchanting young lady as my guide and her fabulous friends who had welcomed me so warmly into their circle.

As the evening progressed the chatter became even more enveloping, punctuated with shouts of names or joyous renditions of staged lines. The smoke got thicker above our heads and swirled round hanging tankards, old photos of teams in sepia brown, broad shouldered rowers on black and white rivers who watched with silent fortitude our revels and japes.

Barmaids scurried through the standing stones of deep discussions propped up in corridors, or hurried between listing tables, while they carried towers of stacked glasses; like circus performers.

Eventually the bell above the bar would toll, amidst groans of horror and a sudden rush for Last Orders. Ten minutes later the death knell would ring and the crowd filtered out to occupy the pavement, finishing long cigarettes while making life changing decisions as to whether it was the student bar, the curry house or Fish and Chips? Hands were held in loving hands, arms and scarfs tied in serpentine union as groups disappeared off in every direction.

I knew after hours pubs too where the owners were dear friends and the drinks would be on the house. They knew I'd do a gig or a party for them anytime. It's the deal with musicians, they don't always bring money to the table.

There were a couple of sweaty night clubs available but the crowd there were more a mix of locals from the suburbs and tourists. The lure of the college bar was more appealing, for once within their walls we were safe to behave as appallingly as we wished.

As Summer unbuttoned the coats of Spring, the pubs with tables outside would become a new focus of speculation. Warm cubby holes were exchanged for open courtyards; bicycles superseded busses, railings stacked with countless fairly crappy models. Most bikes had already completed years of service at Public School and had names stamped on their frames or painted on mudguards.

The trick was to have a bike that rode really well and yet looked as if it was about to fall apart at any second. The theft of bicycles was an apprenticeship taken very seriously by Oxford's 'Non Elite.' I'm sure kids as young as six and seven were given orders like 'young bloods' in African tribes, to leave the suburbs behind, enter the jungle of alley cat streets in town and not to return without scalping a bike.

These stolen perambulators were then pulled apart, sprayed and rebuilt to disguise their origins. It was a perfect training ground, advancing one day towards a decent career in Car Theft. Bless their little 'Bolt Croppers.' Boys often accepted a theft as a way to upgrade the old model; while girls would be reduced to paroxysms of grief that their dear friend had been kidnapped and was, at this very second, being sat on by somebody else's fat arse.

Added to this were the 'Small Time Traders,' who dealt in bits and pieces they could hack off the body. Lights, bells, saddles, grips; they would even take a whole wheel if the chain wasn't looped through it. A quick wander round some of the second hand shops was usually the quickest way to retrieve any stolen property. Many students just shrugged and claimed off the insurance as though it was simply inevitable.

The prevalence of bikes made cars unwelcome. Eventually the Council changed some of the roads to precincts and made parking so expensive it was cheaper to taxi in by helicopter. Thus Oxford, around midnight, exuded a deafening whisper where the thunder of cars had trolled by all day.

We would wander up the middle of the streets, fully knowing they were our jurisdiction now; arms linked in arms, waist to waist, our dreams squeezed tightly in the sweaty palms of our loved ones. The huge gates and high walls of the college grounds on either side of the road would open every now and then to pull a few staggering shadows inside, until just a few of us would remain, teetering ever so slowly towards a last drink at the last bar.

The silent windows of laboratories and museums watched our infant play with the disdain and yet the forbearance any master has of a gifted child. They had observed some of the greatest men and women from history play hopscotch on the same flagstones. Who was to say that one of these mewling minions wouldn't achieve the same distinction?

What made it so special was that our eccentricities were therefore accepted, even expected within that context. To wear a Batman Cape with full college regalia was seen as a stroke of genius, not mere tomfoolery.

I have partied and loved in Oxford and Cambridge, but I always found the former to be warmer, its high walls and turreted halls seemed to embrace our faltering steps as we wound through their historic shadows, following the steps of those heroes and heroines who had felt the glory of this ambience.

Their names were often proudly displayed on small blue plaques, long since sunken into the creases of weathered walls. Thousands more, the 'Unnamed,' were no doubt stacked in silent rows, on the dust laden shelves of those rooms within. Accompanied by the tick of an old Carriage Clock, the tock of a gold watch, or the sigh of a gutted sofa surrounded by crumbling antiques that celebrated those ancient tomes.

The writers and thinkers, the scientists and chemists, the anthropologists and biologists, the mavericks and maniacs. We were all of those in our beer soaked minds, wandering from this pinnacle of possibilities out into that vast wasteland of the world littered with all the previous defeats we would then have to conquer.

My only problem, with a brace of Belles under each arm like some Viking marauder, was not to bang my head too hard on the clouds above as we waltzed back upon the melody of their voices, the refrain of her laughter in mine and the Song of Solomon.

A distant church bell echoed above the tree tops and ramparts of this Eden; it reminded me of bells that had rung through my life. The Sunday sermons, the Monday mornings; a bell to rise, a bell to eat, a bell to school and a bell to break. Bells for tea time, bells for Prep, bells for sleepy heads to go to bed. A bell one day to mourn a death.

This is the power of such a place, imbued with the sense that Time could so easily become timeless, caught in the spines of those ancient volumes, their leather backs burnished in shafts of light from the exalted windows.

TAU

Sunday morning, Oxford. She was sleeping the way young people do, especially students who fulfil half their studies in a coma of somnambulant repose; deep, motionless, purring, untroubled by strife and unlikely to surface for hours to come.

Even the gentle hiss of the kettle didn't rouse her, I looked out at the early summer morning, the recent rain had made the leaves almost iridescent green, glossed over with fresh dew. The coffee was Instant and awful, so I made it strong, chucked a sugar in and slugged it down. The birds and the sunrise were calling to me, my old friends from many a dawn.

I studied her lying there, oblivious to everything but her dreams; the curve of her shoulder beneath the blush of her neck wreathed in curls, the pout of her milk white breast, enticing, entrancing. I considered gently sliding back inside those tresses, but there would be time in the lazy late morning. I had learnt in life to let sleeping dogs lie and never wake a woman up too early. Anyway, I was keen to run, to explore.

I was a natural cross country runner as a schoolboy and despite my addictions I ran regularly. It was another High. I left a note, closing the door silently. I reckoned I had a couple of hours. I knew the lie of the land from walks with Rose and watching her row on the river. I knew a good track along the Thames at Port Meadow. I waved cheerily at the porter and found the Cortina. In the boot I kept my trainers and kit. The CD Walkman was in the glove box.

I took off down St Margaret's Road towards Jericho. The streets were still sleeping, their curtained eyes closed tight against the first shafts of sunlight. I swung right and left and took the footbridge over the railway line. Crossing it I saw the expanse of green pasture beyond and my heart leapt.

I turned left, following the curve of the field until I came to the barges and boats moored up at Medley Bridge. I slowed up to inspect the colourful artwork, the plant pots and bicycles that festooned their decks. Past Fiddler's Island and Bossom's Boatyard. Then past the Sailing Club, with various old dinghies facing every direction except the river, some with fresh coats of paint, others wearing sun bleached, peeling T-shirts.

I left them behind and carried on into the thickening mist coming off the river. At places it obscured the water's edge, until suddenly the cackle and hubris of two Swans or several Ducks would bring them flying out, a phalanx of feathered rugby balls, arcing slowly upwards amid much kerfuffle and kerfuckin' hell.

My lollopping jogging would give chase, tripping blindly on tufts of long grass and dipping into soggy puddles as the birds inevitably and laboriously arced backwards, splashing down about fifty yards further up the river with disgruntled quacks. As soon as I arrived there the whole process would repeat itself until either they ran out of patience with this silly game or I ran out of steam.

The air was moist, cool on the throat, until I swung back from Godstow Lock, by then the morning sun had taken the edge off the river's chilly skin and as I exhaled my breath warmed my rosy cheeks. There were cows and ditches to negotiate but the ground was perfect, not too hard or too soft; my running became effortless and my mind wandered. In the distance the outline of the 'Dreaming Spires' scored dark ascending lines against the horizon.

The Thames, in its infancy still, reflected the blueing skies above, knowing nothing of the great men and women that strolled her banks, or sailed abroad on her grey back; some to their death, others to return vainglorious with the booty of foreign shores clasped in their palms. Yet, for a few, lurching into Dry Dock, half drowned in salty whisky the treasure chests had long since floundered, daydreams mouldered, limpid wrinkles of weathered hope, hung round their necks in barnacles of Fool's Gold.

I considered my own voyages, the pearls I had brought back and those I squandered on bitter mud to fill the gaps in sun baked memories. I wondered what kind of a young man I might have been running these trails all those years ago. Too late to go back. So I made a conscious decision, then and there, to make the most of this chance with Maud to explore an echo from that past era of my life.

I returned to the bridge over the railway and paused at the top to glance backwards; the mist had cleared and the silver skinned Thames was now undressed. I looked at her meandering body as I had the sleeping girl, marvelling at its exquisite grace. I took a deep breath and set off again, looking forwards.

Before returning I slowed up at several gardens and picked the odd flower until I had a poesy. Back at the Cortina I retrieved my clothes and dashed over to North Parade where I bought chocolates, croissants and some decent coffee; three student essentials.

When I got back she was awake but still in bed, the girl from the next room was sitting at her desk.

I smiled at both, "Hi, I've been out running."

Maud's lips pursed up as if she was chewing a wasp, "Jesus, you're keen! Y'wont be getting me out running at this time of the day, now will ya? God it's still morning!.."

"Or any time of day!" The other girl chipped in and we all laughed.

"Croissant?" I opened the bag and offered her one.

"Nah, thanks, I just needed to borrow a dictionary. By the way I love your Top Hat." She got up and opened the door, "Catch you later."

A luscious rather dusky voice cackled from the sheets she was sliding back under, "We'll see you for seven…ish in the bar."

It turned out to be somebody's birthday and the late afternoon was spent with the other girls 'Getting ready.' This involved five minutes with Makeup, four attempts at choosing outfits, three bottles of wine, two hours chatting and one huge Pizza. I loved it.

Even though it was 'The Lord's Day' the college bar was busy, buzzing, bustling with students; the disco lights were whirring away above an empty dance floor while the swing doors burst open now and then with shouts from trilling, thrilling, voices. I loved it even more. Weeks of weekends passed by like this.

As the Summer term warmed up after much Spring rain, the heat of college life rose accordingly. A couple of the girls had found boyfriends and I began to get to know some students from other colleges I was hanging out with, meanwhile it seemed most of the St Hugh's students had learned of the Campus Hippy. St Hugh's took a diverse range of candidates from many backgrounds, more than the traditional college's who preferred to foster their incestuous relationships with certain Public Schools. Thus half of these students had been gathered further afield after much scrutiny and many examinations.

Exams, exams, exams! It was approaching the end of the First Year and fast approaching there was another essential hurdle get over. Failing the 'First Year Exams' would mean expulsion pending any last ditch attempt at retaking them. The purpose of such a rigorous rule was to keep the students on track for at least three terms and wheedle out any unworthy miscreants

I wondered if my Irish lass, after so much consistent partying was really going to make the grade; but she sailed through, with her friends, without much more than, "I'm going to have to do some revision this week. When you come over I'll be in the Library."

As the last weeks of term approached we watched as the different Degree Subjects finished their 'Third Year' exams. I studied the anxious queues waiting to get into the Examination Building. They all knew the next few hours could make or break a future career and also their parent's hopes and dreams.

I noticed some of the students seemed to be at Oxford with a clear cut schedule of study set out by their parents and the fear of God put in them if they failed. These we hardly saw from the beginning to the end of term, every Friday the parents arriving to spend three days cramming and studying with them. Such was 'Their' desire for this holy accolade of respectability, an Oxford Degree to be conferred on their child and ultimately the family. These students had a very different three years to most. They were expected to play their part in the rising dynasty of their family, which is no bad thing. But this heavy responsibility sometimes sank the ship they had put all their gold in. Every year, one or two would fall into the despair of impending failure. They made brief headlines, but it wasn't a story anybody wanted to linger over in Oxford. It's easy to forget that as the possibilities of life extend, the responsibility to achieve them increases.

Our friends had all passed and despite the odd lack of confidence or doubt they now had a mandate for two years studying and student life before the dreaded 'Finals.' Thus they began to make plans for the Summer Holidays, all twelve weeks!

'Inter Railing' was a popular sport for young people at the time, a chance to do their 'Grand Tour' but on the cheap. Tickets were bought for a duration of time, perhaps four or six weeks and the traveller could make an itinerary for wherever they wished.

Some innocents got tripped up and ripped off on these trains, arriving in every major city in Europe, cashed up and mashed up. For some predators it must have been so easy to ride these wagons or to wait at the main terminals and pick off those young people that could be manipulated or were careless with their bags.

Maud was disappearing for four weeks with three of her friends. Her parents were worried. So was I! What if something happened? However, at least she had friends going with her so there was backup.

it wasn't the way it had been for me travelling solo, I never had a ticket back from anywhere, only a ticket to depart. Getting back never really worried me, I would sooner or later, hopefully. Nobody was waiting for me and nobody knew where I was exactly. But being unconnected allows for some freedoms others don't have. I didn't have to worry about my parents being upset if I overdosed or got abducted.

I tried to wise up the girls. I explained the classic mistakes young people make, all the lessons I had learnt on the streets. Who to really trust? Nobody! Never let your guard down, fully. Even people who have entertained, advised, chauffeured, lent stuff, helped mend stuff are to be cautiously loved. Be aware there is no such thing as a 'Free Lunch.'

We also had the 'Russian Ballet Dancer Syndrome' discussion, which went something like this.

"So my lovely," I looked into her eyes, "It's going to be an amazing trip for you all. Which cities are you going to visit again?" She reeled off a list. I guessed all these places would all have their seething dens of iniquity, as most do. "I hope it's the best fun ever, I suppose you are going to meet loads of other students doing the same trip. It'll be great."

She smiled, "Ah, we'll have the craic, that's for sure, but I reckon it's going to be tough going too. There's so much we all want to see." The excitement was running round her face like a cat trying to get out of a pillow case.

I knew that facial expression, I wore it once waiting for The Magic Bus to take me away to Morocco. The chaotic unplanned travels we had undertaken on the 'Hippy Trail' had now been fully homogenised for the younger generations that followed. Probably a good idea. Many travelogues from the old days included horrendous stories of 'Rip Offs' and rapists, mine included. However, the safer you make an adventure the less room there is for the magic of wonderful happenings to occur. Sometimes a traveller needs the sand in their fingernails, a head full of smoke and rusty seaweed to really get the full trip!

"I hope it's the best ever." I paused, "But hey listen, I totally love everything we've got together, I value it and cherish it dearly so while you're away I'm going to look after it. But, it's like," I paused again, struggling to find the right words, "Look, I had plenty of travels and some crazy trips, I met some beautiful people out there and one or two awful bastards, but there's a little something I wanted to say. I kinda love you so much I want you to have the best experience you can have and there's a thing…"

Another pause, "Well, let's call it the Russian Ballet Dancer Syndrome." God this was tough and I was making a total bollox of it, as per usual. "It sort of goes like this. If one night, you're at a party and you find yourself, champagne in hand, on a balcony with a gorgeous Russian ballet dancer and you'd really like," I chuckled, "To screw his brains out! Then I would totally understand."

We both howled with laughter. She gently took my face in her hands and kissed me. "I only want you babe. You're my Beau. Jesus you're enough! Don't worry, the girls all love you too and we're looking out for each other. Nah worries mate." She drawled in an Aussie accent. "You're the best. Simply the best!"

I'm not sure why I came up with that image except that as a child I had been very touched by the story of Rudolf Nureyev and his defection to the West. I was stunned by his resolve to leave his family and all his friends behind, just to follow his heart, his Art. At that time I couldn't know I would also renounce my family, in pursuit of my Art, but unlike Rudolf I was dancing on street corners, dodging coppers.

At that time I also busked at Notting Hill Gate tube station, when I was in London as it helped pay for the trip. Perhaps I was thinking of a guy amongst the regular punters who dropped by to hear me play He was called Marge Mellow and purported to be a ballet dancer of Saddler's Well's fame. Though Maud would have run a mile from Marge and he from her. Bless his gay socks! Maybe Ballet was on my mind? Lord knows, my heart was dancing.

I'd been burnt by love and no doubt started a few fires myself. I'd not had the chance as a teenager to experience a time of Innocence, before Experience took it away with the rest of my childhood.

Somewhere in the madness, between the whoring, the drugs, the cruel deaths and banished children,

I'd lost the formula for Trust. But the look in her eyes told me there was nothing to be concerned about. Having complete faith in someone was a new feeling for me and I never felt otherwise with her.

As the days and nights passed we savoured every moment but eventually it was the last week of term. One of the girlfriends was sitting her last First Year Exam and several of us were going to meet her to celebrate at The Turf.

A somewhat boisterous but friendly atmosphere usually prevailed here. The worn flagstones of the courtyard were inured to the beat of feet and bicycle tyres. The picnic tables outside were draped with bags, purses, scarves, folders, Mortarboard hats and the languid limbs of students basking in the baking hot, beer drenched sunshine.

Maud was already there and it wasn't long before Clarice showed up, with her boyfriend Jason who looked more like an archetypal 90's Pop Star, than most pop stars. His sharp black fringe mopped his handsome brow; his dark eyes scrutinised the world from an aloof place, as if we were being watched by a Leopard. Then, like magic, as if he had just woken, his face would beam, the wrinkle above his eyebrow would disappear and the boy inside smiled. It was no wonder she had fallen for him, I would have, if I was that way inclined.

Clarice's face was flushed from her cycle ride, plus all the emotion of long days and late nights revising. I had met up with the girls several times in the old St Hugh's Library, their heads all bowed in reverent supplication to the gods of the Examination Board.

Her white shirt was unbuttoned by one button too many, the curve of her breasts, slightly crushed into her white shirt, was outlined by the bra beneath. The material became more transparent as the heat of her body moistened it and long shanks of blond hair fell around her bold features, she personified voluptuous attraction. She had the kind of body a Nordic skier might have, strong, healthy, utterly perfect, flawless and with unbeatable stamina. I could imagine the bright, bubbly unbeatable beauty she was at school, scoring goals in Hockey, winning Tennis matches and gold medals.

My appreciation of her beauty had nothing to do with lust. Though her description might betray that. I was just stunned by the commonality of perfection. Everywhere I looked the personification of Youth at its best was on display, draped over tables, perched on benches, propped against the railings; in every state of gorgeous disarray imaginable.

Zena arrived, puffing, out of breath. She had the same vivacious vitality Clarice had, but her's was all streamlined into a thinner vessel. Her sports would have been Long Jump, High Jump or maybe the middle distance races. She was a tough, slightly quirky, cookie. They all seemed to be, perhaps it was an essential quality for surviving those years of intense study. Her perfect wide smile, the flick of her shorter 'Sun In' bleached hair, clear blue eyes which were enticingly beautiful and a voice like Maud's that just seemed to lift and lift and lift, like a rising glider until a raucous, ravenous laugh performed a loop de loop around her lush lips.

Then Lulu arrived. She was shorter, her face was cute, all her features collected economically together into the beauty a Pussycat might have. But don't be fooled by this cat, Of the four girls I had a suspicion that she had 'Inflammable' stamped somewhere on her, next to a small red sign that spelled 'Explosive.'

The four girls summed up the quadrille of loves a man may seek. Clarice was like the Earth, solid, strong, dependable. If Jason built a castle with her it would last forever. She had that simple, dependable logic people who love Sciences seem to have. She was studying Chemistry

Zena, was Air. The most essential thing for Life to exist and yet is untrappable, uncatchable. To grip it, gather it up or try to contain it was impossible. Her's was an ethereal, ephemeral love that entices a man to desire her in the same way he needs breath. If ever there was going to be a maverick, it was Zena. It sums her up somehow that I never had any idea what she was studying. In my opinion her brilliance had that gentle twist that gifted autistics display. She loved The Beach Boys with such a fiery passion and adoration, playing their Greatest Hits over and over.

Lulu was Fire, She was the kind of girl a man would approach in a bar, his feet drawn magically towards her like two magnets, despite his brain screaming, 'No! Don't do it.! I'm gonna get burned.' With every breath a man knew he was going to be loved with a passion that was so strong it could give life to the dying; yet also perhaps death to the living. Such a powerful love may also implode. Somewhere inside all that ecstasy there was a stick of dynamite charged and ready to blow. She studied Law.

Maud was Water. She nourished every part of my being, she went through me, around me. Her love, like her laughter could be poured into any vessel and it would bring life to all, as rain water does. Her love was the best, for me.

Natasha turned up. Her love was like a wild Panther, dark, mysterious, hidden by night in a canopy of shadows. She was tall, angular and majestic, with the limbs of a stage actress. Her hair wasn't black it was Jet black, she had little need of makeup to enhance her almond shaped eyes, the dark lashes and angular brows defined a girl with intent, who wouldn't be easily swayed from her purpose. She would have made a natural Cleopatra in both looks and attitude. Yet this was the young Cleopatra, long before Caesar and Anthony had marched through her milk white deserts and captured her pyramids. She was full of enthusiasm, with the youthful folly of sweet dreams; already aware of her natural powers, the due inheritance of her territories; her birthright. Her voice matched her regal looks, with an inbuilt aristocratic gene rounding her vowels, edging each word in authority. Her laughter leapt like a sprinter at you, wrapping a warm scarf around everything. She was a Biologist.

With true artistic style, Hilary arrived, late as usual, peering out, even on this sunny day, from the folds of her duffle coat. Her striking face modelled her bold features like a Goya, intense eyes under dark eyebrows, such excitement infused them as if they just couldn't wait to experience the next thing. Her verve, her inspiration was intoxicating. Her mind was amazing, whizzing round colours like a spinning top in a paint shop.

I felt such a vibrant artist deserved to be learning her trade in the best possible pool of art, but, in my view, I feel we had just entered one of the bleakest periods of Art, one that leaned towards the head rather than the heart, as personified by Tracy Emin and Damian Hirst. Having studied extensively the History of Art and explored so many museums and galleries in the western World, I found dirty beds and amputated bits of fish, admittedly interesting ideas, but artistically bland and bloody awful. Such art did move my mind and my guts, but not my emotions.

I did meet Hirst, he turned up to buy Toddington Manor one day. I had left my job there by then but I spotted his helicopter from my back garden and guessed who it probably was.

I found two men in the main room on the right as I entered the stained glass quadrangle. One looked very smart, but the other less so. I noticed his suit was stitched inside out so all the seams were visible. 'Pretentious prat,' I thought and turned to the well heeled one, "Mr Hirst?"

It wasn't him of course, it was the tosser in the half tailored suit. I tried my best to say I looked after the Manor grounds for years, that I knew the place better than anybody and had he heard about the curse? Well he hadn't, but unfortunately he wasn't about to, nor entertain this 'Pretentious prat of an old hippy.' I guess that thought crossed his mind.

He basically turned to the sharp suited guy and said pretty much, 'Get rid of this unwanted intrusion.' His face had 'Don't you know who I am?' written all over it. This was ripe coming from a man who supposedly is so much in touch with his humble roots.

So I figured, 'Fuck you.' I went back to my cottage, got a couple of my albums and my book called 'The High Way Code.' It's an 'Arty' book in a magazine format, with photos of me semi naked, shooting up or tied up. I thought that would at least make him see I was a creative soul. I dashed back. They had closed the door on me so I gave the bundle to his Helicopter Pilot.

Some months later Hirst, also famous for the almost plagiaristic resemblance his paintings had to Francis Bacon's and some other ideas perhaps borrowed, published some photos of himself...naked! I can't suggest it was my book that planted the seed in his head but I can say he would have been better advised to keep his badly stitched suit on.

He might have paused a few minutes to hear about the 'Curse of The Manor,' if only for the provenance of the building and that it added, as a Ghost story might, some colour to its history.

The Manor's curse had already begun to work from the day he bought it. What did he achieve with that purchase? Did he restore the Manor to its glory, did he inspire local artists, did he set up any schools or studios or galleries? No, he covered it in scaffolding and white tarpaulins, like the carcasses he dealt in. Twenty years later it is still, similar to his artworks, emotionless, loveless, a ghostly shroud.

Hilary, I suppose, couldn't avoid the swift moving current of Art that defined her era and she created several 'Installations,' another buzz word and artistic movement of the Nineties. These pieces of Art, even in the National Galleries, could comprise of standing inside a badly constructed cardboard box covered with bits of paper, timetables, flyers or magazines, perhaps a dirty cup, a calendar or half a lampshade propped up in one corner.

These works only touched the mind in my opinion. They were an 'Idea,' that another mind judged to be interesting. Where was the emotion and passion in all this? Art should touch the heart and come from the heart. Nothing in this period of 'Brit Art' stirred my soul, other than with dyspepsia.

However it was impossible not to love Hilary and her Art. She was so committed and apparently well respected. Her enthusiasm was intoxicating as was her desire for extravagant expression. I loved that. She was like a rainbow, shining and always hopeful after lashings of wet weather. I don't think I ever saw her without a bicycle and a satchel. She liked me, I think she understood we suffered from similar types of the same incurable disease.

Hilary locked her bike up against the railings and joined the rest of us, now occupying two tables. As the heat of the day built up through early afternoon, bow ties, smocks, gowns and shirts evaporated.

These girls were the core of Maud's friends, as well as the lads, Tom, Phil, Jon, Peter, Clive, Howie and a few others. One of the most beautiful aspects of their characters was a lack of any 'Bitching.' Almost everywhere in life, from Office Girls to Building Site Boys, from Politics to Obstetrics, people slag each other off. They're either too good or too hopeless at their job, too ugly or too gorgeous, too this or too that.

It's no wonder that Mediocrity rules, when the only reward for raising one's head above the parapet is having it blown off. I had already learnt in my life that the truth stinks in a world where bullshit rules, as does excellence appear like a pustule on the leather skin of banality.

Having been a school teacher for many years prior to this time, I had already suffered the slings and arrows of the Staff Room. There's nothing teacher's hate more than somebody the kids love instinctively. I'd also learnt the 'Unspoken language,' women use while their oblivious men prattle on about football and beer; the way they can silently assassinate each other with a sword glance to the left, a dagger look to the right, eyes that could freeze a blast furnace. The red head who enlightened me on that score was exemplary in her own art; I was blessed and cursed to learn from such a great mistress of sorcery.

It's a shame that perhaps it was thousands of years of men ruling the roost that has led to women competing against each other for the best Rooster. They would have been better advised to buddy up like men do and kick the little red fucker out of the hutch.

If I had to offer a reason Maud's friends got on so well it would be that intelligence had something to do with it. Also that the weeks they spent together were so intense there was a lot of better things to focus their lively minds on. Boredom and bitching make good playmates. I was often stunned by the brilliance of their intellect; these students hadn't just gravitated to the top, they had been collected, like uncut diamonds, from the mines we call the British Education System. They had reached the top and in many ways were absolved from the lowly concerns of the populous, for now.

These were the people that would populate the next two years of our lives, including the young lad lolling in the corner with his bow tie and pants at half mast. I felt privileged to be among the privileged, again.

Falling in love with any of these young ladies would have been so easy for any man, they combined their natural beauty with an unnatural intelligence. They were also at that point in their lives, those precious years of blossoming between youth and age, where every facet of mind and body is at its peak. To share in this transition was special, watching the colours fill in over the months, the sketched outline of their personalities revealed in rainbows. Any comparison of the face in their Freshers photo with the end of the First Year picture would suffice.

However, even these belles and beaus, at the top of their game in life were superseded by a clique who were the real 'Creme de la creme,' those at the top of the top, of the upper echelons.

I saw at Public School that most pupils were from Professional or Military parents, yet there were a few who seemed to breathe a different air to everybody else. Some had vague Royal connections, Diplomats or Politicians, Conservative of course, or just plain 'Stinking Rich.' Though wealth wasn't quite enough, it had to be old money, family crests on the gold ring worn casually on the little finger.

Our crowd and theirs were just as charming and beautiful in their own ways. But these young dames and dukes, from so far within the castle walls, had an air of privilege and birthright genetically woven in their psyche. They exuded an inherited aroma from a kingdom no middle class mortal could ever dream of entering. Every stitch of their clothing was perfect, every hair coiffured, every square centimetre of skin was loved and pampered. They seemed far removed from our gritty concerns.

The males of this set, wore arrogance and position comfortably, like a woollen pullover. As the girls had already told me, these guys also had a capacity to come across as complete dorks. Beauty was indeed in the eye of the beholder. I guess some of them were just high spirited and thoroughbred, too well off and closeted by wealth to understand how the rest of us were living. It's an observation that could claim sympathy for both sides. I remembered that feeling from a long time ago, of being beyond any bounds.

Although the courtyard of The Turf is enclosed by buildings, the heat of the afternoon penetrated from above and gradually everybody was cooked. The dozing boy, who must have finished his final Finals, was gently slipping, limply into a supine slumber along one of the picnic tables. He had obviously spent a couple of years practising for this day and he had perfected the ultimate End Of Term Mash Up.

Life went on around him, two handbags and a scarf were propped against his legs. His abandoned shirt eyed the waste bin suspiciously, while his bow tie had long since departed around the neck of another slender nymph. His white flesh belied the hours spent at his studies, his steady breath was calm now knowing in the morning he would wake up hungover, but joyous and sigh, 'My God, it's all over.'

I pondered that thought, knowing full well, like this boy, that my time within these walls, beneath those ivory towers, were possibly now ending. Would our love survive the holidays and once she was home from abroad would her parents lay down the law?

I couldn't blame them if they did. I wouldn't take me home to meet my parents, if I had any.

I remembered the long coach trip from Cirencester to Cambridge when that little bomb went off in my head, suddenly realising I would never be able to take a girlfriend to my home. The thought had never crossed my mind until I spent a weekend visiting the parents of a new girlfriend from my college days in Bristol. Ah well, they'd have only said, 'Run a mile!' or as one of my dear friends suggested once, 'Have you considered getting a Dog instead?'

This was the last 'Hurrah' of the last week for most of Oxford's students, on Monday it was back to just another week for me; trying to make the mortgage, organise Band Practice. hit the gym, have a run, play at the Open Mic Night at The Royal Oak. I put those thoughts away and tried to savour every last drop from this moment in paradise.

The eyes of the girls were even more gorgeous now, misted over with beer, emotion, sunshine and the sheer exhaustion of nailing their First Year at Oxford to the holy cross of endeavour. Two more years awaited them as Undergraduates. The following year was the best. There were some exams, but without penalties for failing, short of worrying their parents.

Their cars would be arriving in a day or so, usually the family Estate, which would be filed with boxes, bags, three weeks of washing and various nefarious trophies from the past term.

I thought of my end of year departure from college in Bristol, leaving my stuff in the Janitor's cupboard, filling a bag with the left over food I could find from the student kitchen, catching a coach from Bristol to somewhere far away.

A girl from the bar returned again collecting glasses. It suddenly seemed the right time to go. Plans were made for the evening; bags zipped, last cigarettes extinguished, hugs, kisses, smiles to the assembled inebriates, buttons knitted, scarves tied, sunglasses lowered, bikes retrieved, locks undone and our small party of blessed souls, somewhat indulged in spirits, wandered off in search of St Hugh's fair lawns.

We passed the Pitt River's museum and turned into the University Gardens. Maud and I both knew the topic nagging our minds, the shadows at our feet, but somehow it didn't seem to matter. We were so happy, so much in love, it would have been churlish to spoil even a moment of it by looking down.

She turned and kissed me, her warm slender curves wound round me, the folds on her long flowing dress licked my ankles; the mound of her curls strewn over my shoulder. I imagined them blowing in a Westerly, wind, towards Ben Bulben, the scent of Sligo fields yonder, the merry pipes of singers, raising to heaven an Irish song, as fiddles and mandolins bodhran'd along.

Those moments would come to pass one day. In that kiss I felt we had settled everything that ever needed saying. She was a very smart young woman and I have no idea how, but she got me in one, she understood my way of thinking and loved me for it.

She never tried to divert me or say no to my creative projects, which still had some hopes and aspirations in those days, the music industry hadn't quite kicked the shit out of them yet.

We had met 'Mum,' and she hadn't run out of the restaurant screaming. Always a good sign I think. I had done my level best to portray my level headed best self. But mothers have X-Ray Radar, tuned to the frequency of bullshit. There was no way, even in my best Tie Dye Flares and jacket I was going to pull the wool over her eyes. Not that I wanted to portray myself as anything but myself. I prefer honesty, because lies always ricochet. I could empathise with her viewpoint; her golden child had achieved for their family something akin to winning an intellectual lottery.

I would have hoped like her that my daughter would meet, if she went to Oxford, a guy around her age, studying more than a Bachelor of Arts in getting smashed and laid.

Despite all these crosses in boxes I guess she could see the happiness in our eyes. I wasn't 'Cancelled until further Notice.' She, like me, probably thought it would all be over in a few months.

The beds of flowers in the University Parks' gardens were Monet paintings, trees in full bloom, basking in a mixture of rain and sunshine, which had washed the city's dust from their leaves. The summer musk kicked up scents as we crossed the paths between each expanse of grass. The Duck Pond waited at the bottom of the slow sloping banks, a great glassy eye reflecting a footprint of sky, the occasional bird traced these reflections with feathers across the sky. A duck paddled poshly by, its beak erect and highly polished, as befits residing in such a prestigious oversized puddle.

Cupid's bow had unleashed his arrow, its tip dipped in a love potion so strong, I felt it coursing through me, a tidal flow I couldn't swim against. Like the duck I kept my head up, looking as if I was in total control, while my feet were paddling like fuck in the mud and squelch beneath me.

I wondered how many other lovers had faced the end of the summer term with the same emotions.

"Gosh, it's going to be so amazing." I lied.

"What?" She smiled. We stopped in the lea of a huge tree and I pulled her down to sit on the grass with me, leaning our backs against the trunk.

"Your trip with the girls. You'll come back feeling different about life, I know I did." Our arms linked.

"Ahh, we'll just be having a good craic and seeing as much stuff as we can; you know, museums and stuff like that. We've got loads of plans and lists of places." Our legs edged together.

"It's what you weren't planning to see that may well be the most memorable bit. My journey's were like that. Just take care babe, remember there's a lot of crazy people gravitate to railway stations and tourist attractions, looking for lost students."

"Ahh, there's lot's of crazy people everywhere," she pinched my nose and laughed, "And you're the craziest motherfucker of them all!" We fell apart laughing and then hugged each other tightly.

"It's my prerogative to worry about you babe."

She smiled, "Whatever that is, I love it." We laughed and kissed until we ran out of breath. She rolled over and I brushed the crush of dark curls from her neck. My fingernail carved a line between her shoulder blades, her skin was perfect, softly blushed and lightly tanned.

I made an 'I.' Then 'L,' an 'O,' a 'V,' an 'E.'

"You," I whispered into her ear, my lips kissing her neck, tip toe'ing to where her bra strap hugged the skin. I tugged at its elastic and growled quietly, like a lion heading towards the light of a camp fire. "I'll be waiting for you babe."

"Hmmm," she purred, "I like the sound of that."

I turned onto my back and pulled her over me, her eyes were moist, twinkling stars at their centre. "You're gorgeous."

"You're not so bad yourself." We danced a slow Waltz with our kisses. She grinned at me, "Come on, let's go for a walk over the river."

We crossed High Bridge and turned left over the stream into the unkempt wilderness bordering the east banks of the Cherwell. We wandered on arm in arm, until we crossed the next stream. Here the path backs away from the river and we found a small curve at the water's edge, hidden by reeds in front and curtained by the trailing branches behind. I took off my shirt and laid it on the dappled shadows. Her long skirt unfolded as my hand moved across her thigh; her slender legs begged my fingers to follow them up to the thin fabric above.

She was perfect. I had found a young woman who's passion, once unleashed like Pandora, was limitless.

She was keen to learn, unafraid, simmering, ready to boil over at any moment. We made love. Her bra strap gave in to my teeth and my mouth devoured her breasts; her nipples, licked, bitten, sucked into my kisses. Awhile later we rested, staring up at the leaves above, the glint of sunlight, the flicker of light and shade. It was all so perfect.

We made love again. As my head came up in an arc of ecstasy, I glanced through the long grass and saw four shocked faces, as though caught in a flashbulb of stilled expression, gliding serenely past on a punt. I guess they heard the song of her laughter dancing down the river, all the way back to the Boathouse.

We dressed and sauntered back in the lengthening shades, held in the space somewhere between the ending of afternoon and the beginning of evening. I felt the warmth of her body, I knew I was inside her. A red scratch followed the edge of her breast, her buttons undone, my guilty fingerprints on every one of them. Her kisses still lipsticked to my neck.

Everybody we met smiled at us as though we were the lucky winners of some amazing award they all knew about, but couldn't tell us. Our love seemed to make everybody joyous around us.

True Love is magical. It is an energy that makes all those close by hum like a choir, things work out, even better than planned, luck is on every corner.

We crossed back over the bridge, the sun was already undressing the day, laying out her red satin pyjamas over the clouds to the west. The settling dust of the city shaded pinks into crimsons, drawing black edges around grey spires. We wandered back across the lawns towards North Walk. Thought in thought, arm in arm, hand in hand, with even strands of our hair magically plaited.

Couples were still on blankets, reclined against the grass banks, some rested backs against each other, one or two solitaries were lost in pondering thought. Yet all of them had their faces raised and noticed us pass. They observed the world happening around them, everyone was gazing into the middle distance of life. Nobody had their heads bowed, in servile reverence of a small screen in their lap, nobody tapped or talked into mid air. They were all here, with us, sharing that sunset.

As the park receded we briefly walked through the real world on its way home or back out again, until North Parade twinkled its coloured lights at us and we turned into this little haven to buy cheese and brown sauce for the sandwich toaster. It was our main source of hot food, other than Ali and his van but he would still be having his Moroccan siesta.

Back at her room we ate. Then slain by the heat and excitement of the day we dozed off. The sunset was long gone when we awoke, but it wasn't dark; the city lights had blended with the rising moon. In the half light we entwined again, unlikely to be disturbed by passing river punts, we dived into each other's naked waters.

The twilight caressed the colours spying through the window at our bodies. It was a moment we both secretly tucked into our hearts to look at, now and then, during the weeks we were going to be apart.

Later we dressed each other, swapping T-shirts and touches of brush stroke. She put on some make-up and we headed to the bar via the phone boxes. There were two downstairs in a corner, usually one would be full, rarely two. Being the end of term many students were checking arrangements for parents arriving, or ensconced in hour long weeping with either past, present or a future boyfriend. As we waited a face glanced from the box and a moment later she replaced the receiver. I wondered if our arrival had heralded the classic, 'Oh look, sorry, we'll have to talk another time. Somebody is waiting.'

Maud called to make sure her father, bless him, was still cued in for pick up. He had an incurable disease which prevented him passing a Pub without some small donation being made to the landlord. He bore his affliction with dignity and grace, never a murmur of complaint. He was truly a beautiful man, generous of heart, liver and pocket.

I knew I would have to be there when he arrived. Man to man. Hand to hand, returning his daughter to his care. I needn't have worried. Maud put the receiver down and came back to my arms. I asked, "All set then?"

"For sure, well so he says. If the feckin' van makes it. He'll better get here or Mum will kill him. Jim is coming too." He was her younger brother, by a few years.

We headed back to the JCR and the mayhem of one last night. Having pillaged Oxford's clubs and pubs during the day the students had all come home to roost till midnight. The music was louder, the pints deeper, the smiles wider and yet many an eye had tears brushed to one side, as the enormity of three months separation hit them.

I felt the same. Would it ever be the same? Some faces would indeed not be coming back, their three year tenure of paradise being over. Others perhaps, due to be posted back in Autumn, would be lost in the mail, by strange occurrence, a dastardly quip of Fate's whip or a foreign News Bulletin.

We played along, danced on and on, singing the songs we had partied to for weeks, until the music faded away. The bar man shaking his head sadly as he turned the volume button. A good friend to us all, but he had to close the shutter on another summer term sooner or later. Wherever that point is, between sooner, later, he took it, locked up, waving goodbye through the descending grill. It was over. Done.

The following morning, suitcases with hangovers from hell and bags full of eye shadow, were being dragged unwillingly across the endless undulating parquet flooring. Puffs and huffs echoed through the high corridors, followed by the odd, bump, bump, bump, as a trunk went down the stairs on its bum.

Maud's father and brother arrived. I helped, smiled, shook hands, was polite, saying the right words up until the only one left between us was 'Goodbye.'

The Transit van paused a moment at the end of the road, I saw a hand wave. it turned and disappeared. The Porter suddenly appeared behind me, "Alright son? I hate this time of year too. Don't worry, they'll all be back before you know it."

"I hope so." I sighed, "I hope I'll be seeing you…"

His hand rested on my shoulder, "Course you will boy. She's crackers about you, mad as pancakes."

"What, er...?" I smiled bleakly.

"Oh, I get to hear it all mate, not that I'm listening of course, but you can't help it, they spend more time gabbing on in my lodge than I do. You'll be fine, trust me, see you in October."

"Christ, it'll be Autumn." I realised.

"Guess so. Take it easy now."

"No chance of that buddy," I laughed.

The Cortina was waiting patiently, I chucked my guitar in the back and considered going over to Gaz or maybe stopping by the Music Box for awhile. But my heart wasn't in it. I put Maud's latest 'Mix Tape' in the stereo, flicked up the volume and set off in the direction for home."

Monday night was band practice. We were keen as mustard on a hot tin roof. I liked to think of us a bit like the band up at The Big Pink in Woodstock with Dylan and Robbie. Except we had no fame, less fortune, hardly any money and pretty much a less than zero chance of making any three of them.

My music was already out of date by the time I'd learnt three chords, but being fashionable never really bothered me that much. I was on a mission. We were going to make an Album. Wow.

The first problem was I had nothing to record it on. Sure, I had a Reel to Reel, but it was only two track and there was no way I could squeeze the cosmic cacophony of my band into such a small space.

I had already done enough quasi journalism thanks to Jiro, to have discovered the power of, 'I'm doing a review for…' Nobody had heard of 'Don't Tell It,' because it was way too creative and edgy for mass consumption, but I knew the form. So I stretched a point or two and pretending to write for some Music Tech mag I blagued a Four Track Minidisc recorder, which were brand new on the scene then, touted as 'The Musician's choice.' I guessed I must qualify for that, somehow.

So I rang up this big company and they were only too happy to send me one to review. I figured I could do the whole album in ten days and send it back.

No problemo! It came, lit up, worked for seventeen seconds, hit a glitch and died with Error Zero Seven, on its little screen. 'Shit.'

I rang up the next day, saying I had this band down from Glasgow, god knows why Glasgow, but we had only five more days to test the recorder before they returned. Bless the poor woman who dealt with me. Two days later a new one arrived and I sent the old one back as requested to their Repair Centre. We kept the machine a week or so, I nailed album, kept the masters and sent that back too.

A month or so later the farmer at the end of the lane asked me if I would pick up the package left in his porch.

"Sure?" It turned out they had returned the repaired machine to me, thinking I guess that I had bought it.

Thanking God, amongst any other deities that might be listening, for this providence I felt duty bound to keep it and use it to good purpose, as one should with any gift from above.

Kevan was usually the first to arrive, well always. He was a brother, as much a friend, as much a member of the band, as much as anyone ever was. We had that sort of love. The type that made Butch Cassidy and the Sundance Kid jump off that cliff!

Only difference with our jump was it took twenty years to descend, interspersed with some very high altitude flying. Boy did we have some sessions. We cooked up music the way it was supposed to be done. Live! Full of emotion, full of life, full of love, including the odd fuck up and a few bum notes.

Miles would dig that.

RHO

Windsong. As the latch on the old back door clicks up a silence creeps out to greet me, the hush and stilled heartbeat from within. He has been waiting for me patiently, my best friend, 'Windsong.' My ally, my haven, my one good thing when everything else was sliding into perpetual shit.

There is no better view of the hills above Stanway and Stanton, adorned by their seasonal shades. White fur coats in Winter and red cloaks for Autumn, Spring galoshes painted with petals, from a palette of rainbows; while Summer lay naked, her green threads worn to gossamer, her pert reds still unripe, a garland of pinks anointing her lascivious fecundity. She too was watching me, her warm arms reaching through the open windows, beckoning me down to the river, where the rush of falling waters covered the sighs and cries from love and life.

As I studied the Weeping Silver Birch that formed an archway from its branches and leaves leading to the front gate, I noticed the small, perfectly symmetrical shapes of the Opium Poppies growing next door. The owners were 'Weekenders' and rarely there, so rare in fact that things could grow and disappear from their garden without their ever knowing. Even if they did nobody calls the 'Cops' over a few missing, dead or dying Poppy heads. My neighbours would come to forgive me a lot, as the years passed and they remained, arriving in Spring like the daffodils and departing with the falling leaves of Autumn.

Without thinking, as if led by an unseen hand, my feet turned into the music room towards the front door. There was a porch with a glass inner door, as I glanced through I saw the pile of letters on the floor; they fitted a common description, either brown or white, tiny slices of doom awaiting my presence. Sadly these were only the latest arrivals, scattered on top of other ones from previous weeks. I clicked the latch up and gathered them all together, and neatly stacked them on a box of records where a previous pile still sat. It could be a few more weeks before I finally opened them.

I had a process for such dire financial conundrums. The trick was to wait long enough, but not too long, for the requisite moment, by which time most of the doom and gloom would have been superseded by updated versions of the crap. So that binned half of it. Then I made three piles, 'Life or death,' letters, seriously needing consideration and possibly even answering. Then, impending crap but not this week and therefore eligible for return to the heap in the porch, with luck they would get through the second round and get answered. The third pile would be advertising or bills I had lost the will to pay with the usual demands from Debt Companies, who made a living out of buying bundles of Defaulted loans at a cheap price and then harassing the debtors until hopefully someone would give in and start paying. Not me.

Finally, I never undertook any observation of my financial situation without getting utterly smashed beforehand; the worse it was, the more smashed I got to cope with it. Oddly enough, with an elephant's dose of morphine bulldozing like a rhinoceros on heat through my veins most financial crashes look rosey enough to smile through another day.

My Irish belle had a week at home in London and then a month Inter Railing. By the time she returned I would have cleansed any traces of this narcotic hedonism from my body. What could be simpler? What would make a great day greater? Opium.

I'd had a good run, surely I could allow myself to indulge in a few days 'Dancing with the Devil?' How the brain mocks itself? How it plays tricks to fulfil its secret desires, winking coyly from the side of the stage, beckoning me to where the table is laid, full of fare I really shouldn't have. But that brain wants it, it loves the dull thud of the opioid, washing away all its sins, cleansing doubt and depression from its walls and windows, as if sweeping the cobwebs away, to reveal sheer joy, immeasurable pleasure, a slow eight hour orgasm running through every synapse. Despite the brain knowing it shouldn't, it draws me closer and closer. What could be simpler?

My hand reached through the fence, I didn't even have to sneak into their garden. I chose about ten or fifteen poppies, that would do the job. Their heads were stained with brittle black beads of Opium, a good sign of potency, while the stalks also revealed the deep black veins of delight within.

All this would go in the pot. I glanced up at the sky as I returned to the front door, a buzz of anticipation already humming inside me Above, a solitary Magpie flashed by over my roof.

The kettle hissed as the sun slowly strolled over the hills, way over yonder, through my kitchen window I followed the elegant lines made by the trees and fields of Dumbleton to the west. I lived in a magical spot, not the best house in the block, but certainly the one with the best views, front and back.

In the back of my mind I knew the poppies would help to calm the ardour of my lust, it would make it easier for me not to stray, lulled by a summer's hot afternoon and a Russian Ballet Dancer? I cut up the Poppy heads and stalks and squashed them down in the saucepan. The Kettle clicked off and I poured the steaming liquid over the contents. I flicked on the gas and watched while the water began to bubble and turn brownish. A good sign. I sniffed the steam, the back bite of a bitter taste burned in my throat, this confirmed the potency. A better sign! Poppies could vary in their strength.

It was so easy, like falling into the arms of an old friend after a long journey. My life always seemed a long journey, ever onwards, no going back. There was no departure point to which I might endlessly return, or even an arrival zone. But Opium provided a station on the line, a stop off point to stretch my legs and let my mind wander. A safe place.

I remembered those end of terms at Bristol Poly, with the Janitor leaning on his brush, chatting and laughing with me, waiting for me to pile the last of my crap in his cupboard, his wave goodbye and the endless summer of wandering from coach station to coach station. Luckily I love such places. One thing I can guarantee is everyone there is about as poor as me, I've never met any wealthy people waiting for a coach, anywhere.

'Home,' those impenetrable four letters, which even shaken up will only knock on a door marked, 'Me? Oh,'...A guilty pause then, 'Sorry but no, not today.' After a time a life of true loneliness loses the ability to seek out or love anything else, other than the hiss of silent air, the final click of a door, closing of the outside world. Clocks are removed, mirrors vanish and the day is spent in anticipation of its long sleep.

People are unwelcome here, they are too loud or messy and belligerent, they just don't understand gentle...ness and silent...ness, they crave the noise of brash voices, the thunder claps, the vent and fury of crowds, they see no benefit in lonely...ness.

With Opium I knew exactly where I stood, what the deal was and what the final cost would be. I poured the steaming liquid into another pan to soak off the heat, then into another and then into a mug with a spoon of instant coffee. A tablespoon of sugar and a dollop of milk made it more palatable, but Pavlov's Dog had drunk enough of this shit to love its bitter rind and brittle peel, the smell of vapours rising from the baths of Elysium.

I understand that it is hard to understand.

How many lovers have watched their lovers fading away, disappearing behind the cold eyes of Opium? It must be so sad to love someone who desperately needs to be loved and yet keeps every attempt to be touched, to be embraced, held back. I have broken some hearts, being like this.

The problem was Opium's touch had replaced all those hands that belonged to my family. Since my expulsion from school and my Mother's death I had been cast out as the Enfant Terrible. I had my sister, my son and daughter out there on a limb, but Clare was in Brighton and the kids in Somerset broke my heart every time I had to leave, after those few precious days at the weekend. Saffron's face and her little hand waving from the bedroom window, it utterly destroyed me, twice a month, every month for years and bloody years. I needed something to freeze these emotions. Junkies have Autistic Hearts, everything felt through a magnifying glass.

As I finished the cup I made another and let it stand. One is never enough, two is too much and three is the magic number.

I thought of the weeks to come, I was working on an album with the band and generally scrubbing along the floor of survival, as per usual. I liked my life and was liking it a lot more as within minutes the glow of contentment spread from my solar plexus, a warm vibrating arm had been wrapped around me.

I guess I won't get the chance to say sorry to those who loved me and lost me, or went nuts somewhere between the two, unless they read this, but some of them have already died. It would break my heart, as well as theirs, when I knew I had to score, like really had to score and there went fifty quid I couldn't afford to some guy for five rolled up Rizzla papers and some brown dust. Years of that had passed and years were to come.

I appreciate it is also hard to understand how a man who loves freedom so much would yoke himself to the shackles of drug addiction. Well, the truth is the chains went on before I knew they existed and the marks on my wrists and ankles just never faded. Yet, within my bubble, Opium in particular offers another kind of freedom. Within its embrace those letters in the porch are forgotten, or even considered to be surmountable. Like a lone General on a battle field, surrounded by dead or dying troops, I still believed victory was possible, somehow, someway, maybe if I got a break, a chance of real success, something to make all this crap, all that Past, worthwhile.

The world beyond my window suddenly seemed a better place, my body sang inside with excitement, it wanted to run again. Later, I would go, up the hills, effortless, racing the horses, free in my wilderness.

I only offer this explanation because I will reach this point time and time again, overlooking Paradise and yet I just couldn't leave that Devil alone. As the years became decades it changed too. The first ten years of drug abuse was a playground game compared to what followed. One earthquake after another storm, hanging on the same cliff edge, but now the rock face was floating in an abyss of nothingness. No connections with life on the ground, nothing to grasp while the drug oozed slowly out of my pores. As the years went by it took longer and longer for the body to cleanse itself.

Enough thought! The warm 'Slush Puppy' of Opium was sloshing around the inner courtyards and quads of my brain, messages were going out to the far colonies to expect a 'Rush.'

This is the moment.

This is it.

I changed into my running gear.

The grass beneath my feet began to blur as I ran, heading across the fields to the tunnel under the Railway Viaduct, a colossus of arched bricks. Under this, over the fields to Stanway Cricket Ground with the thatched pavilion, where I had fantasised about boarding the African Princess. Then left along the lower fields of Lordy's domain, bordered by ancient trees to Stanton. Over the stiles, through the gates, down the track, onto the road round the chicane and into the flower bedded, butterscotch and rose garlanded walls of the village.

I passed 'The Vine,' which was the quintessential Riding Stables locally. Its fit, sleek and well groomed horses were exercised by even fitter sleeker and well groomed stable girls. They all seemed to have long blond hair and that discerning smile which promised the world, or at least a view of the dreamy hills. How I lamented my inability to even sit on a horse without feeling distinctly seasick. However, the girls, some of whom were daughters of the family living at the Vine, at least graced us with their presence up The Mount. Although considered an 'Outsider' as I wasn't born and bred in the Cotswolds I became dear friends with one in particular, a real peach among the prunes, if ever there was one, called Bubbles. A young woman with more character than a Shakespeare play, yet sadly with probably as much drama, not all good.

With such diamonds in our goldmine, we added the farm, or the estate boys, with the colourful locals, the odd millionaire or two. Now and then folks from London would descend. Outside The Vine I noticed a couple of cool cars; which had the unmistakable sheen of vehicles living in London.

The 'Pop Stars' were back. Perhaps, around seven o'clock, as the sun melted over the thatched houses and cottages I would be having a pint with these lovely people, standing two steps from the music business I desperately hoped to be part of. I may as well have been in outer space. Which is where most of them, bless their Gucci's, thought I'd come from. Generously, they appreciated my guitar playing and enthusiasm for all things marked either 'Life, Love,' or 'Liable to blow your brains out.' They were the next generation and I was definitely the last, or maybe the one before that, or before that. Fuck.

I took a deep breath and turned right through the village, onto the grass verges that fronted the stone arches and steps of several magnificent houses; weathered by wind and rain, built with a stone that could tell a thousand tales, if only we could read those centuries of light and shadow.

The hands that hammered and stroked the contours of every one, coursed and quoined. The grubby little fingers of children running their rattling sticks down the lines of history. The warmth of farmhouse fires within, defrosting cold backs and frozen bums, feet stamping out the cold, kicking off the stable yard manure or steaming dry the summer dew.

One day, we will read those stones, with the chatter of the farmers, the laughter of their wives, the growl and gristle of Gloucestershire accents, so thick they couldn't be stirred with a stick, less still understood. 'Old Gloster' is about as broad as it is long, like the stone at sunset, it melts deafness over an eardrum like a ladle of butterscotch honey.

I passed Sir Richard's windows, the Staffordshire figures he loved were perched studiously on the sill, their backs betraying sideways glances. The upward slope was effortless, the road forked and I swung right, then sharp left past Pixie Cottage, its thatched roof larger than the cottage beneath, roses climbing the clefts in the sun soaked stone. I waved to an invisible Rosie and Ollie inside as I weaved left and right where the road petered out and the trail began.

In those days it was no more than two tractor tracks winding up the most gorgeous hillside imaginable. It had dingles and dells, hummocks and dips where I could hide with lovers and while away the blushes of summer afternoons.

There were always horses up there too, as well as the occasional squawking Pheasants, raised in their thousands to be shot in their hundreds, for fun.

Oi Barbaroi! I once came across a shooting party, led by a great pudding in his new Barbour coat and posh wellies, trumping down the hill where the path runs under the trees and narrows. There was no escaping our collision. I was used to coming across such parties or groups of horse riders out on a hack. He had his chumps with him, all dressed similarly as though out of an advert in 'Country Life,' that bible for everything except real country life. You wouldn't find the stable girls, the farm hands and the old hands that had ploughed with horses an unforgiving land for centuries between those glossy sheets.

It wasn't until I was a few feet away I saw the little girl by Mr Chump's side. She was perfectly beautiful, wrapped up in a fur collared coat and boots; but as I glanced closer I noticed two birds hanging from each tiny white hand.

I couldn't help myself.

"My God!" I said. For one moment the Chump troop thought this half naked, long haired idiot with his Walkman and headband was about to pay them a compliment. They were wrong. My emotions burned, I couldn't help but ask, "How can you put death into the hands of that innocent child?"

I didn't wait for a reply. I could sense one wasn't forthcoming, so I disappeared up the trail. I had made my point.

I just couldn't understand this mindset which encouraged hunting with its barbaric consequences. The ridiculous social pomp and circumstance, just to nail one fox's tail to the woodland floor and then remove it, so the blood can be daubed on the newest, youngest recruits. To me that seemed like sour cream on crud cake.

This heartland of huge tractors and Porche drivers with all its entrenched customs and attitudes was perhaps one of the worst places to shipwreck a 5 Star Executive Beach Bum with bohemian taste and hippie flares. Just my presence near a Point to Point

Meeting was enough to ruffle the country feathers of these folk.

I prefer not to denigrate somebody else's way of life, nobody really has omniscience; but faced with that awful image of such rose like innocence holding the limp bird's on a piece of bailer twine irked me.

My problem is a dreadful inability to shut my gob, when opening it will do me no favours. I often think to myself whatever happens don't mention that, don't say that, they're gonna want to kill you. Less than five minutes later out it comes and all hell is let loose. I seem to have a pathological urge to tell the truth, which can be fatal in mammals.

As the woods thinned out I came to the upper green banks where the trail had a beautiful loop carving up the incline in a hoop. It was at this spot one morning years before when the mists were filling the valley below that I came across 'Bubbles' descending on a huge horse, coming out of the fog like some Norse goddess with long blond tresses flowing behind.

I was dumb struck by this epiphany emerging from the mists and for once I could only totter by smiling inanely. That evening she turned up at The Mount and I was hoping she might have been impressed by my energetic jogging and my 'sawn off' shorts. I ventured to enter into some sort of conversation with her. Not with a view to picking her up, as I was a lot older than her and her boyfriend looked a fiery chap, but just to bask in the glow of the moment. So I came out with, "Hi I was just thinking, you know, haha, if we ever got married you would be called Bubbles Smiles!" God! Where does this verbal tripe appear from? Needless to say I never saw a girl's face express so unequivocally a look of pure horror as that thought entered and swiftly exited her mind. If only my tongue could edit my brain!

But friendships are born from such clodhopping mishaps and we still laugh and cry about those shorts. Twenty years later we'd ascend the same hill in a 'Four by Four' on a misty track that was a mud slide, four minutes going up that hill I'll never forget. Trying to get a roll up together in the back while feeling I was on one of those wild horses as we took bend after muddy bend to reach the film crew she was working with. I kept praying silently, 'It's good to live life on the edge!'

The Levi shorts, to be fair, I had found abandoned on a hedge after a Glastonbury Festival, some years before; the fact that they had probably belonged to a teenager didn't really worry me, just everybody else!

Finally, having curved round the graceful hoop and puffed up the last bit of the track I arrived at the top of the hill. I turned back briefly to view the fields and the thatched roofs of the village in the valley below and beyond all this the distant, ancient Malverns.

From there I cut along the brow of the hills, heading south for a mile or two, following leaf strewn paths through the woods. Once I was above Lordy's estate I climbed the slopes across the last few fields, past a derelict farm, to The Throne Of Trees. This was a magical circle at the peak of the hill. I would use it in my book Baradour.

I circled clockwise around the Oak trees, stopping at last in front of the one that looked over the valley below. It had a seat formed from a bolus of wood at the base of the trunk. From this vantage point I surveyed my kingdom. The exhilaration of the run, the beauty of Mother Nature around me and the Opium all thundered through me like a steam train.

I guess the hill was a few hundred feet above sea level, but I was cruising well above that. I still had a lot to learn about long term drug abuse. I clicked the Walkman back on and some heavy rock began to flood my heart with blood. I took off, my winged feet flying down the hill, now aided by gravity. The sheep plodded out of my way while the odd horse sniffed disconsolately in my direction, they'd seen me run by before. Within minutes I was skirting Lordy's lair, making my way down, round his grounds, to the cricket pitch far below, under the railway viaduct and back towards Windsong.

At the main road, I went left up the incline until the small triangle of grass welcomed me to turn into the lane, its Poplars standing proud, then the Chestnuts, leading into my driveway, dropping conkers below.

I slowed down and turned to go round the back of my cottage. I flicked the music off and opened the back door. As the latch locked, the silence within hummed inside my ears. Sunshine flooded the floors below the windows. A faint galaxy of rainbow stars wobbled on the walls as the breath from the back door set the glitter ball in motion, sun dancing on its round back.

I showered and dressed. Shorts and a vest T-shirt.

My guitar, still in its case was singing to me. Band practice was tomorrow. I flicked open the catch and lifted my baby out.

The chords began to suggest a few words and suddenly I was riding on the back of my muse, I could feel the song coming, the trick was not to pull too fast or too slow on the thread. I had a rough verse and two lines of a chorus. I kept fiddling and diddling until the rest came through. All that was left was to bridge it together, nail the 'Intro,' the 'Outro' and write it in the book.

Three days after we'd met, I had written 'Touch Me Twice;' my song book lists it as the 21st of May, '96. It was mid summer now, the heat of the afternoon added to the thump of my opiated heart. I strummed chords, while outside, beyond the music, bird song filled the silences of Windsong.

I was blessed, very blessed considering the melt down of my teenage years. How easy it would have been to end up out of my depth with a nasty punter, or on the end of a dodgy deal, reeling out of some toilet with the Devil tearing the bloody shirt off my back. I'd seen that happen and too much darkness to ever worry about the rain or starvation. However, my days with the devil were far from over; he had a few tricks up his bloody sleeve to come.

Meanwhile, reality would always be suspended on a thread of hope that somehow, some blinking thing might just work out, justification for so much that was lost or taken from me.

I wrote the words down, jotted the chord shapes next to them, I would come back to it later with the band and see what happened. Not content with the labours of the run I decided to go for a swim at the Lido in Cheltenham; I could pick up some dope on the way back.

I painted this picture to capture a good day, the day that everything was fine. There must have been a day like this, many I'm sure. How could I have back pedalled all the way to Hell? But the drugs that lit the fire in my heart on that day were going to burn down my future one day, smoulder by smoulder.

Nobody wakes up one morning and thinks today I will begin a trail of tiny events that will eventually destroy my life, my love, my home and career... But shit happens.

"Pint of Lager Colin, a BB, a Cider and er," The pretty young woman at the bar paused, blushing, making herself only more gorgeous, "two Orgasms and a packet of Crisps."

Colin, the landlord of The Mount Inn, smiled, "What flavour would you like...?" He began to reel off the crisp options, but nobody was listening anymore, they were waiting to see what two 'Orgasms' were going to look like in her hands. However, a few minutes later, when this vision of Venus turned round holding her drinks aloft, the other customers all politely studied their beer mats or the flagstone floor, as if this were just a regular occurrence; which it was during the heady summer months, for some years.

The 'Band' were outside, perched on the wall or standing around the table they had commandeered. The young beauty delivered the 'Orgasms' and pints to outstretched hands, then disappeared the get the crisps. She had refused the offer of a tray from Lyn, preferring to shimmy back through the packed bar.

All the men politely looked askance, yet their eyes couldn't help but follow the backs of her legs as she returned the second time; it was too much for any man's retina to refuse. A moment later the side door swung shut behind her and ten sighs sank back into ten pints of bitter Bitter.

One aspect the 'Pop Stars' loved about the village was it didn't blink, though it might occasionally stare for a moment. People were obviously curious about who was, 'down this weekend' but nobody was star struck enough to embarrass them for autographs or a cozy chat. They'd seen it all before.

The Cotswolds had always courted the rich and famous, drawn by the beautiful scenery and the horse racing at Cheltenham. Brian Jones was a local boy and Mick Jagger used to pop by Lordy's as did Yoko Ono and others from the top rank of music, film and showbiz. The Mount at Stanton refreshed them all.

The flowering of the New Romantics had dovetailed beautifully with Thatcher's 'Go get it' economy in the late Eighties. An era of indulgence and opulence had coloured in the glossy magazines of that era; flowing on into the early nineties of Britain.

Of course it wasn't there for everybody. Back in the cities factions were rioting for their basic wages and working conditions. However, in our beautiful valley, up a backwater, somewhere within the holy 'Shires,' life carried on as normal; the sound of distant battles muffled by endless hills and woodlands.

If it was a choice between living in a high rise flat in Peckham, or a thatched cottage in Bourton on The Water you'd have to be made of wet concrete to get that wrong.

I knew what a city could offer, but I realised it would never sustain my soul or rather it would slowly nullify my free spirit. Years later I realised even the country wasn't enough and I needed the coast, the wild sea as a panacea for all my shadows.

I felt blessed to have stumbled into buying a home in the Cotswolds. It's ironic how in one of England's finest Rose gardens a dope plant had self seeded. However, by the same token I stood out like a sore bum in a font.

As the years rolled by, the young women carrying the drinks for the pop stars became the wives and then the mothers of their bottled bundles. Until these prodigies grew long enough legs and arms to be the new wave of kids tottering towards the bar.

I watched their lives come and go while living pretty much the same type of life as them, just without the money and probably a load of hassle. In those days I used to joke that if I became famous on Monday by Thursday I'd be busted and Friday would be the last you would see of me. I was very lucky I never ended up in prison considering the amount of opiates, in all its forms I was taking. I thank my guardian angels for that. I knew what would happen in there. I couldn't go through that again.

With my pint of Guinness, perched on the wall over looking the thatched rooftops of Stanton I stared in reverie at the sunset. Behind me the laughter of pop stars and beauties blends sweetly with the guttural 'Glarshercestershire' accent of the locals.

"Oi, oi Smiles!" Three young lads came bounding down the steps, one tapped me on the shoulder as they went past, "How's it going Smiler? That was awesome on Wednesday. Ledgend! You be up this week?" He was referring to The Royal Oak Open Mic night run by Mike Finch and his friend Martin, a great Mandolin player.

"Ahh, cheers guys. Yeah, I should be, god willing! You never know though. You know you know me!" I smiled, fooling around with the banter, I was secretly hoping one of these 'Stars' behind me might be listening to this accolade and wonder if the 'long haired nutter' was indeed worthy of some musical investigation. Sadly, there were no back doors onto their tour bus.

My style of music, the dreaded 'Singer Songwriter,' was long over in popularity before I played my first chord. Worse still, when it made a comeback years later, by then I was way past my Sell By Date.

It seemed like Life, with its damned vicissitudes had driven me to experience many delightful scenes, but generally at the wrong time, in the wrong order. The party was either about to wind down, hadn't started, or was never going to happen at all. It was like attending a series of Fancy Dress Parties but always being one costume behind or ahead, of everybody else.

In the end I gave up waiting for a miracle, creating the whole deal myself. It would never have the thrills and spills of the extravaganzas these wealthy bands could pull off. But I had the same dramas they had, the highs and lows, the good gigs and 'Shit arse Charlie' gigs, the only difference being they used to walk out on stage at Wembley, whereas I used to get to busk the queue for the Tube.

I would have loved their trip and I'd have done my best to tear the sky down from above; but as I mentioned fame and definitely any fortune would probably have been a death or prison sentence for me. So I just stuck to my dream and my albums.

As the sun began to smoulder over the smoking thatch roofs, the scent of Ash and Oak logs on stone hearths was permeating the evening breeze. Colin lit the fire from time to time in the summer and if there was ever a smell to bottle forever it was that first whiff of the 'Welcome' up The Mount.

Colin was about the best barman or landlord a pub could ever wish for. In all the years I knew him he was always a calm, smiling presence behind the bar, he might have had the worst day ever but none of the customers would ever know that, he was as level headed as a pool table He was ably assisted by his wife Lyn, the landlady, who sorted out the food side of things as well as everything else a bloke can't do! They were like old friends, dependable, trustworthy and somewhat amused by the antics of those that frequented the pub.

From my vantage point on the terrace outside I watched as vehicles puffed up the steep incline to the car park above the pub; there was a knack to getting it right and occasionally some poor bugger would entertain us by stalling half way up. It also meant that everyone outside could see the incoming vehicles and forewarned is forearmed, particularly if it was the 'wife' or an irate girlfriend on the way up.

Should the Police decide to park up at the bottom of the village there would be a discrete call to the pub. Some time later the 'All Clear' would sound and a few 'Undercover Beer Lovers' would escape into the early hours and the misty country lanes. Owners of Land Rovers could even just trot off over the hills to the next village. This was not unknown, anything to escape. I think there was also a local tolerance of idiots, up to a point, too much tomfoolery would no doubt initiate another discrete phone call. This was how village life had worked for years, better to get a clip round the ear from the local 'Bobby' than a prison sentence.

The villagers worked hard too, those horses didn't saddle themselves, the fields were unforgiving and the woodlands forever tangling in weeds, threaded with Pheasant runs, patched with ponds and fallen down farmyards of olden days.

The Pub was often the only break in their labours. It doubled up as the 'Office' for many and in the days before mobile phones were prevalent this was the next best thing. With some people Colin could set the clock by their arrival. Rodger the Dodger, a local builder, was infamous for his seven o'clock arrival. Colin would glance up at the clock and lift the appropriate tankard off the hooks above the bar and begin to pour. Inevitably, as the 'Head' settled, the sound of the door in the 'Outer Lopers' bar would precede a body appearing around the corner of the 'Inter Lopers' bar and a shout of 'Hello' or some similar curse.

The characters were endless and in those days I felt at times as if I was on a film set. Unfortunately, there was no real part for me and I had no right to be there in the first place. But hey, as a man said to me on a beach in Morocco in 1976, 'In all the beautiful places of the World, you will find the rich and you'll find the freaks.'

It was a dilemma though, not having lived there or anywhere long enough, I was never a Local. I didn't play Cricket either, in both senses. The thought of spending Sunday morning and most of the afternoon banging a leather ball about when I could be playing similar games in bed seemed absurd.

Not belonging to anywhere, or really anyone…was ingrained in my psyche.

I had to work really hard to get into some of those circles, but ultimately I was never a full member. You needed stuff I couldn't provide, heaps of money, an extended family, a Cocaine farm in Columbia, maybe an Emerald mine in Africa. Still, I had them intrigued and I certainly cracked the glass ceiling in the end, but like a summer holiday, just as I was leaving.

If I had never spoken a word to any of them, the countryside itself was enough to fill me with daily wonders. The colours, the multitudes of wild life, the variety of trees and flowers through the changing seasons was an epiphany of Nature. It inspired my Muse, it made her happy and I have always had a need to feed her first and me second, otherwise it would have all been pointless.

The sun sank a little lower. The skies to the West over the Malvern Hills lit up a distant sea of low lying clouds, their flaming waves scorching the horizon.

I sighed with wonder, still wondering?

Maud would be leaving soon. Her mates had come down or up to London and the holy trinity was about to set sail, or rail rather, in the next day or so. I could sense their excitement. I was truly thrilled for them as I loved them all, their youth, their innocence and their inestimable energy.

She would call from somewhere, as and when. That was cool and about a week later she did. I could imagine the box in the railway station, squashed full, huddled bodies, straps, rucksacks, dangling bottles of water, perched sunglasses, screams and squirms as fingers held small pieces of 'Holy sacrament' on which were the numbers of friends and lovers. While others determinedly pressed an International Dialling Code and entered the digits.

Then, "Shhh. Shh! It's ringing." Breathless pause.

"Oh my God. Oh my God! Mother Mary and all the blessed Saints." A pause. "Shit. Where is he?"

"Hi, is that you?" All I could hear was laughter and squeals, it sounded fun, "Where are you?"

"Just heading into Paris, I thought I'd ring before we leave the station and find somewhere to stay."

"Ahh thanks babe. How you all doing?"

"Err,' I heard her giggle uncontrollably, "We're good, just not had any sleep yet and this rucksack weighs a ton and a half, to be 'fecking' sure!" More laughter.

I could hear the beeps going in the phone box... "Hey babe love ya, take care, hi to the girls. Kisses."

I vaguely heard her voice, 'I'll call you...' Then the click, the phone cut off and I returned to the silence of my cottage from the bustle of the 'Gare Du Nord.' I knew the station fairly well and I could imagine the three of them circling amongst the heaving masses of kids and adults embarking on, 'Tours of Paris.'

It was going to be a long month of phone calls.

In the meantime I had to keep my whiskers clean until my darling returned from her travels. But dawn can be as enticing as dusk when it comes to the urge for passion, sensation, immersion in the holy waters of an immaculate conception. The sight of those innocent flowers bobbing their Poppy heads in the neighbours garden would entice me back again, sooner or later; that was as sure a bet as death and taxes.

The melody, a theme from an old movie would echo against something I touched, awakening the devious desire with a whisper. Again and again this process came to challenge me, a demon I couldn't let go.

It was still early when I left the pub and I let the car take me to the roundabout to stop at the shop on the corner.

As I strolled in the display rack caught my attention with a new 'Don't Tell It' magazine, its dramatic, arty cover was sensational. It was so unusual among the copies of 'Farming Daily,' and 'Shooting Monthly' I just had to buy it. I remembered the first time I had seen it, how I knew what being an 'Outcast' was like in these Shires, how I felt I had to pick it up out of sympathy. I really knew how that magazine felt. Some muppet had delivered it by mistake to the outer zones of sensibility where it would only be slandered and pilloried. God I knew that feeling.

The more I investigated the pages the closer I had bonded with it. If I had tried to make a magazine this was along the lines I might have taken. Every photo screamed from the page, each headline blistered the synapses. Ironically, bizarrely, like some oxymoron,

Jiro had called it, 'Don't Tell It,' when it was all about telling it to the World!

I had bought the copy, expensive as it was and the next day I had rung the Editor, complimenting him on his Editorial. That was Jiro and thus began that adventure when he didn't put the phone down on me, asking if he was interested in any freelance writing or reviews. I mentioned my stunning career as a blagger and reviewer with Venue Magazine in Bristol.

"The who?" He sounded foreign, he was.

"I'm a musician and I also write books, though not yet published, quite, yet." I was stumbling, rambling on but he graciously helped me up. We kind of liked each other from then on. I reckon he had done a lot of stumbling and rambling on.

"Books? Hmm," That had caught his interest. "How do you feel about doing a Book Review for me so I can see some of your writing. Then, if I like it, we'll take it from there."

"Sure, that would be utterly amazing. Cool. Shall I leave my dress with the secretary?"

He should have replied, 'What Secretary?' But instead he said, "Er no, give it to me now."

I went through the process. 'Windsong,'

"Nice name, did you call it that?"

"Yeah." I could tell he was becoming more curious, I finished the address.

"Brilliant." I'l send something off later."

I had put the phone down and done a little whoop and holler. This was great, another connection with the big city where my sweetheart lived, it seemed a good omen.

A couple of days later a package arrived containing a book with the Publisher's blurb on a sheet of paper about the Author. My brow wrinkled before I'd even reached the book. It was a popular style of fiction in the Nineties, 'Cheapo, weirdo novels,' where blood and gore need spilling, preferably over a screaming dying woman by page three. Not my bag.

I admit I am naturally against such brutal aspects of creativity. The gratuitous use of one more severed head on top of another chopped up body just left me cold, on the mortuary slab. So I diligently worked on my review, over and over, until it was as tight as a Gnat's butt.

It had begun, 'Fuck me!'

Which was, cunningly, a quote from the film, 'Wild At Heart,' followed by, 'This book scores a mighty 8.3 on the Rectum Scale,' or something along those lines. Then I gently went on to say what a travesty of justice it was that trees were being cut down to print this violent trash. To which I added, 'Be careful what you fill your head with.' It's ideas like this that proliferate more ideas like this. What ever happened to just wanting to get fed and laid once a week.

The sad thing was books like this sold well to the moronic minions who read them, in the comfort of their armchair arrogance. Ironically the publisher was actually delighted with my turn of phrase and wanted to quote the '8.3 on the Rectum Scale' on the back of the book for the next print run. I hope someone wised him or her up on that one. I don't blame the writer for his output, who knows what his trip was or where he came from, such awful violence may have been his daily backdrop. Also, no doubt the 'Publisher,' wanted a certain sellable product.

It wasn't just books that were heading down this road. The new 'Computer Games,' the 'Zombie' craze, the extreme horror movies all seemed to be pushing the border further and further towards the dark side of life.

I really believe this crap does not help children to grow to love one another. Surely there's enough time for them to discover this shit for themselves without handing it to them on a graphic plate. The Nineties were one big push towards that line marked '2000.' Somehow, excess fuelled excess.

A couple of days after posting my review off I had a call back from Jiro, 'Hey Smiles, I'm loving your style of writing. When are you next coming to town?"

I replied, "I could be coming to town anytime it might suit you boss!".

He laughed, "I'm around all the end of next week, finishing up the next Issue. Your review is in there. Maybe catch you then."

"Sure. Thanks man, I really appreciate the chance to do a bit of writing." I was buzzing to know I'd made the cut.

"You know where we are?"

"Nah, but I'll find you, I'm a man of the world you know, I'll get there."

He laughed again, "I think you will. Wherever it is you're going." That was sweetly deep. Jiro was like that, a really smart, cool dude, with enough energy to fire a rocket into Space and just about enough left over to make the next print run of, 'Don't Tell It.'

I drove up to London to visit the magazine's HQ. I stayed at Andy's and we were both curious as to how things would go.

The night before we had a couple of smokes and a Gin or two, talking for hours, listening to CDs on his stereo. The guys he had employed to do Elton John's music system had recommended the set and requisitioned the gear. Within his huge basement flat the sound was stupendous. We both loved music.

He had designed the whole flat around a sofa which was massive, supremely comfortable and great to sleep on. Its previous owner had also lived in London and was reputed to be friends with the Dalai Lama, who visited for Buddhist conventions, staying with this guy and sleeping on the sofa. Needless to say, it was either the essence of his presence, or perhaps Andy's Gin and Vermouth, 'Screw the Tonic' routine that guaranteed a good night's sleep.

The next morning I set off on foot to find the HQ of the magazine. On arrival going up the steps I passed a Fashion Model coming down, carrying a large leather satchel, no doubt with her Portfolio in it. In those days trudging from office to office was the only way aspiring models could get jobs.

Jiro's large open plan office was much like himself, colourful, cool, sexy and somewhat crazy. We had a chat and then, true to form, I got my guitar out of its case and delivered a song about God knows what. It was, according to Jiro, 'Memorable.' Most 'Journo's' carry a notebook, not me!

The long and the short of that first meeting was we got on fine and he said he would keep sending me books to review but he had other ideas, people he wanted me to interview. That sounded interesting. As I was going he pointed to a pile of tapes and CDs on the floor, carefully filed Jiro style, "Hey, help yourself to that lot."

It was a pile of stuff from bands like mine, but with some sort of Record Deal, complete with photo packs, freebies and so on. Shit. I knew then I could never compete with all this. No wonder my tapes got lost at sea on the way to Tottenham Court Road.

I gushed, "Wow! Far out!"

"Far…what?"

"'Out' man. You know? Hippy shit dude."

Jiro just smiled as I dug my way deeper into some Sixties kaleidoscope of terminology. "I like that. You really are what you are. Hey, I love your writing too. Call you soon."

I bundled a selection of stuff in my music bag and made my way out with my guitar. It was only really then I noticed a guy at one of the desks, he seemed friendly and was to become another lifelong buddy, Mark Olden.

There was the occasional jaw dropping lady who moseyed in and sashayed out of the office while my eyeballs did the 'Can Can.' This was going to be an interesting universe to explore even if I just made a couple of issues. I hoped the nearer I got to the hub of London and its artistic community the better my chances of finding somebody to help the band get out of the fields and onto the tarmac, maybe.

I walked the summer streets back to 'Olympia,' I was in no rush. Andy was out until later that day with Adrian buying material for some of Elton's chairs. It wouldn't be fair to mention the costs involved, but they summed up the era. I did actually see some of the stuff one day. Andy ended up with a tiny square, the little piece of material sat there glinting in the sunlight, appearing different velvety colours from every angle. It was truly special. Probably a couple of grand's worth in my hand.

As the bleached pavement disappeared under my strolling bones I caught glimpses of past lives on the corner of this street or that. Maybe a Tube Station or a shop doorway reminded me of some night, some scene, or something. A Seagull of memory swooped by. As soon as I saw it, it flew by.

I let the sun play on my face, the trees huddled in tiny front gardens spread their dappled green leaves.

Life was picking up in all directions, despite no real income and none on the horizon.

I had realised early on I would have to pay my own expenses for this trip, as I could tell Jiro was just about breaking uneven each month, but I reckoned the free VIP ticket into some of the clubs would be worth it. I was right.

Andy's flat was rarely without visitors or somebody planning to drop by for the evening. They were, in the main, either dropped in the cream, dripping with it, or feeding off it. The world of 'High' Art, Antiques and 'Caring for the Rich,' comes with a huge amount of 'Emperor's Clothes' syndrome attached. Literally! I loved them all for the fact they pulled it off and could manage the tantrums and the bloody tiaras. It was a vast game of cards at times. It took only one to fall, to rumble and tumble the rest into disarray.

I loved the camp Antiques Runners, as they were known, the boys who did all the footwork finding stuff too buy before websites were even invented, searching out hidden gems in the 'Shires,' or more likely Lewisham, for the city shop owners.

For a Gay man Andy had many lady friends, some of whom seemed to have a certain 'Laissez faire' about them, even more so after a couple of Andy's Gins or perhaps a brief 'Toot in the Loo.'

Coke was becoming more accepted as part of the lives of business people at the 'High' end of the market. It had yet to reach the poorer outposts and villages. Once it had been mainly the preserve of drug addicts and Rock Stars; now, for sixty quid you could fly Five Star like anybody else, dressed in a diamanté smile for twenty minutes, until the next little hankering for a powdering of the nose.

It created the scene for some extremely wild parties verging into some fantasy of pleasurable insanity.

The latter half of the Nineties for many people was an almighty practice session for the big one in 2000, the Party of the Century, of the Millenium.

It was beautiful in some ways to see a civilisation getting ready to dance off merrily into the moonlight, but it was also the greatest missed opportunity for some deep reflection on how far we had really come in Mankind's history. I just hope Womankind can do better with the next one.

But all this was still so far away and yet so near. It coloured the back of many people's thoughts, where would they be in the next millennia? What would they be doing?

I don't think anybody was planning to pick up a 'Smack' habit and end up homeless again.

OMICRON

The hours ticked away the days, phone calls came from breathless cities, kisses from across the far off continent, distant cathedral bells chimed the hours of the weeks, until at last a month evaporated in the heatwave of several railway stations.

I waited for the call that finally came, without a rush of coins being fed into a box, the background noise carpeted and double glazed. She was home.

That summer we made love. In the quiet hush and crush of the couch downstairs, the courting Cortina or the wild fields of hot afternoons. Sultry twilights, bitten lipstick red at dusk upon a quivering mountain of quilted silks and satins, all slung upon the lilt of birdsong outside the windows of Windsong.

Our love was a diamond of sparkling sand laid out on an Oyster's palm, from which a Pearl slowly grew. At that moment only a few rainbows were wrapped around its heart, but even then I could see the perfection, the shimmer of paradise within.

We had time that summer, until the early autumn, to create our world beyond the heady dreaming spires of Oxford. We explored the villages I knew so well, the country pubs and riverside bars. Much of this was a delightful revelation to a girl from the suburbs. Though she knew Ireland well, as beautiful in many and different ways, she had never seen what villages blessed with centuries of wealth had created in the 'Shires of England.'

From here we travelled west to a beach I have loved all my life, which waits now, stretched out in the bay. Dark blue waters, tinged with greys, the stray crests of waves meeting the sand banks in the estuary.

Everywhere we went she was loved, as her laughter lit up the faces of all those who met us. The power of lovers to adorn a place with joy was held in our embrace. It was refreshing to be with someone I felt so at ease with. We made Love.

Yet these hours also became days that brought us to the last weeks before college began. Behind the high walls and the Porter's portcullis'd gates, I had discovered a haven within those Oxford walls and the gardens that bordered them. I had returned to a place I should have been long before and found something I had lost in the back streets my teenage years, with this girl, her innocence and the cast of fresh faces that adorned and adored her

Love like this is similar to a new song. We were both listening intently to the melody, not wishing to miss a beat, creating the music that followed. Although we had only made it to the first chorus, there was a sense of crescendo to come.

Everybody who heard her beautiful laughter, echoed by the smiling buffoon in her arms, was moved. Like all true lovers we had an energy between us that pervaded everything. Those that watched from the wings were curiously in awe.

Perhaps knowing I was so blessed made me never forget those less fortunate, the weak or damaged. I could have wound up there. Without a fair state of health nothing good could happen and I had played

Russian roulette with mine for years. It developed in me a keener empathy for those not so lucky.

Following Rose, who was training to be a Doctor, in previous years to lectures at the start of her day in hospital, I had often wandered slowly back, past the endless grey corridors, glancing at those caught in a web of tubes and needles, whose spider eyes blink red, beep, flash red, blink, beep, flash red, off.

While my Irish four leaved Clover had been roaming Europe I returned to the sanitary world of Hospitals again, but this time at the bedside. It was a chance remark by a barmaid at The Royal Oak on one of those mad open mic nights that she was visiting a local man from the pub who'd been in an accident. To be honest I'd have quite happily spent a day at a Waste Disposal Site with this particular barmaid if Maud wasn't on the scene, however I asked who? It was one of the Green Welly Brigade as I called them, Young Farmers and proper country people. He was in a coma after a head injury.

I didn't know the guy other than he was one of the lads who used to walk past me as I wailed away on Open Mic night, with a look that said, 'I know what I'd do with a dog if it made a racket like that.'

Rob Gilder had made one bad split decision that summer. There had been a party at Home Farm, a place where tragedy had struck before; coincidently a property within range of the curse from Toddington Manor. Previously the farmer's son had fallen in the grain silo, either first, or in pursuit of his mate. Both dead, drowned in dust.

The party in the barn had spilled out onto the lawns and driveway of Home Farm next to the main road. On the other side, the fields stretched out gracefully along the trickling Isbourne, a rare stream swimming northwards. The skies would have still been fairly light with the midsummer midnight glow from the Moon and the orange radiance of Cheltenham's lights beyond Bishops Cleeve Hill.

Somewhere between, the rooftops of Winchcombe were rattling with the lust of beer bellied blokes and buxom wenches, the last songs of the disco from The Sun Inn were making the thatch over some old oak beams gently deposit their dust of the centuries on those below.

I wasn't there, it wasn't the sort of crowd who might have invited me. I can only recount what I heard had happened and poor Rob remembered nothing.

But I knew every scent of that village, every mood of her seasons, her damp winter willows and radiant summer roses. I could imagine the throng gathering outside on the lawns as Land Rovers and Range Rovers began leaving with their excited occupants, in search of a bed, or more booze and coke. As one vehicle trundled towards the road, Rob had made a quick decision to jump into the back. Almost as soon as he was in, it turned left onto the main road. It had only just begun to straighten out when Rob made another split decision and changed his mind.

He jumped out. No problem. He landed. Not much problem. He toppled over, partly from momentum and probably disorientation, as well as a few beers no doubt, as many do. Not a major problem.

But there were no bystanders to catch him, the road was notoriously dangerous, the remaining party folk were clumped in drunken huddles on the other side of the farm's fence, on the soft, dew damp cushion of green grass. They watched helpless, with laughter cut short and shock as his body fell. His head came down and hit the unforgiving pavement with a thud.

The corner of the curb lay beneath his head. There was a moment of terrified silence. Rob fell helplessly and hopelessly into a further darkness. As voices rushed towards him his eardrums frantically beat the blood backwards, sending 'SOS' messages inwards.

But his brain lay slumped over its desk. A ticker tape of diminishing meaningless messages began to gather round its ankles, spreading up the body, until only the cranium slept, almost but not quite, dead. Touch less, taste less, sense-less with just a hint of life clinging to his skin, like perspiration.

Rob had been carefully packaged and wrapped that night in a coma, then delivered to Fenchay Hospital, one of those hospitals renowned as any patient in there was obviously in serious shit.

He was returned to the Intensive Care Unit in Cheltenham, after three months in Frenchay, to be closer to his relatives. There had been some debate as to whether he would ever make that return trip, or if it was going to be worth it at all. But Rob made it. He was a stubborn bugger like that. However, he was in a right old pickle.

The barmaid and I eventually found the ward and the bed he was in. There were tubes coming in and out of every available orifice, including one into his neck. I stared at the tiny tube, as the flicker of breath and mucus tried to work its way in and out; it was so thin, as thin as the thread of life Rob was hanging onto. The saliva choked valve was taped to his skin, the white plastic nozzle gasping for air it seemd, but his body lay still, lifeless, with his hands and fingers curled in tightly towards the wrists. I looked at his face. I didn't recognise it as any chap I'd spoken to up the pub. But that didn't matter. He would have heard me, or definitely seen me, it was hard to miss me with my somewhat loud, more like deafening, sense of dress. I was probably the last hippy seen in that pub for a long time. So, although I wasn't his friend, I knew when he, or if he, came out of this he might remember me. I only hoped that didn't send him back into a coma!

He had large mechanic's hands, now wrench less; with his clumsy bundle of fingers that looked as if they were tied together tightly, they tapered gently, now grease less, to nails that needed cutting. Finger nails like his would usually have been worn down with the work he did, day by day, week by week, fixing the lorries of his elder brother's haulage firm. The Gilders were a firm that transported livestock and often had the Animal Welfare protesters camped outside their yard. I don't think it's possible to find two people further apart socially than a vegetarian hippy and a meat haulier's mechanic. But that's how life just works out some times.

I could tell from the broad trunk of his body and the swooping branches of his shoulders that this was a powerful, hard grafting, dependable man. The lower half of his torso was covered with a hospital gown; from which a tube emerged to fill a waiting bag, not the kind of thing any man wants to be attached to.

Next to him in the ITU Recovery Ward was a man, minus one foot, his right one. With the same regard and respect I have for victims anywhere, which means I never slow down to look at an accident, I never ask for details of any man's misfortune. They'll tell me soon enough if they feel the need and if they sense the compassion in my eyes is honest, not just curious or prurient. This man didn't want to.

Sadly, a few weeks later another man had what seemed to be the same injury. I only glanced at him briefly, but his eyes were already waiting for mine.

"I came here on holiday, you know." He suggested, rather than spoke, as if he was half way through a story. "The Cotswolds sounded dead posh. All them old villages and country pubs. Looked beautiful." He paused as if he was reading a guide book, which suddenly fell from his grasp. "Then this." He nodded vaguely downwards, "I tried to brake you see. You have to…"

He sighed and nodded as if acknowledging an holy truth, "The Mrs and the daughter. See, we were…" his accent was changing to more northern. "Down from Lancs' you know." the word has passed his lips so many times. "Not quite The Cotswolds ay? But you see," he looked desperate, "You have to brake like. Can't stop it. Instinctive." His eyes were red, "Especially with the bairn in the back. You know?"

I didn't know. I couldn't. "Lancashire," I whispered affectionately, not really having any tales from there, but trying to sound as if I loved the place. I had no need of filling the space. As Rob lay, unconcerned in his semi coma next to me, I had a brief run down of the chap's trip and the accident. He kept repeating, without knowing, "The Mrs and the daughter see."

Less than a hundred yards away other wives and daughters would be having a day out in Cheltenham. The Sandford Lido would be rippling to the splashes of children, watched by their sun drenched parents. It was a beautiful day, summer was still baking the tree lined back streets, I knew the shortcut through the lane. Within ten minutes of leaving the hospital I could be diving in its turquoise waters, amongst the blessed.

How little we value those simple things in life. One left foot. One right. Matching size. How fortunate we should feel with every step. I knew this man would dearly have liked to join me. He clearly wanted his right foot back. Now! He wanted to wake up from this chaos, this stupid dream. It can't be him. Worse still, as he wakes from the slumber of morphine he feels the twitch of his foot beneath the blanket. For a moment he believes it's there. His heart leaps to the skies, 'It was all a bad dream.' Then one eye glances at the missing lump below his knee. The blanket has betrayed him, it refuses to make the simple shape of a foot. 'Bastard!'

Thank God and Mother Nature for Morphine. It's the only thing that might put a bandage on that wound for awhile. Then he'll have to fight another long war, returning from the 'Comfort Zone,' to the 'Guess what? Nobody really gives a fuck zone.'

However, by another twisted token this chap was solaced in some way by dear Rob, who had both feet but no Nerve Controller to work them. He said it as we both thought it, "Could be worse." Nodding sympathetically at comatose Rob. He attempted a laugh, then added, "Ay, I could have lost both feet."

I smiled my best Intensive Care Unit smile, we both knew it was a crap line, but it was all he had to hang onto. I couldn't take that away from him.

These two men were the first I met personally who had suffered this cruellest twist of fate. I figured it couldn't get much worse. I was wrong. I resolved to keep visiting. After all, I had two feet, walking was easy for me, even up and down stairs! Rob didn't know me from Adam and despite both of us living in the same county we couldn't be further apart. There was a universe between us that somehow collided via this tragedy.

I looked at him. The small white tube still sucking and blowing air through, somehow keeping him alive while we all waited. Everybody waited. Everybody talked, in hopeful whispers. We watched his hands for the slightest movement, its tangled grip. a mess of snarled nerves, leading to a brain that was, 'Shut, for essential repairs.'

The Doctors were hopeful, within their hopeless diagnosis. Everybody was praying.

Then one day the fore finger on his left hand moved a fraction. Sometime after that, an eyelid flickered. Rob was moved from ITU to a Rehabilitation ward at another hospital in Cheltenham. It was there I met Gordon, for the first time. He came in with a couple of large nuts and bolts, which he hoped Rob might respond to. But he was a long way from holding a teaspoon let alone a spanner. He put them gently on the bedside table. If Rob was big then imagine his older, bigger, firstborn brother. Nearly as broad as he was tall, over six foot, with huge fingers that could no doubt unscrew wheel nuts by hand. He filled one side of the sitting area. I would learn Gordon had a heart to match his size, he had in fact pretty much brought the family of seven brothers and sisters up after their parents were killed in a car crash.

We eyed each other over the body. He had heard about my regular visits. 'Some Hippy guy.' To which somebody had probably added, 'You know, that long haired nutter who sings up the Oak.' His initial doubts were no doubt confirmed on first sight.

"You must be 'Smiles,' I'm Gordon Gilder. The boys told me you've been coming in to see Rob. Thanks. Seen any more change in him?"

I told him what he already knew. There was some improvement, but not a lot. It would take time, a long time. "At least we're in Rehabilitation, not ITU." He knew what I meant. He was as active as me, in a very different way, but knew the value of health.

I worried I might be seen as intruding on their grief but I realised quite soon that it was useful for the family to have a non relative in this situation. I could listen to their concerns and they knew it was already a forgotten secret between us.

Rob needed me too, because despite his head injury, he desperately wanted a cigarette.

The amazing staff in that hospital got Rob to be able to sit up eventually and cope with a wheel chair. So we began our 'Escape Plans.'

Like two soldiers in a Prison Camp we peered over the bleary fences around us. I wandered with him round the grounds, pushing the heavy chair, pointing out colours and shapes, giving him a monologue I'm sure he could do without. Luckily there wasn't a great deal of feedback from him early on other than his nodding head, but that was probably lack of muscle control. He could well have been trying to shake it, or say, 'Don't you ever shut the fuck up!'

But, every now and then on our trips he'd get a bit excited and press his fingers together. It took awhile before I noticed it was happening when we passed someone smoking.

So, a coma patient. All those months gasping for breath, for life. Breath by breath by breath. Now he wants a fag. Shit.

Of course none of his family are going to do that for him. They're too close and they know it's against the rules. Medically it's about as advisable as hitting him on the forehead with a blunt hammer.

But, there was another factor about the whole deal I used as my excuse to myself for sorting him out. Not that anyone ever knew, I certainly didn't blab and he couldn't even if he tried. A cigarette was a symbol from Rob's past. Smoking was allowed in the pubs in those days and common amongst the young and old community. It went with many jobs, particularly ones like Rob's, as part of the 'Macho Man' image.

I knew Rob wanted to feel for a moment, a minute, what it was like in his life before the accident, by just having a fag, 'Five minutes off from this bloody bollocks.' How many times had he done that? How many times lit up, puffed, stared at the sky, then at the ground as his foot stamped it out? How many times he had shared one with a beauty from the bar?

"Ok. Ok." I said to myself as much as him. "Next time I visit, I promise." A few days later armed with three Malboro cigarettes and a lighter, I wheeled him as far as possible from the main hospital building, round to the back of a maintenance hut.

"Ok. You sure about this?" He rocked forward and nodded. "You're going to get me killed if Gordon finds out." He nodded even more vigorously. He had a sense of humour even then! "But it's ok, 'cause I'm the only fucker who's going to do this for you and you're going to keep your mouth shut." I put on an American New York dockside accent, "Or I'll have to blow you and this whole stinking town to Hell!" He nodded. I guessed there was no turning back now.

We tried putting it in his mouth first but he couldn't mange the puff at the right time to light it, so I lit one and went to put it between his lips. He grunted. That meant, 'No.' His hand twitched, the arm moved.

'Ok, you wanna do it. Cool. You only gotta ask.' I laughed at the ridiculousness of this situation and the corny line. His chest humped a couple of times as somewhere inside that cavern he laughed too.

I stuck the smouldering fag in between his fore and index finger. They were still crooked and stiff as bricks but it wedged in neatly. I straightened up and looked around to make sure no nurse was on patrol in our direction. "All clear."

I looked back at him as the arm slowly raised the hand with its smoking fingers, towards the waiting lips. It was quite simply, 'Pure Poetry in Motion.'

There can be no finer or exquisite gesture than a cigarette rising to the lips. It has every inch of the Kama Sutra in it and all the love and lust a ballet company could ever muster, in one, brief, action.

At last he got it to his lips. I was breathless, as if watching a high diver, unable to take my eyes away for a second.

Like a lot of things in my life it went totally against every rule and stricture. But I would go to the Old Bailey and defend my case as the totally right thing to do at that moment. Life had put me in the place where I was the only man that could achieve this thing for him. I had to do it.

After three or four puffs he held it out for me to recapture. "Thanks buddy." I said, "You saved me the butt!" I saw his chest heave with silent laughter. I stubbed out the fag and we emerged like two school boys from the back of the Bike Sheds, our faces covered in wonder and guilt.

We had another 'Unofficial Escapade' at that hospital. One day I thought it might be a good idea to show him the Cricket and Rugby pitches just a few streets away from the grounds, which had stunning views of Leckhampton Hill. He loved sport and maybe it would fire up a memory or a brain cell.

We trogged off happy as Larry and Harry. One man and his wheelchair patient. I was unaware my simple plan was misinterpreted as abducting the patient. All hell broke loose and the staff were just at the point of sending up the 'Police Helicopter' to look for us when I strolled up the main drive, chirruping away to Rob about everything and nothing in particular.

A nurse came dashing down towards us with a horrified look on her face and all was revealed.

"Er, sorry." I could see Rob's chest heaving. The only thing better than him getting in trouble was me.

Summer was ending, the schools had all returned and Cheltenham sighed a huge collective sigh of middle class relief. The Lido was empty for hours now until the 'Runaways' or early leavers turned up. The college staff at Oxford were making final preparations for Michaelmas Term. My weekends and weeks were drifting in that direction too as early students returned and to be fair nobody needs an excuse to visit such an historic town.

By chance Rob was also on his way to Oxford, to the Rivermead Rehabilitation Centre. Now closed or relocated. Highly respected at the time, it dealt with all the head injuries, strokes and so on from the surrounding counties. The main entrance was one I always felt blessed to be driving away from.

It led to the toughest landscape of all, where, at those moments between day and night, between night and day, the voices of Hell cried out. Sounds from a crypt that were unimaginable. The wail of a person trapped deep underground, unable to move, unable to talk, unable to see clearly. From that horror a torturous sound was manufactured, desperation, disbelief that 'Life,' that precious gift, above all else, had been amputated.

Once before Life had been an easy commodity to fritter away. Minutes and hours, sometimes whole days, wasted in meaningless tasks, to return to the start, at the same point as the previous week, or was it the previous year. Yet also the dreams, the peaks, the mad ambitions to achieve the unachievable, all gone, destroyed in twenty or so seconds, ironically by something called a 'Stroke.'

I was to glimpse the coldest cruellest wilderness of all in this place, by the bedside of a man who had in his past sailed the Atlantic solo. I had never heard such pain turned into sound before. It echoed down the corridor to the dayroom where Rob and I looked at each other wondering what it could be. It was a cry from inside Hell itself. Poor John.

There was another factor during those first months visiting. I watched how the faces visiting the patients gradually reduced in number. I began to understand how 'We' protect ourselves from grief. Rather than pay a dying friend many visits, we have learnt to shy away from trauma, not through any lack of empathy or courage, but our brains have discovered how to 'Shilly shally' around the subject and curiously avoid making the time for grief, for the painful visit. The brain's ability to protect itself is almost on a level with our ability to destroy it.

However, I had none of this grief. I had not lost the old Rob, the brother or friend. I had found an injured man by the side of my path through life. I just knew as I had at the birth of my adopted son, that this vulnerable person needed me at that time in his life. I was aware also that if I gave my help it would have to go with a commitment…A lot of commitment.

After the first visit with the gorgeous barmaid we had parted and I had followed the back lane that crossed the carpark and eventually led to the entrance of the Lido. The 'Boys,' were already outside and gave me a wave, "Alright Smiles?"

"Sure guys, how's it going, 'Big Ron about?"

"They'm all there, usual sport." He meant 'Spot' but the 'Gloster'shire drawl' dripped off his tongue like honey. They were a nice pair of lads, young men now, but basically fairly straightforward lads. Totally devoted to the Lido and all things Ron, as all the regular swimmers were. He had saved the pool, god knows how many times from defeat and ruin by the pumps, heaters and leaks. However, the worst of all being the Council's decision, with their bull headed wisdom to turn the place into a carpark.

Ron was a true bronze chested swimmer, with eyes that never missed a thing, or a swimmer in trouble. I rarely did my length under water if he wasn't about. Fifty metres is a long way and despite swimming towards the shallow end it was always possible, as with most things in my life, for me to monumentally fuck up underwater as much as I did on land.

As I entered I gave 'The Ron Family' a wave and strolled past the fountain to see how busy the pool was. In those days there were never any lanes. People who swam, as opposed to 'Paddlers,' were a rare breed. The heating was not as efficient and heat retaining covers hadn't really been invented. It was fairly quiet, early afternoon, just about the best place in the whole world to be, for me.

As I changed I thought about Rob. Even getting his pants on and off was going to be a struggle for him now. Poor fucker.

Despite taking more hard drugs than the population of a small town, I have nonetheless rigorously tried to maintain my body over the years. In those days I didn't even smoke Tobacco, I just ate dope or injected heroin. I ran every third day, religiously, even if it meant clearing a path through eight foot high snow drifts. Also, I had swum like a fish all my life. It was my favourite sport of all.

I grabbed my goggles and earplugs. The flagstones were hot under my feet. I wandered to the deep end. I had a system. For some reason if I attempted the length underwater from dry it seemed easier. Maybe my body kept a little air sucked up through the skin. No idea. But I had a system.

I sat down on the side wall, I began emptying and filling my lungs to minimum and maximum. Nobody taught me this, I just worked it out. I had a system. I was allowed four steps and dive. I had done the length from an 'In the pool' start but that was really tough. I wasn't up for that today. 'Tough,' would have to do. I had a system. Eventually I stood up, dipped my goggles in the water and carefully paced the four steps back from the edge I was allowed. There had to be some consistency. I had a system.

I didn't need to check Ron was there, but I saw him. I could rely on him tracking me. He knew how hard it was. On a visit years before 'Tarzan' the actor Jonny

Weissmuller, had managed a length and a half, but he had dived off the top board. They had long gone. I'm pretty sure Ron watched him, as he did me.

I grasped the last puff of air I could and zipped my lips shut. One, two, three, four, dive. The coolness of the water glided down my body, the holy turquoise universe below the surface opened up before me. Beneath me the deep end glided away as I began breast stroking slowly forwards. I'd tried fast before, that didn't work. I had to stay calm and proceed at just the right pace, stroke by stroke.

I though of Rob, caught underwater in his coma, unable to get to the surface. Unable even to scream. I stroked on, this part was easy, beautiful, no strain at all. I passed the halfway mark. I could see kid's legs in the distance, thrashing about but away to the right where the plastic slide was. They wouldn't be a problem. The lane ahead was free. Diving in from the shallow end was forbidden and also could be fatal.

With every breath I thought of Rob. I realised, not for the first time, how blessed I was, considering I'd spent half of my life intent on blowing my brains out and the other half screwing it all back together. Poor Rob had just made one bloody awful split decision. I'd made millions.

The burn began, deep in the lungs, then my brain started shouting, screaming at me, 'Get out of the water!' But I couldn't hear it, I mustn't. If the voice got inside me, I would give up. I carry on, counting now, thinking to myself, 'Ok, get to ten, that should do it. Three, four strokes. The burn is brutal now, every muscle in my body wants to leap out of the water. Six, seven strokes. I can see the far wall now, closer. Nine, nearly there. Just three more strokes. It's overwhelming now. My chest is burning but the body still obeys me.

'Come on!' I hear countless, faceless teachers from my schooldays calling, down the touchline. 'Come on!' I reach out and grab for the wall, the lip in the smooth tiles catches under my fingers. I haul myself up into the air. My lungs fill. My mind explodes.

I glance to my left and see the shape of Ron and a small, unnoticeable wave in my direction. That was worth all the 'Tea in China' to me.

It is only now, as this sentence leaves my mind, that I have realised Ron and Rob are just one consonant apart and that Breast stroke and a brain Stroke are just one word apart. I understood that this immense joy I had, was one of the many blessings in my life. Rob was short on blessings. I figured it wouldn't be too hard to share some of my wealth with him.

I made that commitment. I stuck to it.

'Staircase Six' would be the centre of the Second Year's legendary era at St Hugh's; a period even the Porter remembered fondly, some time after, "Ah, yes," he mumbled, "We don't get students like that anymore," and as my eyebrows raised he added smiling, "I miss those days."

The return of Maud's long haired boy friend seemed to meet with approval from everyone. The other students were honest in their affections and I felt our love had become a little pot of real gold they all valued at the centre of St Hugh's ancient heart. I would learn so much watching these fresh lives stumble forward towards the real world from this Ivory staircase. Most had two years to go, during which time I saw them change from youth to adult in Fast Forward. It was a pleasure for me, having been through these trails of growing up, to add some encouragement, reassurance or experience.

It was not easy for them, for having attained the highest academic accolade possible and entered the 'Holy City,' the pressure was on to make the most of it all. Unfortunately, they only had a limited time to cram in as much experience as possible. The terms, Michaelmas, Hilary and Trinity were split into two blocks of four weeks; with the Half Term hangover and recuperation, or 'Reading Week' its official title, in the middle. They were up against a simple law, how much of this precious time to devote to study, to sport, or to socialising; not forgetting they had to sleep at some point in the middle of all this mayhem. Staircase Six led the valiant charge.

Tom and Phil were in the two ground floor rooms, Natasha and Loulou above, with Maud and a guy at the top. It seemed as if those few months of the previous summer and the holiday had woven the threads of all our lives together effortlessly.

I spent so much time there over the coming months that several tutors actually thought I was a student. Fortunately I was at my best fitness wise and photos from the time don't betray that the man in the bright paisley shirt is roughly sixteen or seventeen years older than everybody else.

The thrill and the challenge of being with young intelligent people, pulled what was left of my brain's socks up. My mind and senses were energised into some sort of renaissance. I had missed being among such keen thinkers since my schooldays; this level of natural excitement, of hope, of anticipation for the future was rare. Every society is beautiful on its own merits, but I had longed all my life to return to the libraries and wood panelled corridors of my youth; perhaps believing that if I got back there, all the way to the past, I might find the future I'd lost, or maybe it was the people I lost. How desperate and utterly hopeless our efforts at reconciliation with our demons can be.

I began to live in two, possibly three worlds.

The unemployed teacher in his cottage muddling along with his music and pile of Final Demands. The boyfriend of Maud in the hallowed halls at St Hugh's, a careless world without real bills or mundane cares.

Then, once a week, perhaps twice, I would dive into the brutally cruel reality I witnessed at the Rivermead Rehabilitation Centre, sitting at the bedside of a man in hell, whose future had been cancelled, whose limbs refused to work, whose only communication with the world was the blink of an eyelash.

Some days I would inhabit all three. It gave me a real sense of our precious life, health and every day was, how integrity could be the only gold handrail to hang onto in such circumstances. I've never held life so dearly in my palms.

Having been so far down that I'd lost sight of Up on many occasions I already knew what a blessing every day was, but this period in my life affirmed that forever; even if they didn't always feel it I knew what a glorious experience all those students were having. So I took note, I remembered as much as I could, I carefully soaked up every possible view, every moment of the mad nights and sweet days, while the other students, in their innocence, casually picked up and dropped their weeks. I stored those precious leaves in my mind. Furthermore, I wasn't a drinker then, until the girls initiated me into 'Vodka Night.' This meant I recalled all the nights before, which they in their youthful folly forgot, because they were perhaps slightly too inebriated, indeed I was occasionally sought out by one of two students who would ask me with a blush, 'So what did happen last night?'

Alcohol seems to light the fuse of life and yet dim the memory of its explosion.

However, the higher the walls of paradise the longer the shadows they cast.

Dusk, dawn, half light, early mornings shrouded in mist, dreams disturbed by midnight bells; echoes from the bare feet vanished from bathroom floors, the outline of steps disappearing into the big world, like history dissolving in a long forgotten wilderness. The footsteps of all those gone before, unechoed.

I felt those ghosts of the Dreaming Spires from time to time, especially in the Pitt Rivers Museum, or on the worn flagstones beneath some arches; tiny back rooms in snug pubs where famous faces are framed, somewhat disdainfully, in black and white or sepia. Also in the Botanical Gardens, which seemed to me like the 'Last Stop before Timbuktu.' Full of valises, vases and trunks stuffed with seeds, specimens and bulbs from the deepest, darkest, jungles of beyond. Plant names that conjured up galleons on high seas, brave pirates of adventure, or long lost languages on corked tongues.

As I listened to the frenzy of conversation between the students, I remembered the squats and the cold shooting galleries, the dirty toilets and the dirtier men, the bitter chill of four in the morning, The sweat of Cold Turkey and the twisted sheets draped from the cliffs of madness that I climbed during darkness. None of them could guess this.

Meanwhile, it was technically the best year of anybody's degree, no First Year Exams or Finals, the ultimate nightmare.

Recurring horrors of loosing coursework or missing deadlines were features I discovered many students experienced. So much of their lives as teenagers had been driven by the next hoop to jump through; with an inherent fear that up to then they had just been lucky. I could hear the frantic whispers of their nervous tongues, recalling the spider webbed vaults of endless words and endless tests.

Against this was pitched the laughter of daytime TV, trips to town for shopping, meals created on old cookers and the warming sound of voices from home in the hall telephone. These were the comforts that sustained the lonely hidden amongst the crowd.

I was also fully aware of my responsibility towards these young and beautiful people. Many men would have taken advantage of the situation I found myself in. But, such a man would never have lasted among these innocents, for despite their youth they would have found him out.

It has always been like this in my life, I have had many young beautiful female friends whose intimacy has always been respected by me, whether they are drunk as a Skunk or not, thus our friendships lasted.

All of this swirled round my head as we made our way over to Clarice's one night. I was going to learn how to drink Vodka! Had it been a Joint Rolling Contest, no problem.

I'm always uneasy amongst crowds of very drunk people but getting inebriated with students is less intimidating. None of the boys there were going to try to jump me, hump me or punch me. Clarice's room wasn't on the infamous Staircase Six, it was in a corner of one of the older buildings overlooking the main road.

The chatter reverberated from the room before the door was even open. As Maud and I entered shouts of joy rang out, as if now the party could really start. My Irish belle had that effect everywhere she went; people were always pleased to see her. Then the colourful clown with his long hair would play the fool for them and it seemed as if we added laughter to every conversation.

There were about eight or nine girls and Jason, Clarice's new boyfriend. On the table in one corner was an array of bottles and a huge soup tureen with a ladle.

The girls with prior practice were downing 'Shots' while I sipped the fire water. Then I had a glass from the mixture in the tureen and the warm fire of alcohol gradually crept up my chest to my head and melted my brain. It was fun. Half an jour later we were merrily singing and dancing in a circle, everyone was hugging. I was surrounded with happy gorgeous laughing faces. It was unreal.

They wouldn't be aware that further down that main road a guy would be bedding down on cardboard, while another was still out hunting for the next ten quid packet of oblivion. Why should they? The ugly streets beyond their haven would be there for always, there was no need to rush to see all that.

We spent an hour or so dancing and trying various mixes of Vodka drinks until the volume of music and laughter peaked at 'Let's go!'

Apparently it was just the start of the night. We left the smiling Porter with exuberant waves and headed down the road on wings of pure ether.

Somebody suggested getting the bus. We jumped on the next one and I took swaying photos of our happy clan trundling towards the city centre.

As the last of the twilight vanished to the west, the orange glow of Oxford illuminated our steps as we fell off the bus; the neon wash of streetlights tanning our smiles with a radioactive glow. The girls were far more practised than me at sailing the Jolly Ship Vodka up the narrow tributaries of Broad Street. I followed the dancing bobs of blond or dark hair, the sparkling eyes, nutmeg, emerald, opal and azure on their unblemished mascara shores; where soon, the hot hearts of young men would beg to lay down their reflections in their affections.

The arm around my waist held me close, the fingers on the hand at the end danced. The others were a few steps ahead of us. We looked into each other's eyes. I whispered, "One, two, three." We kissed until our lips hurt while our legs marched on, following the sound of the laughter up ahead.

We were blessed in late autumn with many warm and tender nights. The winds that arrived upon the Oxfordshire plains were befuddled by the Dreaming Spires and petered out over the roofs and maze of backstreets in the outskirts of town.

We were greeted from afar by the hubbub of voices gathered outside a pub with the endless ramshackle row of bicycles, chained up or just abandoned to its railings. The students hugged and clutched their beers. Somewhere, a gap opened up in the throng and we followed the others into the smoky crush of raised voices and clinking pints.

It was elbow deep to the bar but the girls pressed on. I watched as young men melted in their stares, not even knowing they were stepping backwards to allow us through. Before long we were returning, arms aloft, hands holding pints like lanterns to lead the blind drunk into a corner.

Before long some chairs scraped the floor and we dived for the table. Once seated, I quietly leaned my back against the wall whilst the girls were huddled deep in some potential debate of scandal.

I glanced round the pub. I saw the innocent delight of 'First Year' students, so freshly hatched they still had fledgling feathers. The 'Second Years' enjoying the best time; while the 'Third Year' students already wore the shadow of looming exams around those far reaching stares.

From my vantage point, tilted back on my chair and two decades of life experience ahead of them all it was a revelation to observe this rite of passage. In a year or two most of these gorgeous children would be tucked up in offices, with enormous salaries, still unaware of the real world beneath their castle walls.

I remembered the rich men from such offices who came down to the 'Dilly' for some fresh flesh in their lunch hour, or some company after work. I recalled the other boys on the Meat Rack, the cruel and kind men, the Monk, the Doctor and the three Arabs that stole everything.

How could I share this? It would be unfair to tarnish their perception of the world with the one I had fallen into. I knew how valuable their innocence was and I strived to protect it.

The girls had finished their second drink while my first pint was still loitering half full. "Come on. We're off to the White Lion."

There was no way I could finish my pint off in a hurry, I was struggling as it was; so with the skills I'd learnt shoplifting I quietly tucked my glass under my shirt and presented it one sip later at the next table in the following bar.

The girls thought that was hilarious, somewhat cunning, so nobody minded when my second pint followed us to the third pub. One advantage of being semi sober was the girls could rely on me to gather up any stragglers from our group. I guess it was a period in their young lives during which they had to discover their own limits, for themselves. I'd already discovered mine years before in pursuit of what Jim Morrison aptly described as, 'No laws, no limits.'

Everything was wonderful and full of wonder.

After diving for the fourth time into a labyrinthine of back room bars and people crushed together in drunken harmony, hip to hip, shoulder to shoulder, our bedraggled group was ejected in disarray on the pavement. We waited awhile for 'Hill's' to pop out below the huge doorman, her large dark eyes glowing with mischief, such was her artistic delight.

As we strolled around a corner the queue for a club was trailing up the opposite pavement. Girls dressing in sequinned nighties and boys in tight trousers with tighter shirts. Yet either side of the doorway, a little way off, the blanketed waifs of the night were tucked up, only their pale palms on thin wrists, up stretched, evident in the shadows.

We crossed the road and I let the girls get ahead of me. I stopped at the last hand and delved into my pocket, "Here buddy. Good luck man."

A voice mumbled, 'Ta Guv'nor.' I noticed his shoes, they confirmed he was truly homeless, the grey stain of endless pavements washed like a tide up to his ankles, the soles of his shoes dirty, edgeless on the outside from days sitting crossed legged in hope.

I felt the chill of the air cool the perspiration on my back, we had been dancing earlier with her twirling eyes and lip sticked smiles flashed across my eyes. I looked down at the shadow again, "I was there once buddy," a pair of eyes glinted upwards, "Take heart buddy, never give up hope, life changes." I stepped back. That was all I could give him.

I heard the voice again, this time with the smallest grain of hope in it, 'See ya…?'

"Maybe bro'." I caught the girls up and entered their casual conversation as though I'd never left it.

Yet I had jumped back twenty years for twenty seconds. I marvelled how I had come to find myself in this other role. The guy on the street presumed I was a student, like the others; when really I was him. I may have got off the street but somehow the street never got off me.

Even now I would prefer to sleep on a blanket on the floor for three reasons. Firstly it isn't as bad as it seems, once you get used to it. Secondly, because I never want to get too comfortable or complacent. I like to remind myself the street is only four inches away and it doesn't take much to push a man off his royal perch. Thirdly, I can't fall off the floor.

As we walked up the road the milling crowds of pub less people began to recede behind us, only the swoosh of the night bus passing disturbed the descending calm. The girls were linked, arm in arm, swaying gracefully up the road to St Hughs, dipping in and out of the tree shadows cast by the Victorian street lamps hanging outside some of the grander houses. I clutched my warm angel to my side and wondered how this Irish schoolgirl had performed such a miracle.

I lapped up every moment and memory of those halcyon days and nights, every chance I had to dance, in the sun or the pouring rain, amongst these blessed children, beneath those Dreaming Spires.

Meanwhile our tottering footsteps came to a gentle halt at Ali's Burger Van, our smiling faces had eyes like stars, from a distant Galaxy.

Orders were placed and some ate hungrily while others waited, pinching chips laden with cheese and garlic sauce. It was the perfect beer soaker and we all lapped up our share; drifting off slowly as the last warm tray came over the counter.

Ali smiled at me and I remembered Jaffa in his small cafe in Essaouira; the Tagine pot and the steaming kettle, the old men lying on the rush mats, puffing silently on their Kif pipes, staring at the blond boy. It seemed another lifetime away. Then a flash of the picture of Gerard setting light to bottles of Elixir Paregoric, the huge flames almost reaching the ceiling and the thick brown liquid at the bottom of the ladle that we carefully filtered and then injected.

I hugged the warm waist next to me and pressed my cheek against her soft hair. The silhouette in the Porter's Lodge waved cheerily, despite the late hour, happy perhaps to have the last of his flock home to roost. As we entered the inner corridors the laughter rang down the hall, accompanied by hiccups and 'Shhh!' Until we reached the building for Staircase Six. Hugs and kisses signalled the departure of some, then others, until the two girls below waved up the stairs and we disappeared into her room.

The Lava Lamp I had bought for her birthday was warming the bedside table with its red glow. The desk was piled with books and A4 Folders, half an essay seemed to struggling down one page, to the point it reached a tea cup stain. A chocolate bar and an open packet of Marlboros stared at each other.

The Vodka had long since passed and the Guiness wasn't destroying me, I had survived relatively well. My lover was less well pitched and as I gently took the items of clothing from her she curled up and closed her eyes. I squeezed into what was left of a student single bed and closed my eyes while she melted her shape into mine.

Sometime later the bells from North Parade rang out, 'Two o'clock,' or was it 'Three'? I lost count and consciousness. I dreamed of fields that ran down to beaches below skies that never darkened, stilled at the moment between day and night, here and there.

The following morning we queued on the pavement with other students outside the Baguette Shop in the North Parade. The staff, like our Porter, looked after the hungry hung over faces they saw for three years at a time. One of their baguettes could resuscitate the dead and feed an entire army of adventures.

Life that first term of the second year was so idyllic I kept looking over my shoulder just to check from time to time. While I waited for her to finish in the Library or return from a tutorial I would run in the University Parks or down to Port Meadow, perhaps spending some hours in the Pitt Rivers Museum or wander off to The Music Box to chat with Gary and Keith, who always chided me, 'Aren't you famous yet Smiles?' We went to endless parties and dances. If nothing else was planned, St Hugh's student bar always had music on.

What could possibly go wrong or blemish this perfect place? For us, nothing awful seemed able to break our ring of love. But as Christmas approached Nola's story reminded us how fate could infiltrate even these hallowed halls. Nothing was sacrosanct. Her mother died unexpectedly.

Nola was a close friend of the extended family of that congregated around the group of girls from Staircase Six. Her room was in the main building, high up, looking out over St Margaret's Road. The girls took me to see her because they knew I had lost my parents and I seemed to have some words of wisdom, experience or something to say, about almost everything! She was weeping, sobbing, heart broken in bits. Here she was, no doubt having worked so hard to attain this pinnacle of education, no doubt to please her parents and family. But now her mother, the almighty Mother, was gone.

We talked. I told her that from my experience the mourning would never really stop, but it would find a place in her soul to be at peace, locked in a small golden box like the one I had. She smiled at that. Here, it could be safely stored away.

I told her of a Radio programme about Grief, I had listened to driving home, east to west, from Tania's in the early hours. An old lady had rung in, talking about her father's death. 'Never a day goes by I don't think of him. Even now.' I knew that feeling. She had never forgot the day he died, despite being ninety years old and a lot of months! I smiled at this.

I told Nola the only thing she could try was take a part of her mother's life and weave it into her own. I mentioned 'We live as we dream, alone.' We must respect every life is measured out individually. We share what we are given.

I also suggested that perhaps some parents felt better able to guide and protect their children from 'Beyond the veil.' I thought this was true about my mother. We both cried at that.

Also, I mentioned a parent is present most of the time when we are young, especially as babies, then less so as we grow up until finally as adults our visits usually become less and less regular. However, if a parent has died they are, in some way, with us all the time, continually, all the day and all the night, waking or sleeping.

I hoped it helped, but I knew a plaster on this cut would only last an hour or so, this wound would be seeping anguish for years to come.

It was the first intrusion of reality on our merry band of young revellers. There would follow two more moments when the pristine glass of these lives was shattered. My young friends would have to learn there was no escape from those damn vicissitudes of fate. Moreover, that dastardly seamstress seemed to take a sheer delight in aiming her despair at the blessed and privileged; as if to say, 'So you think those high walls can keep me out?'

'Death' was becoming my specialist subject in life. I returned to the cottage after that long weekend and the meeting with Nola in a thoughtful mood. I sat down at my desk overlooking the fields and trees and began writing.

The white, unlined sheet of paper slowly filled with a few words at first, until, at some given moment, it was just pure emotion that carved blunt black lines into the shape of letters.

I was lost, as I often am during writing, between the thought and the process of the pen scrawling across the vellum. I was entranced, following the marvel of letters as they spilled on the page, scouring its emptiness with the dry blood of old emotions. I swayed like a trapeze artist between Nola's experience and mine, the two mothers, now cast forever, as fading photos.

Grief

...and the wracking of the body, the detuning of the spine, the notes bending, shuddering hopelessness in the soft white neck as it falls, helpless, the electric storm inside her eyes ricocheting again the tender folds of the heart. She is gone, she drops, colliding into the pavement, some nemesis of judgement. Still she falls. No terror, no voice, just the helplessness of the Mother's call from beyond the cleft wall. This is Hell. ...and the wracking of the body.

It was seven years before I cried. Seven years of Silence. Footsteps walked up and down the curtained corridors, but no light, no life. No sun. No son. No words. I waited.

I am lost, I am never to be found again, in the same way. The boy in my heart, with bruised knees and scuffed shoes, stops to help the fallen girl.

We carry her back to the room where last year's birthday card is just a poignant mockery of today's day of birth, when really all she wants to do is die. To die deep inside this hurt , where the longing comes in no more, where the fire takes everything back to the earth, ashes to ashes, dust to dust, strung upon greying portraits on a wall called, 'Forever.'

We wait for the rattle and bone of her body to cease. We caress and smooth the broken blankets of childhood, the lost Comforters. We wait because surely this is the last. But there is never a final breath except the one that claims us, never a last sorrow.

...and in his chair the groaning of the ocean tempts the slumbering Captain onto deck, where he looks about to see the grounded boat, the dry dock, the pale colourless magnolia of the hospital walls. More walks, more windows, more doors. None of these things belonged in his sea world, far far away.

Then the howl, the waking, breaking, slaking cry of the waves as they punish the conscience, burnish the sweat from the eyes and tarnish the ward in gloom. Far up the estuary the sea birds walk on dry mud, the tinder of their wings blown away.

"Bye bye," the Mocking Bird sighs.

...and the wracking of the body, its poor parts washed away, the spendthrift driftwood of muscle and fender. No good. No work. No nothing. No no.

These are our hells, our laden bells that sing out across the wuthering heights, the moorlands with tears wrung from the young girl's eyes, sung dry mouthed by the old women of hurrying boys, late by years, late forever and always. There is no escape. This is final. We are walking, like the waking dead back to dying Gethsemane.

But over there, to the right, beyond the grey mist, the arc of a rainbow appears above the endless rain. Is it morning or mourning? Hope? We have survived another night, broken the terror, wounded the pain and in its bleeding, healed some darkness.

She sleeps in the valium dawn.

The Captain stares, seeing only the old sea through his closed eyes.

We hand over her limp heart, hardly breathing to the Porter of Daylight. We hurry back to our refuge at the top of Staircase Six, to fuck from sheer relief at life, at love, at being spared the victim's role on this sodden hour.

Still I miss her. There's no love like Mummy's.

She watches. She will watch.

The nutmeg eyes surrounded in midnight.

The ivory desert, the sand dune breasts.

We are no more, lonely now, hidden, crumbling in our quiet solitude. Never to see. Never to feel again.

We talked this dark black night through to the light of curtained blue morning.

At Christmas, as Irish voices filled the kitchen in Maud's house, I had my moment too wondering how I ended up in the life of this family I really knew so little of. Her mother came up the stairs, perhaps she heard me sniffle or felt my despair, you know what mothers are like.

She sat next to me and put her arm round me. "It's not fair, I know." She held my anguish tight, "When, you fancy it if you feel like it, I've a mountain of mash waiting for you."

She wasn't joking. I followed her downstairs and joined the family at the table. A plate, looking more like a temporary volcano appeared, its potato cone filled with carrots and sprouts.

As I looked up she doused the whole thing in thick gravy. "There you go. A lovely vegetarian meal!"

NU

The New Year, sprung like a Deutsch Butcher's dog, into the limelight of 1996. The band was cooking on gas, rocking with a veritable strawberry topping.

We were ready to make our album. Despite all my endless knocking on Music Business doors, there was no company interested in helping a peace and love hippy band in the middle of the aspirational Nineties. My music according to the usual response was, 'Very good, but sadly very unmarketable.'

No profit meant no interest.

A couple of years before, faced with this dilemma I had made my first solo album, a double cassette, called, 'Troubadour's Home Coming,' 'THC.'

Like thousands of other musicians I prayed it might land on the right desk in Tottenham Court Road one day. It didn't. I could hardly compete with the up to date Recording Studios in London, but what I lacked in knowledge and hardware I made up for in sheer lunacy and an endless stream of unfounded belief. I was possibly the most hopeful man ever, in the most hopeless pursuit of a Record Deal.

Making the cassette had been an adventure which had all begun a couple of years before with a Miles Davis poster.

There was a fancy Bang and Olufsen shop, upstairs in the Cheltenham Arcade, which used to seduce my dreaming eyes, stuck like limpet shells to its window display. My Swedish father owned a B & O Record Player and ever since listening to my Grand Funk albums on it I had been devoted. However, as well as being the coolest brand of Hifi available at the time it was generally the most expensive.

Garrard and many others turned out just as good systems but none of them had the 'Space Age' look of B & O products.

One day as I peered in the shop window like a love sick child at a chocolate shop I noticed Miles Davis staring at me. It's an iconic shot of him glaring with the depth of a million sharps and flats into your soul. His face was like a book falling open in the wind with sheets of music tumbling out, his hand was lined with life, hard living life.

I had to have that poster. I had seen him live in January, 1972 at The Royal Festival Hall with my parents. My Mother was a big fan, my father thought he was. a bit of a 'Ponce' or something similar. But anything to do with my mother was sacrosanct.

I hesitated a moment. I was hardly in the market for buying much more than a paper bag in this shop, especially as I was, 'In between careers,' at the time, unemployed, or odd jobbing, ducking and diving as best I could. 'Penniless' might have been a more succinct way of putting it. Still, I figured they were not going to charge me for looking.

I wandered round the shop at first, ogling the fabulous speakers and music equipment. I noticed Miles' stare following me. Eventually I stood in front of him. The words below his penetrating eyes read, 'Miles prefers Revox.' I looked at the Reel to Reel Tape machine beneath him, which leant gently backwards on its stand. It was so beautiful. A dream machine for anybody into recording music. The Revox was priced at four grand, which was about three thousand, nine hundred and ninety three pounds and seventeen pence more than I could lay my grubby hands on right then. However, I could always have a punt for the poster.

I studied the guy behind the desk and moved in for the hussle. "Hey buddy, I was wondering if this poster of Miles Davis is for sale? Or could I put my name down for it when the display changes?"

This was an old game I played at Record Shops years before, when I would beg the owner to put my name down for some band's new promotion, maybe a poster or sometimes a model made of cardboard. Usually to be told, 'No. I already promised that to so and so, or somebody else.'

The guy smiled, "Sure, it's for sale..." My eyes lit up at once, "it comes with the Revox." I turned round and the four thousand pounds price tag gave me an a somewhat cruel and yet ironic grin.

"Ah well, that's ok. Thanks anyway." I gave Miles a smile and shuffled like a penniless tramp towards the door. "Cheers."

The shopping precinct brought me back from my reverie and I wandered down the row of hideously expensive shops. There was about as much chance of me buying that Revox as a Rolls Royce.

Anyway, I watched that machine for months. Every time Miles would taunt me with his stare. 'Come on you motherfucker, buy me! Before some creep takes me home.'

Miles and I had a lot in common, we shared the same bad habits, we went about our music and composition the same way. We also walked that fine line between keeping it all together and the entire pack of cards coming tumbling down in some almighty drug fuck up. I bonded with him over that.

I had read a lot of stuff about him, watched and listened. I remembered the stalking figure, crouched down at the side of the stage, like he was hunting his band, stealing through the undergrowth of amps to ambush them with Sharps, Key Changes or sudden Flats. When you are hunted, you play like your life depends on it; which was all Miles wanted from them. It keeps the band thinking on their feet if they never quite know what's coming next. I will admit managed to nail that much for my band!

One day I saw the Revox had been reduced in price by a few hundred quid, but that was still way out of my league. I garnered hope that it was at least going down. I visited the shop more frequently after that. A few weeks later I noticed it had moved further back in the shop. I wandered in to have a look.

"Hi buddy, how's it going?" I smiled at the shop assistant and took my hands out of my pockets to show him I wasn't carrying a gun. I get that look occasionally. My eyes shot back to the Revox, Miles was watching me closely. I could already see the price tag had moved from its spot and as I zoomed in I saw a '1' where a '3' once proudly stood. I held my breath and tried not to sprint the four steps that remained between me and my recording career. It was true. One quid short of two grand rather than four. "Hmm," I mused thoughtfully, not that I had two grand under the floorboards.

"Hey, er, what's happening with the Revox man?" As I spoke the guy came over, even from where he was standing my face had 'Sold' written all over it.

'Must be your lucky day, it was only just reduced, the boss wants the space and it's not really current to the 'CD' generation.' He waited while I took this in but he could tell from the words 'Lucky day' I had enough confirmation the deal was for real. "It comes with a load of Tapes too."

"Sure. Right. Wow. Okay." I didn't dare look at him, I ran my fingers over the smooth casing, I touched the edge of the reel and said, "Will you give me until midday tomorrow, possibly later today to sort the money out? Twelve o'clock latest, I promise."

"Sure, what's your name?"

"Mr Smiles! Miles of smiles! Wow, thanks a million buddy, awesome." As I said it I noticed Miles staring down at me smiling. "Ah, er, you remember I asked about the poster and I think you or the other guy said it came with the Revox?"

"Double lucky day." He was grinning too. It must be like selling candy to kids when a dreamer like me stands in front of a shop assistant. "Yes, that came with the machine and goes with it."

I can't remember how I found the two grand, but when it comes to life's necessities it's amazing what you can pull out of thin air. It began a journey which took me to spaces in music that Miles would have understood. I'm sure his spirit helped me get that deal and make my first solo album on cassette.

My cottage was now 'Windsong Recording Studio.'

*

Dawn. Low mist hangs over the fields. A distant bird breaks the silence for a second, until just the purr of her mute breath remains beside. The cottage is stilled, no breeze disturbs the dry flowers on the windowsill. It is too early for anybody except the long shadows to be awake.

But a distant school bell rung by a hand poking out from a brown corduroy sleeve had woken me from the sea spray of my bleached beaching dreams.

My foot slipped out to touch the old floorboards. I knew every bare foot of them, every creak and groan of their aged limbs. Deftly, I stepped left and right avoiding the knots and burnished cracks, noiselessly descending the stairs. Maud, being a true martyr to sleep, was purring away quietly in Dreamland.

The kettle hissed and spluttered until it clicked off. The coffee with molasses smelt like toffee chocolate. Alone in the kitchen, I turned a half circle from the dawning east to the slumbering west. I knew these times were blessed. If only life could have repeated the coming year forever with its banal thrill of four seasons. If only I had learnt to stand still, instead of constantly seeking out some faint rhythm in the far distance, to which my spirit gravitated. I hadn't yet discovered the contentment and true enlightenment that would come eventually with years of relentless crap and failure.

Maud would be sleeping for hours yet. It was the fatal flaw in our relationship, I was a Lark and she was an Owl. Upstairs her dreams were still galloping across the pillow plains, while next to me the kettle whistled its serpentine tune.

I was Eve while Adam slept. I held the 'Apple' in my hand and span it gently round, until I crushed the dry Poppy head between my fingers and crumbled the pieces into the small pan. 'She won't even know...' ran through my head like a mantra. 'Just a little bit...'

'Sex and drugs and Rock n'Roll.' We had loved until love was loved all over, until our lips burnt. Next topic, drugs. I was, like any old drug addict, highly adept at disguising my habit to the world and of course to myself. How many times I put the blindfold on and walked down the plank to self destruction, diving gladly into the becalmed seas of Morphia, knowing full well I was bound to cause my own breathless demise, bedraggled on the beach in ruins. But for now...

The seep of warm Opium crept through my blood. As I lay back on the couch I saw Miles staring at me from the other room, he knew the score; as did so many musicians and artists. There was a connection between prowling the wastelands of life, the out reaches of an musician's life and the lure of getting stoned. You had to get out there to see the distant stars, nothing could be gleaned from the streets of banality or from weeks of safe and steady routine.

The headphones were sitting crosslegged next to the Revox. Final topic, Rock n Roll. I plugged the jack in and clicked 'Play.' The seamless silence gave way at last to the harmonics on my guitar. I usually preceded any recording with this, it was my way of calling up the mystic energies and basically logging whether I was in tune or not. There were times I wasn't.

For a moment I looked up, the valley beyond the cottage was filling slowly with sunlight, it was going to be a beautiful day. The guitar began to resonate as the song began.

My life was perfect, there seemed so much more to come, I was still feeling as if I was beginning, not ending, dissolving. The rush of the Opium and the ricochet of stereo strings melted my imagination.

Was it right or wrong to seek these moments of pure perfection? Opium was an old friend to me, a needy mate, but one in whose company I felt forever reassured. I wasn't going to stop now. Miles knew.

I was also going to make an album with the band. It didn't have a working title, other than, 'The First Album, Man.'

When it came to the time we had to chose we spent one mad night, crying with laughter as the band, plus Proper Job Nick and Texas Tim came up with possible names. Most of which were highly appropriate and very inappropriate. In the end I wanted 'Smiles' in there somewhere but 'Cosmic' being our theme tune song was also possible. Having chucked everything else out we decided to hedge our bets and put Cosmic and Smiles on the cover. We reckoned it would soon become clear which name would stick. None of us guessed that everyone would presume the band was called Cosmic Smiles. So that was it. Fate decided.

It would have been just the name of a crazy band, but years later, when it was necessary for me to fade into obscurity for awhile in Wales, it would become my used name, in all matters work, life and love, until I became more Cosmic than Geoff. However I would never relinquish Geoff totally as that was the name my mother had chosen. She was sacrosanct.

In the meantime I would make ten albums with the band, before the walls of 'Windsong' came tumbling down in debt around me. Naturally, it wasn't quite that simple, those damn vicissitudes of fate would have to play their part, they liked me too well to leave me alone or bring my demise about with one cruel stroke, as had happened to those poor people in the Rivermead Rehabilitation Centre. I was kind of thankful for that.

The years would be filled with amazing musicians, sessions and performances, as well as the 'Shit arse Charlie' gigs.

The best thing about my sleeping princess upstairs was she never said no to my dreams, she even helped them find a foothold in the real world. Yet, I was never destined to succeed, like Captain Scott I was doomed from the first day the plans hit the table. I was out of date, out of time and most likely out of my head.

We got so close at times, just enough to tempt me a little further down the road to nowhere and it all began with Miles Davis and the Revox Reel to Reel.

During that year the band gathered each week at the cottage. It was usually the main reason I had to leave the warmth of St Hugh's expansive welcome.

Kevan would always arrive first and Andy the drummer last. In between Colin, the keyboard wizard would arrive and any other assorted singers or players. The band, beyond the main members, was always expanding and contracting, new characters with fresh energy kept the music evolving.

It didn't matter how good or how bad you were musically, how old or young, there was nothing that could prepare anybody for the experience of playing the way I liked. Miles knew that too.

With music you either depend on the mathematics and step by step practise, or you learn to 'Float the Goat.' Even musicians who knew all the notes still found the freedom we played with difficult to master at first. Until I mentioned the trick was not to master anything, because the second we knew the song it would cease to have the spontaneity I desired. If you make it live, it feels live to the listener.

I tried to do for other musicians what I'd always hoped somebody might have done for me, take me into a studio, get the best out of me and say, "Here, your name is on this album." Age or mental health was not a consideration, we had teenagers and one old chap who was nearly eighty.

I had met this old violinist doing a job for his next door neighbour. I told him I had a song that I'd like some strings on and asked if he was interested. Apparently he had a grandson who was keen on music and the old guy thought this would be a lovely thing to present him with. When he showed up he was so nervous I couldn't record him clearly without without picking up the sound of his shoes tapping the floor. So I stood him on a couple of bits of carpet. That didn't work. In the end he played in his socks and I got the recording.

I was so chuffed to stop at his little terraced house in the middle of nowhere some months later and give this old guy his free copies. That was one thing I got out of it, giving the music away, usually for free, making a small dream come true for people that they thought was impossible.

That was the deal. Free copies of the album was all I could really offer by way of payment. I never had any money to give musicians and one look at my fridge was enough to reassure them I wasn't lying.

Buskers I met became band members, singers came and went, lasting on average three albums, while Kevan, Andy, Colin and I got on with it. The music that came out of that cottage was truly extraordinary, perhaps not note perfect, but utterly true to the most honest way of making music. Miles would have loved it. He would have prowled round the edges like a Tiger, snarling and grinning from ear to ear.

I usually had a vague idea of a couple of songs I wanted to try to record on any particular night. The session would begin with a warm up song, often 'Nobody's Fool.' From then on anything could happen.

'Cosmic,' was the name of a long improvisation, based on a riff I played with a particular Echo loop. It would be true to say, as any good band knows, the sum of the total was more than the parts. There were moments when the sound melded, as if the last piece of a jigsaw had just been fitted in, then the whole starship almost elevated in front of us.

Riding those seconds and minutes was like gliding over a cliff face, picking up the necessary winds from the fatal depths below whilst keeping just in sight of the safe green fields of sanity. We tipped over that edge so many times and always managed to fly back on the last note.

After which there would be a pause, our breaths held, I would glance round to check the machine had been running and recording; not always the case. Then a sigh of relief, we would look at each other until finally someone said the classic, 'What the fuck was that? Where did that come from? Like, what just happened?'

To which I would often reply, "That's jammin' man." It could be so magical if we were lucky. At the end of every session I would thank the Spirits for blessing our poor mortal souls with their energy. It really felt like that some nights, as if Miles, Jimi, Jim, Janis and so on were all passing through, listening to this music which was so free it allowed us to touch the space they owned.

The songs we recorded were all written by me as they were created from my life. I never decided that I had to write a Love song or a 'Not In Love' song, they would come and go as the women that inspired them did. Everything was done from the heart and with all my heart. I had nothing else to offer.

Over that Spring and Summer, we religiously tried to capture some of our best moments until I figured I had enough on tape to mix it all together. I learnt the maximum time you could get on a CD was seventy seven minutes, so I was aiming for seventy six and fifty odd seconds. Miles understood.

There were a couple of things that were against us, as in I didn't have clue about sound dynamics, other than what I heard sounded good or bad to me and the equipment, despite Miles, was almost as out of date as I was. But maybe it was my lack of knowledge that meant I had to just fiddle about until I discovered something that worked. Colin taught me a lot but he was still learning his trade and the area of music he was keen to make a mark on was Techno, which demanded a different approach, as far from what we were doing as you could probably get. He'd spend three months carefully building up his tracks from samples and getting the best tonal resonance. Where we should spend eight minutes creating eight minutes.

I was lucky enough to capture some of his piano playing at its best, before 'Pro Tools' got him. He was a lovely guy too, huge long dreads in his hair and the vibe to go with them.

There was never any arguments in our band, no major scenes, I couldn't stand that crap. We left our lives and worries outside on Band Night. We went in there and communed with the spirits, experiencing something beyond our ordinary reality. For a few hours we played at being the Gods and Goddesses we had worshipped all our lives. If we couldn't play at their level at least we could aim in their direction.

I'm glad I was naive, hopeful and so full of music I could burst. As the year progressed we did a few gigs, but the main deal was what was happening in the cottage and in my life. You could hear the light in it as I had so much love and life in me. I had a new song in my heart. I was hanging on and we were creating something awesome.

Listening back it has become even more extraordinary and special with time, every minute was worth a brick from my house. All my life I've encouraged musicians to finish an album, capture the era, the year, the band as it stands. Don't wait for anybody else to fill-in the gaps.

With my occasional forays into London on behalf of 'Don't Tell It,' I had been punting my wares about, gigging at the Twelve Bar Club, Bungies Cellar, the Troubadour, wherever I could blague a spot.

The more I saw, the more I knew we were screwed trying to compete with the professional bands, their music companies spent more on one night of entertainment than I earned in a year. On the other hand what we had wasn't for sale in Harrods or any other place. It was priceless!

However, I followed every lead and every possible connection to get a deal or a Showcase gig for the music business people. But nobody in the business was interested. The words Cosmic Smiles and Profit just didn't go in one sentence. Miles understood.

I figured the best policy was to forget the whole business bit and just make the album.

I did it all, I got the musicians together, recorded all the album, mixed it, designed it and paid for it. It was my trip and I didn't expect the band to shell out for the first one. It was my baby and I was buying all the nappies.

Even if I'd known that ten albums and several drug addictions would eventually sink my cottage I would still have taken every step.

If I ever feel lost I go back to the albums. My old bones hear the rhythm of the music and start to vibrate, I sense the joy I owned.

I pulled it together for the following Spring, spending days listening through the recordings, doing the overdubs and playing around with the blends and effects, creating the Trip. A good album should be more than ten tracks, it ought to take the listener on a journey to somewhere, with a few unexpected deviations before arriving back.

In the middle of all this I had a chance to play my music on stages that musicians I had worshipped all my life had performed on, in New York City.

"It's the trip of a lifetime," Chris said. He did the artwork for the first album and was the father of Emily, a lovely girl from the Bluebell Woods of my memories. He was a brilliant artist as well as one of the early victims of the treatment for Polio. In those days they removed the shaking leg muscles to help the symptoms, but such a process was as barbaric as it was useless. The moment I met him years before and the family it was like coming home, for awhile.

I remember thinking, 'You gotta be joking. Surely this isn't it.' But sitting here, with the change in the immigration process and my colourful history I know now that was it. Andy, the band's drummer, 'Jazz

Sticks,' bless him, had planned to visit his sister Suzanne who lived in New York with her husband Steve. He was a drummer of much renown, who had toured with Boy George, among others and no doubt added to many a session in the city's famous studios. Not only that, they had a flat in Greenwich Village, which couldn't be more central to the Mecca of Bleeker Street where the Beatniks, the Folkies, the Blues and Rock performers had come to find fame and make some of the greatest music in America; including classic artists Dylan, Hendrix, Simon and Garfunkel.

There was one problem though, one sorrow, which was Steve was dying of AIDS. The other thing that really moved me was I never saw a couple so much in love. One other small detail, somewhat pertinent, always part of my journeys, was he had a flat full of Morphine. Bless him.

He was also my age and of my persuasions. I saw him for about a week over the three weeks we were there. We borrowed one of their friend's flats but spent a couple of night on the floor at Steve's.

We arrived a few days after Christmas. Maud was happy for me to go off on this adventure. She knew what it meant to me. I have rarely known such love with complete freedom and trust.

A normal flat in Greenwich Village would be better described as a medium size living room with several cupboards attached. One contained a bathroom, one a kitchen and the last contained winter coats and everything else. Steve also had a 'Drip' for his Meds set up and boxes of paraphernalia. No drums.

One night I woke up early, I was half in and out of one of the cupboards. I went to the toilet cupboard and creeping back looked at the couple asleep on the bed. The lights of the city meant it was never quite dark and the usual orange halo of neon lights came up from somewhere below. There was no need for a sheet as the temperature from the building heating system kept the place really warm.

They were a perfect mirror of each other, in long well worn T-shirts, their bodies crouched like little Squirrels, holding their palms up to each other as if they held an Acorn between them. But at the top, their faces dreamt, staring with closed eyes at each other, even asleep, in case one might lose sight of the other. But most moving of all, was their noses just touched.

Such devoted lovers, entwined in their dreams; it was so poignant knowing Death was sitting on the doorstep outside. It was the late Nineties, AIDS was still a hopeless scenario, no treatment was as yet successful. Also, it carried the stigma of a disease only Gay men and Intravenous drug users had to worry about; and the people they had sex with. Like any disease it had the ability to grab sections of the population before they got wise. The Haemophiliacs were one of these, hospital workers and litter pickers could all end up 'Spiked' with this curse.

Steve knew the girl he had got it from in Thailand. He knew the kind of sex he had with her was risky. The whole deal was wrong really. But I guess he was on tour and no doubt there were many other factors that brought him to that bed. Miles understood.

He confessed one night to me, "There was this look in her eyes, I knew something was wrong. I didn't realise until later, when I got ill that she was dying of AIDS." He sighed. I admired his honesty, there can be no lies when Death is listening at the door.

In the end it comes down to good luck or bad. John Coffee, one of the first AIDS victims that took the American blood supply companies to court, had merely had a transfusion; one to save his life that killed him. The Blood Banks were supplied by desperate people who often sold blood every week to maintain a drug or drink habit. The companies fought John Coffee, with 'Delaying Tactics.' Until he died. His story made a column in The Times which I read during a coffee break at work, which was why I remembered his name.

But all this joy was ahead of me. Before we left, as well as the Christmas expenditure, I had a couple of weeks to save some money up for the journey. I did a few jobs round the village and stumped up ninety quid, for three weeks in America. One guy, the last job, seemed slightly gobsmacked I was off with less than a hundred quid, so he gave me twenty on top and said, 'Have a beer in Times Square for me.' I did.

We flew out just after my thirty ninth birthday. It was night when we arrived and we both pressed our noses to the small plane window to watch the lights of JFK ascend towards us. I was vaguely worried the Customs may not let me in, I was carrying a battered guitar case which usually got me searched. But I must have met the right Officer at the right desk because he didn't even blink as he looked me over and studied my name in the Passport.

With a smile he pronounced, "Welcome to America Mr Smiles.'

MU

The Yellow Taxi driver was thrilled to have two Englishmen in his cab. He gabbled away merrily as we watched the freeway signs flash by and buildings start to rise as the city got closer. It was still fairly early in the evening, the flickering lights and brightly illuminated shop windows were entrancing. I had to unstick my nose from the window a few times.

New York City, gosh! How many lives had passed through this place, how many in search of fame and fortune, the American Dream, 'If I can make it in New York I can make it anywhere.'

It would be thrilling to think this was the start of a fairy story and somewhere in the chaos a chance was looming for me to break on through to the high life. But it was never my destiny. Every biography of a band has a moment when somebody, outside of their circle, provides the last link in the chain. This would never happen for Cosmic Smiles. However, I would come away from America utterly convinced I was doing the right thing with my music and writing; but it wasn't due to some Record Executive offering me a deal. It was somebody far more worthy.

We bundled out of the taxi and headed up the lift to the floor where Steve and Sue lived. Because we had been following the sun west there was still time to meet up with Steve's parents and go out for a meal 'Downtown.' To be honest it wouldn't matter what time it was, now we were in the 'City that never sleeps.' Sounded good to me.

The dinner was fine and it soon became clear Steve and I had lots in common. Both of us being a bit older than Andy and Sue we both had similar music histories that reached further back in time. It wasn't long before we decided we liked each other. My heart was touched by his fate, such a nice guy, such a lovely lady and such an awful lack of any future ahead of them. It doesn't and it didn't make sense.

After the meal we shared up the bill. My bit was about forty dollars and I watched roughly thirty percent of my holiday spending money disappear within hours of arrival. Shit.

Still, there was always the chance of making a few bucks Busking with my guitar.

The next day we wandered around Times Square, in and out of the monstrously huge department stores, doing the tourist thing. Andy bought a camera.

Back at the flat night descended as the street lights ascended. I knew somewhere down there Bleeker Street was beginning to sing and I wanted to see if I could get a gig. Steve, Sue and Andy were happily reminiscing. I chirped up, "Er folks, I think I'm going to head down to Greenwich Village and see if I can sort out getting a gig while we're here. What do you reckon?"

Steve nodded enthusiastically, "Sure, you want to go down to the Red Lion Pub, they always seem to have some cool bands on. Maybe ask there."

"Thanks man. I'll take my guitar and stuff with me just in case I have to demo a song." In those days my guitar and me were pretty much inseparable.

"Good luck." They all chimed as I left.

Apparently after I'd left Steve sighed and told Andy I didn't have a hope in Hell of getting a gig. He knew the scene, it took ages to get on the list to play those venues, they were top class spots and there was no shortage of eager nuts like me waiting in the wings to perform.

It only took a ten minute walk to get there. As I approached I saw four black guys, dressed in sharp suits like Barber Shop Minstrels, singing harmonies on the corner. I stopped to listen. Their voices were amazing. Shit, I was really up against it if this was the standard of the buskers. However I felt I had two things in my favour, they certainly hadn't heard any of my songs before and I was British, English!

I turned into Bleeker Street and saw a row of Pubs and Bars stretching as far as the eye could see. Under their flashing signs small posters advertised bands or performers. Some had shivering queues waiting to get in, huddled along the 'Sidewalk,' or groups stacked together up flights of stairs.

I found The Red Lion, it was busy. A five piece band was kicking out some tunes on the stage, all the tables were packed full of people, drinking, smoking, chatting, all enjoying the Christmas holidays.

As the barman brought me my Guinness I piped up, "Hi buddy. Great band. Hey, I was wondering what the deal is about getting a gig here. I'd love to play." I quickly added, as if he hadn't already guessed, "I'm just over from England."

"Sure, no worries buddy." My face lit up, "You gotta speak to Frankie about that. He sorts the bookings out." I looked around hoping Frankie was behind me or would appear miraculously. He didn't.

"Er, cool. Thanks." My hope was escalating, "Er, is Frankie about?" My face added a few more lights.

"Nah. Not tonight buddy. He comes in about every two weeks, maybe next week, who knows." My face suffered a power failure and all the lights bombed.

"Ah thanks man. I guess I'll have to come back. Problem is, I'm only here for three weeks." The bar man had another customer and as he sidled off he just smiled that 'Sorry dude' smile at me.

I took my pint and went to sit at one of the tables. There were other people around it but they made way for me and my guitar. A short while later one of the guys in the band headed off to the toilets, passing our table on the way. "Back in a second." I said to the other guests. Out in the toilets I made sure I caught the guy at the sinks and I asked again about the deal for getting a gig. 'Frankie.' Okay.

I went back to my table, despite the disappointment I was enjoying the music; I got out my collection of Harmonicas, fiddling about until I found which key the song was in.

Almost immediately the people at the table got excited. "Hey, thats really cool. You should go up and play."

I explained about 'Frankie.'

But they shook their heads, "Nah it's cool they love people getting up and joining in."

I explained the politics of gigs and that it was very uncool in England to just turn up and try to sit in with a band. But they weren't convinced. "Go on buddy."

I relinquished, "Ok folks, see what happens." As I had made contact in the toilet with one of the band, I kept staring at him until I caught his eye, hoping he'd remember me. Then I waved the harmonica at him. When the song ended I saw him chatting to the other guitarist. Then, he looked back and nodded.

By the time the singer had announced, "Hey y'all, we got some English guy here who wants to come up and play a bit of harmonica on a song," I was already up at the stage. The guy looked me over quickly, "What keys you got?"

I flashed the rack of five harps at him, "Pretty much everything, 'A, C, D, E,' or 'G.' I swiftly added, "Thanks man, I really appreciate it." In England I would have got that 'Fuck off you wanker' look. But the guy didn't seem uptight about it at all.

"Ok, grab your 'D.'" The song kicked off and I knew how to blow, enough, but not too much, never step on the vocals, dance round them. It went well. The audience ratcheted up a notch, the band seemed to be digging it.

I chanced my hand, "Hey buddy, could I do a Blues with you?" To which I added, "Before I go." Hoping to reassure them this British bum wasn't going to be on stage all night with them. "Er, something in 'E?' I knew lots of Blues song were in the guitar Key of 'E' and there was a good likelihood they'd know one.

"Sure thing, I 'spect we could do that." The guy turned round to the bass player and said something, nodded to the drummer and played the first chord. I slipped the 'A' 'Harp' out of its Lee Oskar box and grabbed the first note I hit.

You can't learn the Blues, you earn the Blues by living through them. Of course you can play every song out of Alabama note perfect but it still doesn't make it the Blues. It's something you either have or you don't, like rhythm, it comes partly from what is in your soul, partly from life experience, but mainly out of the ether. You really have to connect with something you just can't plug a lead into.

This is what Robert Johnson's story about going 'Down to the crossroads' is all about. I mean, two roads meeting at midnight? But that's it precisely. Out in the darkness, out in the Blues, you have to walk that road until it crosses the other one, the one that leads you off in another unknown direction. Yet, no matter what the story, the simple test is whether the audience get it or not. You can fake a lot of styles of music, but not the Blues

I took that first note and weaved my way into the guitar, bending and grinding it, my whole body becoming the sound of that note. Then I took it up a half tone before breaking it down on the floor again. Up, down, in, out, the notes built like a wave coming into the bay. But all the time I was watching the main man out of the corner of my eye. He was watching me and he knew I was on it. He nodded over to the guitarist and the band went through the Intro a second time.

I saw his foot move, the head ease nearer the mic. Then, as he breathed in, I blew out the last note, tearing it down and down with my solar plexus, until it died as the first word hit the singer's lips. There was a ripple from the crowd, the band felt the buzz and suddenly the whole vibe in the place went up a notch. We were rocking with a strawberry topping!

Rule number one playing harmonica is, 'Don't step on the vocals.' The human ear can only really take in one conversation at a time and it gets annoyed listening to somebody butt in all the time.

The trick is to hover like a Hummingbird, to chunk away like a Hammond organ in the back of a church; then as the singer falls back you come in on wings around his back, wrap his last note up and fly.

As soon as the singer has gone I listened for the guitars. Following the Bass, but leaving just enough room for the Lead to be there too. Stomp on the Lead guitarist's ego and you will get 'Marshalled' off the stage. There was none of that.

The band felt the excitement and I could sense them listening to me as I took the first break and worked the solo up. The second time I sat back and let the lead guitar take it away. Well there was no stopping him now. Everything went up another notch and all the while the audience knew I was coming back in. They're on their toes, waiting, anticipating. I move nearer the mic.

"All the way from the United Kingdom," the singer smiled at me, "On harmonica…" Of course he didn't know my name, but it didn't matter, the roar from the crowd drowned him out and I launched into the last solo. Somewhat encouraged, I took the mic off the stand and went wild, jumping up and down, burning those notes down with the harp in my mouth.

As I've said to many a young performer, 'A good musician knows went get on, but a really good one knows when to 'Get the fuck off.' For a second the band held the few chords, building and then bang, one, two, three, smash. The drums, guitars and harp all stopped on a Dime. The audience went nuts.

Before the guy had even looked round I had packed up my harps and was off the stage. "Well folks, what can I say. That's what we love about gigs. Thanks to our English friend there."

Back at the table I sat down with the other people and almost immediately a Double Bourbon appeared in front of me. The Barman I had spoken to when I came in smiled. "I'll let Frankie know you're around."

I smiled, "Thanks." But I knew that was a long shot so I bathed in my little glow of joy and sweat about three tables from the back of the room as the band carried on. We'd taken it up a level, they were on fire now, maybe too much fire.

A few minutes later I saw the guitarist flinch as one of his strings broke, flicking across his hand. At the end of the song, he went up to the mic, "Er, we're gonna take a short break now, while I fix this string." He looked over to the barman, "Hey, could you put the House Music on."

By the time he caught the barman's attention I was already in front of him. "Hey man, I could fill in a song for you. While you retune?" He looked at me, there must have been a murmur of encouragement from the crowd.

"What's your name?"

"Mr Smiles! I beamed.

"Hey y'all. Looks like we have another treat from this guy, all the way from England." He paused, "He says he's called Mr Smiles." The crowd all cheered at this. As he passed me he added, "Cool, enjoy. I'll be about five minutes."

I swung the guitar strap over my shoulder while the other guitar player handed me a lead. One brush of the strings. "That'll do." I was in tune. I sang a song I'd recently written that had a cute 'Country Blues' feel to it. It seemed to be the right song for there and then.

As I played I looked at the crowd from the dizzy two foot high stage, glanced at my watch and thought to myself, 'Wow, less than an hour or so in Greenwich Village and here I am performing live on stage.' Miles would have loved that!

It was awesome, a train of tiny events made even more amazing because if I hadn't done the Harp bit they'd would never have let an unknown musician jump in like that. Everybody loved the spontaneity of it. That's what the best gigs are all about.

When I finished the song, the guy came up and asked the crowd if they wanted one more. They did. I played Hummingbird, which is perhaps the song that says the most about me and my life. I was so happy to lay that one down on Bleeker Street.

I didn't even loiter for a third. It was enough. Know when to stop, know when to get the fuck off. I thanked the band and the audience and made my way back to the small table. There was another Double Bourbon next to the other one.

As I've told many a young musician, its not learning the chords or writing the songs thats hard, it's living the life that takes its toll. I slung one of the Jacks back and smiled at the family opposite. "Hey, thanks for kicking my ass to get up there."

One of the guys smiled, "Loved that, through and through boy. You made our night. What's your real name dude?"

"Geoff Smiles. It is my real surname, my mother's maiden name," I paused, "Didn't wanna carry my Dad's name, he kind of...we kind of..."

"Cool name. Good luck with all your music, are you in a band? I can tell you they all been through here."

We chatted for awhile and enjoyed the music from the band. I could have stayed longer but I'd nailed this place and there wasn't much more I could do to top that. I was keen to get out and see what else lay further on down Bleeker street.

I came out of the Red Lion Bar, smiling from ear to ear. The band gave me a nod, they knew the score. I could have hung around like a lost puppy hoping for second helpings, but it is more important to respect the unwritten etiquette of gigs that exists between musicians; not that they all adhere to its strictures.

The thing is those guys might have planned months for that gig, it wasn't fair to expect I could share the pie they'd spent so long preparing. Its about having Respect. This is even more prevalent amongst the Blues and Jazz musicians, where having a reverence for the 'Elders' was a central creed; because even if you think you know better, you haven't earned the right to say it. Not until you had lived it and survived. I had learnt this from my early forays on the gig scene in London and reading plenty of biographies about musicians.

After the heat of the bar the winter air was crisp and chilled my face. I didn't have to look far for the next tvenue. A few feet from where I was standing a flight of steps led up to doorway beneath a small sign. A few people were going in. I checked the name above their heads, 'The Terra Blues Club.'

I followed up, inside a few more stairs brought me into a large dimly lit room. The bar ran along the far wall and to my right a stage, about three feet off the floor, filled the end of the room. A few booths with high sides were set to the left, towards the back wall in shadow. On the stage an old black man, sitting on a chair, was playing guitar, singing a really nice blues song. My ears pricked up as much as the hairs on the back of my arms.

I ordered a Bourbon and sat at a table about three from the front. The place wasn't that busy but it sure wasn't empty either. I had a direct line of vision to the guy and I studied his guitar playing closely, while occasionally glancing at his expression. I really don't know how those guys do it, but with fingers like fat sausages, voices that croak and a beaten up guitar they break every bone in your heart.

This guy was good. I hadn't even bothered asking about how to get a gig at the bar. I had a 'Plan B' now. I watched long enough to suss out that the guy seemed sweet; I caught his eye a couple of times and he didn't blank me. I quietly got my harps out of the bag and laid them on the table. When he came to the end of the next song I caught his eye and waved one briefly at him. He continued chatting to the crowd and then his eye came back to mine. He paused for a moment and I saw him nod at me. I ducked reverently to the front of the stage. He lent down and stared at me, saying nothing.

I whispered "Hey, buddy, I was wondering if I could sit in on a song with 'Harp?' I'm from England."

He looked at me for a second without a flutter of emotion then straightened himself up and brought the mic back to his mouth. "Hey folks, seems we got a guy who wants to play a song with me. He's from England." That was my cue. I grabbed the rest of my harmonicas, jumped up on the stage and came round to his right.

He lent back off the mic and without looking at me muttered in my direction , "You got a G?"

"Yeah."

"Ok. You got one song. If you're shit you're off. You got it." He reached round and picked up a spare mic and handed it to me.

"Ok, I got it." I looked out across the room.

The stage lights below us blinded everything but for a silhouette. All I could see was the silver shine on the top of people's heads somewhere back there.

I watched his arm as it began to strum the guitar, listened for the first few seconds and then pitched my notes in. Gently, gently, I caressed the chords, weaving respectfully between his fingers and thumb, finding the spaces in between, filling them slowly with molasses and cream. I saw his shoulders relax and the guitar settle into his lap. The sheen on the turn ups of his shiny suit polished the shoe which tapped a rhythm out. I linked my heartbeat with that toecap.

After one of the harp breaks there was a hoot from the crowd and the black man's shoulders dropped a bit more. He sang the next verse and then gave me a nod to play. He ran through the chord sequence twice before the last chorus and we ended on a soft wavering wail. The crowd loved it.

His face turned round and he winked. "Ok, one more, maybe two. You got an A?" I nodded. "We're off." He played the next two songs calling out the Key to me and checking I had the right harp. The crowd enjoyed them and one or more silhouettes seemed to have appeared somewhere out there. After the second song he announced, "Gonna take a break now for a few minutes. Let's all give a hand to this here harmonica man from England." He turned round to me, "What's your name?"

"Mr Smiles," I grinned. He knew the significance of the Mister.

"Mr Smiles." There were a few cheers above the applause. I went back to my table and packed my harps away. At the bar the guy just handed me a huge glass of Bourbon and waved his hand.

I was getting to enjoy the feeling of the Sour Mash burning inside, but I had to keep my shit together. I wanted to play here too. I went back, sat down and waited until the musician came over. I figured after his smoke or whatever else he would pass by.

Sure enough he did, "Hey Mr Smiles. Nice playing. You living here?"

"No, sadly not, just on holiday. Thanks for the spot."

"No worries."

I seized my moment, "Hey, I suppose you wouldn't trust me to open the next set with a song?" I pointed to the guitar case half hidden under the table, "It's fully loaded man." I laughed.

He paused and looked at the battered case. "Okay, same deal, one song, any good you'll get a second."

"Oh wow thanks. Cheers man, I'll give it all I got."

"If you're half as good as your harp playing then it should be great." He smiled.

In the end I played two songs and finished with a third, an instrumental. All went well, but it wasn't my gig and the guy had to run the show. As much as I'd have liked to share more I knew when to get 'The fuck off.' Afterwards, I spent another hour there, feeling it disrespectful to the guy to leave before his next break. I thanked him for the spot, he told me he was back in a couple of weeks and I was welcome to drop by. I told hm I wasn't really sure where I'd be, but maybe? He laughed at that. I shook his huge warm hand and made my way back to the street.

The air seemed even fresher now with a warm layer of sweat right through the shirt on my back.

I strolled down the street. It was still fairly busy with people passing me, huddled in twos and threes or hand in pockets, shrugging off the cold. It suddenly occurred to me I had no idea what time it was.

My watch had been adjusted to East Coast time, it was just coming up to two in the morning. 'Shit.' The others will think I've been mugged. Sue, bless her had told me not to venture past this Subway and to watch out for that area and basically, any problems call her at home, anytime, whatever. She was lovely.

I can't tell you how much I wanted to ride past that Subway she mentioned.

However, I had only really turned the corner into Bleeker Street, so I picked a spot in the distance, headed down to that and turned back. I noticed even at that time the music scene was still going strong. I knew in England we'd just be getting off the last bus or tube, standing into the 'Chippy' queue, drunk as a skunk and hungry as a horse. New York was still bright and bushy tailed.

Somewhat reluctantly I made my feet head home.

Back at the flat I crept in noiselessly, Andy was on the couch, Steve and Sue on the bed; I reversed my guitar and me quietly into my cupboard and lay down. My head was still filled with all the people and lights, the thrill of the night tingled inside me.

I know famous bands come over and get to play the great venues and go to fabulous night clubs with other stars afterwards. But the fact that I had scored two gigs on my first night, by chance and both going really well, was a story no record executive could manufacture. In the first five available nights I was in New York I blagued and blazed seven gigs.

Just before I felt myself falling to sleep I looked up and out the window next to their bed. The orange neon sky twinkled with the few remaining lights from distant skyscrapers.

Perhaps it was then, that I first noticed the sleeping couple, curled up like two squirrels, with their paws in prayer. It was such a touching sight, knowing their love was ultimately condemned to death. It was so moving, that even if they'd been naked, the vision of them together, with its poignancy wouldn't have portrayed an ounce of sexuality, for it was so pure, so full of unconditional love, so tragic, so beautiful, it went beyond all earthly concerns.

I thought of John Coffee, I knew Steve wasn't going to make it, but I felt, having met him, that for the moment he was going to be fine but he wasn't going to escape like Gerard. He was already wandering off on some days between our world and theirs.

I sighed in stunned admiration, lay my head back and fell asleep.

Steve and I rapped a load about the music scene the next day. Everyone was amazed I'd managed to even get a note let alone the chance the play, twice.

One of the days early in that week, Steve and I were left alone in the flat while Sue and Andy went out shopping. "Help yourself to the Morphine if you want dude. I guess you like the stuff. I wish I was taking it for all the wrong reasons too." We both laughed. It was good for him to have somebody he liked but not too close he could really off load to.

He told me about the girl, and some of the concerts and tours he'd done. We just melded and welded.

A thought occurred to me. I had been initiated into Rosicrucianism and taken part in many ceremonies at Rollright Stones, Avebury and Stonehenge. It had given me a keen eye for other energies in the body and spirit. As I looked at Steve I could almost sense the flame of his life's candle, it was going to run out but I felt it was burning strong for now.

I wondered if I could bring any of the energy I'd felt in those circles to him, whether I could set up a little link between the two. Every time I looked at him I saw 'Life and Death' in his eyes. I pitched in, "Hey buddy, listen I've never done this before but I feel I ought to offer you some kind of healing energy from the spiritual circles I share with others over in England." We talked about it, I explained about the Druid gatherings and he got it, he didn't dismiss it.

I had no idea what I was doing, but I knew I had to do it. Then, when I began I knew exactly what to do at every stage. If you had asked me at the beginning what I was going to do I would have shaken my head and admitted, 'Not a clue.'

But I knew, second by second, minute by minute Never a moment's doubt or loss of concentration. I weaved into the big structure of his body energy, the electric egg that surrounds us, then delved down into the layers; trying to bring the force from those Circles I knew through me, like a radio signal which I then broadcast through his body.

I must have spent twenty minutes or so like that, moving left and right, feeling the heat around his damaged skin and exhausted organs, dissolving it into me and then going to the sink where I placed my hands under running water to cleanse away the negative diseased energy.

I also knew exactly when to stop, like the gigs. It was done. I'd already told him to chill for awhile after I finished, I would go for a walk and be back in due course.

When I returned I fully expected him to be polite but nonplussed about the whole trip.

"Er." I laughed, "How was it for you man?"

"Wow, it really blew my mind." He smiled.

"What? You're joking?" I was shocked, I hadn't expected much more than to try and share his pain for a time. I added, fishing, "Really?"

"It was unreal, I had a total 'Out of body' experience like nothing before, not even like Acid or something. I was floating up there in the corner of the ceiling," he pointed up, "There, I could see you and me, it was fucking crazy but I knew it was ok, I was ok."

It was the start of many 'Healing' sessions I did over the years to come. I never once spent five minutes at a 'How to Heal,' course, nor did I read about other healers. I just kind of knew how to go about it and I did get better at it over time.

I never went around saying, "Oh, come and see me the 'Great Freaking Healer.' But if I came across somebody who was ill or damaged I felt beholden to offer them the opportunity. Some people I worked on even without their knowing.

One was a nurse from Cheltenham Hospital, in the Royal Oak at Gretton. I had seen the bandage on her knee and while I was sitting at the table with her friends I did the energy thing under the table without any of them seeing. But later in the evening she had come up to me asked what I had done with her knee? "What do you mean?" I played dumb.

"In the pub? When you were sitting there I felt this heat and cold going through my leg. It wasn't the draught either."

"Well, I er..." I stumbled through some explanation.

"Amazing." She replied. "It worked, it's fixed." Then she told me she was a Nurse. Something must have been working through me, which is how I feel about it. I am only an antenna, picking up a broadcast from a higher energy. I just have to keep moving about like 'Dad' with the old Black and White TV aerial, trying to keep the signal and the picture clear.

LAMBDA

The plan had always been to do a 'Drive Away.' This involved delivering a car from one place in America to another. The idea is to pick a desired destination and wait for a vehicle that needs taking that way. There is always an allotted amount of time to get there, perhaps three or four days. The trick was to hurry as fast as possible to the arrival point and then to have the car for a couple of days sightseeing. Or to add a detour to the journey. We did both.

We spent our first week in New York doing many of the things tourists are obliged to do. It was a lot of fun and NYC still had a vibrant expectation of good things round the corner. Andy had come with me on one of the Bleeker Street expeditions, we had been to a really cool party, a fab flat with a huge balcony area outside. I met a lot of interesting people, but it was a bugger knowing I was just 'Passing through.' But I had my cottage and my Irish lullaby waiting for me back home.

It was the first week of January, the middle of winter and we decided a Drive Away south was better than west. Also Andy wanted had always wanted to visit Cape Canaveral to see the old Lunar Space Rockets and maybe catch a launch. So when a vehicle that needed taking to Florida came up we jumped at the chance. We headed off to find the little Drive Away office, up some huge side street full of back to back laundries and rows of trucks dropping sacks of washing off by the ton.

The deal was we had to put down a four hundred dollar deposit, I only had the four so Andy added the hundreds and signed all the paperwork.

Within an hour we had picked up the vehicle, which in fact was some massive vehicle masquerading as a car. I could have made two English cars out of this one chassis. We did all the necessary checks and then the guy calmly handed us the keys to fifty grands worth of a spanking, shiny Dinky Toy. "Take it easy boys," he advised.

We nodded, somewhat dumbfounded, excited and slightly terrified. "Sure Boss." I drawled in my best Americana like a comedy stooge. We waited until he was out of sight before we started jumping for joy and hollering. "Wow!" Somehow we hadn't realised any car for delivery had to be at least worth the cost and effort; I had thought it would be an ancient Oldsmobile, clunking and rattling all the way to wherever, or some family car full of sticky sweets and the aroma of old dog and stinking nappies. This car was on steroids and would be perfect for a long journey.

Our timing was impeccable. We had four maybe five days allotted journey time. We said fond farewells to Steve and Sue who reminded us that if we had any problems or got separated to liaise through her in New York. I'm sure she figured I'd end up wandering off, getting lost or arrested. Me? Maybe I had shared too many stories of my past monumental cock ups.

It was late in the afternoon and was already starting to get dark when we set off. The plan was to drive straight down to Florida pretty much, sharing shifts at the wheel through the night. I knew Andy was an Owl and I was Lark, so we decided he would drive through the night until he felt tired and then I would do the early run into the dawn.

We soaked up all the sights as we drove over the Hudson Bridge, heading west until we picked up the Freeway south. About ten o'clock we were making good speed. Despite the odd flurry of snow and reports of a storm coming east we seemed to have a clear road. Steve had secretly handed me a small brown container before we left and said, "These may come in handy. Enjoy!" He knew the score. I opened the lid quietly and slipped a couple of the tablets of Morphine in my mouth and crashed out on the back seat as the buzz enveloped me.

What a trip so far. All the people we had met and the places, especially the music venues, had been awesome. 'New Yorkers' were almost kind of 'Super extra shiny, they really had that 'City Slickers' look about them, even the staff working in the little shops seemed brighter and larger than life.

I'm not sure how far we had traveled when I took over the wheel; it was still pitch dark except for the lights on the Highway. The car was easy to drive, an automatic. While Andy tucked himself up in the back I downed a Coke with two more of those little white pills and set off. Some time later the dawn began to creep out of hiding, trailing long lines of deep orange across the huge vista in front of me. In the rear view mirror the sky remained deep black as if dawn had forgotten the northern skies today.

Andy had mentioned to wake him up at some point for breakfast. He liked his food but looking at him curled up in the back I figured he would enjoy his sleep more so I drove on until mid morning. The sky refused seem to brighten up much, after the dawn had made such an effort, but that didn't seem to matter as we were just 'Passing through.'

I'll never forget that first 'Truck Stop' or 'Diner,' by the Highway. I'm a frugal, slim guy; poor is another word for it; I like to keep a tight rein on my appetite so my belly remains inside my belt. I'd met a few 'Big' people in my life and one or two somewhat 'Bigger' people, but nothing or nobody had ever prepared me for what I witnessed in that first restaurant. Some of the people that literally had sort of waddled sideways in and out of that place were on another level of 'Bigness' that really was quite astonishing. How their poor little hearts coped with such a huge frame to support was a mystery to me. If this was the result of KFC and MacDonalds Burger culture it was appalling. I never felt happier to be a Vegetarian.

Andy stared bleary eyed at me, "You getting food?"

"Nah bro, just coffee, more coffee and maybe some coffee to take away." The sight of those folks was just too much for me, too much from every angle. Also I didn't want any food to get in the way of those little white pills doing somersaults in my stomach. I was by this time cruising sweetly at altitude.

Meanwhile Andy was on a mission, for some reason he was determined to source the best or the biggest burger in America. He liked burgers and this trip was an opportunity to try some of the best I guess. They were also fast and easy, cheap and cheerful, with no washing up.

He had a breakfast which could have fed both of us but my tummy department just wasn't open so I let him work his way through it unmolested. I did have to glance around now and then, just to make sure I hadn't misread the vision. Nah.

I looked at Andy's disappearing food and thought, 'Jesus this stuff is more addictive than Heroin.' I remember thinking this is like America's Opium, the dark round burnt burger.

We didn't do much more than refuel and head south again. We had a map but it seemed like one long line going down the page. I'm sure Washington went by somewhere on the way. I carried on driving as I was wide eyed and bushy tailed while Andy slept again.

All day it remained dark, as if the sun just never quite got its ass out of bed. We didn't care. We were heading vaguely towards Daytona Beach, Florida.

On the way we did a brief detour to check out Atlanta which was hosting the Olympics later that year. It was one of the few times I have actually been stunned by the beauty of Skyscrapers. The colours, their designs and the enormous sheets of glass which reached up to the heavens above were a sight for tired eyes.

Andy had another burger, I probably had a bagel which became my staple food over there and of course a coffee. We took off south again. Eventually we began passing billboards that advertised the 'Sunshine State' and endless fields of oranges. The landscape in January didn't quite reflect the posters, but we didn't care. At last we arrived in Daytona and ran up and down beach like two schoolboys, racing imaginary Hot Rods. The sea looked nice but wasn't swimmable, even by my freezing standards.

At some point we headed off to a Motel to get a decent night's kip. We still had the wheels for two more days, having made better time driving south than we had reckoned.

The guy in the Reception was typically chatty in a non chatty way. "Passport. Where you boys from?"

We told him England though our accents must have given that away and that we'd just come down after spending a week or so in New York.

He looked up, "New York!" For once he had a bit of passion in his voice. "Haven't you boys heard?" He could tell by our dumb stares we hadn't. "About the storm? The blizzard? The snow?"

As we had run South a snow storm like none before had blown in from the West. It became famous as it brought New York to a standstill for four days and there was, for the first time in recorded history, no crimes committed during that period.

Just shows the power of Mother Nature to chastise and educate her children.

The news was all over the British Press and our friends back home believed we were stuck in New York unable to move. They had to be informed some weeks later that actually we were running up and down Daytona Beach playing 'Sports Cars' in the weak Winter sun.

Of course this was before the Mobile Phone Era. While travelling the only form of communication was a Phone Box. In Britain, every call concerning life, death, love or disaster could be handled with a two pence or a ten pence coin, in the States it was a Dime or a Quarter. Nobody knew where we were or what we were doing. That was part of the thrill.

The Motel was a typical Motel, the only character in an otherwise drab building would be the guests. There were none, except Andy and I. Who, in their right minds goes on holiday to cold Florida in early January? Only us it seemed.

The place had a swimming pool which we both were sorely tempted to try, but the water was more freezing than the sea and full of an entire Autumn's worth of leaves and dead insects. Plus the sign that warned to check for crocodiles was slightly worrying as apparently they like a pool swim too; I figured they wouldn't be so picky about the leaves. Still I think we took a couple of photos of us lounging by the pool on Andy's new camera.

After getting our room sorted we went out again to explore and found the famous Copacabana Club, or one version of it, but it was closed. Everything was shut, unlit, boarded up, deserted, sleeping, strangely empty and yet full of the ghosts of vanished Summer visitors; shards of old coffee cups, shreds of 'Miami Vice' hats and shrouds of windbreaks, caught at the back of the sea walls.

The following day was the last we had the car so we drove over to visit Cape Canaveral and the Kennedy Space Centre. We went in to have a look at the exhibition of previous missions into orbit and to the Moon. I remembered being at Seascale Prep School and being brought down to the dining room in the middle of the night to watch the first moon landing with all the other boys. There were only forty two of us in the whole school, huddled round a tiny black and white television.

At Cape Canaveral the first thing that struck us as we drove in was how tiny the Space Rockets were. From years of watching the Lift Offs on TV I had a feeling they were bigger, longer, wider...Surely? But as we entered the main building the capsule of the first Apollo Mission to land on the Moon was there, parked on the right side of the massive entrance hall. It looked the size of a small car, a really small car. We hurried over to look inside the open door.

Gosh, those astronauts really had steel balls to get inside that and go any further than the Corner Shop. I couldn't have remained in such a small space for more than three minutes. I would estimate the area wasn't much bigger than the inside of a Mini Cooper. One of the old, original Minis. Terrifying.

I think most of this was 'Free to Enter' and we went to see a film the Imac Screen, something fairly new in those days. It aimed to give a life like experience by wrapping the screen around the viewer.

The film opened with a helicopter hurtling along a sandy landscape, then suddenly it dives over the edge of the Grand Canyon and starts to weave. There wasn't a person in there that didn't gasp and lean back in their seat at that moment. Awesome. Typical Americana, the biggest and the best.

The documentary covered the history of all the space missions and became like a Planetarium. For twenty minutes we were tiny astronauts in the vast universe. Incredible. The icing on the cake for Andy was the imminent 'Blast Off' of another rocket scheduled for that night. He sat up for hours until he eventually saw the tiny stream of silver and exhaust climbing into the dawn sky. I had long given up and gone to bed.

The next day we had to drop off the vehicle as late as we dared and get back to the Motel. Whatever, we figured we had nailed this 'Drive Away' business and the plan was to pick up another car and head slowly north, vaguely to New Orleans or perhaps Nashville. We were on a musical adventure after all.

We discussed how we were going to get to Fort Myers, which was further south down the coast, where the next Drive Away was located, apparently above the Thrifty Car Hire office at the airport.

Andy had known I had come over with limited funds and had reassured me several times not to worry, if I ran out of cash he'd lend me a bit to go on with and I could pay him back later on our return. I hadn't discovered Credit Cards yet! However, I wasn't really going to ask him for money outright, I always had busking to fall back on.

In New York I had busked the Subway steps mainly, either the bottom or the top. It was mid winter and freezing, my hands had to go back in my pockets in between songs, but this also meant my potential client was also less willing to take their hands out of their pockets. Nevertheless, I had made a few bucks up there, outside the Carnegie Hall had proved good but that was nearly gone now.

We'd been too busy travelling for the past four days and busking deserted summer resorts was never going to yield much. Plus I'd noticed some of the people on the streets down there looked desperate enough to steal the laces out of my shoes. Anyway, I still had a couple of dollars and I followed Andy gamely round the massive supermarkets. While he was shopping I was quietly shop lifting. We'd both arrive at the till, him with a basket of stuff and me with a couple of Hershey Bars.

The truth was I didn't want to admit to Andy that I was already categorically broke, technically destitute in America. Basically I couldn't afford a bus ticket to the next town let alone Fort Myers so I cunningly suggested it would be just be a bit of fun and save money if we tried Hitch Hiking.

The short and long of it was I had hitched all over Europe but I doubt Andy had hitched more than a lift home from the pub. Still, no worries. What could possibly go wrong? I was also naturally a fan of Lou Reed and a 'Walk on the Wild Side,' hitchhiking across the USA seemed cool to me.

I reckoned we were somewhere east of Lakeland, maybe Lake Wales, from there it would be pretty much straight south through places like Lake Placid, Venus and La Belle to Fort Myers. All we had to do then, was get out to the airport. The distance was about a hundred or so miles. Far enough but only a couple hours or so drive in a decent car.

We set off mid morning and pitched up together by the roadside at a reasonable spot. Nobody seemed to be stopping, or even really looking. I guessed two guys together ruled out a lot of lifts so I suggested Andy stay there in the prime, first come first served spot, while I wandered further down the road in the hope of second helpings. Andy looked a 'Nice man' as opposed to me with my long hair and of course a guitar. Though we decided if he got a lift before me to try to get the driver to pick me up too. We agreed it might not work, but whatever happened we would meet at the Thrifty Car Hire office, near the airport. What could possibly go wrong? If there should be a hitch, haha, call Susan in New York and liaise through her.

I quipped, "See ya later buddy. Take a walk on the wild side!" I wandered off further down the highway. The cars were getting faster on this stretch of road so I carried on walking, looking for a better spot near a junction where the cars normally slow down. Pretty soon Andy was out of sight. A couple of hours later I still hadn't got a lift or seen Andy go by. But 'Rule Number One' of Hitching is patience.

I had learnt the 'Art of Hitch Hiking' back in the Seventies, having spent many hours by the roadside with plenty of time to think. I had realised there was no way I could hurry up the guy, having a shave at home, who two hours later will give me a lift; he'll arrive as and when he does. It did mean, believe it or not, I discovered, through learning patience, an amazing peace of mind while hitch hiking.

Rule Number One of Hitch Hiking was nothing could speed that guy to me any faster, I just had to wait. However, I was concerned for Andy, he wasn't as road worthy as I was. Anyway, I figured he had enough money to book into a motel. if he got stuck and he could always get a bus.

As ever, just when I thought I better start walking back to see if he was fine, a car pulled up and I was away. I can't remember the first few lifts, but I was steadily making my way down south. Naturally I didn't have a map, or a mobile phone with Satellite Navigation, just a thumb and a mouth. I really had no idea how far I had gone, or how far there was to go.

I was feeling good, Lou Reed was there in the back of my mind, it wasn't quite sunny California, more like freezing Florida, but hey I really was hitch hiking across the USA, well, down a little bit. The winter blue skies were pleasant and by early afternoon it was warm. I was on the side of a fairly busy road, but it had a gravel hard shoulder.

I noticed a white convertible go flying by. I heard the crunch of stones beneath the tyres. I saw the car was reversing back towards me through a cloud of dust. As I ran to it the car stopped, for a second I thought it was going to speed off again, a favourite game 'Rednecks' used to play with Hippies, I had experienced that a few times before, but it didn't.

The driver got out, shortish, tubby, almost bald, in a cream suit, two sizes too big for him which flapped around. He shouted over the traffic, "Hey, stick your guitar in the boot, Jump in."

"Ah, thanks buddy." I looked at the back seat of the convertible, it looked just the place for my guitar case. 'Rule Number Two' hitch hiking, 'Don't let your bags get locked in anyplace you are not locked in as well.' Rule Number Three. Idiot! Don't get locked in anywhere if possible! As for my guitar, I'd rather hold on to it. "It's ok, I'll stick it on the back seat." As I looked over I saw he had odd boxes and stuff but there was plenty of room.

"Nah. Stick it in the trunk, more room." He insisted. I hesitated for a second, I knew this wasn't a smart move and if it had been just me I might have said forget it and I would have waited for another lift. But Andy was probably already in Fort Myers and I didn't want him to have to hang around waiting for me. We would need to find a motel at some point before dark. So regrettably I put the case in the trunk and got in the front seat.

A roar of the engine and one dust cloud later we were flying down the highway, the music was on and this guy seemed 'Fair to middling,' to use old Cotton Picking slang. He was talking away at a rate of knots which was usual, but in his hand he had an Eau de Cologne bottle, which he kept dabbing under his chin; then he would rub it left to right under his jaw until it came up round his face and then he started putting it in his ears. 'Hmm,' I thought. Quirky?

I was doing all I could not to notice this, but it was so strange it was weirdly hypnotic. Anyway, I've met a lot of crazy people, really crazy people and he didn't seem that bad, but my 'Alert Warning System' was already moving to 'Amber. Caution!'

We were coming up to a junction, I was keeping an eye on the road looking for signs to Fort Myers and not seeing any when suddenly he turned sharp left. This wasn't good. We were leaving the highway. My Alert Warning System went up a notch to 'Red' but I had to stay calm, I didn't want to piss him off. I piped up, "Hey, man we're leaving the main road, I can get out here and catch another ride if you like. Man, I need to keep heading due south."

He didn't slow down, "Don't worry kid, I'm opening a Jewellery Store today, I just gotta pick up some boxes of stuff. I'll take you right back to the highway. It won't take long." All the time he was rubbing the bottle with more and more gusto around his face, under his nose and almost up it.

Hmm, I wasn't filled with confidence by this but my guitar was in the boot and there was no way I was jumping out at the lights or any crap like that. That guitar and me live or die together; Lord knows we'd died on stage enough times.

About twenty minutes later I'd just reached that point where I figured it was all going to be fine when he did another unannounced departure left.

We drove through a narrow gap between two high hedges into a yard. In front of us was a dilapidated bungalow, on its left was a pile of junk nearly as high as the roof, spreading out in every direction. I just had time to take this in when I noticed a huge black Mastiff guard dog come lumbering towards me. Luckily his chain, which must have come off a ship, kept him a few feet away from me.

"Don't worry about Hemingway," the guy said. I was just praying Hemingway wasn't pissed as per his namesake or just pissed off. I turned back to the car once I was sure the dog was out of reach, to see the trunk lid opening and my guitar coming out. Hmm, this wasn't part of the deal either. "Hey I wanna have a go on this here guitar of yours boy. You don't mind that. Do you?"

I did mind. He smiled at me. I was about to say something, but he was off with it, down a path along the side of the bungalow.

I thought to myself, in between prayers, 'Follow that guitar.' My Alert Warning System was now flashing 'Red Red' like a James Bond movie.

The guy opened a side door And I followed my guitar in. The first part of the room which I could make out through the gloom created by the closed curtains was just a messy kitchen, piled up with dirty cups, cutlery, plates, boxes of dog food, tins of crap, cereal and fuck knows what everywhere. At the end of this area was a fridge and a door to a corridor. As I scanned the living room over the pile of trash on a dining table to my left I saw with horror every single available surface was covered in dust, paper, books, magazines, ashtrays, bits of this and bits of that. I was trying not to betray my horror when I noticed the artwork around the walls, huge dark purple and brown canvases covered in garish sexual designs, mainly breasts and close ups of mutilated genitalia.

Hmm, warning alert went to 'Red! Red! Red!' Which in my Rules of Hitch Hiking stands for, Rule Number Nine, 'Get the fuck out of there!'

But he was already undoing the belt on my guitar case which I had to use to stop it falling apart and out came my Yamaha. I was running along with the game, but not liking it. Then, having told me earlier of his proficiency as a guitarist, I realised as he began to play he didn't know an 'A' chord from his arse. Shit.

I checked my Rules of Hitch Hiking to see what four 'Reds' on the Alert Warning meant. Hmm, no four 'Reds!' Presumed dead by now, employ any strategy left, no matter how dumb or crazy!

In this situation the only thing to do is let the guy know I was aware of his game and that maybe, just maybe, I could psyche him out that I was possibly crazier than him. That I could manage! Also, refuse any drink, any food, any anything. Be aware of every everything. I was, in between 'Red's going off in my head.

So I gently prized the guitar off him and started to play. I kept staring at him, making up these lyrics that just got wilder and sicker, somewhat twisted and semi demi hemi psycho. Suddenly he stood up and vanished through the door into the shadow of the corridor beyond. I put my guitar in the open case and quickly strode over to try the kitchen door. It was locked. Fuck. I went back to close the guitar case; I was fully expecting him to return any moment through that door with a pair of handcuffs, a 'Gimp' suit and a shotgun pointing at my balls.

But he didn't. He came out and headed straight for the side door. Without even looking at me he flicked the key in the lock and said, "I'm going now."

I dived for the door, pulling the guitar case shut. I didn't even wait to pick up the belt. I grabbed the door handle just inches before it shut. Luckily, I must have put my travel bag over my shoulders when we got out of the car, because as I came round the front of the bungalow, keeping an eye on Hemingway's snarling teeth, I saw the white convertible disappear in a cloud of dust through the gap in the hedges.

Shit. Now I was miles off the highway. I had no idea where and this huge black Mastiff is looking at me like I'm two hundred cans of Prime Dog Food.

"Cheerio Hemingway. Nice boy, that's it." I backed away from him, hoping his chain was still on tight and fixed to a ton of concrete. I backed through the hedge and looked around, sighing with relief for a moment, but not for long. There were woods as far as I could see with some grubby run down shacks along the side of the road. I knew which way I had got here, but guessed by where the sun was in the sky that the road wasn't heading any further south. I asked the first person I saw the way to the highway. With a typically non plussed 'Jerk Off' jerk of his head he pointed towards a dirt road across an open area of rough grass on the other side of the woods. I started walking. The highway could have been miles.

It wasn't looking good for hooking up with Andy either. Then the thought suddenly dawned on me that I had told the crazy driver I was meeting up with an English guy, trying to give the impression I wasn't hitching completely on my own. But with horror I suddenly had the thought that maybe the mad guy was going back to get Andy. Double shit!

As I walked, like any wild animal, I surveyed every detail around me, checking to see if a 'Hippy Lynch Mob,' was round the next corner. They weren't. They were quietly sitting on their porches, under baseball caps and chubby rolls of check shirt, drinking beer and polishing their guns.

Every now and then a steroid pumped truck would scream by. I didn't bother sticking a thumb out. I decided it was safer to walk to the highway than risk getting picked up by another nutter in the woods.

A mile or two later a small car with a woman driver pulled alongside. She wound down her window and asked where I was headed. She offered to run me up to the main road. I did give her a second look over, I wasn't taking any chances on her having a pistol in her pants. Then she said something about her son being a guitarist. I got in. I wasn't listening, I was busy thanking my lucky stars.

The kind lady dropped me next to the highway. I thanked her profusely though it wasn't a great place to hitch from as the cars were flying by at full speed. I walked along until I was standing opposite the turning for a big 'Trailer Trash' site of static homes. It seemed to stretch forever into the sparse woodlands on the other side of the road. I looked behind me, there was only an endless flat marsh of long grass with clumps of brown Bulrushes poking up. To the left I noticed a sign on a wooden post. I wandered over to have a look and saw it stated bluntly. 'Beware of the Crocodiles.'

What the triple fuck? My Alert System flashed a last 'Red' and I moved swiftly up the road a bit.

Beyond this swampland I noticed the sun beginning to get lower in the sky, I had maybe a couple of hours of daylight left, after which I knew catching a lift on anything more that an Croc's back was seeming less and less likely.

Just to make sure I had a full grasp on the situation I decided to count my remaining money in case I needed to eat before I got eaten. Forty two cents. Hmm. Anyway, what could possibly go wrong and scratching around in my head for any semblance of hope in this dire pile of crap I remembered, perhaps because it was relevant to my mode of transport, that, in the Hitch Hiker's Guide To The Galaxy, '42' was the answer to the 'Meaning of Life.' I almost felt a small glow of reassurance.

Glancing nervously over my shoulder every ten seconds, I stuck my thumb out. It got later and later. I knew I couldn't rush that guy having a shave, but boy I wished he'd get his ass out of the bathroom and down the freaking highway to me.

The sun was setting, to the north a dark pillow fell over the sky, to the west a grey line of cloud dimmed on the rim of horizon and faded slowly into black.

Triple, quadruple Fuck!

The cars were going so fast. Nobody wanted to stop. Everybody was finishing their day and heading off to their evening, except me. Then I noticed a car pulling up a few hundred yards down the highway. Ahh, it was so far away I guessed it had nothing to do with me, but I watched it anyway, like a hawk. Then the reversing lights came on. I picked up my guitar case and ran like the wind.

For one mad moment as I opened the passenger door I thought it would be Mr Eau de Cologne again. It wasn't. The driver had a sense of urgency about him and motioned me to jump in quickly. This time the guitar went on the back seat.

He smiled, "I don't know why I picked you up? I'm going to dinner with my new girlfriend's parents and I'm late. But I had the strongest impulse as I passed you that I just had to pick you up. I tried not to!" He laughed and accelerated back onto the highway. "Here. Grab a beer." He passed me a Budweiser from a four pack on the floor. I never drink Lager and rarely any alcohol before seven in the evening but I drank that stuff like it was pure nectar of the Gods.

The oddest thing was, when I had a moment to catch my breath and look closely at my saviour he was a carbon copy of my best friend Greg back in the Cotswolds. A truly uncanny likeness in looks and as it turned out his personality, an angel for certain. He explained that it was his first meeting with the parents of his girlfriend and he was a bit nervous, quite a lot nervous.

I studied his face, thinking to myself, that was probably why he took so long shaving! Then I saw a small razor cut on his chin and smiled to myself.

The guy dropped me at Fort Myers, but obviously no airport is ever located in the centre of town. He showed me the road I needed to follow and added. "Hey dude I gotta pick up my girlfriend but we will be coming back this way in about half an hour so if you're still here I'll run you up to the airport."

"Wow man, you are so kind. Thanks so much. You saved my Hippy ass back there, that's a fact." Sure enough I was still there when he returned. So I had a chance to tell his girlfriend what a saviour and what a beautiful guy he was.

About nine or ten o'clock I finally walked into the Thrifty Car Hire office at the airport. No sign of Andy. None of the desk clerks had seen an English guy come through, though they hadn't been working all day. This was the night shift. I sat down and waited. An hour or so later, approaching midnight, I decided it was getting too late for anyone, let alone Andy, hitch hitching, I was worried Mr Eau de Cologne was already feeding bits of his balls to Hemingway.

So I made the call, as arranged, to liaise through Susan if we had any problems.

"Hi. It's Geoff here." Just me calling up was enough to panic her.

She went from nought to Triple Red Alert in a flash. She didn't waste any time on pleasantries. "What's happening? Is Andy there?"

"Well, er, no." That wasn't the right answer. I could sense a quadruple Red Alert being sounded in New York City. "The thing is we decided to hitch hike…"

"You did fucking what? Hitch Hiking! Are you crazy? Nobody hitch hikes in the States. Are you nuts?" I could tell she wasn't happy.

"But, you know," I pleaded, "I thought, well, er, you know Lou Reed and all that."

"Jesus fucking Christ this is the Nineties not the Sixties. There's loads of crazy people with guns out there. God Almighty!. Where's Andy?" I could sense she wasn't being reassured. I heard Steve saying something in the background.

I tried to smile down the phone, "Ah, er, well, that's why I was calling you. I was hoping he might have phoned you? That was the plan?" At least I'd done that right, hadn't I?

"No, he hasn't." She was starting to get worried, I could tell. "Where did you last see him?"

I explained what had happened that morning and thought I better tell her I was a little, tiny weeny bit, worried that the psycho who gave me a lift might have gone back for him. That did the trick.

"Oh Jesus!" She had passed pissed off and angry now. She was really worried. "Ok. I'll call the Cops. You stay in the Thrifty Car Hire place and wait." The receiver clicked and went silent.

I gave the phone back to the nice lady behind the desk. She smiled at me, "Everything alright, y'all?"

"Yeah, I hope so." I explained, "His sister is a bit worried so she's going to call the Cops, er the Police and see if they can help find him."

She looked at me as if to say, 'Don't get too hopeful about that.' I sat down and waited some more.

Around an hour later the double doors of Thrifty Car Hire blew wide open and the massive hulk of a Cop walked in, like he'd just got of a horse, stiff legged, hungry as a mule and staring straight ahead. His gun was bulging on his hip. Although there was only one person in the room, me, apart from the lady behind the desk, even though he was looking for a missing guy, he didn't nod a flicker of acknowledgement in my direction.

He drawled at the lady behind the desk, "I believe you got us an Eeeegleesh man here, who got a friend who's gone missing." He cleared his throat as if it was full of venom, "These boys been Hitch Hiking!" The way he said it made it sound like we'd been out mud wrestling with Crocodiles. He still didn't even glance at me. It could not have been anybody else. However, he waited, staring at the lady until she pointed me out, in the empty room, sitting on the bench.

Slowly, he turned round and looked me over, "So that'll be you boy." He tried, with a convincing lack of success to cover up his distain, before he added, "You been hitchhiking, huh? You got split up, huh?"

I nodded, "Yes, we arranged to meet here but he hasn't showed up." He took a couple of details from me but I could tell he'd already giving up looking for Andy by the end of my sentence. I mentioned the weirdo but that didn't seem the least bit surprising to him either. He looked at me with that, 'What do you expect? This is the Nineties not the freaking Sixties.'

The double doors blew open and shut behind him and I figured that was the last I'd see of him. Luckily he hadn't asked how much money I had on me or technically he could have locked me. The law in America stipulates you need at least ten dollars to your name not to be classed as a Vagrant. I was nine dollars and fifty eight cents short of that.

The lady behind the desk had seen me eyeing the snack machine, but nothing was on sale at forty cents. Awhile later she came over to me and said,

"Hi honey, we had a little collection in the office and here's a few dollars for some food."

""Ah, wow, that's so kind of you." I couldn't believe their lovely gesture.

She added, "You can stay here if you want all night, but we can get one of the Taxi drivers to run you up to the airport if you like. She added quickly, "For free. They got plenty of cafes up there and you'll find a better place to sleep."

"Oh thank you, that would be really kind. Thanks so much for the money." I knew the airport would be a better place to find a bench and get some rest. I was saved. My third angel of the day.

The following morning another taxi brought me back and I waited for the Drive Away office to open. It was signposted up some stairs from where I had waited the previous night. I sat down on the bench wondering if at any moment the Cop was gonna blow those double doors open. He didn't. The ladies behind the Thrifty Car Hire desk had all changed but they looked at me and they all knew I was the guy from England who had lost his friend. Oh dear.

At some point the man who ran the office showed up and took me upstairs to his tiny office. We went in and he looked me over, "What can I do for you?"

"Well, first I have to wait for my friend to arrive but we're looking for a car heading north, back towards New York."

The news wasn't good. "Sorry, but we haven't had a trip up that way for a couple of months. There will be no chance with the snow they got up there now." My disappointment must have been palpable because he said, "But anyway, you wait outside, you never know, something might come in."

There were two chairs, I sat on one, praying for a miracle, a vehicle and for Andy to show up. I must have been there for an hour or two when I heard the man put the phone down in his office and exclaim. "Mr Smiles, you gotta be one of the luckiest sons of a bitch I ever met. Guess what? I just had a Nissan truck come in for delivery north of New York, but the client says they'll happily come down to the city for the pick up. Suits them fine they said." He could hardly contain his joy, "Jesus, you are one lucky son of a bitch."

I had to nod to this. He was my fourth angel in twenty four hours.

Even better, about an hour or so later I saw a disgruntled Andy dragging his heels up the road towards the office. I ran out to meet him. He wasn't a happy chappy.

"Listen pal." I didn't have time for any crap on this deal. "Thank God you're here. Look, cars going north are rare as rocking horse shit but, by some miracle, we've had a bit of luck. Doesn't matter what's bugging you buddy, we just have to go in that office, stay cool and sort the paperwork out for this vehicle. There is only one available. It's just come in. He said there hasn't been a car north in months. If we don't get it they might not have another one."

Realising he could be stuck in Fort Myers with me for months he suddenly got his head out of his ass and we went up to the office. Andy produced his passport and four hundred dollars for security. A few signatures later the guy took us to his car and drove us off to pick up the vehicle.

As we got closer we passed several 'Gated estates' and huge houses. Unbelievably, we stopped at one. The black guy in the Sentry Box scrutinised us and then raised the barrier to let us through. There was nobody at the big beautiful house, one of several in a large semi circle, all with columned entrances and garages as big as my cottage.

The truck stood proudly like a new bar of soap on a toothbrush clean driveway. It was huge. It was brand new. Less than a hundred miles on the clock. It had an eight speaker Stereo System. Wow freaking wow!

The guy handed Andy the keys, "Take it easy boys. Enjoy the ride." A moment later he was gone.

We looked at each other and smiled.

I gave Andy a big hug, "Hey man. Take a walk on the wild side."

KAPPA

I gave the Sentry a cheery wave as Andy drove past him. We headed out of Fort Myers north and then pulled up at a parking area to take some photos and sort out the truck. The stereo was awesome and we set about finding some cool radio stations to listen to. Everything sounded better with an American DJ. We were smiling from ear to ear.

We opened our map and scanned the names of cities we knew so well from films and music videos. So, where? We knew the time we had been allowed with the truck from the Driveway was another four or five days to get to New York. We soon realised that New Orleans and Louisiana were a bit far west but Nashville was possible, Lynchburg, home of Jack Daniels, the Blue Ridge Mountains of Virginia were all within our range if we just made a swing west as opposed to a left turn west on our journey north.

We had three days and nights driving north which were all memorable. Andy had some tummy trouble that was getting progressively worse. He was sadly suffering from a common complaint in the States, 'Burger's Revenge.' For almost two weeks he had only eaten burgers and they had backed up inside him to a standstill. Traffic jam, no movement.

We bought some Bourbon and some laxatives, but he felt so rough we just chilled in the motel the first night. We had a second floor room and I went out to the drinks machine for some Coke, where I met a couple of black guys working on the railways.

One came back to the room with me promising he had a smoke of dope; but he just seemed to drink a lot of Jack and chat a lot. Eventually he said he was off to get the dope but asked if he could take the Jack for his mate to have a shot. I could sense a 'Rip off' coming our way so I figured I better do a damage limitation. I couldn't stop the guy but I could let him know I wasn't as green as he figured. I just followed him out the door, rapping off to him all the way back to his room. He kept looking at me. When we got there I knew there was no 'Mate' inside but I clocked the number, "See you soon, dude."

We waited long enough to know he wasn't coming back. At least we hadn't parted with any money, but I was pissed he was taking the piss. Jesus Christ, is there no respect anymore for a long term drug user by these punks? That's a dark joke.

So I thought, 'Right you motherfucker, I'll have you.' One thing I knew about railway workers is they start early. I figured he would be gone by seven or eight, nine at the very latest, then all I had to do was get into his room. I'd done that before .There is always a way in, if you are keen enough.

The next morning I decided to do a 'Walk by' and check out his room. As I came round the corner to his floor I saw the trolley of a cleaning lady parked up in the corridor. Bingo! Her voluminous black body, pinned in a tiny white apron, was perched precariously over a bed in the room she was busy cleaning.

I took a punt with my best British brogue. "I say? Hello? Excuse me? Madam?" She eventually glanced over her shoulder, obviously not amused to be interrupted in her work. "I was wondering if you could possibly help me out for a minute." I paused a second as the round face came full circle to see who the hell was bothering her, "Ahh, bless you. I was having a drink with the man in...," whatever number it was, "and I left my bottle of Jack Daniels on the side. Sorry. Just wondered if you would mind if I picked it up." The English accent was working its magic and I was stretching my best 'lost puppy' expression over my widening smile.

I could tell she was suspicious, but curious. Lucky for me I have an Innocent face, or so I've been told, usually only when I'm sleeping.

"You boys drive me crazy. Jack Daniels you say. The rest of the bottle is in his room? You want me to get it?"

"Yes please." I don't know why, but it always comes down to a split second between doubt and trust for a decision to be made.

She sighed and straightened up at last, staring at me like I was an unwelcome disease. 'Ok. But if I get any shit for this..." Without further delay she went to the door I pointed to. She unlocked it. Held it open. Luckily, thank the holy spirits, Jack was right there, on the table next to the bed. By the look of it he hadn't drunk any more either.

Before she had time to smile or change her mind, I took one long step past her, grabbed the Jack and reversed out of the room. "Thanks so much. It was a great night. Say 'Hi' to him from Mr Smiles." That did it. She ginned, her smoky white teeth appeared for a moment. Then the door shut.

I was praying I wouldn't turn round and see the guy coming down the corridor. All cool. Back at the room I wasted no time. "Come on. I got the bottle. Still half full. Let's go." Andy came out the toilet with a somewhat frustrated look on his face. We left.

We drove on for most of the day and were getting closer to Nashville, we knew this because there were already at least thirty Country and Western Stations all vying for our attention on the radio. We tried a few. Why not? But it was endless Cowgirls whining and wailing away for Cowboys; or Cowboys pining away for Cowgirls long gone, long dead or just long gone dead.

The music was so smooth and well produced it was a joy to hear at first but eventually just hung on my ears like thick molasses. By the seventeenth Cowgirl I was ready to burn the ranch down.

I can't knock it, Country and Blues traditions weave in and out of each other. I had never heard such good, proficient musicians either. Obviously they do a lot less drugs and alcohol than the Rock n' Roll boys, so I guess they remember to turn up at their lessons and actually learn something. It must be so inspiring to have such a lot of great musicians around and no doubt relatives or friends who play instruments too.

Finally we spotted Nashville on the horizon. It has a stunning, though oddly demonic, skyline. In the middle of the usual skyscrapers are two spikes of a building, lit up in bold red, that look exactly like the

Devil's horns. We parked up somewhere and walked toward the centre, we were going to see this famous city, even if we couldn't stand the music.

We wanted to have a look in particular, from the outside of course, at the 'Grand Ole Opry' that bastion to Country and Western. I was naturally keen to get on a stage anywhere, just to be able to say, 'I played Nashville.'

On the way down town we found a venue called 'Music City' and I noticed a band setting up. "Maybe we'll come back here later?" I suggested.

The next corner took us into the main street. On the far side, half way up, we saw a sign for the Opry; but a few steps up the road from us was a guitar shop and we wandered in there.

I don't know what I stole, probably a Harp, but as I left the shop, the alarm went off. Bollox, balderdash! Quick as a flash I reopened the door and shouted, "Sorry dudes, that always happens with me," as I dumped the Harp on a shelf. No alarm. Andy was elsewhere in the shop and utterly oblivious to all this drama.

Outside the Grand Ole Opry seemed a great spot to busk. A queue was forming along the pavement for an early show. When Andy finally came out of the shop with some Drum Sticks I think, I told him I was going to get my guitar and he would find me near the Opry.

A guy like me, at my level in the Music Industry, the 'Basement,' can only hope in his wildest dreams to play the classic big venues. In the meantime nothing is stopping a musician from playing as close to them as possible. Thus I've done the Albert Hall Bus Stop, the Carnegie Hall steps, Wembley Stadium car park and Tube Station. I did get to play Wembley Arena once, at a Music Tech show accompanying the ego of 'Britain's best Didgeridoo Player,' boy how do I manage do I find 'em.

The guitar was back at the truck so Andy went off in search of some food while I got my stuff. There was an alcove next to the Opry entrance where a black guy was sitting, selling Lottery tickets. I asked, "Hey buddy, do you mind me busking here?"

"Hell no! I busk here myself. Where you from boy?" As if he didn't know.

"England."

"You going in?" He nodded to the Opry.

"Nah. Not really my thing and anyhow, even if I wanted," I paused, "I still need to make a couple of bucks first."

He smiled the sort of cracked smile of a man who knows the meaning of having to 'Make a couple of bucks first.' "Sure, I can dig that. Hi, my name is Velvet Thunder." He thrust out a huge black hand from the shadow of his alcove. What sort of music do you play man? You look a bit of a Sixties guy." He eyed me sympathetically, "You know, back in the old days, I jammed with Jimi and with John Lennon in Central Park."

My eyes must have widened a foot; but just at that moment somebody stopped and bought a ticket from him. He passed over the change and delved inside his jacket. A moment of two later a photo appeared in his large palm. "There you go."

I peered at the old colour photo, a Polaroid that had been caressed so often the white border was now curled and frayed. There was no mistaking Lennon and the two black guys, one was Jimi and the other a trimmer, younger version of Velvet Thunder.

At such a moment of epiphany, in the company of a man who has communed with the Gods, I felt it best to offer some devout words of homage and reverence, "Wow! Man."

I kept looking at the picture and this huge black man in the small recess on the sidewalk. It wasn't hard to believe. I wanted to ask loads of questions but it's kind of uncool. He would tell me more if an odd moment allowed. Meanwhile I had to get my sorry white ass in gear and make a few of those 'Bucks.'

I returned the photo like a poor man giving a bible to the Pope. He smiled up at me. "Velvet Thunder's my name brother. Don't forget me." I don't know why he said that. He went on "So, anyways, what kind of music you play?"

"Well, I guess you're going to find out in a couple of minutes," I laughed, "I hope I don't spoil your ticket sales dude. All I can say is I play with the spirit of Jimi and my songs have a lot of Lennon's peace and love vibe in them; though naturally I competently and professionally murder them both." I beamed, putting on an American accent, "But hell man, I'm gonna keep on keeping on."

He laughed with me. "Come on then," I could tell I hadn't filled him with complete confidence, "You set up other side of the steps. I'll send 'em your way, you send 'em mine." Then he was gone, back in the shade, another black hand selling 'Tickets of Hope' on a white man's street, raking in the dollars but only taking home the dimes.

I got set up and started playing. A few minutes later I heard a grunt from the shadows, "That don't sound so bad boy. You got some real spirit in there man."

I must have made some money, but I was hardly looking down at my case. It was early evening. The road in front of me began to get a flurry of open back trucks, huge 'Four Wheel Drive' beasts, so shiny the neon lights were reflected on their bonnets in coloured diamonds. But what I'd never seen, or ever heard before was young women, hanging out of truck windows, or perched in the open back, just hollering. Hollering just for the sake of hollering it was incredible. Anybody doing that in Cheltenham would soon be locked up.

It was a wonderful expression of joy, enchantment, release and happiness, something between a yodel and a bugle, being blown down a drain pipe by a hand grenade.

Just as I thought it couldn't get any better I heard the sound of an old 'Casey Jones' Steam Train, blowing its whistle, coming down the line, cutting right across town. It was an American Dream.

At some point I looked round and noticed the hand in the alcove had gone, with his photo. I was hoping Andy was going to show up and I could have got a photo of Velvet's photo; which in turn would be lovingly thumbed by me for years until the white edges had worn away. But he hadn't showed up yet

I had collected five dollars or so and that was enough to keep me going for a couple of days. I packed up as the queue to the Opry started to file in. Time to move on.

I rounded the corner at the bottom of the street and saw Andy. He was on fine form now. He had just met a guitar playing horse!

"A guitar playing horse? What! Where? How? You haven't been eating any dodgy mushrooms have you pal?" I was amazed.

He laughed, "It was literally just a couple of blocks back there." He pointed down the street.

It was the direction we were heading to the Music City venue. I was really keen now to actually get on a stage in Nashville as opposed to just the sidewalk.

Sadly the horse had buggered off home to score some Oats or Dope so I had to take his word for it.

Once we were in the Music City we got a beer and watched the action. Like the radio stations we had listened to driving in, it was wall to wall Country and Western. Why not? This was its home town. My problem was as a dedicated non lover of this music, with little or no idea about its technicalities, I still had to blague my way up there on stage as if my entire life had been directed to this one and only purpose. A six or seven piece band had taken over from the duo who had been playing and I knew this would offer me more of an opportunity to sit in.

"I'm going to go up and ask if I can play a bit of harp buddy. Won't be a minute." I hung around with my 'Lost Puppy Dog' face on, until the guitarist noticed me. I mumbled in his ear about playing some harp.

"You play 'Cross Harp?" He looked up expectantly.

To be totally honest I had the vaguest idea that Cross Harp meant something to do with blowing the thing more than sucking and bending the notes. Country songs have enough wailing in them without a harp breaking their hearts too. Maybe the idea is to blow true notes, while everything else bends.

"Sure man," I tried to look confident, looking him directly in the eye. Meanwhile I was peering at the rest of the band, figuring how much mess they would make of me when they found out, as far as my knowledge on the matter went, a cross harp could just as well have been an angry one.

"Okay, I'll give you a shout. You got a C harp?"

I nodded, "A to G, no B or F though." That seemed to reassure him. "Thanks man. One song would be beautiful."

I did play one song, maybe two; but I remember struggling to get into it, as much as the band were struggling to get into me. I made a pleasant sound, but it wasn't Country. These guys knew all the notes backwards and forwards, I guess they could smell a renegade Bluesman. "A big hand for our harmonica player, all the way from Great Britain," was my cue to get off.

"Phew." I smiled at Andy, "That was tough. Still, it counts as playing Nashville! Sort of, I guess? Wow, what a place, it's nuts! Guitar playing horses? Wild." We finished up our beers shortly after and with a humble nod to the band disappeared into the night.

I'd never witnessed a band do a collective sigh of relief, until then.

We were pretty fucked, Andy still wasn't quite right but getting better. We headed back to find a motel for the night on the outskirts of town, heading east.

The plan was to visit the Jack Daniels Distillery on the next day and then drive over the Blue Ridge Mountains of Virginia, en route to New York.

The next morning was January the nineteenth. The further north we had come the deeper the piles of snow were from the storm that had blown through. Shops and buildings had drifts almost as high as they were; but the streets and the highways were swept clean with continual traffic.

The Motel room was pretty dingy. Two thin beds, a small television hanging off a bracket, above a shelf with a kettle on it. In one corner another oversized cupboard contained a shower, sink and toilet. The door was shut and Andy had been in there for ages.

I was all packed up and ready to go, watching the small television. It was so old and battered it only delivered a lukewarm selection of colours and was generally black and white at times. The News came on. I paid a bit more attention thinking they would broadcast the weather sooner or later.

I don't know why but some things seem so blatantly obvious to me about life, what is important and what deserves respect, yet I often seem in the minority, in today's materialistic society. My simple aim has always been to try to leave my patch of the planet in a better state than I found it and to leave behind memories of a 'Gentle man.'

My other dream, to spread a bit of 'Peace and Love' throughout the World, like some quasi John Lennon, or Dalai Lama, has obviously been derided by many people as naive; often with such classic comments as, 'But don't be ridiculous! What difference can one man make?'

On January 19th I discovered the difference one man could make to the World. On the tiny TV screen I watched as crowds of people marched on Washington; huddled in their overcoats and walking steadfastly towards the White House. Martin Luther King Day had been celebrated that year, for the first time, by this historic march. Later, that same day, I would see how one sixteen year old boy had also made his mark 'Spiritually' on the planet.

The Jack Daniels Distillery is one of those rare places to visit that I would recommend on anybody's 'Bucket List.' Andy and I arrived there later that day and followed a few other folks into a small reception room. Chairs were lined up in a haphazard way that suggested the last visitors had just scrambled out. A large 'Guest Book' was open on a table and some people were writing in it. I thought that might be a cool idea. I went over and signed it. Under a section marked 'Occupation' I put, Musician, Writer, Artist, Missionary of Peace and Love.

A few minutes later a guy looking like a retired Cowboy came in the room and gave us all a warm welcome in the broadest, widest, thickest, bluntest Tennessee accent imaginable.

"Well, gee, y'all. Hi there, sure is good to see y'all coming on down this here ol'distillery, where the process that Jack Daniels used as a boy, to patent his very first liquor, is still used to this very day. The same Spring he chose for the water to add to the Sour Mash is the same we use today." All the time he spoke his 'Ten Gallon Hat' was bobbing merrily on his head like it had lived there as long as he had.

The sound of his voice was like having warm honey poured over my ear drums, each word melted onto the next, its final consonant softened, like a pat of butter hitting a warm frying pan. It was enchanting.

After the introduction he handed us over to another guy who was going to do the walking and talking tour. We filed out politely behind him, until the first cowboy shouted to him something along the lines, 'Hey Jed. See y'all down at the AA Meeting tonight? Same as usual?' We all burst out laughing. From that moment on it just got funnier and better, then better and funnier.

Our small group were led gaily round the immediate site and to the Spring where Jack Daniel's statue stood proudly surveying all he had created. I wonder how it looked to him the first time he filled his bucket with water to use in his brewing.

Then we entered the actual distillery up a flight of steps, following a raised walkway that suspended us above the big copper vats; these were entwined with finger thin and arm thick pipes, disappearing and reappearing, in and out of their shiny hulks.

Our guide explained every process with a glee that was irrepressible, especially considering he lived in a 'Dry State.' It's hard to believe but the sale of alcohol is forbidden in the place that created one of the world's biggest selling alcoholic drinks. Indeed, there would be none of the usual sampling after the tour, which mortified many visitors, including us.

Exiting that building we were led round the massive charcoal making fires and sheds which were stacked with logs. Various characters, wearing the obligatory lumberjack check shirt, cowboy hats and sporting the same big smiles, worked on fork lift machines moving stuff back and forth in the yard.

Finally we were loaded into an old Charlie Brown School Bus, with an equally cheery driver, to see the buildings where they stored the barrels of Bourbon for the appropriate period of years, until eventually they were shipped out across the planet.

I doubt there is a country out there that does not have a bottle of Jack stashed away somewhere.

The sight that greeted us as we entered the first barn really took my breath away. As far as the eye could see in the half light, barrels were racked up, probably four or five stacks high, row after row of them. Thousands of barrels, from which every drop would be carefully bottled, labeled and ultimately decanted into millions of people.

All of this was started by one sixteen year old boy called Jack. His first Patent was registered at that age. It struck me so clearly, after witnessing the Martin Luther King march that morning and this incredible achievement by another solo performer, that one person can make a big difference to this little world, morally and spiritually!.

That was two men. The third man was of course John Lennon.

It took us the rest of that day and night to cross the Blue Ridge Mountains of Virginia. But we had a rendezvous with the vehicle's owner and we kept on driving until we arrived in New York later that night. It was still piled up at every corner with snow drifts ten feet high and was bitterly cold. The owners of the truck arrived and were happy to see it in one piece, as was Susan when I returned Andy to her.

We all laughed, "Hitch Hiking in the USA, are you fucking crazy?" To which I just nodded meekly.

The next day I went off to visit the Lennon memorial 'Strawberry Fields,' in Central Park. It was sweet and yet sour, great but sad. I remembered Velvet Thunder and thought of him jamming here one long Summer's day ago. I took out my guitar and had a play; but Central Park in the late nineties still had the reputation of the Bois de Boulogne in Paris, not a place to loiter about with no particular reason. I moved on to find the Dakota building, which stared down over Strawberry Fields.

The entrance was on 72nd Street, just across the road from the park. It was getting dark already and the traffic was slowly slushing up and down outside. In the impressive entrance a Sentry Box housed the usual black Porter. His uniform was immaculate, his indelible smile below eyes that must have seen a lot a famous folks pass by. He was fairly old.

"Hi?" I looked at him. He looked at me. He knew I wasn't likely to be renting a room there. "I suppose you wouldn't happen to know where John Lennon was actually shot." I was just thinking what a dire request it was, when his smile changed into an unofficial off duty smile.

"Sure, I can do that for you. You a fan of his?"

My face must have lit up, "Ah, he was a God to me, along with Hendrix. Man, what he gave to the world was so special. 'Peace and Love.' That's been my creed ever since." The guy looked at me and my guitar, he could believe that, he didn't need any more convincing.

He stepped down from his box and joined me on the sidewalk. "Come on then dude. I'll show you the exact spot. I was here you know." We both looked at the traffic. It wasn't very busy. A gap appeared and we stepped out quickly between two cars, heading diagonally a few feet across the road.

He stopped. He looked down. He pointed. "Here dude."

He turned away before I could thank him. I called out, "Hey buddy, thanks! Means a lot to me."

I heard his voice, "I know."

He was gone, back in his sentry box. The traffic was coming towards me. I nipped between two parked cars and opened up my case. I knew the song I was going to sing for John. It was called, in a moment of cataclysmic inspiration, 'Song for John.'

The strap went over my jacket. I shoved my hands into my pockets for a minute to warm them up and waited for a gap in the cars. It came. I walked out to the spot, almost in the middle of the road and began to play, for seven or eight minutes, as my songs are all about that long.

The traffic slowed down and weaved its way round the crazy Hippy singing his little heart out, tears streaming down his face. But nobody ran me over or even hurled abuse at me. Some even slowed down to listen. I guess they knew.

That was three men who had all touched my heart in those two days and given me a clear example that one man can definitely made a change in the World.

Some make such a large mark it can be seen for ever. Others make smaller marks which however, combined with other small marks, can I'm sure also last forever.

I resolved next time I was accused of being naive to tell this tale. Needless to say I've told it many times.

I was touched the cars hadn't run me over. My cold hands put the guitar back in its case and wiped the tears off my cheeks.

I had vaguely asked the Sentry if Yoko happened to be available for a random visit from a mad Hippy passing by from England? Oddly enough, it seemed she wasn't. I did meet her later that year or perhaps early in the next at Oxford in an Art Gallery. Sadly, there was no ladder to climb up to gain her attention but I did manage to get through her minders and thrust a copy of my album into her hands.

In fourteen seconds I gave her a full appraisal of what Lennon had meant to me, my performance outside the Dakota and so on and so on and so on. Until, she weakly smiled, whispering, "Thank you, John would have liked that."

Her entourage wrapped her up within their circle of coats and suddenly she was spirited away.

As night settled in over the skyscrapers I wandered slowly back to Greenwich Village. We had a few more days in New York and then the flight home. Andy and Susan were making the most of their time together. She was much relieved to have him back from our trip to Florida in one piece and was still utterly flabbergasted that we had decided to hitch hike that day. We had a standing joke now, "Are you fucking crazy?" To which I'd reply, "But man! Lou Reed?" Then we would all fall about laughing.

Steve knew what I was on about and we waffled on relentlessly when we were left in the flat. I went out busking again, but it was so cold after the snow I could hardly last thirty minutes. At night I went off to blague more gigs in a similar fashion as I had before.

There was one last 'Confirmation of Belief' for me. I would find myself years later, like Velvet Thunder, with a tattered photograph forever with me, of some black dude, clapping his hands and smiling in a bar. The venue was 'Arthur's Jazz Bar.' Sadly, I don't remember the man's name. He played trumpet. Miles would have liked that.

It was my last night in New York. What a trip we'd both had. I didn't think it could get any better.

I went to play at Arthur's as I knew from gigging before they would at least give me a slot to play and maybe even a Bourbon. Indeed, as it was my last night they gave me quite a few songs and quite a lot more Bourbon, until the plaster started to rattle on the ceiling with my harp playing and the cells started to fall off the inside of my brain.

It was fantastic. There was an entire life that existed for musicians between ten in the evening and four in the morning in New York. There was no platform for us like that in England, the audience would have long departed, catching the last tube or bus.

It was a great evening of music, all the guys playing were black They were Jazz orientated in the club but Blues had its place in there too. We had a wail of a time. It gave them a buzz. It gave me a buzz. It was a buzz. It was a hive of energy up there.

Around three in the morning the crowd thinned out and I knew it was time to go. I had to get back, get some sleep, get up and get to the airport with Andy.

I was sitting on a bench watching the band, nursing my Bourbon. The black trumpeter I had jammed with earlier came over and sat next to me. It was a small mark of respect. I was touched. The whole deal with this tradition of music and musicians was about the 'Respect.'

The band finished the song and while they hustled up the next one there was a pause. This guy turned to me and smiled, looking me right in the eyes like a parent or a teacher does when they really need to know they have a kid's complete attention. I was paying full attention.

He grinned at me "Mr Smiles, I gotta tell you something, right?" I wasn't sure whether he was asking or relaying the message, but I was all ears. "In this business Mr Smiles, as a musician, I can tell you, you either got it or you ain't." He let that settle between my ears before he added, "I can tell you Mr

Smiles, you got it. So you go out there and you give it brother. Good luck to you."

That was pretty much it. He said if I wanted to come back to New York in the future I just needed to come to Arthur's Bar and find him. He'd find me a sofa somewhere until I got on my feet.

I was so moved. I toasted him and told him he'd made the three weeks trip end on the best note ever. "A 'C Sharp!" I joked.

When the band finished I went up and thanked them all for the music, before closing the door behind me and making my way back through the snow laden streets to the flat.

A few hours later we were back in a Yellow Taxi Cab heading out to JFK.

IOTA

America. What a wonderland. The musicians I met, the people on the street, the vast landscapes and the vaster skyscrapers. The beautiful couple who gave us a true Greenwich Village welcome with their love, which was truly a Shakespearean play, upon a small stage with a slow heartbeat beating backdrop, revealing romance, tragedy and even farce. How we laughed together, wearing rose tinted sunglasses to keep away the sight of patient death in the distance.

I have seen many couples this much in love, but rarely has happenstance revealed such expressions of unconscious tenderness.

Steve, as I had felt, was not done with life yet and he fought his way on for a period of time measured in years not months. But ultimately the drugs, the treatment and his time ran out.

In many ways their love summed up America, a fast race of mixed races that made some of the best Art, Music, Films and Love the World has ever known. We are blessed, I could never have survived the lonely moments of childhood without Walt Disney, Peanuts, Grand Funk Railroad and Batman. Yet, under some beautifully polished chrome Fords there seemed a bottomless underbelly which sagged and seeped black oil into the dirty, litter sown ground.

Being desperate or down at heel in The States was a brutal life with slim odds of escape, as well as no Health and less Welfare. This was a long time before Barack Obama changed so much, only to see his hopes of a decent social welfare future, like Steve's health snatched away.

I've always felt America looks like a paradise from above, but if viewed from the side there was no bedrock reaching down through centuries of time, no ancient history at the core to give it real roots, as I feel there is in Britain.

Yet the events at start of the new millennium have somehow added all the depth and shadow a nation could bear. In the Present it has somehow, for me, found a Past. I wondered if any of those bright eyed sparks I saw passing me in the streets of Oxford were among those fallen. But this was yet to come and if only we could have known how innocent and beautiful our lives were at the end of the Nineties we might have danced longer and laughed louder.

I had a bit of Jet Lag and probably a comedown on my return from New York, but somehow the words of that Trumpet guy kept ringing in my ears as they still do now. I wish I could have gone back, slept on his sofa and done the whole trip; but I had a little cottage to look after, my Irish lullaby and two darling children I couldn't quite leave that far away.

About three months after returning from abroad, a large envelope appeared in my porch with an American stamp and the Jack Daniels logo on at the top. I opened it up to discover that I had been awarded a Title Deed to a piece of land at the distillery. I was also enrolled as a Tennessee Squire. It came with a laminated card that swore any Squire to always entertain another Squire, something about 'Riding High on the Hog,' and drinking the 'Mellow waters' of Lynchburg, after they had been distilled through Jack's hands of course. Also there was a calendar and a photo of the land I now had some ownership of. If it was all a PR stunt then it lasted thirteen years and was the best, funniest, most spirit lifting piece of PR I ever came across.

Andy however didn't get anything through the post. I remembered that at the start of the tour, before the guy's drawling introduction there had been the Visitor's Guest Book I signed. I remembered that in the section for 'Comments,' I had added, 'Drinking Jack Daniels is like sipping on Heaven.' I think this must have swung my membership, or just pure luck. It was oddly sweet, that having busked around on cents and nickels, I was given a priceless chunk of Real Estate in the States.

Some months later another letter from Lynchburg turned up. For some reason they always came on a Tuesday. This time it was from W.D.Clayton who ran the Lynchburg Hardware Store. He had written to tell me all about a local scheme to extend the Railroad from Nashville through to Lynchburg. This would improve business opportunities in the town and he reckoned therefore the price of land would go up too. Obviously a big concern of mine and of great interest! After much malarky and chat over two or three paragraphs it came down to some forms being sent to the residents of Lynchburg that needed filling out. To which he concluded at the bottom of the page, 'Us people here in Lynchburg Tennessee don't take much kindly to filling out forms; so that's another idea gone straight in the bin. Yours faithfully,

W.D.Clayton, Lynchburg Hardware Store. All Goods worth price charged.' Priceless!

After that I had letters from folks digging worms for fishing on my land, or inviting me for a barbecue, others that got their dog or cat stuck up my tree. Then at Christmas the Jack Daniels Calendar arrived, every year for fifteen years, until I eventually ran out of an address to send receive it. But that also is to come.

The trip during January had offered my young lady a chance to concentrate on her studies. After a glorious, riotous second year we had somehow reached the point where this was now the last six months countdown to her all important Finals. These would be held in the voluminous panelled hall within the gothic edifice of the Examinations Building. This cruel building mocks every drunken student to and from Magdalene Bridge and puts fear in the dancing footsteps of Freshers and Finishers alike.

The previous summer we had enjoyed the unbridled freedom that 'Second Years' inhabit. It was one long hot, sunny, beautiful drinksdiscoballpartydinners and puntingpicnicdressupdances. We pranced like princes and princesses, dancing all over Oxford, from hallowed lawns to silent libraries and dimmed living rooms.

It was a halcyon time that everybody knew couldn't last forever, so we lived and loved every occasion.

I didn't realise until much later that some of this joy was suspended on a thread and funded by a thing called a Student Loan, which would eventually snap. We didn't go mad, certainly not able to spend the way some of the well connected did, but we made up for any lack of funds with bags of imagination. Youth and our passionate love which added a sheen of gold leaf to everything.

However, some students were more blessed in their heritage, Howie was one of those lucky guys in our group, his father was apparently a Banker of some esteem, in Singapore. Thus I believe Howie was able to play the Playboy to the max. He had organised countless outings and events but the coup de gras, or perhaps the Pate de Foie Gras was dinner and a sleep over at one of the most prestigious Hotels near Oxford. As many as ten or twelve guests must have gone with him, just before Christmas.

At the beginning of the following term he presented a video at St Hughs of that event with bits of other parties and discos from the previous terms.

I thought it was fantastic that he had spent so much time editing endless footage together, then adding the music and getting it finished. I knew only too well how hard getting any creative work of art actually finished was.

I'm not sure why, but I remember not everyone was as thrilled with the results as he and I were. Perhaps some begrudged him his status and popularity. I just really loved the guy; he reminded me of a boy I once knew in Prep School called Bauhaus. A jet black shock of swept back hair, olive skin, eyes that smouldered and a broad beguiling smile that he would casually throw over his shoulder,. He had an air of nonchalance, as if he didn't have a care in the world, but underneath I sensed his Latin pulse.

One day shortly after the screening Howie caught up with me in Canterbury Road and asked me over to his room. It was blissfully untidy, the way a boy would love it, with cameras, expensive toys and screens strewn about everywhere, jeans and shirts draped over the corner of a very unmade bed. We chatted about his Finals and what plans he had? His father was presumably keen that his son should follow him into business. At that time the legacy of Thatcher's Financial Services Industry was still handing out Porches on a Friday to staff who had performed well that week. The Millennium promised endless big booms and even bigger boons. It was obviously the sensible career for Howie to choose.

"But Howie," I suggested, "All of that will still be there for you, in a year or two man. It's not like you have to get a foot on the rung of a ladder and work your way up. Man, you're starting three rungs from the top!" We both laughed. "I'm sure your Dad has plenty of contacts and offers of jobs for when you show up." I paused, "I was just wondering whether you had thought of maybe doing some travelling first, seeing a bit of life, having a few adventures before you go into the Big City scene."

Howie, along with others could not have failed to hear me blathering on about my adventures hitching abroad as a teenager, also I had just come back from the trip to America. With all my experience, good and bad, I was viewed to a greater or lesser degree as some sort of Campus Guru. I had often been asked my opinion by students when it came to concerns of life or love or whatever else. I used to gabble on with one of my stock sayings, 'What do you want to know? I've probably either had it, done it or know someone who did. So what's up?'

Howie was strangely non committal in his reply. He appreciated I cared and was interested in his future. He nodded as if considering the idea but I sensed he had family responsibilities and plans that were already mapped out for him. He obviously took them seriously. This boy was dearly loved.

"Well, whatever dude, enjoy your trip, wherever it takes you. Work hard, play hard. Make the most of every day. I'm sure business can be fun too." I said with an exaggerated lack of belief, "Remember also to 'Keep Smiling' brother," I giggled, "'Cause that really pisses 'em off!"

He replied, "I'll keep chirpy."

We both laughed like cats visiting a Dog Pound. Then he delved around in a suitcase jammed under his bed and took out a Video Tape.

"Hang on." He looked at me, "I want to write on it." He rummaged around his desk until he found a thick black felt tip, then he wrote down the video's spine and handed me the box. "Here you are bro, your own copy, for you and Maud." He smiled.

I hugged him and glanced at the dedication. We both laughed. "Hey, see you later dude. Ah, that's classic man. Thanks so much. I'm touched. Cheers."

It read, 'Geoff, I hope I'm having as much sex as you are when I'm your age. Howie. X'

I discovered a year or so later, there was a terrible irony to those words. I would return many times in my thoughts to our conversation and wonder.

For their final year several friends in Maud's circle had secured a house in Canterbury Road to rent and she had one of the three basement rooms. The front door exited to the road while the back led to the gardens of St Hughs. It was ideal, the room was huge, Matt the medic was opposite, a Norwegian guy next to him, Upstairs Lulu, Natasha and a lad with blond curly hair who had recently fallen in love. I ended up writing a song for him one day.

It was a voluminous house, filled from top to bottom with love and happiness. Everybody seemed to be coping with their workload of lectures and essays whilst keeping up with the demands of playtime. The girls often congregated to watch 'Friends' the American Sitcom, upstairs in 'Tasha's room, Xena and others might drop in too and add their peals of laughter to the throng.

The run up to Christmas had been oiled with bravado as regards the looming Finals; but with he new year and Hilary Term the gloom of the inevitable doom was now inescapable; as if great storm clouds were parked up on a far horizon, just waiting to roll across the Oxford plains. I wanted them all to do well and encouraged worried faces and drooping shoulders to raise their sights.

My return every long weekend brought some relief as I was out of the loop. I often played songs in their rooms or at house parties. They knew I had a band and nobody was surprised to hear me say I was busy recording our first album.

I had done my solo cassette, but this was a new venture into Digital. At that time the CD format was at its most popular, until finally Neil Young, amongst others, promoted Vinyl Records back to their rightful place. Many weekends were spent playing songs on my guitar and writing, while Maud worked in the Library preparing for her impending examinations.

The days began to lengthen after the Christmas holidays, everything was under control, life was calm and studious. Down at the Cherwell Boathouse late frosts dusted the grass with silver and tongues of ice licked the dilapidated jetty at the river's edge. Friendly's paw marks, or should I say 'Lonely' trotted off to the river and back again, though he was rarely seen; occasionally a sleepy head and somnambulant gaze would appear at his round window to survey the chilly river and chilled visitors below.

In the distance shouts, whistles, cries and thumps could be heard diving and tackling through the leafless trees from The Dragon School. The playing fields scattered with boys hurling rugger balls about and crossing hockey sticks in mortal combat. From here and beyond the hum of traffic on the main road gradually rose, hissing round the lanes, under the majestic trees, whistling through wrought iron gates and stone pillars with Pineapples or Eagles aloft.

At the edge of the fields, beyond the park gates the Department of 'This' and the Faculty for 'That' had usually left their lights on, through the brief greying afternoons, tucked behind diamond recesses of leaded windows or beneath the black beamed and red tiled turrets of roofs roaming the dark horizons of those 'Dreaming Spires.'

Students on rickety bikes disappeared into these Laboratories, Lecture Halls and Seminar Rooms, calculating, verifying, adding and subtracting hours from their lives; until their thinner legs pressed on thicker pedals, entering or exiting, courtyards and quads, Porter's Lodges and University Gardens.

I was of course absolved from all this. I could only observe the lambs as they were fattened daily for slaughter, brains bulging in a cerebellum of statistics and high lighted Pritt Stick notes; their synapses soggy in a soup of conceptual hypothesis, nerve endings stuck in endless traffic jams, or recurring thoughts just going round and round and round the same roundabout. Until Eureka.

It seems a tame territory, the Brain Game, the worst injury that can happen is a paper cut, stabbing a finger with a pencil or sitting on a drawing pin, unlike the rigours of a building site in mid construction. But there were casualties and deaths every year from what can only be described as Exam pressure. Added to which might be the responsibility they felt for not letting peers or parents down.

Every year the same story came back to haunt the Halls of Residences; somewhere, somebody had cracked and fallen. It's not just the exams, that's too simple. Its the whole deal, the intensity of it all, the here and now and whoops it's all over, of it all. The almighty bloody edifice of British Education, that climbs towards these ivory towers as if it was Mecca, dependent on new bricks to support the old. There are a lot of traditions and ceremonies which are dependent on fresh blood to fodder their finery

To break the line, to challenge the rule, to dare to dare and thus be expelled was the most heinous sin of all. I had done that, felt that shame, the horror of failure, branded by some a fallen Lucifer for always and ever after and by others a Pied Piper of doom.

It was time for the students to produce the efforts of their labours and I used that as a challenge for me to do the same. I chose a date and told the band that what we had in the mix on that day was going to be it. I wanted the CDs ready for friends at St Hughs to take away on their future adventures. I knew I was unlikely to see many of them ever again.

'Sounds Good' was the firm I chose to produce the finished CDs for me. I had taken my precious Reel to Reel tapes to Henry, the sound engineer there, when I had made my first cassette; now I had a small box of Minidiscs, the 'Musicians Choice,' in my bag.

The minidisc was another bit of luck. At 'Don't Tell It' magazine I had learnt the power of the 'Writer Reviewer' to procure stuff for an article. Many of the music companies included free VIP Club nights with promo CDs, or books from Publishers came with invitations to launch parties. These events, for anybody that puts them on, were often judged more by the amount of free drinks and the quality of the sandwiches than the product itself.

I had decided we may as well record digitally if we were going to produce a CD. I rang a big company, bless them, selling music stuff and blagued a brand new Yamaha 'Four Track' from them, supposedly to review for some music magazine.

Unfortunately, on arrival it died after seventeen seconds of recording. I rang up the firm and mentioned a band had come down from Glasgow to try out the machine and we were keen to get on. God knows where I got the idea of Glasgow, but I conjured up a gory vision of some very pissed of Scotsmen about to rampage over the Cotswolds.

A day or two later another Four Track showed up and I duly sent the buggered one back to their Repair Department.

Encouraged by the fact that The Beatles brilliant album 'Sgt. Pepper's' was recorded on a four track, I pushed all the boundaries and nailed the album. I had the Reel to Reel and cassette tapes all fed in by a stream of lines and leads, adding effects or sound scapes. There was a moment during mixing when I had four machines set up, going on and off, on and off, pumping Cosmic Smiles music into the minidisc.

After I had mixed, mixed again and mixed it again, the machine went back to the company. About two months later old Mr Sharpley, the farmer from next door, turned up on my back step, complaining the Postman had left a parcel for me at the farm. Would I like to collect it?

I had no idea what it could have been until I saw the shape of the box. It couldn't be? Back at Windsong I unpackaged the repaired Minidisc player which they had returned to me, by mistake I presumed. I'm not sure as I never quite got round to finding out. The band recorded the next few albums on that until we moved up to the dizzy heights of an 'Eight Track.'

Being the story of the greatest band nobody ever heard of, my trip to the hallowed place where the minidiscs were going to be compiled on a Master hard drive, was as equally nondescript. Most bands would have had a proper studio, a keen engineer and somebody to plug their leads in and chop lines of Cocaine for them. Then a runner would have despatched the Master Tapes for the band's manager to check. That would be me too. Then the Art Department would provide several options for a cover; that'll be me also. A few weeks later the finished product would be in most record stores and played on the radio while the forthcoming tour would be announced.

I tried all that too, but Badlands Record Shop in Cheltenham was hardly a universal outlet, the radio stations wouldn't touch it as their 'Playlists' all came from some mysterious distant Head Office. while our tour would comprise of a couple of local gigs, some in London and a Festival or two in the summer. But hey, we were on the road to Wembley in our dreams. Sadly, over the years we got lost somewhere going round the North Circular for the umpteenth time.

There was only me to make all those things happen, minus the coke. Anyway, full of hot nervous energy mixed with a dreadful fear the tapes would all be magically blank or unreadable, I turned my Cortina limousine off the M4 at Theale. To be honest the firm 'Sounds Good' looked like any other beige and grey factory unit next to rows of other beige and grey units opposite. They might just as well have been making teddy bears, yet it was my 'Abbey Road.'

All the way there I'd be praying I didn't break down. 'I'll walk back,' I'd promise any God with a sense of humour, but the Cortina never let me down. Henry the sound engineer, my 'George Martin,' was also a guitarist and we bonded over that. He had the best speakers in the world and patiently fed my discs, one by one, into his 'Sadie System.' I would watch the line of sound making a reflected lake of Pine trees, ascending and descending as the song went along. After loading the songs we checked the starts and ends, 'PQ' points and fades. Then it was done.

It felt like giving birth in many ways, minus the pain, plus the palpitations. Months of effort, moments of magic and endless listening, wondering, planning. At the end there was relief and exhaustion, elation and a 'What the fuck do I do now' feeling.

However, I still had to pay the nice lady in Accounts and finalise the cover artwork with Jim. There was often something we had to line up, maybe a barcode to add, depending on how hopeful or hopeless my dreams were at the time. Martin, Jim's father, ran the business and was always pleasant to me. They didn't get many musicians actually turn up at the factory and I guess it broke up the week with a bit of cosmic madness.

I saw Jim, paid the lady and made my way back to the M4 heading west. The sun would often be in my eyes, a Master Copy to check was next to me on the seat and I was the happiest little Rock Star dreamer in the World. Maybe this album would finally get us noticed?

Maybe? Maybe, maybe? I'd already wasted several years on 'Maybes,' though I never really cared much about all that. I couldn't force it, I knew so much depended on luck. For me, as nice as some success would have been, it was always just about making the music not the business; I knew I was over fifteen years too late or too early for the current trends.

The Acid Test was yet to come, that evening I would lie on the studio floor, with Miles staring down at me from the Revox poster, Janis, Jim, Jimi, Joni, so many 'J's' stuck in a collage on the wall all watching me. I pressed 'Play' on the remote and listened to the new album. If it made me cry at some point and go 'Fucking wow' at another I knew it was good, good enough for me and the band. The first album was great. They all were, each capturing the music and my life as it moved inexorably towards the precipice. I would make eleven albums in all, the last one paid for as my house disappeared beneath me under a pile of debts. I have never regretted that decision, to give everything to the music; though I never expected the music would take everything and leave me back in a van, semi homeless, well totally home less. But all those joys awaited me.

No matter how I was judged I can vouch the music was original, honest and so unique in its way. I never wrote a song about falling in love without falling in love, or out of it. I never wrote about being strung out at four in the morning without being strung out. I wrote nearly three hundred songs and every one of them came out of my life and heart, each one bled from my veins.

Meanwhile the Parties and the Balls continued at Oxford with the usual frenzy of energy. Yet the 'In between times' were now given up to fevered study in the Library. Some students managed to seem oblivious, either through sheer genius or terror, while others, in fact most, trembled.

For example the two lads opposite us played Rugby on a new computer game up to the week before Finals when one, Matt, calmly announced he must start revising for his Medic exams. Needless to say he sailed through with a First or as good as. There were miracle minds in these fertile allotments, some on the road to Canterbury, others…to elsewhere.

The buying of a Tuxedo suit for one of the balls was similar to my CD experience. No excited mother or entourage accompanied a beloved boy to the Gentleman's Fitters, no experienced hand tied the Cummerbund round my waist. The dear ladies at 'Just In,' the fine dress shop in Winchcombe, did as much though. They seemed just as excited as me at the prospect of my first proper Ball and fussed over me like clucking hens.

The St Peter's College Ball was blessed with clear skies during an otherwise damp early summer. It was filled with the cream of Oxford's crop, milking one last 'Hurrah,' from the champagne bottle of College life. It was halcyon, magnificent, beautiful, a night like so many others from those years, full of vigorous discussion, beautiful young people, wide eyed fervour and inestimable hope. For, of course, they had every right to have hopes.

I wandered around while the girls were dancing or at the bar, knowing I was coming to the end of this magical time; nothing would ever be quite the same; such is the nature of life. Tuxedos and ballgowns twirled on small lawns, laughter bounded up and down on the bouncy castle; everywhere glasses and bottles were pitched up, propped precariously on walls, window ledges or steps. I took every last drop of the Champagne in with my eyes.

We had to go at some point. I never stayed until the end of a party if I could help it. Get out before the dawn betrays everybody's makeup and the haggard stares of bleary eyes reflect my own. We walked out into the damp street, arm in arm through the neon plume of mist gathered at every lamp post. It wasn't far back to St Hughs. A church nearby tolled three bells. "Ah 'tis the holy number, t'ree, the trinity, just for us darling." I joked in an awful Irish accent.

Early the next morning, at a time when nobody ever knocks on a student's door, I heard the urgent tap and shuffle of feet outside. Maud was fast asleep so I slipped out of bed quietly. As I got to the door I heard feet going up the stairs. I figured somebody needed sugar or milk or something, I went back to the warm hug of the bed.

However, in the middle of this ascending crescendo of waking emotions a few hours later we found out that Lulu had taken an overdose of Paracetamol. A really bad overdose and she was going to need a Liver transplant in the next couple of days. Which meant brutally that somebody, somewhere else was going to have to die tragically and also be a match.

We all knew then, that although the college year and the examinations weren't quite over yet, the blissful idiocy of youth was.

She had survived the initial 'Knock Out' of the pills. We all waited for news, we could think of nothing else. She was in the John Radcliffe Hospital and a couple of the girls went up to see her.

Twenty two years previously I had done the same thing, having tried to get stoned or just cause mayhem at Public School, by drinking a huge bottle of cough mixture I had nicked from Matron's office and taking thirty or forty Paracetamol. Shortly after I collapsed in Science class and had to be helped up to the Sanatorium by two lads. The Nurse there had put me in a dormitory and in my drowsy state I had been wandering around the room. I spotted a small plastic beaker next to an empty bed and curiously went over to look at it. At the bottom was one Paracetamol pill. Where that came from I will never know? But the sight of it immediately turned my stomach over and made me dash to the toilet and puke up the others. I was so lucky.

The cruel twist of Paracetamol is that the initial blast of the drug doesn't usually cause death; the patient often recovers fully for three days, but meanwhile the liver is slowly dissolving until it just shuts down, defeated by an innocuous little headache pill. Unable to process its toxic waste the body poisons itself to death. No doubt many people who attempt suicide like this spend those few days mourning the stupidity of their act, while witnessing before them the horror that their death will have on those people, their family or friends, who love them.

At the John Radcliffe the girls visiting watched the eyes of every passing nurse, in case it was news, feeling the eyes of her parents; knowing they starred back from hell. Maud returned later that day to say Lulu was being transferred to London that night, with the view to giving her a liver transplant. It was her only hope. But meanwhile, in another lifetime, at another death time, somebody else had to die by misfortune. They would also have to have signed a Donor Consent form and also be a perfect match for Lulu. There was so much that could go wrong or not go at all, so many 'What if's' and so much at stake. Then, should fate decree that somebody's life was to be lost and Lulu's possibly saved, there was still the operation itself, usually lasting seven hours with all the risks that involved.

Chiaroscuro, light and dark, sunbeam and shadow. They collect on the walls of our daydreams, spiders crossing one thought with another, mixing the palette of past and future; meanwhile, we struggle to see the colours daubed across our present.

The next day about seven of us got on the coach to London and made our way to Guy's and St Thomas Hospital. That was one coach ride I never want to take again.

We congregated on some grey plastic benches near the coffee machine, in one corner of the huge foyer of the hospital. We were not allowed on the ward but from time to time Lulu's Dad or Mum would come down and appear with some news.

I peered into the despair in her parent's eyes. I knew only too well how lucky I had been. It could have been my parent's praying anxiously as they did, it could have been me with three days waiting to die, faced with an operation that may have been my last. Though when I was at school it was only five years previously that the first liver transplant had been done successfully in Cambridge. So much could easily have gone wrong.

Clarice, Xena, Natasha and Maud were red eyed tearful wrecks while John, Howie and I stared into morose nothingness.

We waited. The Pre Op. We waited. The operation. We waited. The Post Op. We waited. Then Mum and Dad appeared, we knew from their faces Lulu had survived the ordeal. Now it was just a question of a million possible things that could go wrong. Would the new liver be rejected. How would Lulu cope with all the medication; a lifetime of medication.

On the coach back to Oxford we all sank into our seats, glad of the darkness to hide our weary faces.

Lulu wasn't going to be back in her room later, growling with a hangover, clutching a glass of white wine in solace, her college year had ended. But the silence from her door filled the stairs and corridors between ours.

Reality, the real World, those damned vicissitudes of Fate had cut the Ivory Tower from our far horizons.

Seeking some return to normality in between the build up of those weeks until the summer exams, we scurried off to the lawns of the Boat House and the bobbing punts, searching for the cat Friendly.

Branches over the river had lost their blossoms and the leaves of Summer contentment spread out over the lazy waters. We went on a roller coaster of emotions during that time, knowing our friendships would separate. Yet in between everything and the trauma of Lulu's departure our love was a golden nugget and we warmed our hearts around it.

Finally, only a few weeks remained, staggered with the timetable of dates for exams and the mad dash to find Examination Gowns mixed with hours of late night cramming. Then the joys and woes of every exam, the post mortem pints and counting the days to the final Final. For Maud a couple of weeks or so remained after the last exam until the end of term, which we spent in halcyon afternoons punting on a river of endless aspiration and sparkling wine. It was all done, all over, all except the goodbyes.

My band was booked to play the St Hugh's last big garden party for the leavers. The College and JCR photos had been taken-on the lawns. I managed to be in the background for the first one poised with my guitar and joined them all for the Fancy Dress photo, perched on the benches hoping not to fall off.

The day of the Garden Party remained dry, although it wasn't the best of summer months and everything went on vaguely as planned, yet it was almost surreal and hard to believe this would be our last grand event together. Never again would this blend of characters dance the night away, as we had for those three magical years. Tears of passing joy and joy passing are sometimes the warmest and wettest.

There would naturally be the Degree Ceremony and one or two events to come, but essentially the main act was over, we would always be visitors from now on. It seemed ironic the walls which had cocooned our lives in paradise were now turning against us. The bird's nest tipped up and we all toppled out.

On the day of the party I had given into temptation, taking a few poppies from the college garden and making some Opium Tea. Perhaps I did it to give me the extra strength to perform, to create the hysteria of ecstasy they expected of me, or because, like the others I was sad that the greatest experience of all our combined lives was ending. This would never happen again. The word 'Final' now revealed its true nature, its truth, its nemesis, its damning verdict on us all. We were at the end.

In the photo of the last 'Hurrah,' taken later that night, so many eager faces look upward, bathed in a haze of mixed emotions; some drunk with the relief that the Exams were finally done, the endless essays and assessments over; some deep in their thoughts, a studious expression behind radiant smiles, some just happy and some just sad.

The few days that remained were spent making last visits to everywhere and almost everybody, including several stops at the Gardener's Arms, while all the posters came down, photos were unpinned, fridge magnets unstuck, floors searched for sticky sweet wrappers, cushions found, lost sheets and pillowed blankets removed; lava lamps, candles, teddy bears, sandwich makers, mugs and CD cases; small TVs, large stereos, Ghetto Blasters, coats, dresses, hats, scarves, single gloves, odd socks and old muddy trainers located; books and magazines, files of A4, sheets of A4, crumpled and folded A4, blank A4, filled with doodles A4, rucksacks, handbags, carrier bags and suitcases filled up. All gradually gathering together in one corner of a denuded room, awaiting their exodus and their lonely exiles.

We paid homage to the classic haunts of those years. It had been by many accounts a vintage era for students, as regards a self confessed ability for revelry and living the life to the full. The new intake of 'Freshers' seemed tamer and so much younger by comparison.

The world was changing faster than we dared to think and much of this change in lifestyle was due to a new phenomenon, the Mobile Phone. As the last weeks had passed many students, with a view to staying in touch after college, had made an effort to get these devices. They had been around awhile in brick form for ten years, but now they were small and affordable.

We all thought it added security and better links to people, but in fact some element of freedom was lost. We could no longer just disappear, no longer excuse ourselves from being away from the phone, or for missing an important call. Now we were traceable, followed about by Nokia and Blackberry everywhere. As the number and volume of the Ring Tones increased, the hubbub of conversation died down.

In The King's Arms we gathered around tables and sat on sofas that seemed, once upon a short time ago, to be ours forever; yet now other students were there. In The Turf the walls seemed a little closer, in The White Horse the ceiling lower, The Chequers was a riot of energy that overwhelmed us; the music and the crush of people was too loud, too raucous, too vile, too young for us.

In the cobbled backstreets the high walls were no longer within reach, the Porter's Lodges now barred us entry to the Quads. Our fugitive steps led us into the open spaces where the Isis wormed its snakelike reflection or the Cherwell lumbered beneath a tree, beyond a fence, the city lights dimming behind us, the shadow plains of distant dreams, hardly in sight but somewhere in front of us.

The girls Maud, Natasha, Xena, Clarice, Nazia, Lulu, Julia, Alex, Plum, Anna, Sara, Clare, Philippa, Lucy, Charlotte, would never lose touch. Who knows what happened to the boys? Tom, Phil, John, Ben, Jason, Dominic, Daniel, James, Jonathan, Stuart, Andy, Acland, Richard, Jon, Matthew, Robert, Jonny and Peter; tragically, with a percentage of students following careers into 'The City,' lured by the huge salaries on offer, I'm sure some of those bright young folk had friends in the Twin Towers or were in fact there on the day the World's dreams for a new century were exploded.

Meanwhile there would still be gatherings at parties for birthdays, new jobs and so on; but they would be in rented flats, or on distant lawns; no longer was the hallowed turf of Oxford growing under our feet.

Those few years we shared were the sweetest, their warm soft centres, the endless variety of people and events, all played out beneath the Dreaming Spires.

For me it was the most unlikely of experiences, to arrive a wandering Troubadour, hired to entertain the queue and then being part of the queue, to fulfil the wishes of my mother twenty years after her death was comforting, amazing, but ridiculously poignant.

In many ways the future didn't really matter to me at all. I wasn't leaving with a degree and a reference tucked in my belt, I wouldn't have the advantages that such a golden card offers. But I had stored the experiences like gold bars in my mind; the delight of being in love, being loved and basking on the banks of those heady waters, the Isis and the Cherwell.

Scenes from our adventures punting down the long endless summer afternoons into the arms of the warm summer evenings would never be forgotten.

The corners of streets, the arches, the lodges, the pubs and pathways, the high walls, the beautiful stone work, the graceful railings, the ever reaching upwards of roofs and turrets, the weather cocks, the mists and dawn runs, the hot and the cold breath of seasons, the melt of kisses on lips during the winter, the sweat of midsummer bonnets and tuxedos, the cold clammy hands of the black robes, wreathed in palls around the hung shoulders of examination candidates. The laughter and tears.

The swift passing of 'First Years,' the ever limitless wilderness of the 'Second Years,' followed by the cruel calamity of non stop marching by 'Third Years' to reach 'The End.'

The teas and coffees, the beers, the cheap wine and expensive champagnes, the Marlboro Lights, the Vodka nights, Friends, Narnia and The Beach Boys, midnights, mornings, dawns, dusks, musky scents, cuddled up love, the bedside tables, empty cups, undressed reflections in heart shaped mirrors, addresses on fag boxes, crumpled dresses, biscuit crumbs, crusts, crimpers, chipped cups, plates, glasses, ravaged chocolate boxes, savaged sucky sweets, creams and empty boxes of headache pills, the Pill, sweet packets and furry jackets.

All of this, passing inexorably through millions of seconds and thousands of minutes, until the hours were tolled, one by one, from the first to the last, by the bells of North Parade.

THETA

The queue for the Prom Club was knee deep in gorgeous young people. I used to warn male friends who hadn't visited Cheltenham before that the first thing they would see driving into town would be not one, but two or three utterly stunning women, for they roamed in packs. It is still true; even the dogs, furry ones, are good looking! Having lived in areas less blessed I used to marvel at this phenomenon, which I attributed to either the good fortune of generations of wealthy people not marrying 'Utter Munters;' or there being a factory hidden away in the depths of GCHQ, our local international spy listening centre, which churns out drop dead beautiful, five foot eight, blue eyed, long legged blonds by the dozen. Such are the deep thoughts of young men confronted by life's unfathomable mysteries.

The Autumn evening had been warm and most of the girls were standing around in posh frocks, made from possibly three or four handkerchiefs of material. The boys likewise, were strutting their stuff in smart trousers and slick shoes, open shirts, gold bracelets, big watches and bigger eyes. They shuffled on their leather soles, scanning the crowds for friends.

Everybody was relaxed, there was hardly a group without somebody smoking or lighting up, cigarette packets lay next to posh handbags on the tables behind the ornate black railings. Maud and I waited, slowly approaching the steps to the terrace.

These were guarded by two off duty Bulldogs; their emotionless eyes searching the oncoming bodies for T shirts or trainers, which would be refused entry along with their disgruntled owner. The bouncers could afford to be picky, sometimes they even insisted on a tie, however badly it might have been dragged on. I remember dashing back to the car one night to get a work tie, just to get up those steps and into the club.

There were also some young men who had 'Trouble' written all over their grimaces. Inevitably, when they were turned back there would be the endless threats of reprisals as they faded into the back streets and the early hours of the morning.

There were a couple of guys I noticed, with three or four stunning girls, already looking hot and sticky from dancing inside, one of whom spotted me and waved us over. We were next in line to present shoes and clean hands to the burly bouncers, but the one on the right saw her gesture and noticing the two men next to her waved us straight in, as though we had suddenly become VIP's.

"Hi." The tall dark haired woman smiled at my Irish moll, "I love that dress." She was the wife of a friend and obviously out with her girlfriends. She looked at me. "Do you know James and Charlie?" I shook my head. "Fantasia? You remember the rave at Sudeley Castle?" I nodded, smiling at the guys.

"Ah yeah, great. I didn't go myself but I heard about it. Apparently it went really well, loads of people! I'm amazed you got the permission sorted."

"Wasn't easy," one of them replied, 'fancy some Champagne?" A bottle and two glasses appeared by magic. "So what do you do?"

I explained forty years of madness in four minutes, but stressed that I was a musician, had a great band and an album.

"We've just released this." James handed me a CD.

Maud and I smiled as the DJs surname was familiar to us. "Is that your long lost half brother Jeremy from Sligo?" I quipped. Then I explained Maud's surname and the DJ's were the same, while she laughed at me as if to say, 'You do talk some top bollocks." As usual, everybody round the table seemed instantly entranced by my belle.

I scanned the cover and the track list. "Looks really good. I'll play it on the way home. My stuff is a lot more 'Old School' I guess. Hippy music man." I drawled. The music I made was about as far from these boys as you could get in its creation, but in many ways very similar. I knew I had to bluster my way through this initial interview, try and create some kind of cool impression, based on the fact there was very little to crow about, I was out of date, out of funds and way out of luck.

The inevitable one of two questions was coming, this I knew from past experience. He chose the first one, "So what kind of music is it really?"

"Well, fuck me man, that is the twenty four million penny question. I wish it did fall into a category but there just isn't one that fits!. I know, I looked in every Record Store. I can't find it." As they started to smile I went on, "Its sort of bluesy, jazzy, funky, spacey, kind of thing." They were nearly laughing, so I did a quick air guitar solo and added, "But definitely and always, without a shadow of a doubt, rockin' with a strawberry topping man!" That cracked it. They all howled and we clinked our glasses together.

We all shouted, 'Rockin' with a strawberry topping!" With that we became friends.

The other question I encountered was inevitably, 'What is the Band called?' To which my reply would invariably get a look with as blank an expression as ever seen on a human face. To be fair, who's ever heard of 'Cosmic Smiles?'

A year or so later I was in Corfu, playing my guitar on the balcony of the little apartment block, when a new friend I'd made that holiday, Ashley Craven, came sauntering over the lawns with some young guy. Ash was in fact the lead guitarist in a Punk Band called 'The Exploited,' which for a time were signed to a real Record Company and quite famous. Ash was on holiday, at his Manager's expense, with the aim of decreasing his Heroin habit; not exactly going Cold Turkey, but maybe Tepid Chicken, drop down a few notches and level out. We had bonded over that.

So on that day, I really didn't want to blow my street credibility with this guy, but the longer I played the song I was doing, the more apparent it became to me that at the end of it the guy with him was going ask me, 'So, what's the name of your band?'

I wrung some idea out of the ether and played the last chord. Having complimented the song he came straight out with it. I knew I had to come back with something more than, "Er, Cosmic... whatever.'

I leapt onwards and outwards, rapping off the top of my head. "Well, you know my friend, I see you like hanging out with Ashley, which I guess means you're a pretty wild dude and if you're that wild you're gonna get out on the 'Edge' sometimes. Well, you can spend all the time you like on the edge but one day man, I can assure you from my experience, it's inevitable you're gonna fall over that edge dude. Well, half way down the cliff, if you look on the left you'll see me and boys 'Cosmic Smiles' playing on the last ledge!"

That cracked it. Ash and I also became firm friends and I made every effort to get up to London and see him when I could and his lovely lady Sophia. I tried to encourage him to stay clean, or cleaner. But we both had the hunger still. However, he seemed to be free from 'Dancing with the Devil' for awhile.

At the small resort called Arillas they have cliffs made of ancient mud, the base of which are as hard as rock. One sleepless night when the 'Wild Turkeys' were keeping him awake, Ashley had gone down to the beach and carved 'ASH' into the grey stone as dawn broke. I took a photo of it which I cherished for many a year as the cliff was washed away.

The door to the Prom Club kept opening and letting out the sound of the pumping music as a few people left. We chatted about the next album they were making and the rave scene. Having finished our Champagne I nudged Maud and wove my arm round her thin waist, "We're going to nip up, dip in

and rip up the dance floor. Maybe see you up there."
They laughed.

The Prom Club was basically a house knocked into a club. It was impossible not to feel you were going up a private staircase, but every room was a blaze of spinning lights in a smoky haze, loud music and the broad smiles of the bar staff tucked behind a vast row of pumps somewhere on the back wall.

Half way up the stairs a bored bouncer monitored the queue to the toilets in a vain attempt to separate the Sniffers from the Pissers. However, though he might catch one or two of the young lads who were bouncing off the carpets before they even got in there, a few of the guys he didn't even look at, to be fair I wouldn't have asked them to tell me the time, let alone what they were doing in the toilets.

It was the late nineties, Cocaine was tolerated to a degree, depending on who was in charge. After all, to be in the Night Club business in those heady pre millennium days, a Coke habit was almost seen as an occupational hazard, like a Pub Landlord being a member of amateur Alcoholics Anonymous.

We brushed past the bruisers and went to dance in the main room upstairs. The high ceilings let the smoke rise above the heat from the bodies. It was packed, but not quite like sardines yet. By midnight it would be heaving. After a bevy of songs we were roasting, we bought drinks and went downstairs to sit outside beneath the orange glow of streetlights in the trees above us. Our bodies gently purred and steamed in the cooler air.

My friend's wife came out for a cigarette.

I called over, "Hey, thanks for the champagne."

"No worries, James loves meeting new people. He's having a party at his place in Leckhampton next weekend. He said you're both welcome to come."

I glanced at Maud and she nodded, "Sounds great. Yeah. Where is it?"

She explained and assured me I couldn't miss it. The last mansion on the left, up such a such road. Seemed easy to me. James was still in the process of leaving his Prestbury apartment and I called in a couple of days later with my CD and have a chat. He asked whether I fancied a job in Ibiza, handing out leaflets for Pasha. I had to say it sounded great, but I had the responsibility of keeping the cottage up and I couldn't just leave my belle for weeks at a time, so I ruefully declined.

We finished our drinks slowly, watching the crowd of sweaty revellers falling in twos and threes down the steps on their way out and those still turning up, keen to get in, waiting for a nod from the bouncers. Maud stubbed her Marlboro out and awhile later we headed off across town in the vague direction of where I'd parked. I liked to be on the side of town heading homewards if possible. Within minutes we could be over Bishops Cleeve Hill and back in the safe womb of the valley beyond.

But there was still an hour or so before the Clubs shut, so we skipped down a side street to bring us round a corner into Regent Street. We could hear the thud of the '21 Club' pounding out and saw up ahead of us a bunch of young stragglers hoisted or hooked on the railings, holding Pints that seemed to pendulum at the end of their arms.

Pissed as newts, poor buggers, not quite got their wings yet but still determined to fly. One of these lovely boys would be leaving his Mum's diced carrots and half a kebab somewhere down the Lower High Street.

"Fancy a drink here before we go?" I suggested.

"Does the Pope pray on Sundays, or what?" We both laughed and slipped past the lads and down the steps to the club. The basement room was tiny. The ceiling was inches from my head. The bodies were mashed wall to wall. The music was deafening. Everybody had a glass in one hand and a fag in the other, raised up to shoulder height. Everybody was talking in a semi shout, lip reading, cupping hands over ears, leaning on shoulders covered in sweat. The available small space above our heads was a Cumulus Nimbus of thick smoke, tinged with puffs of Dry Ice occasionally. Movement in any direction, except up and down, was slow.

I nodded at the bar and my Irish 'Beerhound' slid away between two people. It was four deep to get a drink but she was back soon enough. I think it must be a skill she acquired in College or perhaps it was an innate Irish trait.

We slithered slowly through the morass of semi insane, semi clad, damp writhing bodies to a corner, parked our drinks and had a dance. More of a glorified giggle really, as merely standing still in the crush of bodies made the sweat run down our backs. By the time we'd danced for a few songs we were dripping. I began to realise why some of these girls obviously went out almost naked, a bikini might have been a better idea.

It was manic, loud, fabulous, beautiful, ecstatic, hot. I loved it, the wildness, the free abandonment of any division between people. We were all loving the music, letting off steam, literally. There was no sense of prejudice, dancing like lunatics, united in having a good time, right here, right now. We were going to be doing this, building momentum to the Millennium.

It began to feel like that, parties and events became trial preparations for the big one to come. We kissed and cavorted in an almighty joy, all of us looking forward to a new 'Thousand Years.'

That was something so special and we felt blessed to be on the planet Earth to witness this rare occurrence, to be its bearers, going forward.

Personally, I hoped most societies would have had a good look back over what they had achieved and what they failed on. It wasn't just the 'End of a Year,' or 'End of a Decade,' or even the end of a hundred years, this was a rare deal. I prayed for true change. But sadly, we all just partied and got pissed.

Following my rule, I always leave any club event before the final curtain. There is nothing worse than a crowd gone mad in a rainbow of loud music and strobe lights suddenly exposed with all its brutal flaws in the cold white silence of House Lights.

We squeezed back through an even tighter mess of smiling faces and over energetic expressions, until the first draught of air from the door froze on our damp skin. At the top of the steps the lads had all gone, leaving their beer bottles and a couple of empty fag packets wedged between the railings.

The night was suddenly cooler now; I remembered the dreaded hours of the early morning before dawn when I was living rough on the streets. "God help the homeless," I whispered.

Back in the car we were soon leaving the glow of Cheltenham streetlights behind, hurrying away to the breathless silence of the star filled skies above the shadow of Winchcombe; weaving through the slow curves of the medieval capital, its soft cumbersome butterscotch blocks of stone melting leaded lamps.

A few miles beyond we turned off the main road and followed the shadow of Poplars, then under the Chestnuts, over the gravel drive, to arrive home.

Windsong was sleeping soundly as we approached, the eyes of the back door were closed tight, the chimneys snoring, the breeze brushing the Virginia Creeper, like a lost forelock, back and forth across the walls of pebble dashed dreams.

We crept in on tip toes, as if we didn't want to wake Windsong and disturb his peace, or awaken the ghosts of parent's past. Even the wooden stairs couldn't manage a creak.

We undressed in the half moonlight, gathering our stumbling bodies together, fingers and thumbs, lips and tongues, arms and legs, into a woven heap beneath our quilted breath.

We made love, a ballet of limbs beneath the glitter ball of remembered bodies in the night's mirror.

Our breaths became breathless, until they ached as one. Our sighs became sigh less. The kiss of hearts.

We pulled the quilt up, tight over our sleepy dreams. We slept, touching and touch less.

The following Saturday we trundled up a tree lined avenue in a posh backwater of Cheltenham. It was the last house, it had to be, there was no room for any more. We parked my wreck between two rather shiny sports cars and set off to enjoy the hospitality James and Charlie were so well known for.

Dancers from the regular crew of Fantasia were there and loads of people that were I guess vaguely connected with the rave scene.

It didn't seem to matter who you knew, or didn't, it was an easy atmosphere. I guess with our usual understated look, floor length coat in electric mauve faux fur, Ocelot pattern shoes, Maud in Dalmatian, it would be hard to overlook us. As anachronistic as I was, even then, these guys seemed to enjoy the cross over. I never got that, 'I am the big star' trip which goes with a lot of music business people and performers, or the boneless Promoter.

There were Record Decks set up in various rooms and people randomly dancing. The toilets were just off the pool room and we joined the queue to 'Line up.'

I liked the whole vibe with Fantasia, the music was good and accessible to guys like me, not too 'Hard Core.' I would end up spending my Millennium with them, but sadly not at Toddington Manor where they had planned to have the party, of all parties.

I dipped my toe into that world and its drugs, after all I had taken just about everything else what was a bit of Ecstasy and a few more lines of Coke. But I have never been enthralled with Cocaine, its effects are far too short lived and the continual craving every twenty minutes for another line is tiresome when compared to one hit of heroin which would knock anybody out for hours.

As a hardened and long serving drug user I had my doubts about Ecstasy, the 'New drug on the block.' Despite medical views, I was never truly convinced. I looked on it the same way a dog does at a puddle of clear but contaminated water. It smells okay, seems okay, but nah, something just ain't right. I don't want to argue the science of it, or the morality of it. We all make personal choices, but it wasn't mine.

I got into several of the wilder and more 'Way out there' Clubs through 'Don't Tell It,' in London. I went to quite a few events through friends in Bristol and one night the 'Toddy Lads and Lasses,' all boarded a coach and headed up North to one of the most famous of all the clubs at the time, called Cream.

It was here that I saw the other side to this whole movement that the parent's of Leah Betts had found. The walls of the club were so wet with condensation it ran down to pools along the floors. It was rammed and pumping. We all went off and explored. Girls took pills or packets out of their bras or knickers and fed the boys. Everybody was drinking water, faces twisting in a munched up mash up of emotion.

Each floor had a different beat of music kicking out, most of it super fast high energy Techno. I didn't see much in the way of chill out areas. The floors were slippy and shrouded in Dry Ice, cigarette smoke highlighted the Lazar display splitting the prism of multicoloured beams from glitter balls and spinning lights on the gantries above.

A couple of hours later we were dancing on one of the main floors when there was the usual scuffle of two or three Bouncers heading through the crowd. We were used to that, there were often a couple of lads who had to spoil it for the rest, kicking off as some bloke has looked their way too long or jogged their elbow. A few moments passed and the dancers to either side seemed to slow down to a stop and step back. We did the same as the bouncers returned with a young lad who was motionless. Frozen in his stance, caught like a Still Life photo of a runner just out of the blocks, pouring with sweat.

The guys carrying him had grabbed his body at both ends like a sheet of plywood. He hung there between them like a frozen mannikin, unbending, unmoving, unstuck, unmasked, unlucky. As he passed us we could see his clothes were wringing wet, his hair was plastered flat and he was probably unrepairable. An expression was die cast on his face, of terror confronted with utter hopelessness. Minutes earlier he had been dancing like all the others. Maybe he would die right now, as his glazed eyes strobed past us, or perhaps on the stairs down, or in the Ambulance; or possibly in an hour or two, in a small frantic heap of tubes and bleeps in Intensive Care as his parents watched, helpless to help.

There was no way he was coming back from that. I knew that look, as a drug user I'd seen it before. It was the expression of a guy who had just shot up the wrong, or the strong, shit. It was so fast, like a blaze of Napalm going through an old hay stack on a summer's day. The rush had just blown the central control system of his brain to pieces. I'd been on that runway, watching the guy in front slam on the tarmac. No coming back from that, no antidote, no god or goddess, in reply to any mewling, is going to fix that.

That was proof enough for me, as regards Ecstasy. I felt vindicated in my suspicions, in future I would stick to what I knew and trusted, Opium, Heroin and Morphine; the Holy Triumvirate.

Though naturally air, water and abstinence would have been a better idea they hardly set the tone for an interesting story, other than Ecclesiastical. As time has passed the use of Ecstasy, like Cannabis, has gained more credence in medical practice; but their controlled micro dosing is nothing compared to a turbo charged 'Mitsubishis' we used to take.

The saddest, cruellest most ridiculous part of the whole four minutes between the rush inwards of the bouncers and their hurried retreat with the boy was the music never really skipped a beat. However, the dancers nearest the corpse all fell into slow motion as their lips turned from smiles to gripped tight. We all stared into his look less eyes. As the last bouncer left, the space behind gradually filled and the bodies began to speed back up. Five minutes later all trace of the tragedy was removed, as if a small slice of one hour was secretly removed, its history rewritten.

We had also dropped some 'Mitsubishis' that night, a fairly popular type of Ecstasy, tried and tested by thousands of Clubbers; but nobody can really tell how each heart will react.

Having spent years with a syringe in one hand and a bag full of 'Gear' in the other I knew only too well how much of a lottery taking drugs and surviving is. Death is an 'Occupational Hazard,' with addiction. Whether it's Heroin or Paracetamol, the wrong dose is fatal. If it came from a pharmacy I could at least add up the milligrams. Powders, potions and lotions that come from an unknown source are an unknown quantity, until they're inside you. I think that was the last time I took 'E's.'

I knew how to reach Nirvana, my way, I had several ladders propped up against that mountain; why on earth would I want to risk a rope swing? If it came down to having to participate fully in such events then Cocaine was an adequate tool and less likely to kill you with one glance.

At the start of the girl's Third Year the Millennium had seemed so far away. They all had so much to think about the subject was shelved, except for the inevitable dinner party where people shared dreams of what they were planning to do, if they could get a babysitter for less than a grand, if they had a baby at all.

Merely a year later, the ex students were beginning their careers and suddenly the Millennium was going to be next year! Everything had moved so fast, from those blissful fields of careless timelessness to this countdown of minutes and seconds to zero.

Most of our friends from Oxford had headed to the big city, while we returned to little Toddington, that renowned centre of non commerce, based on one shop, one pub. Opportunities in a Media Career for Maud, which was her goal, didn't go past being a Barmaid in the Local. Not good. I knew her mother would kick my ass for that. But luckily a girlfriend of mine got her a start with Eagle Media in Stratford.

Then my daughter Saffron came to live with us, in a caravan in the garden. My sister Clare had bought a house in Brighton. I felt blessed all the women in my life were happy. Meanwhile, it was endless events, trips, clubs, parties, weddings, birthdays, filming, gigging, recording, writing, open mic'ing and loving.

There must have been a day back there, many days in fact, when everything was pretty much perfect, as perfect as perfect ever gets.

The band extended with another Sax player, a singer or two and a host of guests who came along to have a go at a song or just enjoy a session.

The band name was fixed as Cosmic Smiles. It came about by indecision. But everybody presumed the band were called Cosmic Smiles when they saw the cover of the first CD; so we were stuck with it. Ultimately it would stick to me and I would become Mr Cosmic Smiles in a future life. That was never part of the plan, not that I ever had a plan.

The second album 'Freedom Road' featured a cover with photos from the John Lennon Peace memorial in Prague. We had taken them on a trip there. It was a fortunate occurrence as the following year brought huge floods to the city and all the artwork and graffiti was destroyed. Emily, who had got Maud her job with Eagle, had an artistic father Chris, who did a sterling job computerising the cover. Meanwhile the band and the music just got better and better.

Then I heard about a Viola player who lived next door to my dear Canadian friends Greg and Linda. He was Malcolm Henderson and the longest serving member of the English Symphony Orchestra. He had actually played the Albert Hall and the Carnegie Hall, whereas I had only played the Bus Stops. He knew all the notes and exactly in what order they went.

But jamming with the band and our way of making music was a revelation to him. All his life he had played his viola, faithfully following the notes on the stave. He remarked that he had never turned up to a practice session to be presented with basically a blank sheet of paper, an unwritten Score. No Time Signature, no Key, no Sharps or Flats, no Notes. He admitted to me that many of his fellow musicians would struggle with that, despite all the years of training.

He also said after a particular song, that I had broken every rule in music by changing from one chord to another in a particular sequence; but that the effect was stunning. I was pleased with that.

Malcolm came along to help add another flavour to the third album 'Love Love Love.' At the time his partner was a very famous business woman. She, sadly was dying of cancer. The mother of my children, Sandie, was very ill too.

You can feel the all the 'Love, Life and Death' in that album. We worked on that one during the years before and after the Millennium.

The excitement of anticipation and the ever hopeful dream that somebody, somewhere out there in the music or art world would hear us and pull us up to the next level was palpable. We were pretty much as good as anybody else out there, just maybe not as commercial. I knew it wasn't enough to be good. I needed a bit of help from the gods and no doubt the goddesses of Fortune. How I prayed for that bit of luck, all my life.

The World crept forward to its biggest party, people planning on either spending, earning or wasting the moment. I had tried to organise Fantasia holding their party at Toddington Manor. We just might have pulled it off. I warned the brothers not to advertise it in the local press until the last possible moment, as the Manor was owned by a Sheik and one of his assistants was living in the bungalow next to the driveway on the estate.

I had hoped to win 'Ronnie Raphael' over, or just prayed maybe he would be away with the Sheik at that time and we could quietly sneak five thousand ravers, the rigs, the marquees and light shows, in and out of the building without anybody knowing a thing.

Ahh, the joys of naivety.

A feature story in the Cheltenham Echo put the cat amongst the Pigeons and the word came down from London that there was to be no chance of any party happening. Even with a huge sum of money being offered for the hire of the venue. The problem with a Sheik was there is no price high enough to tempt such a rich man out of his comfort zone.

So the Fantasia event was moved to another stately home, not so far away, towards Stratford on Avon.

It was a good time to be around on Planet Earth. I had begged many people to think about the issues of progress and regress, how far we had really come as Human Beings. But it all fell on deaf ears. Most people were either intent on blowing a fortune, making a fortune or just blowing their minds.

Christmas and my birthday passed. We had been to London to see Maud's family and our friends up there. Xena had departed on her round the world trip and as far as we knew Howie had also left to do the same thing. As they were sort of an item once upon a time I suggested they might meet up somewhere out there. It never came to pass.

There were new jobs, new lives, new everything, all poised for this great moment. The media was full of it, the TV and Radio programmes were relentless in harping on about what was going to happen and whether all the computers in the world might crash at midnight? Would planes fall out of the sky and all the knowledge stored be lost?

People were being paid thousands just to sit and watch the screen, in case something went wrong. I heard of people supposedly going round 'Millennium Proofing' computers. Which meant little more than turning up at an office, fiddling around for a couple of hours on the screen, making sure not to change a single thing, whilst looking studious and concerned. Then heave a big sigh of relief, pick up an enormous cheque and disappear. I think I missed my one and only opportunity in the computer business.

When it came to the actual night, New Year's Eve 1999, it rained. Typical, Mother Nature was going to add her scorn to the whole event.

We parked up in a field for the Fantasia event, next to hundreds of others. We had a free entry. Sadly the event wasn't held inside the Manor House as we had planned to do at Toddington. It was basically a massive marquee, next to ramps of floodlights and toilet blocks. The queues for these became one of the most entertaining parts of the night as everyone tried to max out their dope and Coke in the final hours leading up to the big moment.

We were inside. The whole tent was full of writhing half naked people, trying their best to feel this was one night like no other. It had some great moments, but ultimately it came down to the final Countdown.

Hundreds of us, all screaming. "Ten, nine, eight, seven, six, five, four, three, two... One!"

Happy New Year. 2000.

ETA

I turned left onto the motorway at Tewkesbury and headed south towards Somerset. It was a typically busy Friday, the weather was fine and perhaps it was a school holiday too, thus all three lanes were bumper to bumper with cars, coaches and lorries. I pottered along, slower and slower until the vehicles in front were at a stop. Start. Stop. Standstill.

I waited, I knew it would be like this as I had done the journey a hundred times before. Usually it would clear a bit, slow down at Bristol, speed up and chug to a grinding snail's pace past Weston Super Mare as 'Kiss Me Quick' tourists headed for the ice cream parlours and slot machines on its famous pier.

Unusually for me, I turned on the radio to get some travel news. It was a pot shot in the dark whether I would wait five or fifty minutes for the next update. A short while later I heard the motorway was jammed from Stroud to Weston, all the way.

I was used to riding these things out, but even more unusually for me I decided to bail and turn off at the next exit. There was no rush. I was heading down to visit Sandie, the mother of my daughter and adopted son. I had been down a couple of months before when she was in hospital, during a severe bout of illness. We were always friends, she trusted me and knew I would walk across hot coals for the children. She looked thin, her skin was always slightly tanned, but now it was tinged with an airbrush of yellow.

We talked about Kane for awhile. His real father was always a point of debate for us as he had resurfaced from America a couple of years previously. We were both concerned he would show up on the doorstep unannounced, but he hadn't.

"Heard from Bill at all?" I asked.

"Nothing since the last time. Maybe he's given up, thank god." She sighed, she had always told Kane that I was his real father and that was that. I always gave Sandie the last word on anything to do with the kids. I am a fervent believer that the mother's view should be respected, above all, when it comes to decisions about the children.

"Phew. Well that's one less worry." I held her hand, it was thin and weak. "But hey, what's happening? What are the doctors saying? Do they know what's wrong with you yet?"

Sandie had been ill for many years to a greater or lesser degree. Her physical problems stemmed to a degree in some way from being generally broke and at the tail end of the drug distribution network. She had always enjoyed opiates, as I did, but her options were limited by no transport and less money.

The fact is by the time a drug reaches the outskirts of the suburbs or villages it has been tampered with. 'Cut' and then 'Cut' again. The more this happens the bigger the chance that some of the powder used to cut the drugs would be toxic in its own right. By the time Brown Heroin reached the outer villages of Somerset it could be mixed with anything vaguely brown. It was a war of attrition. Attrition won.

"Well they said it looks like my liver is pretty bad. It probably is, but they reckon it's at least three years before it becomes really serious," she paused, then added, "and terminal." Sandie didn't seem to be too concerned about it. In hindsight I wonder now if the doctors were being totally straight with her, or had they just diagnosed her badly?

Saffron had already left home to work with horses, Kane was fairly wedded to his work in a bike shop and spent much of his free time with the family of his best mate in 'Bridgy.' Then Simon, her partner who had lived at the house in Bawdrip for years, left. He had been just a lodger for most of that time and then they had fallen in love out of the blue. It was intense and so beautiful. They loved each other in the way teenagers do, it was as if they had never loved before. Sandie rallied and was perhaps at her best during that time. Then it crashed. I have no idea why. But I guess that broke her already broken heart.

I came off the motorway at the next roundabout and found a lay-by. I sent a text on my Mobile Phone to say I had turned back as the traffic was grid locked, but I would pop down as soon as possible, on the next available weekend.

After years of having to ring the neighbour's phone and ask them to pop next door, it was now so easy to send a text. Too easy.

I hadn't heard much from her or the children. She had become weaker faster than expected over those few months since my last trip. For years thereafter I regretted nobody had told me, perhaps I should have asked, but I didn't suspect anything. I had rekindled my teaching career and was dealing with the chaos of a 'Special Needs' school. I had been asked to fill a temporary post for two terms in Woodwork, or Design and Technology. Then the PE Teacher, a big presence in the School left suddenly and I took over his job. Plus I had all the ex curricula activities of my life, Maud, the band, the gigs.

Of course, no matter what the excuse I should have realised, or intuitively known that the situation was deteriorating. Some of these thoughts occupied my mind as I turned back home.

I stopped at a garage and noticed the date on a digital display blinking '2000! 2000!' as I filled 'Trusty Rusty,' my Cortina, with twenty quid's worth of fuel. I wondered? A new century. What would it bring?

A few weeks later I got a call, from Nadja, Sandie's best friend, her 'Soul Sister.' I knew from her voice that something was wrong. Sandie was dead.

I had missed her. I was so upset. The fucking traffic and god damn fate had denied me that last meeting. She was a heartbeat I had shared once, the mother of my children. Oh God? The children!

It dawned on me that History was in many ways repeating the experience I had with my mother. This was happening to the children as it happened to me. Circles of death in life. The reoccurring nightmare. I had missed her.

It I had made it down the motorway and seen her, she might well have been able to tell me that a short time before, during an argument with Kane, she had finally admitted to him that I wasn't his father. I might have been able to talk to him before he shut me out.

I had missed her and therefore knew nothing of this until just before or after the funeral I think. I can't remember whether Kane came up and questioned me about it, or if I was told by Saffron that he knew. Bad memories are sometimes blurred.

I remember everybody was kind to everybody at the wake. That was how Sandie would have wanted it. Her parents were there. We all knew we had lost a beautiful friend, a special lady. It is the worst thing a parent can endure, to lose a child seems inherently wrong, the old should go first...Willingly!

Sadly, ironically, I may as well have buried my son on that day too, for it would be the last time he ever spoke to me.

Thus goes the story of Life.

Sandie had made a couple of bad choices in her life. Her marriage at an early age to her husband Steve was one; he had been cruel to her and maybe that sparked her wildness and some of her sadness, her need to fill a hole in her heart. Their marriage didn't last. She had worked successfully in London as a Seamstress making Hippy clothes for Pop Stars and suchlike, but for some reason returned to Kent.

We had met on a crazy stage, full of electric tripping visuals dripping off the walls, or more accurately, 'Tripping' on Acid in a squat on the London Road in Maidstone. Jim and Nadia had set up the place, he was such a talented artist in the line of Renaissance Fairy and Goblin painting, spending hours, days, on 'Speed' or 'Coke; drawing intricate pictures.

While in the back room we hid like stealth bombers, unfolding the packets and the paraphernalia of our drug use. The trip we shared, the life and death of it all was intense, thirty six hours flying, two dawns, straight through. But then a friend Bernie and shortly after Jim fell through the cracks. That was a loss of an amazing artist, but also a man muddling with relationships, games in games, shattering the crystal ball. Bernie's death was just plain awful. He had such an attractive girlfriend and a beautiful baby boy. One night two Irish junkies were over at his flat and Bernie had passed out, way too stoned already. The story goes the guys decided to steal his drugs, which they did. They shot him up, injected him while he was asleep to make sure he didn't come after them. He never woke up. They had overdosed him and killed him. He was the first of my junkie friends to die, Jim the second, there would be so many more, too many and now Sandie.

Sandie had always been on the periphery in the London road squat, she was Bill's girlfriend; that was cool with me, I only wanted her friendship, I was way too on the outside of 'Outside' to have any inkling to get fucked in that place. But one night we were both tripping on the bed and she asked me if I wanted to make love with her. Well, firstly she was Bill's lady and secondly I was flying Astral Airways at the time. But we did have a moment of communion that night on some other level of being, I remember feeling as if we had joined our souls somewhere between the kissing and fondling. Then I thought no more of it and went in search of the next fix.

London Road was hippy commune in the vaguest of terms, which having lived on one side of the road, after Jim's overdose, crossed over to the other, literally and metaphorically.

I preferred the original basement warren of rooms. Usually in Alan's room with Gaz, getting high and then wandering off to the Photo Booth in town and taking some mad pictures, covered in makeup and smashed across the universe. They took the tripping Trip to the very last Terminal on an Unguided Tour of the Universe; while I pushed my body relentlessly as far as the needle could go. I had no fear and less brains. It's a miracle none of us blew a fuse.

We were honestly, completely, all crazy then. It was as if, inspired by the stories of famous adventurers during our childhood, Scott, Mallory, Cook and the greatest of all, Captain Kirk of the USS Enterprise, we also had to, 'Explore strange new worlds…to boldly go where no man has gone before.'

I did see and experience some events, either outside or inside my mind, that are inexplicable in ordinary language. I have wandered through scenes which mimicked Tolkien's vision. I've met those fairies and goblins Jim drew and fallen through the volcanic crust to the Orcs and 'The Horror.'

Those excesses of physical experience will never be repeated by any generation, for we were literally flying blind, en masse into the unknown. Men and women had conquered land, sea and air before, but nobody had set a rocket off inside their brains and followed the trajectory as far as possible.

I like to imagine some crazy scientists, before even Owsley started the whole LSD thing, in some lab with crazy smiles on their faces suggesting, 'Hey

Professor, let's give the rabbits some of this new psychedelic candy and see what they make of it...'
The next day they return to find the Laboratory is in ruins, all the bunnies have vanished and Pandora just blew the hinges off her box.

If Sandie hadn't come along a year or so later, pregnant with Kane, minus Bill who had then run off to America, I would no doubt have lost it, run out of my luck somewhere between eighteen and twenty one. I had so many near misses with death, as well as the paracetamol there was the day I sat with an ampoule of Adrenalin from my father's doctor bag thinking, 'I wonder what will happen if I shoot this up?' Also the times I just took anything with 'Poison' on the label, crushed it up and shot it up. It should have been me not Sandie that blew a fuse.

But I never thought the boy Kane, who I loved as any father does, willing his successes, lamenting his failures, would dump me so profoundly. I nicked him his first bike for fuck's sake. Boy I loved that boy.

If Sandie had not told him the truth I guess I might have admitted it, unless she had made me promise on her death bed not to. I would have obeyed her as she was the 'Mother.' I respected her dominion. It was like that from day one and would always have been like that. Her child, her decision. I was sure he would come round one day. He didn't. He hasn't.

The drive back, leaving the children, had always been awful, the Sunday afternoon departure, the mournful morning, the pit in the stomach, the wave of that small hand at the window destroyed me. I'd spent years, forever leaving. I hate Goodbyes.

All those weekends and all the heartbreak, the pain of trying to give a month's worth of love to a child in a weekend, the constant wondering and the sorrow, down and up, distant parenting, the indistinct voice on the neighbour's phone, the touch less, hand less, finger less, kiss less, hug less, 'Love you, love you.'

Introducing new girlfriends, lost that one but got this one, the rooms, the old motorbike and the cars, all come all gone. All a picture to hold in the mind as the telephone stared faceless at the reflection of the wallpaper in the window by the door. I missed one of those damn visits and lost my boy forever.

I drove back slowly from the funeral. The view from Sandie's front room was gone forever. The garden where Killer the cat was so clumsy he used to fall off the wall, Sam the dog, who was so big he was really a small bear in disguise. Olly and Oscar at the table, Dave, Plug, Duncan, Simon, Nad, Bev, names frayed in kohl cotton or fading like old Levis by endless washing in soapy memories.

I loved them all.

The hill between Bawdrip and the motorway wound upwards into the sky. I glanced in my rear view mirror at King Sedgemoor's Drain glinting in the cold sun, a silver arrow across the marshes of my heart.

I thought of all the years, over now. The hundreds of visits and yet I had missed the most important one, the last one. That's Life's way of building a regret for the long grey afternoons of old age. I can scream, 'It wasn't the way I planned it man,' to the silent hours, through the bleak violet hours, but nothing can be rewritten, retold, reworked, which is dead and gone.

I returned to the cottage, to my life as a Special Needs Teacher which had taken off in a big way the previous year. The 'CDT' was a laugh because I was as clueless as the kids, I was never a Handyman, despite all my years on building sites. I wasn't the kind of guy you would find cobbling something up in his shed, I never had a shed. However I knew where these kids were coming from and I had one big advantage I was probably about as far out and wild as they were.

Just before I began this part time job, a few boys from the 'Romantic' bands had been down to the Cotswolds riding horses at The Vine and goodness knows what else. All the Jack Daniel's calendar had written on it for that week or so was 'Cocaine Daze.'

However, in accordance with National Guidelines I must have straightened myself up and made a good impression on the boys and staff. However, nobody mentioned to me the stuff we made all our designs out of, 'MDF,' was reasonably toxic, a popular kind of composite board made from powdered wood and glue. Needless to say we spent months in a dust cloud of this stuff, knocking up CD boxes and funky bits of useless crap. I knew where these kids heads were at.

It was quite a good deal for me as there was no real commitment to the staff room bollocks. I was billed as 'Long Term Supply.' But that all changed towards the end of the Summer term when a chance remark led to me getting a permanent full time job as the P.E. Teacher. A dream job.

This was another subject I technically knew nothing about, other than I owned a body and had survived endless PE lessons as a schoolboy myself, but hey, I could find out all I needed to know in the textbook. I was used to being about a page or two ahead of the students in some subjects I had taught. As long as it was that way round and not two pages behind.

Computer Studies was the limit of this strategy I knew nothing about that and I relied totally on subterfuge, or simple bribery and blackmail of the kids to survive a term of that. In fact I recently met two young men outside a shop in Winchcombe I vaguely recognised. "Hey, Smiles, do you remember me, you used to teach us Computer and Information Technology?" I looked at the name of the Plumbing firm emblazoned on his overalls and thought to myself, 'That figures.'

The previous 'Head of PE,' had been a key member of the staff in the school; I was warned once or twice I had 'big shoes' to fill. To which I replied, 'That's ok, I'll provide my own trainers.'

However, it was unmistakably a full on Full Time job, demanding a lot more than just turning up, covering a few lessons and going home.

The first year, from September to the next summer was flat out. Including all the millennium stuff on the go. I had to learn a new subject, run the curriculum, suss out the Examination process and basically blague my way through it with no broken bodies or major disasters. Sandie died in the middle of this.

It was crazy, busy, hectic and majorly stressful in the way only Special Needs teaching can be, as it was called then. The first thing I did was install a huge sound system in the ceiling rafters of the gym connected to a multi CD changer so we could have music all day. Then I painted the walls with targets and patterns to look really funky. My Form classroom had one wall totally covered in a collage of pictures from magazines: including cars, watches, speed boats, planes, models, stars, and super stars. The boys thought it was great, super cool.

We battled on. Of course there was a small catch with this new job, Ofsted, the dreaded government school's inspection bureau were descending on us just before Christmas. I took the job on reckoning I could get away with only months of paperwork as I had just started the job. Other teachers were not so lucky, trying to provide the backlog years of Lesson Plans they had never written or taught anyway.

They had my sympathy. I can faithfully say I hardly planned a lesson past morning Break because I never knew what was going to happen, so much depended on the boy's moods, the in school politics and whether someone had a vendetta planned for that day. The only thing I could predict reliably was an air of impending doom, threat or general chaos.

Although the classes were as little as five to ten boys in number, every one of our boys was worth a classroom full from any other school. We demanded a high pedigree of student, if they hadn't burnt down their previous school, tried to stab a teacher or pupil then they really were not up to our standard. On the other hand, despite Ofsted, it was quite a liberal era with exceptional conditions for teaching children.

Some years later, teaching became the sterile, pre programmed, grey dirge of regurgitated Government dictated, nationwide slop it is now. Lessons dreamt up by some moron in an office who had never taught kids like ours. It was a bland system designed to quantify and specify children, to give them an across the board, unilateral dose of the same crap, at the same time of the year with every lesson scripted. Children do not learn or function like that, especially the young characters I taught.

There are three ways to motivate and control a child at school. One, 'Do this task and I will give out the chocolate.' Two, 'Do this or I will take the chocolate away.' Or, Three, 'Do this because I have made the task so interesting and relevant, also I have earned your respect to such an extent that you want to do your best, willingly for me.'

I fathomed this out teaching English at the first place I worked in called Adlestrop Park School; as mentioned in the famous poem by Edward Thomas, near Stow On The Wold. Maths, Geography, Science and so on can all be added up and subtracted as subjects; there are facts to learn and facts to recite. However, to get a child to use their imagination is not something that can be wrung out of them. A teacher can make a child learn ten new words, spell ten new words, but it is impossible to force them to use those ten words imaginatively. There had to be another way to inspire these children. I discovered the third way.

It is the same with Sport. A child chasing a stick will run, a child being chased with a stick will run faster, but a child running to impress their parent or teacher will always run the fastest.

Usually everything and everybody in their lives had failed these boys at their previous schools, so it was down to me in my little PE Department to try to rebuild them.

I knew the body and the mind were closely linked and I began to try to raise their expectations. But there was no way these kids were going to do Press Ups all day, or train at Gymnastics. I had to work round their prejudices against anything 'Boring.' I bought a complete Gym, about twenty machines, from an advert I found in my local newspaper and we started 'Weight Training.' This was viewed as a far more 'Manly macho' pastime and before the little buggers knew what had hit them they were starting to get fitter and stronger.

In general my pupils had the physical attributes and a natural talent for sports that was just short of next to nothing. It was hard In some ways for me, with a natural physique and having played top class sports at school, to be teaching this set of three legged, six toed, goggle eyed Muppets, bless them! I'm not being cruel, but playfully fairly honest, though I do appreciate that teachers, even retired ones, referring to children as, 'Six toed Muppets,' is not current 'Best Practice' in the modern curriculum for all things blinking 'Politically Correct.'

However, as a cultural observation, one would still have to remark that the boys I taught tended to be either malnourished or over nourished, super tall or rather short, ridiculously fast or inordinately slow. There wasn't one that fitted a vague approximation of being 'Normal.' Every one of them was a winner, when it came to losing.

However, in amongst the crew were a few boys who defied the trend, but often only in one small vista of achievement. They were perhaps good at football or basketball; but this didn't mean a full grasp of the game. It was more due to a case of hyper, continual, obsessive, compulsive, repetition of one behaviour. Delroy B was a great footballer, but too good to be good, he almost just couldn't get down off his cloud to hit the pitch. I wonder if he ever made it? He did however give me one of my teaching highlights, which was through massive coercion, corruption and bribery he managed to get an 'A' grade at GCSE a rare event in schools like ours.

But the best of all was a Basketball player called James Flecknor, nick named, 'Flex.' We were always generally getting slaughtered playing matches against other schools, as we had forty boys to choose from and they often had four hundred; even with my pleas for leniency to the opposing Coaches and the teams themselves. I often had to sneak over to the opposition's changing room and ask that once they were 'Five Nil' ahead, maybe they could ease back a bit. These 'normal' boys had no idea how cruel a defeat could be for our boys, how crushing for their dreams, especially when they usually only compared their day to day efforts against our other Six Toed Sloaths. But one remarkable day, we had our moment of glory that was worth all the defeats.

At Blockley School both teams trouped into the big gymnasium which doubled as a Basketball Court. We had a couple of benches to sit on along the side and the lads gathered round me as I gave them their 'Pep Talk.' They didn't really need that! Already instilled with a complete dearth of confidence, they were however full of bravado, bouncing about as if this was going to be a walk in the park. Of course, it was an act to cover up their lack of any real hope.

As I blabbed on, trying to be positive, I noticed Flecknor was quietly watching the other team and paying no attention to my speech. "Ok guys, you know the score, just do the best you can. I think you're amazing and remember what I told you."

"What was that, Sir?" A small thin scrap of a boy asked.

"That?" I looked for the face amongst the gangly gathering, "That....Is precisely what I told you not to forget!"

"Er, what Sir?"

"Typical!" We all laughed together. "Go on lads, give it your best shot, just do your best. I promise, if we lose by less than twenty points the Maccy Dee's Milkshakes are on me. Remember we only have forty boys to choose our team from."

"Yeah and thirty of them are wankers!" Chimed in another lad, full of faith in his school mates.

You had to be fast with these apprentice hecklers, so I quipped, "I know buddy, but we got the best ten tossers here. Right?"

He reluctantly nodded. It was a classic case of the 'Special Needs, we are a bunch of crap' syndrome. The ploy is to say, 'I'm a pile of shit,' quick enough, before anybody else gets it out, then at least the boy can claim the credit for his own slagging off, which is better than somebody else having it. The negative, back to front, upside down logic of these boys could be astounding at times and yet, often very astute.

As the two teams of players chosen to begin the match gathered around the Referee, it was so easy to spot the group that were mine. It was a blatant, clear visual representation of 'Special.' The other team all looked to be of fairly similar build and height; while my colourful lot ranged from 'Thin as a rake,' to borderline 'Ten Ton Tubby,' perhaps 'Knee high to a Grasshopper,' or, as in Flex's case, the worst example of a 'Lanky streak of piss' ever seen. He was just one long extendable limb, at the end of which, in or out of lessons, was always a basketball, his only real passion.

He was, to be fair, the main reason I had organised the match. Every boy had a spark in them and it needed careful encouragement to make it burn brighter and hopefully be strong enough to light a fire one day.

If the event was a complete disaster it could have the opposite effect of what I hoped to achieve and kill that flame forever. Dealing with these boys was like skating on ice carrying a flame thrower.

The match progressed slowly through the first three Quarters and into the last. To be honest the game had swung both ways, sometimes we were even in the lead. I can't remember exactly the way the game panned out, except that most of the time we spent catching up their score, only to fall behind again. But we reached the last quarter and the scores were pretty matched, or thereabouts.

During 'Time Out' they huddled round me. "Come on lads," I exhorted them, "We can do this. You have all been playing so well." To see their little eyes light up when I said that was just so wonderful. To be true, they were, with their excitable, erratic and somewhat overzealous efforts managing to pull off some great moves and score some baskets. It was generally Flex at the end, slam dunking the ball in.

Occasionally, one of my other boys would score and I could literally watch his chest puff up in front of me as he went running past.

The chosen lads, basketball teams are continually changed with 'Subs,' went back on the court for the last fifteen minutes. There was no mistaking when the match was going to be over as a massive clock, with an even bigger 'Second Hand,' was located at one end of the gym where everybody could see it.

The minutes ticked away, the 'Long Hand,' slowly heading up towards the twelve. They got a lead of a few points, then we got it back level and suddenly we were in front. The minutes were ticking towards the twelve. Maybe three to go. If only we could hang on to our lead long enough. Watching a national rugby game could not have gripped my sides anymore. I was shouting like a madman. We all were. Even the coach from the other team was off his seat sensing the excitement.

Then disaster struck. One minute to go. They scored. Shit. They were one measly, god damn, little point ahead. One of our boys hurriedly passed the ball out from the back wall, but I could see the look of frustration on his face. These boys were so used to failure they could smell it coming. God, why didn't the other team just let the poor little fuckers win for once.

But that was never going to happen, the opposing boys were just as wound up for the grand finale as mine were.

I didn't know what or where to look, at the players or at the clock. Every second lasted ten heartbeats, ten held breaths.

The Second Hand swung down to the bottom of the clock and passed the '6,' the ball was still in our half.

Flecknor was over on the right. In desperation one of our boys passed it to him, hoping for a miracle. The oppositions Basket was right under the clock. The entire team from the other school were closing in on Flex, trying to stop him getting any closer. Flex, like me, kept looking up at the second hand, darting left and right, trying to nip through a gap. It wasn't happening. They wouldn't let him move. He was getting boxed in on all sides and virtually back to where our basket was.

The Second Hand crept up to the '9.'

'Oh God, please...' I prayed. It reached the '10.'

I glanced back at Flex. He could see it creeping towards the '11.' He had two tall lads trying to block him from the front, the rest were around his legs.

He jumped. Higher than all of them. He aimed. He threw. Every pair of eyes in that gymnasium watched the flight of that ball as it went up and over all the boys.

For a moment, both the ball and the ticking Second Hand, clicking away the last seconds were visible in the same view. '5…4…3…'

Then, with just two seconds remaining, the orange ball fell, fair and square, right into the net. We were a point ahead. By the time the Ref blew his whistle the Second Hand had clicked the '12.' But we weren't looking at that. We were all dashing over the court to hug Flecknor. You could still hug kids and not get arrested in those days.

It was, no doubt, as good as it gets. I guess winning the FA Cup at Wembley on 'Injury Time,' could not feel any more ecstatic than that. Especially if it was, like us, a team from the 'Bottom Division.'

The minibus back to school was a riot of joy. Flex had acquitted himself well and earned his legendary status for all time.

At the entrance of the weight training gym I bought for the school a plaque states his name at the official opening. No mention of Mr Smiles, who got a bunch of boys out of a Beano cartoon to heroically perform like champions, but hey, that's life.

I had taught English at Swalcliffe for several years in the late Eighties and early Nineties, until the Bursar and Governors messed up the finances and had to let two teachers go, as they politely put it.

I remember walking down the school corridor and having a blinding flash of realisation, 'Gosh, I can get out of this Work shit, with an honourable discharge.' To be sacked was awful, but a redundancy was not my fault. Also, I could get back to doing some more creative pursuits.

There were only seven members of staff and all of them except the old Art Teacher Mike Manetta and myself had wives and kids at home. So I suggested to him we take the hit for the others.

He agreed. I had children, but not living with me. My 'Pay Off,' was six hundred pounds and I spent five hundred and ninety nine on a Canon Starwriter. With that I wrote 'EX' the first draft of my autobiography many years ago. But I was back as the PE teacher, with big boots to fill and yet I found I was naturally quite suited to the job.

I spent five days a week doing that, weekends with one foot in the music scene and one on the dance floor. I was also still doing articles and book reviews for Don't Tell It magazine. Maud was happy, often off filming, finally ensconced with Eagle Media as a Production Assistant. Life was full on.

Plus the band, the jams, the albums, the gym'ing, running and swimming, the wild Cocaine parties, the Mitsubishi nights, the Hashish and my usual dipping into some opiate or another.

At the same time as this, another tiny tragedy was unfolding in York at my Grandparents. It was hard to get up to see them regularly, as it was a fair drive and there were always other things I could be doing or was actually booked for. But two or three times a year I would find myself back in York.

For many years, apart from seeing Nanna and Uncle Bill, my main joy had been the Swimming Baths at Yearsley, built by Mr Joseph Rowntree, the famous Chocolate manufacturer of York; or to go jogging up and down the banks of the Ooze river.

I would also be doing the rounds of the Chemists to buy Gee's Linctus or something similar, a pleasant occupational pastime for a drug user. I also loved going to the Shambles and York Minster, a place my mother loved dearly. I enjoyed visiting the second hand shops and looking in the old toy shop where my father had once bought me a Balsa Wood model of an airplane.

My Nanna and Bill had been more like parents to me than my own at times. Now mine were both gone for good they did their best to be there for me. They both loved their little bairn. I was as near as Bill ever got to having a son and he took an interest in my travels and rise from doing exams at night classes to being a teacher.

But as time had gone on, Bill had retired from work or been made redundant, their lives, like most old people became generally poorer and poorer, despite Nanna having a purse about three inches wide with a wad of money she always kept.

Bill was in charge of shopping as Nanna didn't get out much now. Her days as a volunteer at the WRVS were over. She was always sitting in her armchair with the TV on, a cup of tea and a box of Menthol

Cigarettes, Consulate. My mother's suicide must have broken her heart, especially with Jean, her other daughter, semi in and out of depression and hospitals in Canada.

I did finally manage to get up to see them after Sandie's death. Everything seemed much the same, except I remarked they ate mainly, in fact only, Pork Pies for supper. Like many clues I missed it until the situation later became blatantly clear.

Bill became increasingly concerned they didn't have enough money to live on and took obsessive care spending their tiny pension each week. I have no idea whether this was actually true or not, perhaps it was all in his mind as I didn't think they were that hard up generally.

As a 'Health Freak' I knew that Pies of any sort were were not the best thing to live on for an old and weakening body. Indeed, I would go as far as to say Pork, in particular, in my utterly biased opinion, is just about as good as sewage as a form of nutrition.

My visit to York had been no different to any other in the past. Everything looked pretty much as it always did. I wandered off most days, round old and new haunts in York, sometimes busking. I had recently met the colourful homeless guy who had build a Cardboard House outside the main Theatre in York.

But one day I was pottering about downstairs at Nanna's and I met Bill heading along the corridor. I asked him, "Alright Bill, how you feeling?"

You had to be careful around him, he could be very terse and quite curt if he wanted to be. In fact he had become quite irritable as he got older, but no more really than any other old fool.

He stopped in front of me and pulled my head close to his, "She's not your Nanna, you know?" His small dark eyes, deep nutmeg with fear, above his greying moustache. "She's an imposter."

By the time I had registered what was happening he had trundled off to the toilet. Had I heard him correctly? Surely it must be a misunderstanding. But from that moment on I began to watch him more closely and it soon began to be blatantly bleeding obvious he was going mad.

Bill, fearing poverty, had starved his brain and body to the point that, without any proper vitamins, it was rotting, setting off little wild fires in his head, called 'Aneurysms.'

One of the main themes of this book is that nobody in their right mind wakes up one day and decides to begin a train of small events that will eventually fuck up their entire life. Shit happens, monumentally and never coming from just one orifice. While we quietly get on with the day to day business of surviving life the universe and everything else it can throw at us, something often takes place in the wings of the stage that will ultimately impact all the actors. A bit like costal erosion, nobody really thinks one sand dune blown away will lead to a hillside collapsing, but it does, it will and more than that it's bound to be the hillside I just camped on!

Further to this is seems that advice given with the best of intentions can sometimes lead indirectly to a disaster. This was the case with my advice to Howie and perhaps in some bizarre way with Hannah.

Hannah had a smile that could have made millions advertising toothpaste. She was young, beautiful and intelligent. She was part of the 'Toddy Crew' by virtue of her brother Sam Timmings and a girl called Sarah Luckett being her best friend. I was blest to have these young people in my extended family of friends due to my performing at the local pubs and letting them party at Toddington Manor. I also looked after these 'Young'uns' if I thought they were getting into deep water with life; I would offer my advice from the Cosmic Smiles Guide to the Universe, on the basis that I had either experienced what they were going through or knew somebody who had. I had after all learnt a lot about love, life and the other shit death.

It's such an odd random connection of events, but reflects precisely what I want to get across, in that it life's fuck ups are not always our fault, they just happen even when trying with the best of intentions, to encourage a young man to persevere with his quest for love.

So Sarah had a boyfriend, I'm not sure of the exact details, none of my f'ing business, but I do know he was from New Zealand. How they got together in England is a mystery to me but they had and the guy was much in love with her but had to return to New Zealand. At some point after this he had decided Sarah was the love of his life and he was going to propose to her. The only inconvenience was they lived roughly eleven thousand six hundred and seventeen miles apart, coast to coast, as the Crow flies.

However, he got his act together, bought her a ring and told all his friends and family in New Zealand he was going over to England to get down on one knee and do the deed. Which he duly did.

Sarah, however, said 'No.'

His visit had coincided with one of my parties at the Manor and about three o'clock in the morning I found him on the front steps, due to depart for New Zealand, minus his girlfriend and about as utterly miserable as a poor young boy can be.

I tried to cheer him up and offered him my insight on the topic of love. "Hey buddy. Listen, I know you must feel awful about how things have turned out and pretty sick going home to all your folks without Sarah by your side. I guess you're going to feel a bit shit and even embarrassed you didn't pull it off."

He nodded in miserable agreement.

I persevered, "But do you, really and totally, despite this setback, still love Sarah completely?"

"Sure, of course. I've never loved anybody like this."

"Utterly and completely…?"

"Yeah, I swear. Sarah's the one. I just don't know what I'm going to do with my life now. I'm broken."

"Ok buddy. Well don't give up hope, because I can assure you from my experience in life that such utter love and devotion will bring to you another chance. Such a perfect love, such a devoted heart cannot be denied in life. If your heart is totally true and honest life will make another moment happen for you."

He looked up at me, "Do you really think so?"

"I can guarantee that any dedication, such as you have shown cannot go unrewarded by the Gods of Fate." Before he could say it, I said, "This isn't some Hippy dippy shit man, this is really the way the laws of life and love operate. Trust me. Keep da faith and the faith will keep you."

I saw him smile for the first time that night. "Ok, thanks. I guess I could come back again next year."

"You'll never know buddy, unless you try and really believe in that love."

Which is pretty much what happened and this time Sarah said yes. This all sounds so beautiful and yet it's as if life just can't let a good thing go without their being some twist in the tale. Having got married Sarah obviously moved to New Zealand to live with her beau and a year or so later Hannah decided to go out and spend Christmas with her.

I remember a big bonfire we had just days before she left, in the field next to the church in Toddinton where the Toddy crew had once had a caravan. I remember so clearly the darkness beyond the fire and occasionally seeing the flash of Hannah's smile as she glanced over at me. That smile was so bright, so hopeful, so young, so perfectly beautiful.

On this holiday Hannah fell in head over heels in love with a dashing young Kiwi she met who also happened to be a helicopter pilot.

I think it was New Year's day or thereabouts that he offered to fly her over some of New Zealand's scenic landscapes, probably with plans to stop off at some romantic location. What could be more perfect?

But tragically they crashed.

Somewhere in a landscape dominated by steep riff valleys covered in a dense layer of trees and foliage. Despite every effort it was virtually impossible to locate a wreck in that kind of terrain. It would be ten years before somebody stumbled upon the mangled remains of the helicopter.

I can only hope they both died on impact, in each other's arms.

Sadly I have often considered the trail of events and thought that if I hadn't encouraged that young man to pursue his love he may not have returned, they might not have got married and Sarah wouldn't have moved to New Zealand. Thus Hannah wouldn't have gone to spend a holiday with her best girlfriend.

Such is life and love.

Howard Piper, Howie, was a similar notion of regret for me. I often wondered if our conversation about what to do post college had born fruit? Indeed, he had decided to go off on a world tour starting in the east. We used to receive occasional photos from him, dramatically poised on concrete breakwaters or languishing in some tropical bar. But then the news filtered through of fate's cruel betrayal of that boy's future. Howie had gone 'White Water Rafting' in Malaysia, I think it was. The boat had capsized and he had got wedged under a submerged tree trunk. It was a horror story. I thought of what he had written on my copy of his video and his quote in the St Hugh's Yearbook, 'I will remember a video I made that even if no one else does, I will love till I die.' He also wrote, 'I did more things than I needed to and more things than I should have done and had a laugh from beginning to end.' With typical altruism he stated, 'Wishing everybody every success in the future and my warmest memories.'

It was just pure tragedy.

The funeral wasn't much better, crowds of weeping students and after the service when I attempted to follow the hearse to the burial, in another church, I got lost and had Clarice, Xena and Maud all weeping in the back of the cortina. Not my finest hour.

As I've tried to state, sometimes our best intentions in complete innocence lead to the worst outcomes and nobody ever wakes up one fine morning and decides, 'Today I will start a small train of events that will ultimately fuck up my life.' But it happens.

ZETA

I returned from a Christmas visit myself at Nanna's in York to get back to teaching which, looking at my Jack Daniel's calendar from that year, seemed to be all consuming at the time. I can tell from the brief comments that I am not enjoying and resisting the 'Nine to Five' studiously but with little hope of any change. To work with my highly colourful teenage boys, many of whom had a predilection for chaos, violence, or just pure mischief making, was not an easy job. In my heart of hearts I was yearning for those casual weeks spent in the arms of Oxford's charms. I was hating the pressure to conform to some kind of banal routine, but there was no other course for me or us at the time. My debts had been mounting slowly but surely and now I had at least a reasonable salary I could make some repayments.

It seemed almost unreal after the delights of nearly three years living the life of an overgrown, over aged student. Suddenly I was the teacher, not the prodigal pupil. I was thrust back into the prison of Monday to Friday work life. In the back of my mind I could hear W.H.Auden, the poet, muttering that it was a Poet's duty not to work, to find the acres of time needed to commune with the Muse. I had realised many years before, that 'They' could try to get the money back off me but they'd never get the 'Time' back.

However, there was more important things to think about too; I couldn't shake the memory of Bill's odd words. I called my sister and told her I was worried about whether Nan and Bill were going to be alright. I asked if she had noticed any strange happenings on her last visit and to keep an eye out on her next. We were very close when it came to family matters as there wasn't much family to fight over.

In our separate ways we had both been deeply affected by our teenage life at home. I wasn't aware of how off the rails Clare had been, due in her step mother's jaundiced view to the influence of her narcotic brother. I learnt much later that while she still lived with our father she had been in and out of hospital several times as a teenager, overdosing by chance or desperation, no doubt searching for the mother's love she had never really found in the first place.

When David had died she was around twenty years old. She had left home for college in Cambridge, but when that didn't work out she returned to Ilkley and then settled for awhile in Bristol. Sadly this was just about the time I left it, always a theme in our lives.

Then with Mark, her new boyfriend, who seemed pleasant enough, albeit a bit lacklustre, she moved to Brighton. She began her gardening business in earnest and got a mortgage on a terraced house on one of the sloping side streets that crawl up from the famous pink Pavilion. She seemed to settle down and be quite at one with the universe, to the extent she was happy enough to have a child, Jessica.

I never understood how she managed to pay her mortgage off several years later, sell up and have so much money left in equity, until Shiela, the evil step mother, informed me in an off hand way, 'I bought that funny little cottage for her...'

I went up to visit Clare with Maud at some point in the summer of 2000. The house was slightly chaotic with her two Lurchers and young Jessica, but it was a happy home. At a glance Clare obviously seemed to be in charge; she ran her gardening business with gusto and a lot of hard physical work, while Mark held the fort and helped out at a pre school nursery.

Maud and I wandered the happy hippy stalls of the town on our way to the Pier and stony beach. Like a million holiday makers we raced the waves up and down the shore, climbed over the Break Waters and chucked stones a million years back into the sea. We fell in each other's arms as lovers do and somewhere above the roar of the shingle and the music from the arcades our song of love soared.

Never forgetting my art I took a tape recorder with me as I loved recording random stuff for the albums I was making, to use as ambience. I captured the Fairground on the Pier and groups of lads chanting Football hymns, as it was the European Cup that year. I found it an inspiring place, full of the Gay and Lesbian communities that had regrouped here when London became too expensive or too hot to handle.

I remembered the weekends that Dr Barry St-John Neville used to send me down to meet Bob, or some other man, to earn myself forty quid and some fags for an afternoon queening around. On one stroll with Maud I noticed a small corner restaurant Bob had taken me to and then promptly dismissed the thought from my mind. This was a new era, but flashbacks between the extremes of my old and new life were hard to ignore. Although I had long since left the street, its alleys and the undercurrent of life living there always caught my eye. I could still spot the Punters a mile off and the thin wary gaze of the boys loitering about hoping to 'turn tricks' in the side streets or the back of some carpark.

It was never easy for Clare either, she was also haunted by the past, or the lack of it. She told me she had not really known our mother as she was just a bit too young when she died to have formed those memories. Like me, having spent years at boarding school relationships with parents were always slightly unreal. They seemed at times, when we wrote letters home, more like distant Gods we honoured, who we craved an audience with on our homecomings; who, if we had good School Reports spoiled us rotten. They took us on holiday and bought our uniforms, but the day to day life of a family was never something we experienced fully. However, being six years older than her I had a far more intense experience in those snatches of time between school terms.

We were intensely loyal to each other and united in our disgust at Shiela's attitude. She had stolen our Father and his wealth as far as we knew. She lived in his huge house with her successful daughters, while we floundered about trying to keep the Bailiffs away.

When I first met Maud I had been unemployed and scraping through on a meagre income, something I became very good at doing, living on thin air. But her arrival at Windsong had obviously added to the household demands. Quite rightly she expected the occasional cooked meal, hot water, heating and so on; things I had managed to overlook for years. She was, during those first few years in particular, totally unaware how deep in the shit I really was. Some people accrue wealth throughout their lives while I just accumulated debt after debt. I had a theory that it didn't matter whether I made a million or borrowed it, as long as I got through it somehow. One day my ship would come in and all would be well. Sadly, I have a feeling now there was never a ship in the first place, it was just a dream some of us had.

Clare and I both suffered from the misguided notion as teenagers that one day our parents would have passed their wealth on to us; my mother had in fact carefully recorded the Antiques they collected with dates and prices, mentioning this to me, showing me her little note book. We never guessed that her death nullified this. When David died we discovered that legacy was now in the hands of a woman who had her own priorities and we were essentially disenfranchised. I had long been used to having to rely on myself, but I worried about Clare. However, unbeknown to me Sheila had, in her condescending way, remained helpful to her. I don't mind Clare kept this from me, I was just glad she was ok. I would always manage, I'm a natural born survivor.

However having been brought up to believe the safety net was out there, we lacked the killer instinct needed to make a decent and profitable life. We had an innate sense of wealth that was financially unfounded, we were indeed 'Enfants Terribles,' but without parents.

On that particular visit we discussed our limited options as regards to keeping an eye out for Bill's deterioration, while helping Nanna. But with both of us living at opposite ends of the country and being generally broke things didn't bode well.

Much of the background soundscape I recorded in Brighton went onto my next album, 'Freedom Road.' The band had morphed into a larger outfit with the addition of Morgana, a 'White Witch' from Bristol on backing vocals, a young girl called Faith on Sax and Malcolm on viola. Band nights were becoming a little happening in their own rights. Everybody loved the vibe at Windsong and its magic.

Kevan, the Spaceman Bassman was usually the first to arrive, then the singers and Malcolm would come; finally Andy the drummer. What is it about drummers? But it was never an issue, it was just the way he was, there was never any moaning in our band, occasionally one of the singers would get uppity but in general we had nothing to argue about. There was no money to fight over, no royalties, no love affairs complicating matters, just a cooperative will to make some music. I was privileged that the band and the regular guys gave their best as we had a great deal of love for each other. The fellowship that surrounds any creative project is special; Kevan and I made a bond that became unbreakable.

The deal was simple, turn up, add to the music and one day I will repay those efforts with an album with their name engraved for eternity on it, fifty copies for each contributor.

I paid for everything, the equipment, the tapes, the artwork and production; I wrote the songs, designed the cover, did all the running around and phoning up for the gigs. Getting everyone together was the first hurdle, checking on Monday they were all up for Tuesday, if not, how about Thursday. In the end I just recorded with whoever showed up. If someone was missing I would dud them in another day if their bit was essential. The band went on for years like this.

The beauty of my music was it could go any way. I didn't mind if the song ended up with an eight piece band or just a bass line. If it worked, if it captured the essence of the song's emotion, that was good enough for me.

The drums took up the living room and the rest of us were in what would have been the 'dining' room in a more traditional home. I don't think I ever owned a table to eat meals on, unless it was in the garden. I guess that sums up my priorities. I had taken the doors off and as much of the walls out as I dared, to facilitate communication between us and allow the music to flow through the cottage.

I also put a five foot wide, two hundred year old, Chinese wheel in the kitchen wall so we could look through to both rooms, pass drinks and joints in and out. As the pace towards the summer gigs built up and the next album got nearer to being finished, Windsong became more and more a permanent studio and less a house. Some weeks Andy's extensive drumkit with all the microphones set up never left my living room and my cat Friendly would potter about through the maze of leads and cables with a bemused grin on his face.

This era from the second to about the sixth album was probably one of the best times of my musical life. My lovely lady, who never once betrayed my dreams or said no to any of the mad projects or bits of music kit I came home with, was happy to share the band and our hopes. I was well in debt by the time she had moved in. The Oxford years had been great, but she had accrued big Student Loan debts and I had been funding my unemployment with the assistance of any credit card I could get hold of. Becoming a teacher could have balanced that out; but with my inherent disregard for money I also took the opportunity of a salary to borrow even more.

Thus over the years I was able to make the albums, eleven in total at Windsong, twenty hours of music, out of the hundreds of sessions I recorded, until I eventually broke the bank and the cottage too.

When we did the second album I asked if anybody else in the band was up for contributing financially to the couple of grand it took to make the finished CD. Andy, was the only truly solvent member of the band but, bless him he apparently had Cashflow problems at all his Jewellery Shops. He managed fifty quid, but it convinced me it wasn't worth asking anybody again.

To be fair I felt it was my 'Trip,' so I had to fund it. In return for that I kept the full copyright. Though as I wrote the songs that would have been mine anyway. Being always optimistic, I thought that if somebody wanted to use a track in years to come, it would mean I wouldn't have to find every band member to get their permission. The band was my baby and I simply just had to pay for all the nappies.

The instrumental tunes were more of a team effort, sometimes they would just spring up, like a flower suddenly blossoming. Several minutes later the last echo would vanish into the hum of the headphones, we would be motionless, hardly breathing, because my floor boards creaked, there would be a moment's lull, then an intake of breaths, followed by, "Where the fuck did that come from?" Many of those tunes just began with a random guitar riff, or Colin started a beautiful melody and we gushed all over it.

The singers on the recordings just did their thing, I might be warbling away or using the effects to warp my voice into space. Everybody was in charge of their bit. The most I ever did was to suggest the kind of vibe or emotion I was looking for. Sometimes if it didn't work I would say so. But it was a communal debate, never a demonic one. I knew that was the best way to get the best out of them. We felt real magic in those two rooms from time to time. All of us would be playing, interweaving instruments and then suddenly, as if we had created a carpet from those threads, the whole thing just rose up into the air, a sound beyond our sound. We clung on like children to the edges of this heavenly fabric while it billowed and came to life in front of us.

It doesn't get any better than that. Musically, for me, when the magic flows it's one of the most beautiful creative experiences a person can experience. I'm sure it can't feel any bigger a buzz for The Stones.

I decided to make the third album 'Love Love Love' into a double CD to capture more of these moments. I figured the audience already had seventy seven minutes of songs on the first disc so they'd had their fiver's worth, if they paid at all. For I was and still am particularly known for the giving away my CDs for free. What the hell, it was never about the money honey. We really did it truly for love.

It was hard because we never had any big success, the way most of these stories turn out. No, we just had album after album that almost got through the glass ceiling but not quite. It was like playing for a team that never really won a match. Andy was the only guy who didn't have a problem with that, having supported Aston Villa for years. We had to have a very special kind of dedication to continue turning up for practices and making magic knowing it was never going to go much further.

It would have been nice if financially it had kept a roof over my head, rather than blow it off, but it was never about being a Pop Star or a millionaire; it was all about the making the music. The experience of jamming in Windsong, then watching the sun slowly set while listening back to something we had just created that evening was simply the best.

I often reminded them, that the richest man on the planet couldn't walk into Harrods and order a slice of what we had. We didn't need the fame and the fortune to be the richest musicians on earth, we already had that, with the songs, the instrumentals and those moments of pure wildness.

I also used to joke that if I had become famous on the Monday, by Thursday I'd be in the shit, busted and locked up for the weekend. I don't think my lifestyle and drug usage would have mixed well with any more public notoriety than I already had. I was happy to be a little local 'Ledge.'

'Are you famous?' People always asked that, in the old days before they had Google.

"Hmm, big on the 'Underground Scene," I used to reply.

'Oh?' Widening eyes staring at me, fully expectant of some revelation.

So I gave it to them, "Yeah, the District and Circle Line mainly." Then I'd chuckle and say, "Nah, really man, big among Moles and Badgers and I got some really great fans, two should be out of Rehab soon and the other one is due Parole. It's all looking up!"

Meanwhile, back at the reality ranch, I rang every person I knew connected to the music business, went up and down to London with my guitar, a bag of CDs and a battered copy of 'EX.' Touting my wares, knocking on every door I could find.

In fact I used to busk at Notting Hill Tube Station, on the District and Circle Line to fund these trips. Here I met the cross dressing ballet dancer Marge Mallow and a bunch of street urchins who would drop down the steps and sing along with me or just generally have a party. I think it must have been my hippy smile.

But the end result of it all was years of promises, never fulfilled. We even had Release Dates and the CD Serial Numbers set up to go...

Yet back then during the first few albums we still had high hopes that it was early days and maybe our luck would change. That went on right up until the day I took our sixth album 'High Timers' into the Record Company. Probably one of the best albums I ever made.

It had all come about with my frustration that nobody, including my girlfriend seemed to want to assist me push this band up to the next level. I had helped her to get a job with Eagle Media, who did little else than History and Music filming. How come she wasn't trying to get me in on the action?

Thus the boss of Eagle Media Bob Carruthers came looking for me one day, after a filming job at The Lyceum with Jethro Tull and Uriah Heep. I passed on some of my albums to him and we set up a meeting. Some weeks later and several more meetings, during which I had been given the hallowed Serial Numbers of our forthcoming releases, I parked up in Stratford upon Avon and headed to his office.

I had promised to deliver a new album, along with the three CDs they were already planning for release. The catalogue numbers were 0887, 0888 and 0889. I was so thrilled, I liked the triple '8.' The band were excellent at that time, excited about our prospects; we had put our heart and souls into the new album. I'd actually made a very approachable, semi commercial album. All the others had been pretty 'Way Out,' with one song merging into the next, most of them at least eight minutes long; but this one had been straightened out, cleaned up and even de drugged for public consumption.

We had Malcolm on viola from the English Symphony Orchestra and Rebecca Eddolls, whose voice, her brother Martin, assured me had stopped the traffic in Boston. Well it did a pretty good job in Cheltenham too. She had a remarkable tone and hadn't found improvising too hard to pick up. Martin ran a computer company with his father at the time and he had detailed a guy called Stuart Wraith to work on the design of the CD covers, putting my ideas onto the screen, and into 'Zeroes' and 'Ones.'

As a band we knew our chances of success at that time were roughly one in two thousand. For every ten thousand bands in England, five would get a deal, maybe one of two of those might break into the Big Time, tough odds. But hey, this is Cosmic Smiles, one in a million let alone two thousand!

After the 'Love Love Love' album, the next one was 'Groovy' and had been 'Released,' which only meant the pallet of CDs had arrived at my cottage. It was, September 7th. The following week in between classes at school, standing outside the gym, Danny McInnerney came out of the staff room and called me. 'Come and look at this.' Several heads were gathered around the small television, as I looked over the second plane hit the World Trade Centre. Obviously, the world changed that day. An album called Groovy suddenly seemed a bit out of place. There was nothing groovy about this at all. So the next album, 'What a World.' I did my best to reflect what I saw in the World, I felt it was part of my job as a Troubadour. In the Sixties it was Vietnam, now we had Weapons of Mass Destruction.

'High Timers' was the album after that. Everybody loved 'What a World' but it had a sprawling mass of soundscapes and madness in amongst the songs. The new album was tight and tidy. I summed it up by telling people it was the only album I'd ever made that I didn't have to warn them not to play such a such a song if their parents or the Vicar was about.

So I had a meeting set up with Bob for ten in the morning, I think it was a Monday. I duly arrived in the plush offices and spoke to the Receptionist. In my sweaty palms I clutched a box of the new album. She pointed behind me and asked me to sit on the couch, "Somebody will be down in a minute."

I waited to go up. I imagined playing him a few tracks, watching his eyes widen and jaw drop as Rebecca's voice peeled his scalp off.

A young man came jauntily down the stairs to meet me. I got up to follow him back upstairs but he motioned me to sit down again. "Hi. You must be Mr Smiles..?"

"Sure, from the band Cosmic Smiles, I've come to see Bob, I've got my new album here." I waved a copy in front of him.

"Ah, that's the thing..."

He seemed to be struggling a bit so I chivvied him along. "Is Bob in yet? Is he ready to see me?"

"Ah." He screwed up his face into an expression that definitely wasn't conveying 'Yes' to me.

I tried again, "Is he busy or something? It was ten o'clock we agreed, wasn't it?"

"Er, the thing is," He looked in pain, "Look I'm really sorry, this is my first day at work here."

For a moment my face lightened up, I could see this guy didn't know his arse from his elbow or what was going on; he only looked twenty something. I guess he noticed that flicker of hope and couldn't stand it anymore.

He continued, "Er, the thing is, it's my first day at work here and my first job is to come and tell you we don't want to proceed with any of the albums."

While the horror of that moment sank in he added, "Thanks but Bob hasn't got time to see you himself." The guy walked back up the stairs.

I came out of there and walked blindly up the street with my box of CDs, into the nearest chemist. "Hi, I've got a really bad chesty cough. Do you sell Gee's Linctus?" They did. "Two bottles please." I walked into the Charity Shop next door, crouched behind one of the clothing rails and downed both bottles. I was heart broken. What would I tell the band?

I think that moment broke a little piece of the Hope off my heart. Perhaps this was the turning point? Perhaps this was the day it all really started to go wrong, with no hope of it ever going right again.

The situation in York had slowly deteriorated too. Social Workers were apparently involved, a Solicitor had been in touch with Bill for some reason. Clare went up to visit them and find out what was going on.

I was still up to my neck in leather trying to fill the boots of the teacher I had replaced. The pace had been relentless since September with the build up to Ofsted. Then Christmas. Sandie's death and Uncle Bill's madness. Followed by the run up to the exams and Sports Day. My feet didn't touch the ground.

However, I never forgot those even worse off than me and every Friday I still took Rob Gilder to a swimming pool to rehabilitate his legs and balance. The aim was to get him walking as best we could manage.

Clare rang me from York. I was teaching a lesson at the time and had to take the call in the corridor outside the gym, watching the little buggers through the glass door. She sounded upset.

She was upset. "Geoffrey, I'm at an Auction House in York. They're selling all our stuff off! All the things I saved of Mummy's from Ford House, that I left with Nanna to look after. Bill's lost his mind, he doesn't know what's happening, his solicitor has brought somebody in to value everything they own and they're selling it all off tomorrow. Can you come up? I've got hardly any money but I'm going to try to buy back a few bits for us to keep."

Looking at my schedule of work for the next couple of days it was impossible. I knew it was impossible. I could have begged the Headmaster to give me the time off. I should have done. But Ray Hooper was a bullish man and somehow intent on my humiliation. He enjoyed bullying me at the best of times or at least diminishing my achievements.

"I'll see what I can do." But the sale was the next day. I was broke as usual, though I probably could have bought some stuff on a credit card. I was up to my neck in it and I just knew I wouldn't be able to make it. "Give me the address." I said in some vain attempt at giving her a bit of hope.

I can see her in my mind, trying to spread her pennies to buy back a few trinkets from our past. I suppose every now and then she must have looked to the entrance door to see if I had come in. Surely her big brother would help her out. Surely he would come. He had to. There was nobody else. None of the 'Smiles' family from Sunderland seemed to know what was going on.

But of course I never arrived.

She called me in tears to say it was all over. All our stuff had gone except two Staffordshire Figures, The Huntsman, The Lovers and my Mother's table lamp, The Whistling Boy.

I think that moment broke a little bit of the Hope off Clare's heart. Perhaps this was the turning point?

Weeks later we found out the Antique's Salesman and the Solicitor were in cahoots together and had taken most of Bill's profits from the Auction. Nanna and Bill had been assessed by some Social Worker, who, with utter disregard for their emotional welfare, had sent them both off to separate Nursing Homes, apparently for their own safety. Nanna's purse which always had a wad of money in it had also vanished.

It was a disaster. Mr and Mrs Bailey never met again. I think this broke a little bit of Hope off both our hearts. 'Home,' somewhere back there, a place where people at least had known our parents, was now gone, gone, gone forever.

Eventually Summer came with its desultory heat. The Poppies were in full bloom and it may well have been around then that I began to drink my Poppy Coffee more often than not and perhaps for all the wrong reasons.

As the school year came to a close in the summer, there was the ultimate test for the new PE Teacher, could I pull off Sports Day? Having watched and taken part in a few I felt it was just another gig with an amusing Set List. A lot would depend on the weather and the parents, not forgetting the dear boys who might at any moment decide to sod off, 'Kick off' or tell the Vicar to 'Fuck off.'

Any test for the boys, based on their previous experience of life, was an opportunity to fail. It was much easier to avoid the whole subject and not take part. I can understand that. So I had to coax them into a frenzy of energy without setting fireworks off. Somehow between us it came together. I made it so that every boy won a prize that day. The sun shone and I had crowned my glowing Offsted report with a year of sports and successes that went beyond my expectations and no doubt many of the other staff.

All that remained was to see how the exam results worked out in the Autumn. If they were good I would have proved wrong those who doubted my way of working with the boys. I was always naive enough to believe my colleagues at face value, I still retain a childlike faith in humanity.

However, the endless rush of the working week, the three hundred mile commute and the sorrows of my personal life meant I had flavoured the season with poppy tea and now, with the latest album in the bag we would be off for two weeks holiday in Corfu at a small resort called Arillas. It had a magical vibe there it seemed a happy place to be, perfect for holidays; it didn't look built up or over run with Hotels, the people were so friendly and totally trustworthy. If a bag was left on the beach it would be still there or handed into the nearest shop.

The only problem for me was I would no doubt go into opiate withdrawals over there, not pleasant or helpful to my partner enjoying the trip either. So I toddled off to my local friendly GP. Dr Townsend, bless him. He was out of his depth really, with a long term junkie on his list of patients at the comfortable Cotswold surgery. But he was a kind and intelligent man. He listened carefully and let me explain what I needed. Roughly fifteen codeine phosphate a day for fifteen days. Two hundred and twenty five 30mg pills. He would write a prescription for three hundred and off I would go. They never lasted the fortnight.

Then on our return, just two brief weeks later, as September began, the countryside would have changed to Autumn. The smell of decay meant that most of the poppies would now be gone. I could still find some, with enough looking. I drove down the road with one eye in every garden, stopping to check bits of wasteland where I knew they grew. Going round all the places I regularly picked, until eventually there were none. Shit.

Then I'd go back to Dr T. Another three hundred or a thousand Codeine Phosphate later... So it went on and no doubt my dear friend Gerard would send me something from the Thai Burma border at a random moment and before I knew it I had a full blown habit again. But it was the start of a new term, a new school year. I had to either clean up fast, which was almost impossible, or try to gently nurse myself back down to Terra Firma on Codeine and Gees Linctus.

So it progressed. This became my life, the invisible cloak I put on every day to protect me from feeling too much, hurting too much. Despite the small successes I had at school and Maud's happiness, I felt I had failed the people who really mattered the most. Sandie, Saffron, Kane, my grandparents, the band and most of all Clare.

I put so much into the children I taught, I never let them down if I could avoid it. I put all the love and energy I wanted to give to my children into them. But I did get back as much as I gave from my lads.

The problem with even a small drug addiction is that it gradually undermines everything else. It took me years to suss out the way it worked; the subtle differences between me 'Stoned' or me 'Straight.' How it affected my personal life, my work, my health and my gigging.

I only wish that the general populous understood some of the other palliatives we take to make our lives better, paracetamol, alcohol, 'Happy Pills' are all just as bad. Getting off them has its own dangers too, in ways opiates don't.

Somewhere in those years I began to tumble. If I knew which day it was the fall began I would have ripped the entire week out of the calendar. But that's not how life goes. It is the small day to day attrition that breaks our resolve, not the major disasters; they almost raise our game to meet them. Whereas the endless bills, money worries and drudgery of small failures, pitted against an ever ageing and aching body tend to be far more life threatening.

In the middle of all this Ashley overdosed. Having got clean, with the trip to Corfu and support from Sophia his beautiful wife, he had made the classic mistake many do. He had decided it would be fine to have one little 'Hit.' One injection. Gone. Shit.

I knew that hunger. It had never left me. I knew that thought. The little monkey on the shoulder, the devil at my back, whispering, 'Go on.' He had gone for it and sadly misjudged the dose.

The funeral had far too many young people there. Sophia and her daughter, the friends and fans from the London music scene. The wake was a crazy wild affair with many of us celebrating Ashley's life the way he would have wanted. I played a song or two somewhere in the middle and had spoken at the funeral. I didn't know him that well, but I knew him inside out. We had played the same games, with the same music and drugs as a backdrop. We played the way really true musicians do, with every muscle and blood vessel in our busted bodies trying to hit the highest note. We both in many ways paid the highest price to make the art, to hit the highest note, to make that moment for you to share.

THE HIGHEST NOTE

I stare out in the stoned starlight, dead of night,
Running through a Bible black blues, my life.
Dancing with the Devil's blood, you know there's, no laws, no limits,
Immaculate, cold confession and a pale reflection.
There's a song insanity sings now, for you and me,
A sweet white melody to put the Sandman to sleep.
Chorus

People hanging on their jagged lives, both black and white,
Hollow cries from their empty eyes, I see no love inside,
The bad guys are busting their backs trying to male a deal,
While the good guys are fast on their heels, it's a crazy scene.
Chorus

I stare out in the stoned starlight, so you said,
With the rocks and the stardust, running round in my head,
You know I'd have believed 'The First or Last Goodbye,'
If only to have faith that somehow, something wouldn't die,
Maybe thats why I hear this music, in my life,
A sweet white melody to put the Sandman to sleep.

Chorus:
 But you know, I don't lie, when I say I tried to hit the highest note,
 And you know, I won't cry, when I slip into my last goodnight,
 'Cause you know, it was just too much, when it hurts to touch the people you love.
 'Cause you know, it was just too much, when it hurts to love the people you touch.
 'Cause you know, it was just too much, when it hurts to touch the people you love.

DELTA

On Midsummer's Eve, sometime in the late nineties, it was approaching three o'clock in the morning at Sainsbury's carpark, Amesbury, Wiltshire. We had been there for about half an hour, ahead of schedule for once. Cars began arriving randomly around the otherwise vacant carpark. One of two people got out of their cars and rummaged around in boots or back seats before returning to the glow of interior lights.

We all waited.

A short while later, a double decker bus, with both floors lit up came trundling into the midst of these cars and stopped. There was nobody on it except the driver. Moments later, car doors and boots were being open again as thirty of so Druids donned their robes, picked up staffs, perched crowns, tiaras and top hats aloft a varied assortment of heads.

I robed up too, rescued my guitar and bag of bits from the back of the van while Maud got her video camera. We joined the others, gravitating towards the bus through the misty air, full of freshly puffed druidic breaths.

There was no idle chatter, other than the echo of, 'Well met' or 'Blessed be,' from amongst a shadow of shapes now gathered by the bus. We lined up in an orderly fashion as if this was just an everyday occurrence. I whispered to Maud, "Imagine some drunk on the way home stumbles round the corner and lights upon us lot." She giggled sweetly.

Quick to reply she whispered, "Ah, he'd never touch a drop of the devil's drink again." We both laughed and hugged our bodies together to stay warm.

Eventually, magically, the swing doors of the bus swung open with a swoosh and we filed inside. The bus remained where it was, the driver didn't move an inch, he was impassive, almost invisible.

Like children we went upstairs to the front, figuring we might have a better view of the dark night. From below the occasional staccato of 'Walkie Talkie' could be heard. About ten minutes later we suddenly heard the engine of the bus shudder into life and the doors closing. With a few clanks and jolts the bus lurched off towards the main road. The crackle on the Walkie Talkie kept up, but we couldn't hear what was being said. Nobody sitting upstairs made any comment. We all just waited as if we knew what was going on. Nobody really did.

It wasn't until we came over the final hill and the shape of Stonehenge appeared that we realised what all the Walkie Talkie chatter downstairs had been about. The whole area was full of people and the dreaded Thames Valley Police.

Most visible were the Mounted Police on their huge horses, trotting down the road as the crowd parted around them, while the unmistakable helmets of their colleagues pushed into the crowd. As we got closer we could hear was a lot of shouting, see people waving flags, drumming, chanting while hurling what might be deemed derogatory remarks in the general direction of anybody but themselves.

The bus made its way gainfully towards the ancient stone circle but without success. It came to a stand still and a voice shouted up that we had to walk from there. With my guitar and one or two drummers we set off at a march to the main entrance of the Stones still fully hopeful that we would get in to perform our ceremony. This had been the aim of many meetings between English Heritage and the Order of Druids.

Sadly that year the Summer Solstice gathering got hijacked by those protesting, quite rightly for general access to the Stones and the regular 'Travellers,' for whom this was an annual rendezvous before the trek to Glastonbury Festival.

It was also a spiritual moment in a spiritual place.

After a couple of hours shuffling forwards and back again, we were no nearer the hallowed ground. So a few of us peeled off into the field on the far side of the road where I played guitar and a few people danced as sunrise and the dawn passed. Small groups were saying prayers, crosslegged on the damp grass, all staring into the dim distance. But in some reflection of the whole affair it had been a bit cloudy and we hadn't been blessed with those first distant rays of sun.

Despite all the Walkie Talkie discussions we had not been admitted to the Circle for whatever political or police reasons. We turned back, having taken reams of film and photos, to find the bus that returned us to Sainsbury's carpark.

When it stopped some time later and we all got off, several early shoppers questioned their sanity, as the double decker bus full of Druids, Witches, Orcs and Fairies disgorged itself next to the trolley bay.

The following year was different, we were all chosen officially and our names listed, like a page of Tolkien, in a letter with several rules; among which were the edicts that no electric musical devices, drums or instruments were to be played. Well it didn't say I couldn't bring them along, just I couldn't play them. My guitar and I had done all our ceremonies and most of the other important things in life together, so I decided it would be wrong to attend without trying to take him along too. As I edit this we have been together now for forty three years, definitely my longest ever relationship!

My spiritual father Septimus, led the way with about eighty other Druids from Britain and across Europe. My guitar was hung across my back and none of the English Heritage officials took offence as we piled through the newly installed turnstiles and under the tunnel that crossed the road. Those tourists who had coincidently booked a Day Trip to Stonehenge were agog to see our motley crew pass by.

Druid hymns and refrains echoed up and down the tunnel, until we came up the ramp on the other side. Ahead of us the flowing river of Septimus and the others led the way, ushered by an official who parted the ropes keeping the tourists back. Moments later we were on the hallowed grass around the Stones.

We gathered together outside the 'Portal Gates' to the Stones. 'Skinny' and Arthur Pendragon had been allotted as Guardians to the East entrance. Staffs aloft they made an arch that awaited us. Septimus said some words and then led the way between those mighty men into the circle.

It feels different the second a foot falls inside the silenced world of the Stones. Cut off by centuries from the outside it casts an aura of reverence upon all, as any holy shrine does, but the open skies and the sheer presence of the 'impossible' drowns any soul in humility. That any human would think to build such a circle, using stone gathered from a hundred miles away, is the overwhelming emotion that grabbed my heart.

Without knowing how, everybody wandered slowly around until they found their spot in the circle.

I stood at the left of Septimus. He had mentioned to me earlier that he might need a hand bringing the Chalice up and replacing it, so I stayed close to him.

Knowing there was a time restriction on the whole ceremony Septimus raised his hand and began to speak. He called on the 'Quarters,' to beg the spirits and elements to bless our gathering. He asked us to join hands and recite the Druid's Prayer, to which he added another in the ancient language of the Druids. A few elemental chants filled the space between us. Septimus spoke again about how this was the first proper Druid Ceremony to be held at Stonehenge for many years and how significant it was in so many ways. Then there were some Druids who had been allotted to speak and a Bard who beautifully brought to life a long poem, all recited from his memory. He came to an end and rejoined the circle.

Septimus looked at his watch and asked if anybody else had an offering of a poem...Or a song?

I waited, thinking ten voices would have called out, but none did. As Septimus stepped back, I stepped forward, "I have a song. Is that okay?"

He replied, looking studiously at his watch, "You've got six minutes, exactly!" The way he said 'exactly' I realised he meant exactly, for some reason.

All the repressed reverence, the emotions of the day after the disappointment of the previous year and of course the natural power of the Stones were suddenly released as my guitar rang out the chords to 'Live on Life.' As I sang I began to circle the inner circle, faster and faster, whipping up the waves of energy and spirit into a mad whirlpool of excitement.

Many of us who were there had been on the bus the year before. This had been a battle for our rights that had lasted over twenty years, since the dreadful day of 'The Bean Field Massacre' of Hippies, when the police smashed up a load of hippy vans and buses, famously attacking a pregnant woman and children; after which, police policy regarding any access to Stonehenge had gone into lock down. It felt like a breakthrough on a physical as well as a spiritual level and our bodies danced with joy like freed prisoners.

As the harmonica swept back and forth every body erupted; even those men like King Arthur, perhaps less enamoured of the golden troubadour swayed on their heels. It was an ecstatic joy, a thing music does so easily. A moment for the people I respected and loved dearly, fellow conspirators in this world, in our own madness trying to respect and preserve an

Ancient Lore, a Code of Conduct, a Knowledge for the heritage of British Heritage! How ironic.

As the song progressed I calculated roughly five minutes had passed so I circled towards Septimus, who was smiling. A small nod confirmed my time was closing in so I reversed neatly back into my position letting the last chord on the guitar and harmonica die away.

It was, quite simply, a magic moment. There were many others over the years but those six minutes were so special and recorded for eternity in my soul.

Septimus stepped forward and the next part of the ceremony began, the in-ordination of Skinny's partner Veronica as an Arch Druid. There were various moments and parts to this including drinking from a Chalice used in Druid ceremonies for several centuries. As Septimus gave it to me to replace he nodded and I quietly drank from it also.

Many people deride such gatherings as merely a bunch of crazy people dressing up; which you could apply to any religious order, but I have discovered over the years the magic and the heart that is gently secreted within them. My belief was never a blinding flash, nor a blind faith, it came from years of these occasions and being astounded by the magic. Never once did I leave such a gathering without some moment that had touched my heart and my spirit!

After the ceremony we retraced our steps and noticed a large crowd had now gathered watching from behind the rope barrier.

It was one of the greatest gigs in my life, all five and a half minutes of it.

Once back in the carpark, robes were exchanged gradually for jeans and jackets. Staffs, swords and daggers laid alongside wands and crystals, all carefully stowed in velvet rags and bags.

Skinny, who was anything but slim, waved me over to his bike. The Harley gleamed in the sun. "Here, roll one up." He gave me a handful of grass, "Stick the rest n your tin."

"Ah, cheers man." He was like that, amiable, hearty, a barrel of laughs in a barrel of hugs. He worked as a Forklift Driver and was renowned in Cheltenham for nicking one on some occasion and using it for semi criminal and joyriding purposes. It kind of summed up Skinny, everything about him was big, even his nicking sprees. Like a lot of bikers, both Angels and Outlaws he had done his fair share of drugs, sex and rocking down the highway to Hell.

He was the sort of man I loved sincerely in the way that men love each other, with respect, admiration and a certain amount of jaw dropping awe. I would have done anything to help him out and vice versa.

Which was why a week or two later I had an invite from him to come and visit two of his dearest friends Dave and Jane Hawkes. He assured me I would like them and also they could probably help me out for a bit of this or that if I needed it.

Arriving at their house was like coming home.

I suppose the people I met there reminded me of many I had known years before in London, Kent and Somerset, the wild boys and girls who now, like me, found themselves to be older and wiser but still basically doing all the same shit.

Dave, 'Bogey,' was an Angel who was once a 'Copper.' He had run a Veg Shop with Jane for many years down on the south coast and then arrived at Moors Avenue, Cheltenham. The Moors, along with Hesters Way, was always seen as one of the rough areas of town, where plenty of drugs and stolen goods were sold and so on. Having lived in a few big cities I felt it was quite tame really. I knew a couple of the older Johnsons, a family notorious at the time for a spate of crime. They seemed alright if you were alright with them.

Moors Avenue housed the usual array of colourful folks, many of whom I met through Jane and Dave. Bikers and alternative people had found themselves a place. Cheltenham had a history of drug issues going back to the Sixties. Brian Jones being buried in the Cemetery probably sums it up.

Skinny had a weakness, he liked his food and one delight in particular, Pork Pies. I did have the debate with him about all the crap meat in them but he was happy with his equation for life. Some years later he began to get dreadful stomach pains. Knowing I was an old opiate user he came to me for advice on pain relief, beyond the usual prescription drugs.

By that time he had taken up with the Arch Druid Priestess, Veronica, through our ceremonies and the fact she was a biker too. They made a lovely couple. But the pain in his stomach wasn't indigestion, it turned out to be cancer, the type nobody can do much about, except wait.

Having just found love, he was leaving us.

We both knew it but rarely talked about it. As he got worse we made a plan for him to come over to my place for a last blast, to take some heroin and get a bit of pain relief. We scheduled it a couple of times but for whatever reason it got cancelled, then we finally hit on one Saturday, this was going to be it. I knew time was literally running out on him, I felt sure he would show up.

The day before I had gone into town and picked up a few bags of heroin. My lady went off to work and I was left waiting for Skinny to arrive.

He was late. I waited. He was still late. Fuck it. I was waiting to have a shot with him. It's the kind of thing crazy people used to do, get high together, shoot up at the same moment and lean back on the wave of nirvana smiling at each other. He still didn't come.

In the end I thought I may as well have a little shot. I figured I better try the stuff out anyway. Amazing how easy it is to convince a willing mind down the road to ruin.

I cooked up a teaspoonful and filled the syringe. I pushed the plunger in.

But something wasn't quite right.

I rarely injected drugs at that time, to appease my girlfriend who naturally and quite rightly found the whole thing utterly scary. Very wise.

In my excitement I didn't see I had slightly nudged the needle to one side and missed the vein. Usually when that happens a bulge appears next to the needle mark. Nothing appeared, so I presumed it must be either weak stuff or I hadn't used enough.

Fatal mistake. Nearly fatal.

So I cooked up another spoonful, making sure I put more than enough in this time. The acrid smell of Brown Heroin is unmistakable. Smells good I mused to myself. I wondered where Skinny was. I replaced the belt on my arm. I pumped the muscle and dug in through the skin at the same place.

This time there was no fucking about, I was surgically focused on the task. The red cloud of blood burst into the barrel of dark liquid and I pressed the plunger steadily home.

In seconds the rush took my scalp off. A prickle of hot pins began to spread over my skin. I lay back on the couch and breathed in the pure air of nirvana. But something wasn't quite right.

The rush kept coming. I slid deeper into the couch. It was okay. It was doable. I could survive this rogue wave. But I gradually realised the gear couldn't have been crap, it was pretty good actually. Too good.

So what happened to the first fix?

I looked down at the crook of my arm. I peered really closely and I could see to the right of the puncture marks a slight bubble underneath the vein. Shit. I had missed the first fix. Bumped it.

I made a rough calculation. In about twenty minutes the first lot would kick in on top of the second. I had basically given myself an Subcutaneous injection as well as the intravenous one. Shit. There was no way I could back out of this now. I was heading down one hell of a Highway to Hell.

I knew what to do from past fuck ups, keep walking, drink fluids, take Vitamin C, keep breathing! Or call an ambulance and get a dose of Naltrexone, which would reverse the effects; but the ensuing crash would bring on the horror of withdrawals. I also still figured Skinny might show up and I would have to somehow keep my shit together not to disappoint him. I didn't want him to see an ambulance on arrival. He, after all, was really going to die soon. I was only possibly going to die today, if I didn't keep ahead and on top of that wave.

It's not a good place to be; because after the pain relief spectrum of any opiate had been exceeded it begins to enter an uncomfortable place all its own. The pain of a toxic body and a poisoned brain. My head was on fire. I was jumping to fall down.

I kept walking most of the afternoon, listening for the sound of Skinny's Harley coming down the lane. He never came. About five Maud came home to find me half way up the driveway.

I smiled bleakly at her. "Hi babe. Er sorry, been a bit of a fuck up. Skinny never turned up and I sort of, kind of, er sorry babe, overdosed a bit." Quickly I added, "But don't worry babe, I'll be fine." I did feel I was going to be okay, but I also knew every now and then a wave a physical nausea would hit me like a truck and try as I might I would be keeling over, heading for the depths, down to the floor and beyond. I had been closer to death than this before and I felt sure that eventually I would level out. I'd made it through the first wipe out, a few hold downs, they were getting easier to handle.

The only complication, apart from an untimely death was we were due to help out friends at the wedding reception of their daughter. They lived next to Rob, and had seen me walking him up and down the road for years. They gave me odd jobs every now and then as they were property developers. They were not 'short of a bob or two' and the wedding was no doubt going to be a stunner. We were invited to help serving the food and drinks for a couple of hours and then to join the party. The bride was a lovely girl who was deaf. With experience of my Grandfather I had always made the effort to speak clearly to her so she could read my lips and we got on well.

Maud's face had dropped off a cliff, poor girl, "Are you sure you're going to be okay." She said, holding me tight, "Jesus. What about the wedding?"

I gave her a hug, "It's okay, I been here before. It's not too bad. I better just keep awake and moving. I'll be fine. Make some excuse for me, but you better get ready and go darling. We can't let them down."

One thing about Maud was she trusted me to know where I was, despite the odd cock up, when it came to drugs. She always respected me and understood that I was much older and although not wiser was definitely in charge of my own destiny, come what may!

Around seven she disappeared in a black frock to be a waitress. Sometime after midnight she returned to find me still walking up and down the lane next to the cottages. It wasn't over yet. I didn't feel it was safe enough to let my head go to sleep yet. If I was going to lose it now, it would be by asphyxiation in deep sleep; I had to keep going for another few hours to flush the drug through my system. I drank another glass of orange juice and made a coffee.

About an hour later she went to bed. I sat in the living room for awhile and then as my head began to hammer I got up and crept out into the night air. It was summer, the stars were out, we had no street lighting so the sky was crystal clear. The gravel of the drive crunched under my feet as I trudged up and down murmuring to myself, 'Keep breathing. Keep breathing.' Then I heard something. I stopped and listened. Nothing.

I walked on. There it was again. I paused, listening hard, somewhere out there a cat was miaowing.

I made a small clicking sound with my tongue, "Come on, don't be afraid, I'm here," I whispered. Out of the shadows a huge black cat with a white bib and socks, a typical Felix model, came padding out to meet me.

I crouched down and held out a hand, lowering my head. The cat came closer and gave me a good look over. The state he saw me in must have been awful, I was surprised he didn't run away, but his curiosity kept him padding left and right, slowly, nearer me.

Being vegetarians we had nothing meat based in the house to offer him and he had missed the odd day we had fish but I deftly crept up to the kitchen and found some milk and a few bits of cheese. I returned to the garden and placed them on the path.

I went back upstairs to the bedroom. "Hey, are you asleep?" She wasn't. "Come on. Quietly." I said no more and led her downstairs to where I had left the saucer. We sat on the step and the cat appeared. He sipped the milk, sniffed the cheese and came up to us. We gently backed in through the door and he followed us in.

'Friendly,' as we named him brought me back to the land of the living. The pain in my head went and the nausea faded as I caressed his fur. He was massive. Hardly a feral cat but obviously homeless, or 'In Between Homes' one might say. As any cat owner knows they tend to chose their owner, not the other way around. He came to stay. It wasn't the last time he would help me through the darkest hours before the dawn.

There were three outcomes from that night, the cat who came to stay, my agreement not to use syringes anymore, though it was never a vow of abstinence, despite the fact I had very nearly followed Ashley to the grave. The third was that Skinny never did make it over and some weeks later we gathered at his bed in Veronica's front room to say goodbye. It seemed unreal that such a mighty bear of a man was only days from death, smiling, chatting, still with so much life in his eyes.

Skinny, like Dave was a hub that many spokes were drawn to, gathered around and which made a wheel. It was so sad to lose such a lovely, gentle man, one who had really just arrived in my world. Guys like me need guys like Skinny, who need guys like me.

Added to this was the Druid connection, our time in 'Circle' together and of course at the Pub. Yet the best times were probably in the front room at Jane and Dave's. 'Shooting the breeze,' or fumigating it more like with the smoke of fine Hashish.

Usually there would be three on the couch, one on the arm, somebody in the doorway, two in the kitchen and Skinny in the chair opposite Jane. Dave was always on his feet, putting on Reggae albums, smiling like a Cheshire Cat. If you stayed there long enough I'm sure the entire world would have passed through that room. God knows life and death did.

Skinny's loss was much harder for Dave. They went back a lot further and had both been into the life that went with motorbikes. Lord knows what they got up to and perhaps it's best that only he does.

As I was a close friend and Veronica knew I could handle having to stand up and talk to a crowd, she asked if I would speak at the funeral. I could do that.

A week or so later we gathered outside Cheltenham Crematorium, having stopped on the way up from the carpark for a minute or two at Brian Jones' grave. It was always adorned with flowers, badges and cards, tokens of love from far and wide.

Outside the main doors the minutes ticked by, the conversation slowly fell silent while one or two heads turned back towards the road. I strained my eyes to see and my ears to listen. Then I heard it. The roar of the motorbikes following the hearse. It was the first 'Biker Funeral' that I had been to with a full cortege.

As the motorbikes appeared, spluttering, growling, rumbling, ticking over at five miles an hour my knees quivered realising I would be in front of this lot soon. I clutched the card with my speech in my sweaty palm and hugged Maud tightly.

The Chapel was packed, the pews were full, with people shoulder to shoulder against the walls and in the entrance lobby. Veronica held the service. It was suitably Druid and yet open to everyone. I went up at the chosen moment and took the couple of steps up to the Pulpit. I put my speech down and looked up at his friends. It was a curious crowd of people, many of whom looked as if their last visit to any form of church was at Baptism. I smiled, these were my people, the 'The Wild Tribe.'

Whether biker or hitch hiker, we had all consciously stepped out from the centre of life to see what the edge might reveal. We were all unique in our own ways, from opposite universes maybe and yet united in our devotion to non conformism and freedom.

When a member of the tribe has fallen it comes to the point that one of his fellows must stand up and honour his passing. My speech touched the hearts of some there and it would fall to me to be that man for several of the Tribe over the years to come. The sound of those bikes is engraved on my ear drums.

It wasn't just Skinny who was dying. Within a year of being put in hospital Uncle Bill was fading away; Nanna was also in the Departure Lounge.

I went up to see him. Clare had come to visit before I went up to York. It was only then that she told me Bill had abused her when she was a girl. Suddenly, a period of time when my grandparents never visited made sense. I had never known. That must have been a terrible discovery for our parents.

Bill was in a semi Intensive Care Ward, awake but his eyes were half dead, drifting bleakly in and out of consciousness. He had shrunken in size but his red 'Handlebar' moustache, now thickly streaked with grey, was unscathed, defiantly perched under his nose.

It was hard to know what to say. All my life I had believed this man the nearest thing to an interested father figure. He had ferried me as a small boy back and forth across the Pennines on countless Exeat weekends from Seascale Preparatory School, while my parents and Clare were in Uganda. He had given me my pocket money, taken me for fish and chips and looked after Nanna. Going to visit them after my mother's death was the closest thing I ever got to going 'Home.'

I spoke to him. I'm not sure how much he heard. I told him I had found out about what he did to Clare. I said how sad that made me feel and how could he do that to her, Nanna's grandchild? I could feel that those eyes were watching me, like a diver, down too deep, holding his last breath, regretting, knowing he wasn't going to make the surface.

I couldn't let him die like that. I appreciate it may seem hard to grasp that I could find any compassion for such a man, especially considering what similar men had done to me when I was a young. However I had loved him all my life, unconditionally, as a child does, without any doubts, until then. I still loved him. I couldn't stop that overnight.

"But Bill," I never called him that, always Uncle Bill, "I also came to visit because I wanted to say how much you meant to me when I was at Prep School. I would never have survived that without you and

Nanna. Thanks." I smiled, "You take the high road and I'll take the low road." A joke of ours, "Maybe we can stop for Strawberries on the way."

I searched Bill's face for a reaction. I could see the diver nearing the surface, his face distorted by the ripples in the water. I stared deeper into his eyes, diving down to meet his breathless stare. "I want to say thank you for all you did for me, you were never bad to me, I shall always love you for that." The gaze on the diver's face softened and he began to relax, a bubble of air escaped his lips, a last breath. I could hear his voice in my head saying, 'Geoffrey.'

I let go of his hand. I had to return to the surface now. "I shall do my best to look after Nanna." He was slipping further into the navy blue oblivion. I sat next to him for awhile. It would be the last time I would ever see him. I knew that. I had to drive back south later that day. In the end it was the end. I got up and closed the door to his room, "Goodbye."

Nanna was moved to Sunderland to be nearer her son Jack and the rest of the Smiles family. I would do that trip too, visiting the Care Home she was in. If ever there was an injustice it was to see her there.

I know there was no other way, but she could easily have been cared for in her old home if Bill hadn't lost his mental faculties. Everything had gone, it seemed so unfair, such a poor recompense for a life of hard work. Sitting in the row of arm chaired ladies, all with a handbag on their laps, or a shawl, as if they were going out somewhere. But the bags only contained tissues and the shawls were never put on.

She would comfort me in my sorrow. She could see the pain it caused me, the feeling of helplessness, of being unable to fix this. I was forever fighting back the tears.

"Don't worry son." She'd say, "Be soon." That was how we signed off our phone calls as I was always promising to be up for a visit. "Be soon," she would echo down the phone. "Be soon."

Clare would go up. It broke her heart also as Nanna was the closest thing she ever had to a mother. I never knew until too late how little she remembered of our mother, being just too young to have begun to compile her childhood memories, not old enough to understand the awful events around her.

My relations the Smiles, were endlessly lovely to me during these visits up north. It was good to see 'Family.' But it would come to the last day and the walk back from the Care Home wondering if Nanna would still be there when I next returned. It was heart breaking.

Eventually Nanna did give up. She had reached ninety three. She had suffered a hard life and the worst thing any mother could, having to bury a child. She was the only one who never let me down, ever. She always had an excuse for me. "Give over, he's only a bairn."

Then, when the storm had passed she would look at me and say, "Eee our Geoffrey, you little bugger, what are we going to do with you?" Then she'd laugh, light one of her menthol cigarettes and get Uncle Bill to put the kettle on.

She was laid to rest in a Funeral Parlour and I was offered the chance to go and pay my respects for a last time.

She was painted in Still Life. It didn't seem to be her but it was.

I talked awhile.

I held her hand.

I kissed the breathless skin above her eyes and left.

GAMMA

I was heading to the Headmaster's office when I noticed Billy bouncing round the carpark with a cigarette in his hand. As I approached he took an almighty drag and blew the smoke blatantly towards me. He was on his way back to London and seemed determined to stick two fingers up at us as he left.

I'd managed a few good years back in the teaching saddle and could have happily pottered on with it if I wasn't getting bullied by the Headmaster and hadn't experienced a run of injuries from the boys. Some of those were merely from the customary greeting of a punch that was a bit strong, some the result of a boy who had lost his temper and was in full fury. I always used to believe that there was no point in standing in front of a train heading at full speed towards me; it was better to start reversing, hopefully at the same speed and apply the brakes slowly. Sometimes there wasn't enough time.

Billy was a classic case. It was the end of term, almost, a time people would think children might be at their best, hopeful of imminent release to home. Boarding school 'End of Term's' are particularly intense for all concerned. But for some of our lads the end of term was viewed with trepidation and dismay. Perhaps, as they were returning to an unhappy home, or maybe a home with no heating or books. I'd visited many with just a sofa, a TV, only Tea, Coffee, sugar, white bread, margarine and tins of spagetti or beans in the kitchen. That was it.

But perhaps the most heartbreaking thing we dealt with, on several occasions, was the boy left behind. Nobody turned up to take him home. Phone calls would be made by staff as he paced the driveway waiting for his Mum or whoever. Then eventually the news would filter through that 'Mum or whoever,' wasn't coming and in fact really didn't want him home. 'After all, he's sixteen now…' I remember one parent demanding, 'Wasn't there somewhere else we could send him now?'

To see the huge frame of a boy from a tough inner city area crumble in front of me was a sad footnote to any term. Billy was a similar scenario and this was his last term. It seemed a Social Worker was on their way but they certainly weren't hurrying.

Billy was leaving Swalcliffe Park School a week or so early as he had already tested our boundaries to their limits. The general consensus of the staff was for him to go home. It was a shame, we usually had a good relationship, I had taken him with a group of boys to the Gower coast for a week in Wales and he had been great on that trip.

I approached him gently, with a smile, "Hi Billy. You off soon?" To which he exhaled another puff of smoke in my face. "Come on, you know you're not allowed to smoke, especially outside here." I pointed to the Headmaster's office behind us.

He bounced around a bit and replied something along the lines of, 'Fuck yer mum, Smiles.'

"Come on Billy, don't spoil your last day."

He brought the cupped hand up to his mouth and took a big drag; on the way down he triumphantly held the cigarette in front of me and I snatched for it. I didn't get it, but I caught the top. It snapped.

It hung there for a nano second, bent over in his fingers. I heard two staff behind me shout as his fist hit me, then another. I have never punched anyone in my life, let alone a child. I backed off protecting myself hoping he would stop at any moment.

He didn't. I looked round long enough to see two of my colleagues watching, a few feet away, they didn't fancy wading in to help me with Billy kicking off.

Eventually I tripped backwards and fell on the drive. Thus he couldn't punch me anymore and luckily the commotion had brought more staff. One of these was Devon, a six foot four, well built, black man from Dudley! Billy backed off just as he starting booting me. I was fortunate Devon showed up because our boys at full steam are capable of large bursts of energy and massive strength.

I looked at the Math's teacher with an expression that said, 'Thanks for nothing buddy.' I forget who the other one was. A year or two later Mr Rolf sadly got cancer and died; that's when I realised this job could be fatal. It was hard to keep the teaching side of it going, appease the politics in the staff room and cope with the general threat that something awful is most probably going to happen. The stress of being on 'amber alert' for weeks could be harrowing and this war of attrition eventually took some casualties.

The first month of that summer holiday was spent waiting for the bruises on my ribs to heal up. The follow up to that at school was merely to write it up in the 'Daily Diary' and get on with the next lesson.

It's unlike procedures today that at least give the teacher a debrief.

A similar lack of support from the Headmaster came about after another lad Leon had tried to stab me with a pair of scissors. I had spent a day or so waiting for this attack, not that the HM or anybody else felt inclined to react. In schools like ours there were always problems and probably five in front of mine. Anyway, he was only a little lad and maybe fourteen, not a physical threat like Billy who doubled up as a Boxer in his spare time.

I was sitting at my desk as Leon came through the open door next to me and lunged. I leapt sideways round the desk and he came at me again with the scissors held aloft in his fist.

I knew the rules for restraining a pupil and grabbed his raised forearm, pulling down the hand with the scissors. He of course, heaved his arm away from me and in the process of stumbling backwards the hand with the scissors passed his face and must have made a small cut, there was no blood. We both toppled over and the commotion alerted the staff member on 'Corridor Duty.' He came flying in and helped to calm Leon down. I wrote the incident up in the Daily Diary and that was that as far as I was concerned. This was just one of many altercations in the day to day malaise of a Special Needs School..

I had no idea the parents had not been given the full story. I'm sure the Headmaster would have rather talked about the boy's merits with them. I had long forgotten about the event. There had been plenty of other delights since then. Young Tefferson who spat in my mouth, my new mobile phone was nicked, my Mercedes scratched along the driver's side and countless other daily abuses.

One afternoon I was teaching in my classroom and three black men with a woman behind them walked straight in. I thought they were prospective parents.

Before I had time to speak the first and biggest guy said, 'You Mr Smiles?'

"Yes..."

'I'm Leon's Uncle.'

"Yes?"

'I wanna word now.'

"Yes?"

'Outside.'

"...You're Leon's Uncle?" I was beginning to get the feeling this wasn't a social visit.

I looked at the woman behind as she piped up, 'I'm Leon's Mother. We wanna talk right now.'

The big black guy added, 'Outside.'

I'm not sure if this was a question or an order, but any conversation that required taking place outside had in my experience never been an omen of good fortune. But there was little I could do.

I looked at the other lads in their desks, grinning with conspiratorial glee, as bemused and amused as ever, exhibiting for the first time that day an interest in what I was saying. Again, with a bit of luck, one of them had realised exactly where this was heading before me. He had probably more experience at his tender age of the look on a man's face who needs a conversation 'Outside.'

"Outside?" I queried one last time.

"Yeah."

Meanwhile, I was still vaguely under the impression that this was maybe leading to some great accolade related to my skills as a teacher. I was wrong.

We walked out of the class, down the corridor and onto the lawn outside the block where the Autistic boys had a classroom.

I turned round to face the first guy. He spoke, quite forthrightly, "So, we wanna know, how come Leon got this scar on his face from you."

"From me? What?"

"Yeah you!" He stepped a bit closer, a lot closer and with full vehemence in his voice added, "That scar's gonna be there forever."

He looked like he was winding up to punch me too. Whether he was or not, I stepped back instinctively and began to explain. "Look, he'd been threatening me for two days with violence and it happened when he lunged at me with the scissors…"

Before I finished my sentence he demanded, "The scissors! What scissors? Violence? What you talking about?"

"The ones he threatened to stab me with!" I could tell this information was news to him.

"Stab you? His teacher?" The confusion was spreading like a rash across his face.

I went on, glancing behind him, hoping that at any minute the HM would turn up and explain. He didn't. "Yeah. Leon had said all week he was going to stab me. He turned up at my class one day, shouting and screaming, with a pair of scissors in his hand. I had to restrain him, for his own safety. When I grabbed his arm the scissors must have caught his cheek."

The black guy lowered his gaze, I had a feeling he was starting to believe me. "Leon didn't mention any scissors."

"Ask the Headmaster. Read the School Daily Diary. There was a class full of kids there and staff who saw everything." I noticed him step back and turn round to look at the woman.

She spread her arms as if in disbelief, looking at the Uncle, "Leon didn't say nothing to me 'bout any scissors." Her eyebrows raised, "He said this guy done his cheek in with his fingernails. He didn't say he'd done nothing to start it all off."

I figured this wasn't a moment to have a lesson on 'double negatives.' Leaving that thought to one side I asked him, "Does that explain it? Honestly man, I was only trying to protect myself." To which I added, with trite teacher glibness, "…and of course I had to restrain him in case he harmed any of the other children."

This seemed to appeal to his manly sense of justice and suddenly I was believed. The crux of the matter was the HM hadn't explained the circumstances to the mother. Leon had done all the explaining and with a view, no doubt, to securing his own welfare hadn't mentioned the scissors or his threats.

There was a moment's pause and then as one they turned towards the school block. I could hear the voice of the woman shouting, "Leon! Leon? Where are you?" Followed by one or two expletives.

Ah, the joys of being a teacher.

But school wasn't always like that, we had a lot of fun too. At a great festival called Sheep Music, in Presteigne, Powys, I met a wood carver called Harry Thomas, who with one of his mates Andy had started running a 'Forest School' mainly so local teachers could bring a class along for a day and learn the basic skills needed to survive in the Wild. Despite not running a residential course they had considered it several times and had already made some plans. I offered to bring a group of my lads over from Swalcliffe so they could try out some of their ideas. That worked for me and them too.

It went well and provided some golden moments of my teaching career, such as the boy that caught a fish using a stick for a rod and a hook made out of a safety pin. Gosh we never heard the end of that fish, which grew in size every time the tale was related. The midnight walks by the river; setting traps for Rabbits, taking craps, learning about different types of wood to burn and cooking bananas on a fire with chocolate biscuits sandwiched inside. The joy on their grubby faces. The shock of realising they were sleeping under a shelter they had to build the first day with some plastic tarpaulin, a billhook and a bit of 'Bailer Twine.'

I did plenty of music lessons and 'Learning to play guitar' for kids, which in fairness probably meant shut up and listen while I work these chords out. Poor buggers, payback time!

There was the PE lesson I bravely set up the small 'trampet,' a mini trampoline and the big Horse Box. Before I had even time to say, "You must wait for me to supervise your jump and whatever you do never, never, ever attempt a mid air somersault," a little lad had skipped past my back, taken a run up jumped on the trampet, soaring off, tucking his head in as he rotated through the air. I watched my entire teaching career perform a somersault in slow motion before my eyes. Fortunately the cocky bugger landed fair and square on the mat, on his feet not his neck.

Our school was a place of intense colour. I loved those children and put myself on the line to give them the education they really needed. Few of the staff had any idea of what kind of poverty, what sort of mad lives some of the boys experienced at home.

I'd been there, in the living rooms of drug dealers, alcoholics, gamblers, or just plain useless parents with kids; many of whom were actually trying to put food on the table. But any situation like that is liable to intervention from the Police or Social Services. Suddenly 'Daddy' isn't going to be home for awhile.

I never read the boy's files unless I was pressed to. I liked them to have a clean sheet when they arrived in my class and I knew they would tell me what they needed to, all in good time. One of the files I was tasked to read documented a child's torture and sexual abuse of his younger siblings. I found that hard to get my head around, until I read on that the father had abused and tortured him. What a world.

Most of the boys were just desperate for somebody to take an interest in them; they would do anything for a bit of attention. As such, they almost became caricatures of themselves, especially in competition with the other lads. A boy needed a big persona to survive 'below decks' in such a boarding school. I knew that all too well. The weakest lads needed the biggest attitude. I couldn't help but love and admire their courage.

It was also at Sheep Music in 2004 that I met Chris who became a friend and the keyboard player in my band after Colin left us.

Chris was a warning to me of something that was going to happen in my life. I knew it, I could sense it, but it was so dreadful a fate I really couldn't believe my apprehensions. It concerned a decision he had made in regard to his daughter Sylvan.

I was wandering around the Sheep Music campsite and at the rear of a small camper van a guy was sitting haphazardly on a chair. I could tell that he was very drunk, but as I looked closer, he was also very sad.

Being Mr Smiles, it was never my way to walk on by when an unhappy soul crosses my path. I cunningly caught his eye and ventured, "Hows it going man?" Knowing perfectly well it was going in one direction, downwards.

He looked up at me, "Hey. Hi." His voice and upper body drawled a bit, "Come and have a drink."

"Bit early for me pal, but I'll sit and have a smoke with you, if that's cool?" I looked at the lady on the steps of the camper who looked equally unhappy.

There was chair next to him so I perched on that. He turned to me and was about to say something when sadly, the motion, the booze or something keeled over and he tipped sideways. Still perfectly seated, he went over holding his swiftly empty glass and a fag in one hand. I felt the only thing to do was sympathise with the chap. So I duly tipped my chair over sideways and we continued our conversation for awhile like that.

In fact, I don't think he really noticed at all the world had gone sideways, after all his universe had tipped completely upside down the previous January, as mine would a few years later in June.

Then we roared with laughter and righted the chairs while I got on with rolling a big joint. "So, what's a happening pal? You look sort of, like maybe," I was edging forward, not wanting to touch a nerve, "You seem to be having, er, not the best of times, man?"

I wasn't getting the classic 'shut the fuck up' look from the lady on the steps so I pressed on, chirping away like a cracked record, "Well, guess what pal? My name is Mr Smiles and I must have come along today just to find you. Here, have a smile, the first one's free!" I smiled. God I must be an annoying bastard at times. Luckily, we weren't on a high bridge, as such trite slush might just have pushed him over.

Chris smiled bleakly back at me, he knew I was clumsily trying to get across that bridge to him. His voice slurred softly, "Sure." I knew it must be bad. Then he added, "Are you a musician?"

"Yeah buddy, a Guitarist." I held up my right hand with the long fingernails, as if to prove it. "Do you play?"

"Yeah, I play piano." His face lightened up a bit, "In fact I used to play a piano half way up a wall in a restaurant."

Somehow I just knew I was going to love this guy. We chatted for an hour or so and swopped numbers as I invited him up for a jam at Windsong sometime. I explained Monday or Tuesday was often Band Practice. He agreed, like many do. I figured I might or probably might not see him again. I wandered off round the festival to see who else I might bump into.

A few weeks later the phone rang and it was Chris. Could he come up the following week? I was kind of surprised as we had met over an aching wound, but I was thrilled. We had lost our keyboard player that year and were looking for someone new, but I knew Chris lived a fair distance from me in Bristol.

I enthused, "Be great. Come and meet the band man. Bring your keyboard and whatever you fancy. You can kip on the couch if you need to." I heard his reply and put the phone down. I rang Kevan and told him a keyboard player was coming over for the next jam. I always kept him in the loop. Kevan was my 'Right Hand Man' when it came to Band stuff, but oddly enough usually to my left on stage.

The following Monday about six o'clock I started sorting out the 'music room' and firing up the studio, 'Mission Control? Starship No Bleeding Enterprise is about to take off. Start Countdown.'

I was plugging some leads in when the phone went. It was Chris, I thought for a second he was going to cancel, but he started off, 'Er, Hi Geoff, I'm in the village.'

'Oh,' I thought immediately 'He's lost.' But he went on. "You know when we met at the festival I told you about Sylvan's suicide," I'd forgotten her name but it came bounding back at me. From my years studying Latin at school I knew it meant 'Woodland Nymph.' For a moment I pictured my sister Clare, when she used to camp out protecting the wild Orchids.

"Yeah man, I remember."

His voice crackled a bit, "You said some lovely words to me Geoff, thanks."

I could tell he was struggling. I figured something had gone wrong. "What's happened man?"

"Well." There was a sharp intake of breath on the phone, "I was really looking forward to coming up for a jam and I really didn't want to arrive with a dark cloud hanging over me. But man, I gotta tell you…" He paused, then continued "I just, seconds ago, had this call as I turned off the main road to say my best mate has died."

I filled in the silence, "Ah man that's really awful, sorry to hear that."

There was a long pause. "Look man, I really didn't want to bring you down with all this Death again, but also I guess," a longer pause, "maybe I was in some way supposed to be coming to you when I got the news." Short pause, "Sorry man."

"Hey Chris, no worries buddy. Come on up. Nobody is here yet. We can have a chat before they arrive. Whereabouts are you?" He described it and I gave him directions to the cottage. Five minutes later I heard his car pull up.

I went out to greet him, "Welcome to Windsong."

"Cheers Geoff," he sighed, "Look man, it was really special when we met at Sheep music. I was in a bad place man and you just kinda turned up with all that colour and 'Smiles stuff' which helped me to get my head together. Thanks for that."

"That's cool man, it's what I do!" I smiled. "I seem to come across a lot of people who are having some kind of life meltdown. I can usually offer some help or advice. Hey, I always joke, 'I probably had a dose of it myself or know someone who did.'"

Chris's mouth tightened and I figured he was trying to find the words. "Thing is Geoff, I wanted to come tonight and just have a good time without that on my mind. But it's all come flooding back with Tony's death."

I picked up the wine he had brought and grabbed a bottle opener, "Well buddy, I'm glad you have turned up here, I wouldn't want you to be anywhere else when that shit is going down. We'll play some music for his spirit man. Windsong will sort you out."

"Thanks, I just didn't want to turn up on a downer, but I guess I was supposed to be here."

"Well, you remember me saying, Death is sadly one of my specialities. But," I gave him a hug, "Its also, in some way why I live my life flat out, trying to make as much of it as I can. I can't justify wasting one day. Its like death kills us man but the idea of 'Death,' remembering that, keeping it close, can almost give you, like, more life." I smiled.

"Ah cheers. Anyway, I'll get my keyboard and stand. Thanks man. Hey, the cottage looks great."

No doubt Kevan would have turned up shortly after and another night began. Chris fitted in well with the band, seamless. We had a magic session, they often were. Somehow the sum of our parts made a whole we could never have created alone. Also it was fun. Man we laughed, because there was no aggro and no egos, I had that department all wrapped up.

We had talked at Sheep Music but I had also played a couple of songs for him and much of the story of what had happened to his daughter hadn't really been discussed. He mentioned the word 'Suicide.'

Whenever I have met somebody and that word has come up in reference to their life, I have known that I was meant to connect with them. Suicide is one of the cruellest deaths. Most other ways of dying come with the Sine Qua Non that the person is the victim. Its always an injustice, they could have lived another day, another week. Why not? But when someone takes their own life, they and their loved ones are both the victims and the perpetrators of death.

The nearer someone is to the person who commits suicide, the more the responsibility falls at their feet. There is a sense of guilt that we should have seen the warnings signs, felt their distress more keenly. What was the final deed that sealed their fate? Who spoke to them last? I know this too well.

It doesn't really matter what anyone says. Even if everything possible had been done with the advice of professionals to help the victim, there's still a face in the mirror that knows every detail of the case and yet doubts each bit of evidence. It's simply awful.

Chris had done the best he could. His daughter had been suffering with acute depression and confusion. He and those closest to Sylvan had tried to fix her, but in the end he was persuaded to hospitalise her, for 'Her own safety.' He gave his consent.

Within days she committed suicide in the hospital. It is no doubt the cruellest fate a father or mother can ever endure.

It's not my story to tell. However, I should have paid more heed. Such is the misery of hindsight.

Meanwhile, back at the Happy Hippy Ranch, there was an album to make and work to do.

Financially I had been overdrawn consistently since 1983, the day I got my first bank account and there was no sign of imminent improvement. I was managing the bills and Direct Debits reasonably well by robbing Peter to pay Paul, then nicking it back off Paul to pay dear ol'Pete. I was always in the shite financially, it just depended what depth I was in. My Swedish father used to quip, 'Er, the World financial situation seems to be a bit tight at the moment?' So I blame it on a genetic problem!

In those heady days of the last century every week or so a new credit card would appear in the post from some bank, desperate for me to sign the back and start spending their money, money, money.

I sometimes did, revealing in getting my first American Express Gold Card; I felt like the guy off the adverts, except I didn't have his money, his salary or his career. But it always came down to me to cover the slack financially when it came to our life together, entertainments, holidays, dope, coke and running the house, while Maud contributed a bit, well as much as she could manage, which was quite fair I guess, considering her age and after all it was my mortgage.

The problem was sometimes there was a load more slack than I had salary for and Maud had a load less contribution as she was battling with her student loans and so on. So I used the cards as backup.

The more I used them the more they sent me. Every month my credit rating would go up and then my spending limit was increased.

In the end I was servicing about seven cards just to make ends meet and er, knock together ten albums.

I used to say to my Bank Manager, while he took several Valium and banged his head repeatedly on the desk, "Hey man, an overdraft is just the sign of a well lived life. If you're not pushing at the edge of your credit limit you're not really living!"

To which he pleaded, 'Please whatever happens Mr Smiles, I really like you but don't ever repeat that to any other Bank Manager.' He would stamp my loan and tell me to keep an eye on things.

I never did. What went in went in, what came out came out. I never spent money rashly or stupidly. Not that everybody needs a sixteen track mixing desk, but believe me it makes an attractive feature in the corner of any lounge.

I used my money, or rather their money, to make my Art. I needed a roof over my head to keep my guitars dry and my girlfriend happy.

Not that there was always a roof at Windsong. I had some issues with the bathroom that necessitated an umbrella next to the toilet in case it rained. The creeper on the roof had eventually rotted the felt and eventually the whole thing fell through one day. As I was broke at the time I just had to get on with it. I thought it was quite attractive being able to stare up at the stars on a clear night while having a piss!

Poor Chris had the worst of it in that bathroom. I got the ceiling fixed eventually and painted a mural on it. Having had one too many puffs on one of my joints he went off to the loo during a jam session, midway through the track we were playing. He didn't come back. We just carried on regardless.

In the bathroom he had suddenly felt faint and laid down on the floor. Looking up he saw all the fish I had painted on the ceiling and for a moment thought he was underwater and couldn't breathe. Having got over that and recovered somewhat, he returned to the front room. As he came in he saw us jamming away and thought, 'Oh wow, there's a band in here and it looks like there's a keyboard free over there. Maybe I'll just go and join in?'

It wasn't till he hit the keys he actually came back to us. Needless to say the band didn't skip a beat.

Work at school had its good and bad times but I was generally loving it. Stopping on the way back at my Canadian friends Greg and Linda was a nice way to end some days. Watching the seasons pass by as I commuted across the landscape of The Cotswolds was a twice daily joy.

However, for all my efforts and successes in school, whether conventional or not, I kept hearing the HM saying he wanted a younger man doing the PE. Odd really as I don't think there was ever a more childlike teacher than me.

Anyway, I just got on with the job and the boys, I avoided the back biting of the Staff room. My stock response when anybody tried to involve me in their lamenting and bitching was, 'Look, I'm far too much of an egotist to want to speak about anybody else but me.' That usually worked.

But, when an injustice is done to me it's hard not to react in some way. There was a lot of stress that went with the job, mainly handling the personal and occasionally the physical abuse. Some days, when a restraint or situation had been intense the adrenaline was pumping so much my face would turn red from the increased blood flow.

I learned a lot from those years and would never have walked willingly away from that school. But, the temperature had been rising and then a calamity struck. Not massive in the grand scheme of things, but enough of a straw to break the Camel's back.

I was taking a lesson that was just coming to an end. It was the afternoon, one of the lads didn't want to return the last football that was out. We had a good lesson up to that moment, so maybe he wasn't ready to stop yet. He kicked the ball away to another boy who then passed it back to him. But this time he swung round and booted it as hard as he could at me. I was in the gym doorway and couldn't dodge to the left or right.

It smashed me right in the face and suddenly I felt a lump of stone on my tongue. I was just about to spit it out when I realised it was my front tooth. Broken clean off up to the gum.

I couldn't allow the boy to see his victory, for I knew that was how he would see it, so I turned away and covered my mouth. Just then another teacher came down the corridor.

I quickly showed him my mouth, mentioned the kid's name and asked him to get the class off for their next lesson and lock the gym door.

I told him I was going for First Aid but I wasn't. I went to my car and drove home. There was nothing in their First Aid box for me.

When I got home I probably had a smoke and an almighty cup of Poppy Tea or similar. It wasn't good. I looked a mess, my lip was split and swollen. I phoned the school and said I'd email a full Report over immediately but was taking a couple of days off. This was the term after Billy beat me up, I said I needed to recuperate, take stock and see a Dentist. No problem.

An hour or so later the Head of Education rang me. He was a guy who had experienced a 'Breakdown' himself. He was quite new and had never worked in Special Education before. It was me gave him some tips and showed him the ropes when he first arrived at our school.

His conversation was basically along the lines of, 'when would I be back?' He also chose that moment to complain about my wearing of sports vests to work, instead of the traditional 'Fred Perry' short sleeved shirt.

The thing was, as regards my clothes, I didn't stand at the side of the gym with a whistle, I didn't shout, 'Give me ten Press-Ups, jump on the spot,' without doing it myself. My theory was how can you expect a boy to run a mile if you can't. Lead by example.

I remember explaining some of this and then the call was over.

I couldn't believe it.

Something inside me was bending.

Something inside was breaking.

My dentist was a friendly guy and got me straight in to see him. "Hmm, it's just about fixable, but I will have to 'Post and Crown' it." The cost was going to be eight hundred pounds, which, surprise surprise, I didn't have.

I rang the school. Later that day the secretary let me know the school was not prepared to foot the cost of the dental work. I was already deep in debt and now I'd have to find a grand from somewhere.

I couldn't believe it. I said to friends, 'I'd be better of on a Building Site, at least they would have Public Liability Insurance.' Little did I know that was where I was headed back to. After all the years studying to get out of them, I was headed back to the trenches.

That day something broke inside. It was almost as if the animal instinct for survival was coming up and shouting, "Fuck this! I can't take this shit anymore."

Simple as that. It wasn't even my mind, or brain deciding, it was a physical, an emotional response.

I broke.

I slept for three days straight. My mind went to bed, pulled the covers over and dived under the pillows. I was shattered into so many pieces I just couldn't stick them back together. I slept on. I never sleep. I am the world's worst sleeper, it comes from years of drugs and more drugs. I only ever sleep for a period of hours if I have taken a stronger than usual opiate.

It was the end of an era, barre a brief return to fame and glory at Winchcombe School a few years later. But a 'Profession' comes with another Sine Qua Non that it's necessary to stick at it for decades to reap the full benefits. I was never going to stick at any job for decades, let alone years, unless it was writing, art or music. I knew only too keenly how precious each year of life was. To repeat the same ritual of terms, in the same or similar school, causes time to concertina. Suddenly too long has passed to evince a change.

I went to see my Doctor the following week and described what had happened. He took one look at me and suggested I take some time off, not days, but a few weeks, maybe longer.

Boy, did I enjoy passing that information along to the secretary of the school.

Yet really, of course, I didn't. There was my class of boys to consider. They would be lost for awhile without me. But I told myself I was giving them the best lesson, the 'Last' lesson! Which is, 'Nothing ever remains the same.'

The moral was, like a good parent should say to their teenagers, 'Ok, now you have to go and make your own way in the world, a few months ahead of schedule I know, but Life doesn't always tie in with the School Calendar. Best of luck. On you go.'

To which I would have added, with a smile, "I did my best for you, I taught you everything I know," and then, "Do you remember that afternoon?"

It wasn't the plan during the first weeks off to jack it all in but I never did get the chance to see my lads again. I would have preferred that, but 'Life' doesn't always tie in with what we plan for.

As Lennon said, 'Life is what happens to us while we're making plans to do other things.' Which sadly, for him should have read, 'Death is what happens to us, while we're making plans to do other things.'

Which will no doubt be the case for all of us. If Lennon couldn't escape the Grim Reaper there's no hope for us mere mortals.

BETA

I was up at the Mount having a Sunset pint when a friend called 'Dodge' offered me a job. I should have guessed! It was basically humping buckets of mud from the back of a cottage, through a very narrow alleyway to a skip on the road. It didn't seem an awesome step up in my career but it had the advantage of being in Stanton. Working in a 'Picture Postcard' village surrounded by the landscape I had known and loved for twenty years wasn't going to be tough; with a boss who was as laid back as hot butter on burnt toast. I said I'd think about it.

It had been early winter when I had left Swalcliffe. Since then I had not received a phone call or any communication from the staff whatsoever. But just a few days before Christmas a letter came from Ray Hooper, the Headmaster. I thought it was a card or note hoping I would be back in school next term. No, it was a brief statement outlining that a pupil had, after I'd already been gone for several weeks, suddenly made an official complaint against me about something I'd said.

The actual phrase the boy and the Headmaster took exception to was, 'Grow up and act like a young man,' apparently this was disrespectful to a fourteen year old, as he was not yet a 'young man's' age. This bollox was the direction Teaching was going, with my HM pushing it on, merrily down the crapper.

I had to send in a full reply stating it was a stock 'throwaway' phrase used commonly in the English language to convey a general sense that somebody was acting below their physical age; not implying they should really be any older than they really are.

Gosh, it was all bullshit and came to nothing three months later. But it felt like a kick in the teeth again, at one of my most unfavourite times of year, Xmas. Also, I then had another worry to pile on top of the rest of the shit in the crapper.

I stewed myself over that for a few months. Around February I went to see the Doc again and he didn't need any convincing to sign me off for another three months. I must have looked shite.

In regard to all this I rang Mr Hooper and basically offered him a deal. I had many colleagues who had gone off sick for months, even years, or a serial of months and several sicknesses. This was a pain in the butt in Special Schools as Supply Teachers were generally not up to the chaos and would usually be eaten alive by the boys. Inevitably the other staff would end up covering the gaps and loosing 'Free Periods;' these were supposedly used to do marking and lesson planning, but more often than not it was a case of a coffee, a quick mental breakdown and a fag in the woods.

Even with their lack of due care towards me I wasn't going to exit like a wet blanket. I asked to speak to Mr Hooper, there were no pleasantries so I began, "Ok, the Doctor has signed me off for another three months; pay me that in full, which they had to anyway and I'll call it a day from then. You can have that in writing."

He almost choked on his words and hardly paused for breath as he agreed. It was an easy closure for him, he could plan his year without having to keep my job open and get the PE Teacher he wanted.

I actually received a card from the Staff about a month later, wishing me well for my future. They had all signed it. What freaking future I wondered? But that made it official. I was history. A few months later in mid summer I was passing by, probably smashed out of my brains, feeling good. I figured it would be a great idea to pop in to the school and say thanks for the card and the good times we had.

I waltzed into the Staff Meeting, which I knew took place at that time each day, the debriefing! The door was off the latch so I was in there before they knew it. Several chins hit the table, one or two the floor. I must have looked double shite. My shock was the sight of the new PE Teacher, some bald bloke in his neat Pringle T shirt, which couldn't disguise the fact he was not as lean as me and looked much older.

So I took the job with Dodge. I did ask if I knocked out one of my teeth would his work insurance cover it? It did and I didn't.

The mud went on and on and on, but it wasn't a job done under duress. Dodge was the only building site boss I ever saw working in Gucci Loafers, I guess that summed his style up. The other labourer was a young woman I knew well from the pub, who was currently 'Up the duff' and therefore due some time off. He had mentioned the wages, stating he would look after me well, but when the first Friday came I realised I was back in the Third Division again. My

Teacher's salary ended, but the debts I had accrued during that time certainly didn't, including the ones from before then, which were still demanding their monthly slice of the pie. I was in triple shite.

Most of the banks hadn't quite cottoned on that my status had changed as I didn't get round to telling them. Some of them even kept increasing my credit limit every few months. So I was using these to keep my little cottage afloat. I was robbing Peter daily to pay Paul and Tom and Chris and John and so on.

My dear lady was already carrying her Student Loan around like a trunk of lead on a sinking ship to which she had also added one or two credit card debts. It was how life worked back then. We had friends with a deck of cards in their wallets; we all believed that one day when things perked up it would all be fine again. I had no major concerns and kept making the next album, going for the next trip and buying the next thing we needed.

I never spent like a Fool, but I spent like a man who saw these bits of plastic card as merely tools. As long as the job of life got done, we could sort out the paperwork another day; but I never did.

Money had never mattered much to me, as I never had much to matter about! I believed it wasn't the size of a man's wallet that was important, it was the size of his heart and the truly special things in life cannot be bought with money.

I had albums, paintings and books I wanted to create. I had a simple method of going about the funding for these which was to make the thing first. Never presume a project will be completed until it is.

Then find out the manufacturing costs and seek out the money. I always found it some way somehow. I followed the Frank Zappa School of 'Just sign anything as long as it pays for the next album.'

Unfortunately, I didn't have a Record Deal like dear Frank, I just had American Express, or whatever credit card was fortunate enough that year to be chosen by me to contribute to the Cosmic Smiles' mission of spreading 'Peace n'Love' throughout the world.

Which I really did try to do, to the best of my ability. I was laughed at of course for my naivety and foolhardy economics, but I hoped, against all hope, for a miracle. With the current situation in the World there was never a greater need for an army of 'naive' Peace Makers.

Hearing from Dodge that I was a good grafter, Colin at The Mount gave me a day a week mowing the pub's almost vertical lawns. It felt good to be working for people I liked, in a paradise I loved.

With these limited funds I just managed to make the mortgage every month. Rule Number One, 'Don't lose the house!' In my heart of hearts I wanted to be able to leave my children something. It was parental instinct, I wanted them to enjoy what I'd missed, the natural flow of heritage.

It may have seemed like another fall from grace, with a school at the heart of the plot; returning me to the muddy trenches I had climbed out of twenty or so years before. However the work was wholesome, the backdrop stunning, I enjoyed the simplicity of it, the lack of stress or politics and in particular the lack of any paperwork. Oddly enough, unlike teaching, nobody wants to know how many buckets of mud were moved in one day, nor how they relate to the buckets I filled three months ago or the buckets I plan to fill in three months time!

I would be finished by four in the afternoon and could be home in four minutes and twenty seconds. I began to understand that being happy seemed to stem from a simple, yet wholesome life. Being on limited funds removed so many options from life but the experience could be liberating. I wasn't able to plan much further than four days ahead, often less, so I ended up living very much in the moment 'Now.' Ironically this is what countless fancy courses and gurus of enlightenment promise their devotees, at some expense. I simply achieved enlightenment with buckets of mud and a consistent overdraft.

Also at the end of every week I still had a reminder that perhaps it is better to consider what we're spared on a daily basis, rather than what we haven't managed to attain, or buy, or own, or whatever... Rob had been out of hospital some years but we still continued our rehabilitation sessions every Friday after work. We went to the swimming pool at the Evesham Leisure Centre and spent an hour paddling about, back and forth in the water. Over time he had become more stable and the muscles in his legs were getting stronger. He no longer felt like he was falling backwards every time he straightened his legs.

His eyesight was still challenged, he had a sort of tunnel vision that was fairly clear, but one eye was worse than the other. However, whenever a friend of mine from the gym was there, teaching swimming in her black costume, his best eye lit up like a firework. It's a boy's thing. He needed the inspiration to keep trying, when all else seemed hopeless and the end result was never going to be perfect.

Rob made me acutely aware of my own body and senses. He brought home to me again and again the joy of just being able to walk, being able to take a piss without assistance from two burly nurses. It's never really appreciated until it's lost or threatened. My heart goes out to these victims. It is surely the cruellest fate, particularly for the average man with all the old preconceptions about being macho.

There were some bits we both had to get our heads around. I had to help him dress. I didn't like it, I just had to do it. He didn't like it but he just had to go through with it.

I guess it may seem an odd way to end the working week. Hadn't I thought of a pint at the pub? But that was never my bag, I wanted to do worthwhile things with my life; I was so lucky to be alive when so many of my family or friends had died, most of whom had been more careful and circumspect in their lives, but sadly, not as fortunate with Fate.

One of them was Crispin. He was such a lovely guy. We had met in the Eighties and as my drug use went up in the Nineties and Noughties we met a lot more. He had a 'Script' than would sink a ship and the sort of mad chaotic flat where packets of this and bottles of that would appear from forgotten corners. We got smashed a lot together and talked about 'Best Hits' and the piles of drugs we'd consumed. Typical and topical subjects for every junkie, usually consumed with as much passion as a Chef for a Michelin Star. Between us we could have sunk an Battle Ship.

Like many long term addicts with a large, regular prescription of drugs, it was very easy to end up chained by stupor to the bed, avoiding the daylight hours and preferring the anonymity of night, the lack of 'Daily life' outside. The continual assault of drugs on his body had taken its toll. He was getting inactive and podgy due to the effects of Methadone. It saps all the spark out of a human, it acts like a weird sort of anti depressant. it was Prozac before they invented Prozac and had just about as useful an effect on a human, like sticking a slowly filling feather pillow over the head, removing all the Bass, but all the Treble too. It is the road to nullification.

The high level of sugar in liquid Methadone also rots teeth. It was this side effect that twisted his fate.

He was one of several 'Junkie' Writers or Artists I'd known. He covered notebooks with small writing, hundreds of words and doodles crammed on every page. He adored music and had a great collection of records. He got high, played music, mused and wrote. As the world receded his page expanded. This I understood, I had been there too.

I've always loved my close male friends. I am quite open with that, unable to cover up the thrill and joy I get from their company. My buddies became my brothers. I've found many guys like me in the Junkyard, kicking opiates about like old tin cans. I believe our hearts were just over filled to bursting with emotions, not all of which were welcome. The moment the Opium kicked in the sorrows got kicked out. We discovered our tempestuous sorrow could be tamed, lulled by a lullaby in a bottle, frozen in slow motion. I love my close female friends too, but there is something special between guys.

We had been friends for twenty years or so I guess. In the early Eighties I had been employed by his elder sister's husband Vic Norman, an Aerobatic Pilot of some renown, to paint their mansion near to Cirencester. In those days I biked out to work from my girlfriend's house and marvelled as his Pop star friends popped by. Crispin would wander over from his parent's house, which was in the same grounds, for a chat. We soon found out we had a lot in common, too much.

Twenty years later there came a time when running the Cheltenham flat became too much and Crispin went back home to live. His father the Major, had always welcomed me to visit his son. The Mother even more so. But they could see the same look in my eyes as Chris had. On the walls downstairs were photos of the Major scaling the Alps with Crispin, when he was a teenager, still showing the healthy glow of a Public School education.

His room was always the same, the bed unmade, the side table a litter of bottles, fag papers, pills and filled ashtrays; magazines and books vied with piles of clothes for bits of floor space. The curtains were often closed, always closed if I'm honest. Without much exercise his weight increased. My aim was always to open the curtains and drag him out in the sunlight for a walk up to the little lake Vic had put in. Crispin's sister Anne often waved if she saw us wander up the hill. How different their fates had been.

From the outside it would be easy to judge Crispin as a drop out from a prestigious background which he had obviously abused.

Yet it was a car crash that started Crispin's decline and fall. The fatality of the girl in the passenger seat. He was, as I suggested above, just one of those guys with too big a heart to forgive himself or ever move on entirely. I don't know where the blame for the crash fell. I can't remember if he ever told me. But you don't have to be doing anything wrong to have a car crash. Fate has more than one way of pursuing its victims. Whatever the reasons, I sensed this was the fatal flaw that broke his heart.

But I persevered with my persevering , as I had with Rob Gilder. We kept walking and I kept nagging him to get out. Things were looking up, summer was in full flower, we surveyed the lake, smoked a joint or two and all was good.

In an effort to improve his health and his sense of self the idea arose of getting his teeth sorted out, or rather, taken out.

They were basically, monumentally buggered. Drug use seems to show the power of its ugliness in the teeth first, as well as that daily smash of sugar in the Methadone liquid. Apparently it was going to be easier to extract them all, in one operation, at the local hospital under aesthetic.

At that time he was keen to get hold of some Coke to do a few lines with me and something to break up the monotony of his opiate use. With his operation date coming up he had become more insistent on wanting a good blow out and badgered me to sort it out. For someone like him he needed a lot of anything to cut through the mountainside of drugs he was already on. I was always worried in his keen endeavour to get high he'd blow his brains out.

I begged him to take care and I think he actually did, for me. He didn't want me to have the same guilt he'd had all those years.

By chance, I must have known somebody who was able to get some Coke and I took a gram over one day. It wasn't my thing but we had a line together and went up to the lake for a smoke.

He told me the date of the appointment and joked if he died on the operating table I could have all his Velvet Underground and Lou Reed albums. I said, in all seriousness, I'd rather have his note books.

"Nobody else comes to see me man." He smiled. I knew what he was saying. 'Thanks.'

He didn't die during the operation, he was fine. They kept him in hospital for a day or so as he was on such high doses of opiates and to make sure he didn't get septicaemia. He didn't.

The hospital staff said he caught pneumonia. His lungs filled with liquid and he drowned to death.

At that time MRSA was rife in hospitals all over the country, it presents its symptoms pretty much in the same way as pneumonia and I feel it was more likely the cause. Yet not good publicity for the hospital.

The Major wasn't the kind of man to question the Doctors. He was heart broken at the time and what would it resolve? A long vein of pain had been cut.

I bounded along to his house about a month or so after the operation, expecting him to be grinning from ear to ear with his new dentures. I always went round the back of the house to the kitchen door. His mother saw me but greeted me with an expression I didn't recognise at first.

"Ah, Geoff. Come in." But instead of waving me through to the stairs she pointed to the table, "Take a seat. I'm really sorry. We should have let you known sooner. I'm afraid Crispin has died."

"Oh God no, I'm so sorry to hear that. How did it happen? I thought he was fine after his operation?" She explained how and I suddenly realised he must have died some weeks ago.

Without thinking I blurted out, "When is the funeral? I would love to say a few words for him as he was such a…" As I was talking I was not getting the response from her features I expected, I paused. Something wasn't quite right.

"I'm afraid the funeral has already taken place, a week or so ago." She tailed off and stared into the middle distance, before murmuring, apologetically, "I'm sorry. I appreciate you would have liked to have been there."

I was nodding, trying to digest all this information; but as my brain rattled through the evidence it became evident what had been decided.

She went on, as if hearing my thoughts, "We didn't know how to get hold of you."

I sat in silence. What? My name and number wasn't on ten bits of paper in his room? it wasn't in the Phone Book, or Directory Enquiries? A two minute walk over the lawns, Vic or Anne had my number. There were several ways they could have got hold of me. Try Dr Marks or anybody at the Drug Clinic!

I figured the real reason was they wouldn't want a junkie in the congregation to remind them of Crispin's demise and some of their friends were of course from the upper echelons.

Yet, before I could run this dirt track of self pity any further the ponderous voice of the Major called me through to the living room. He was broken. He shook my hand. He would have probably wanted 'Chris' to have his mate there; but it had been a long time since the Major had commanded any troops; those closest to him probably thought it best I was left out.

I stayed a short while. They mentioned a new bench had been put beside the lake where we used to have our smokes, with Crispin's favourite saying on it, which I can't remember now. I took a wander up there, giving a hypothetical wave to a shadow in the window as I passed the house. As much as we could have talked forever, the Major and I had nothing left to say except, 'Sorry.'

Looking back at the calendar diaries I kept at the time, all from The Jack Daniel's Distillery, I can see Crispin's name mentioned over the years, then it just vanishes.

In many ways it was what Crispin had courted with his drug use, a needless death to equal the one he'd lost in the car crash.

It's like that for some of us. I spent fifty years trying to blow my brain to bits whilst studiously repairing it, trying to batter my body as I fanatically bettered it. The guilt of being a survivor can be a recurring trial.

Crispin was gone. His notebooks and records were passed on to his niece.

Reading through these years, caught in glimpses on scattered notes, life at home was a stream of events moulded round work. Maud and Saffron went away on Film Shoots here and abroad. Which I also did, being a 'Snow Technician,' recreating Norwegian battle grounds in the back of a supermarket carpark, in Worcester.

However, I didn't like work. My dislike of drudgery is evident. But everything hung on a rope of hope that one day the band will get lucky or something will work out. We had so many good things that came out of the blue that gave Hope a head start on Rational Thinking. So many unsolicited bits of good news or connections that might possibly get us at least a decent gig, or a 'Showcase.' But all those leads never connected us to the power source.

It was hard making album after album, stretching an already bankrupt household further, only to have each CD slowly die in its tracks; albeit heading in the right direction but Dead On Arrival. It was like being the Captain of a Football Team that always lost. It's hard keeping the morale going with defeat after defeat, year after year. On a plus Andy was an Aston Villa fan and thus inured to such an existence, that helped.

One day I was on the phone trying to get a chance to talk to somebody, who was somebody, that knew somebody in The Music Business. He was listening patiently to my spiel about the band and then cut in abruptly. "You've done seven albums?"

I was thinking I had impressed him with this and was about to tell him all about the eighth, when his voice piped up again. "So, Geoff, how old are you?"

Somewhat unsure where this was leading, but with my head still firmly in the clouds, I told him.

"You've got to be joking?" I heard a peculiar laugh; one that sounded like it was being strangled at birth. I still harboured a thread of gossamer hope that he was on my side, but the voice went on and killed me, "You're too old mate. Forget it." The line clicked and died. A little bit more of the chunk of hope in my heart was knocked off.

I went on to make more albums, but the band had reached the point where it all became pointless. We played now simply because we loved making music. In some ways it was a release from servitude to Hope. But like Polar explorers captured by the Long Night, I guess we couldn't help hoping for a miracle.

The mid years of the Noughties, four and five, were filled with Media work, doing Research for History programmes based wars in Holland and Crete. Then I began writing Rockumentaries for Eagle Media, to go with their reissued and tarted up DVD releases, mainly of 'Prog Rock' Bands.

I loved the variety of the work, the intensity of the filming and doing the interviews. It wasn't a regular enough income to be viable long term but somehow

I managed to make the mortgage every month; even if it was half past three on the last day of the month and I had to cycle the seven miles to get to the bank. I always made it, somehow, some way.

We spent summer weekends on the Gower in Wales and usually a holiday once a year in Arrilas, Corfu. I was in and out of whatever drugs I could get hold of, maintaining a small addiction. It wasn't heroin, but pretty much everything else like it. Endless bottles of Gee's Linctus, Codeine Phosphate and Morphine.

I did some Supply Teaching for awhile and the local school in Winchcombe invited me to take some classes. I had never encountered 'Normal Pupils,' and it took awhile to get used to them doing what they were told and actually being polite.

Naturally the kids enjoyed having a long haired, guitar playing, Kite flying teacher; it wasn't hard to win them over, especially considering how tough all my other pupils had been.

One day the Headmaster stopped me and said he'd never come across a teacher who had made such an impact on a school in so short a time. He said my career would surpass even his, in his estimation. While I got my head round that he added that the Annual Outdoors Summer Trip to the Lake District was taking place in a few weeks. Due to pressure from the students he had agreed to let me go along; though usually it would have been a full time Staff member.

Having done the wilderness training and camping with the Special Needs Boys this would be a breeze. For some reason I arranged to join them at their

Hostel in Ullswater, having first paid a visit to my eccentric Uncle Peter at his cottage half way up a Fell in Broughton In Furness.

I remember it was getting near the end of the week in The Lake District. All had gone pretty well. It was a beautiful morning, I bought a small rucksack and joined the others. We were doing sailing that day. In the evening one of the women staff quizzed me as to why I had not brought my Mobile Phone with me.

I replied, "Well, if I'm away with the kids I like to be fully focused on their week," I paused, "After all, even if I was contacted in an emergency, what could I do up here? I may as well wait until I'm back home and can do something about it." It made perfect sense to me, but I sensed something in her smile which didn't.

It was the last time I saw Uncle Peter, my adopted father's brother. He was the pioneer of the modern Van Life, way before any people had thought about it. Loading up his VW bus and heading off to the sand of the Sahara. He had filled my boyhood imagination with such vigour and wanderlust, or was it just lust? A product of Post War life and a mind far too brilliant for its own good. His peccadillos were many and renowned, his journeys always laden with adventure, hashish and sex. He was never viewed as negative or a pariah, in fact he was feted and loved by all the family, like a colourful, stuttering, mad professor of Life, or was it Love? His beard would gather the crumbs of his dinner until soaked up in the froth of his home brew.

I had found an array of Codeine in his medicine box and pillaged some for my journey. I perused the thick manuscript he had been working on for years. Reams of paper, filling the bottom drawer of a filing cabinet. Most of it hand written in small script. It must have been as long as 'War and Peace' and yet still not finished. I made him promise to let me see it when it was done. One morning, I headed off down the long pot holed drive from 'Browside' to the small road by the gurgling beck, hitching to Ullswater to meet up with the school trip. It was the last time I saw him. It was sad. He was already ill, but he had a Thai wife, who was doing her best to look after him. Still a randy bugger to the bitter end.

Men like him would be derided now; but in those heady days of the 'Permissive Society' I viewed him as a hero, I would dearly like to follow.

'Windsong' had stalled my adventuring, but I had discovered some journeys can take place without having to leave home. Writing, in particular, was one. Having a band was another. Romance too.

I can clearly remember the last miles of the coach trip back to school for some reason. I was overjoyed with life, the trip had gone well. I had been offered a permanent job by the Headmaster, setting up a Special Unit to help pupils struggling emotionally or with their work. I was on the way back up. They had virtually created the job for me to keep me there.

Sadly, it wasn't strictly a teaching job so they had pushed the wage to the top of the relevant pay scale they were able to offer; but still well below what I could earn as a teacher. I had accepted the post anyway.

As the coach pulled into Winchcomb School we all gathered our bags and half eaten packed lunches together. I was at the front and first off the bus. As I came down the steps and looked up I saw Debbie, a 'Biker' friend, was there.

I suddenly remembered that odd look on the woman's face in regard to my mobile phone. Debs gave me a hug, "I've come to meet you Smiles." I was just about to say how kind that was to give me a lift, when she suddenly added, "Dave's had an accident." I knew who she meant.

"Bogey? What's happened? Is he okay? Is Jane okay?" I had no idea what had occurred. I realised then why the woman had quizzed me about my mobile phone. They must have known.

Jane told me about it that afternoon. It was the oddest of circumstances which led to his death, the finding of a Twenty Pound note.

Dave had always been a bit of a drinker as Bikers often are, it goes with the territory, hard men, hard drinking, hard fighting and hard living. But with time the Liver becomes bitter and the tongue follows on soon after.

It had reached the point where Dave's supplies of booze were limited by Jane for the sanity of both of them. One day they were on the way up to the local shop when Dave spotted a twenty pound note on the ground. He picked it up and dutifully gave it to Jane. She knew what he meant. 'I'm not allowed that, because I'll spend it on beer and get pissed.'

"No, you keep it. I trust you." He knew what Jane meant. They went up the shop and came back. He must have nipped out when she was hoovering or in the back garden. He ran up the shop and back with four cans of strong lager or suchlike.

He did his best to mask the smell and the fact he was drunk, but Jane knew the moment she saw him. She was genuinely so pissed off that he had let her down after all his promises and the trust she had shown him by returning the note. What's worse was that he knew it and regretted it, he no doubt knew he'd let them both down, once too often.

He went upstairs for something, the next thing Jane heard was the clatter as he fell back down. We never were really sure whether he just slipped, was just pissed, or just too pissed off with himself.

Jane rang the Emergency Services.

He was in Gloucester Hospital, which is the most unattractive, uninspiring, grey, multi storey building. He was somewhere up there. We were chuffed to find him in his own room, it looked like he was being well looked after. In fact he had MRSA and later on Cdiff, a virulent microbe that tears the stomach apart and wastes the body away.

Unable to digest his food properly he eventually went from twelve stone in weight down to about six. It took seven months, all through Winter until the Spring. Then at last he gave in.

At least 'Skinny' would be waiting for him. Another brother had gone, so cruelly.

Jane had heard me speak at Keith's funeral. She didn't dislike Veronica but wasn't happy for her to do

Dave's funeral and asked me if I would do the whole Service.

"Of course I will. I'd be honoured." I didn't really need to state the bleeding obvious, but I did. "I'll try not to let him down."

A few weeks later later the day of the funeral came. Walking up I stopped briefly at Brian Jones' grave in Cheltenham Crematorium and pleaded to his spirit again to help me get through this. There were a few people already milling about and many more I could see following up the road. Deb turned up with Jane's sister Sue holding onto her arm; both looked frail.

A short while later we walked through the Waiting Room to stand at the other side of the Crematorium to await the Hearse.

From far away, cutting through the birdsong and hum of distant traffic, I heard that inimitable roar of the motorbikes getting louder and louder, until they swung into view through a long line of Yew trees and graves, puttering and spluttering to where we stood. On top of the coffin inside the hearse Dave's Crash Helmet rested in a sea of flowers.

As, one by one, the Harley Davidsons were parked up and turned off, the sound of my knees knocking together got louder and louder. The Bearers were gathered together and Dave's coffin was placed on their shoulders.

ALPHA

Having travelled from Alpha to Omega on the good ship 'EX,' we now return in 'nEXt,' from Omega to Alpha. In every end is a beginning. On reflection however, Dave's death over several months marked the beginning of my end. The decline and fall, the War of Attrition, which lasted six years and sank my little cottage ship.

I had no idea, as I sat by his bed, staring out of the window at the grey expanse of Gloucester sprawled below, that this was just the cold, cooler, coldest, icy waters of the southern oceans. I was unaware these swirling Spring tides, on which the solitary Albatross soared, were just a prelude to the icebergs.

In fact I was drifting in a sea of ice into the bleakest, most godless, awful place imaginable. I was now trapped in an inexorable current, with the ice getting thicker by the day, dragging my bedraggled barque 'Windsong,' ever further, towards a frozen wasteland of antarctic proportions.

Ultimately the ice would pierce my skin and take hold of every organ, quelling the pipes one by one until just the strangled sound of a broken chord was all that remained.

If I had written this book in that hospital room, not knowing my fate, waiting for Dave to die and then decided to write my own future, I could not have created from the bowels of my asshole such a horror story. I had no idea, even with all the sunken ships

I'd already sailed on, how a heart could be so torn to shreds. How thew gods of life could be so brutal.

It is bad enough to lose a loved one, but Fate can't resist turning the knife a half screw, into the bone marrow of emotion. My mother may well have died from any one of the several attempts she made on her life. It was just that Fate chose the night we had argued; my words being the last spoken to her. I was sixteen. I was crazy. I was on all and any drugs. I was into anything or anybody. I was as wild as a Cougar, set free from the school walls, liberated to roam at will on the city streets.

Death seemed to be dancing over my life and through my meadows. Mr Sharpley, the farmer at Lydes Farm, next door, a real old gentleman, died suddenly one morning; his wife took much longer with cancer, over the next few years. This resulted in my dearest friend and neighbour Michael Bunting and his wife Christine being ousted from their 'Tied' cottage. She had worked at the farm regularly and Michael had helped out with all the shitty jobs, literally for years. They loved their cottage and their mad musical neighbour. In my role as a general word smith and all round gobshite I was enlisted to be their solicitor when the children of Mr Sharpley took them to court to serve the eviction notice. It was my briefest career but went extraordinarily well. We got the deal that Michael wanted and life went on. The farm and all its lands with he cottage was duly sold off at auction. It turned out to be the scruffiest man there who paid a million or so for it; Ian Warmington. He had an Eighties leather jacket on and a bundle of wealth apparently from some aunt in America. How fate favours the feckless bastards. I also spoke to Earl Wemys and managed to get a cottage for Michael and Christine in Didbrook.

I didn't think too much about it at the time. I would have done anything for Mike and I guess properties do eventually change hands and families. Sadly we had let the most selfish, petty, nasty man in the valley get hold of the farm and he was to make everybody's lives a misery henceforth and still does. He gave one couple in a self built house opposite such grief over the grass verge on the road and their hedge that eventually the wife also got cancer and died tragically. Stress really is a killer and it seems sometimes there is no justice.

Although we live a hundred or so miles apart now Michael and me are still 'neighbours.' He is one of the loveliest, kind hearted men I've met and truly doesn't have a bad bone in his body. He likes a drink on a regular basis but never turned into a horrible drunk, in fact he's the nicest dipsomaniac I've ever met. There was the occasion when I once asked him about his drinking and why such a lovely man drank the amount he did. There were no skeletons in his cupboard and no major concerns in his life. "Well, Geoffrey," he replied, "I'm just a very thirsty man!" To which there is no response other than a nod and a smile. What a character, like me a consistently and determined pauper, but worth a hundred Mr Warmingtons in my book, which this is!

Then there was Paul's death in London which had another twist of the devil's knife at the end. He was a beautiful, very intelligent man, a Physics graduate I believe; who lived on the King's Road. When I say on the King's road I mean literally on the pavement, under the overhang of the Chelsea Fire Station.

I used to visit him every time I trudged to Rob Corich's door in Edith Grove. He ran Steel Music. I spent three years hoping he would get the band a little break or distribute our albums. Three years of promises, a lot of train rides and countless albums I bought off him. His saving grace was he loved Grand Funk Railroad. GFR fans are a rare breed, hardy to the slings and arrows of bad press about their band. Despite a slanging early on by the music pundits Grand Funk Railroad were a very successful American Rock trio, famously selling out Shea Stadium. I felt certain we had bonded over that and he would help me out. I even planned to learn one of their songs to win him over. As it happened his Record Label should have been spelt 'Steal Music.'

He wasn't so bad I guess, unless killing someone's dreams becomes a murder offence one day.

However, each time I went up to visit him I stopped on the walk from the Tube to hang out with Paul. We used to have a smoke and chew over the fat of the land, as they say. We talked about life and philosophy, people and events. He loved the way I sat on the pavement with him and he called me, 'My humblin' brother.' Except once when I went up, just before Christmas, I was in a rush so I bypassed Paul's pitch of cardboard and blankets.

I was at Andy's in Sheperd's Bush, early the following year, having one of his diamond crushing

Gin and Tonics. It was around the same time as Dave was in hospital. We chatted about the usual stuff and his Interior Design work which was always fascinating.

Then he remembered something and his face changed expression from fifth gear to reverse. "Oh, I forgot to say, wasn't it a man who begged near the Fire Station in Chelsea that you used to know?"

"Yeah, Paul. Have you seen him?" I could tell from the short delay in his response something wasn't quite right.

"Ah, I'm sorry Geoff, but with all the stuff going on with Clare and the Christmas holidays I forgot to tell you. I'm afraid Paul has died."

"What! How? Jesus, he looked great last time I saw him." It turned out that three men had jumped out of a car late one night with baseball bats and broken his legs, just for a laugh, or a dare, or because they just didn't like beggars. Apparently he survived the attack but obviously could not get about so easily. Less movement in the bitter Winter means a body slowly gets colder and colder. The hours between 3am and 5am being the worst. Ironically Paul died from hypothermia, under the arch of the Chelsea Fire Station, in one of the most expensive, deluxe streets in London.

He was right about Clare, my sister. There had been worrying signs from Brighton that she was having a bad time, in fact she had apparently attempted suicide or lost the plot and ended up in hospital one night. Our cousin Ruth, who lived there let me know about the third time this had happened. Not daring to believe the worst, I hoped she was just going through a phase as she did when a teenager. But knowing how things had ended for my mother I was keen to see her face to face and make up my own mind.

Before I visited her I was stopping off in London to touch base with Andy, I always did, he was my dearest brother and one of the few people who knew the home we both once had. He had been there throughout my entire decline and fall, he shared chapters of life with me nobody else had. We left Innocence together in search of Experience. Boy did we find it.

The news about Paul was gut wrenching. If I had seen him that Christmas and known of his broken legs I would have taken him back to WIndsong for a few weeks. If he wanted to keep his hand in he could have gone begging in posh Cheltenham, make a change for him. But I didn't make the stop on that one trip. I was in a hurry, I was late, for what, who knows? It was too late now, another Unsuffered Consequence.

Clare was still in hospital when I got to Brighton. It was an ordinary ward but they decided to keep an eye on her while her wounds, cuts, healed.

As I came in the room I remembered visiting my Mother in the same way, when I was fourteen and fifteen. The look in Clare's eyes was deep and dark, yet vacant. What had gone wrong? I wasn't overly worried at the time because I was sure she would keep going for her daughter, who was eleven and living with her father Mark. Clare had sold the house she owned, apparently her Step Mother had paid off the mortgage some time previously and thus there was a fair amount of profit. She decided to leave her daughter with Mark and explore the world. She planned taking a Round The World Ticket off into the distance.

"But Clare," I remonstrated at the time, "I know how this ends. I've been there. You'll find an amazing place, sunset, a lovely bay, but I discovered I would rather have my children next to me in a local bus stop than be passing through Timbuktu without them."

I had learnt this from a week living in a cave in Cappadocia in Turkey. That really stripped my life down to its nuts and bolts and boy there wasn't much of anything to be proud of, other than those two beautiful children I had shared with Sandie. So I started walking back right then, hitching, walking, hitching, begging, all the way across Europe, back to Somerset, back to see those two children.

I tried to get this over to her the previous year; but she had still left for stage one of the trip to Canada and yet, as predicted, she was back in six days.

I had a phone call from Heathrow or somewhere, "Geoffrey, you were right."

I also had a nagging thought about Chris and his daughter's fate. But Clare knew what the suicide of our mother had done to both of us and surely she wouldn't add to that tragedy. Surely we wouldn't repeat the sorrows of the past.

Yet the Wheel of Life and perhaps more importantly that of Death is unforgiving in its slow inimical progress towards us. I ducked away from that idea.

Anyway, meanwhile back at the ranch I was a busy man, I had a steadily growing 'Habit' to feed. A habit that had become a thirty pound a day or more bad habit. Not big compared to Pop Stars I know, but it's big enough when you only earn eighty pounds a day and have a cottage to run and two decades of debts to finance.

The school job I should have started the September hit a financial glitch, I was told they couldn't offer me the salary as promised by the Headmaster, I would be on the lowest scale. A new Headmistress had taken over and I don't think she liked me, or my hair, or worse still my reputation as a Pied Piper leading the children off the straight and narrow.

Perhaps it was my performances at The Royal Oak, where the History Teacher used to show up, skulking at the back, quietly watching me extoll the virtues of a Hippy lifestyle. The lingering smell of cannabis where all the musicians chilled with me outside the side porch maybe nailed my cross up.

I didn't mind too much. The Headmaster's letter had specifically stated that as it was their mistake he would insist I got as much Supply Work as I wanted. But he wasn't there now and his deputy was another septic sceptic of Mr Smiles. He did his best for me, to set me up for a fall. Neil Hall was asking me to turn some truanting boy around, with a couple of home visits, a few hours a week. This would be nigh on impossible and and also dangerous. Way too compromising. I asked, "What if he or his family are still wearing pyjamas." Quite a fashion at the time amongst certain of Cheltenham's less esteemed residents. It didn't work. It never could or would. The supply work dried up after that.

Then Tewkesbury School invited me for an interview as a PE Teacher. They specified an assessment session in the gym and that I would need to come in white soled shoes and so on for the interview.

"So, Mr Smiles." The Headmaster looked at me, his two colleagues either side of him, "Do you possess a suit?" For one blissful moment I thought he was going to offer me a top job, even better than PE. No, he was disgusted. With a frown he asked "Why didn't you wear a suit to the interview?"

"Well, all I had was a list of the PE activities I had to take part in and the list of what kit to wear. It was stated as imperative to have Non Marking trainers." I was hoping 'Imperative' sounded like the term used by a good teacher.

He wasn't convinced, "Next!"

It turned out a sheet of paper had been left out of my letter, asking me for interview, which would have explained their protocol better. As it was, all they knew now was they didn't need me. Having run a PE Department it was tough not to get a basic sidekick job. I got the definite impression my face, or my long hair didn't fit.

So I kept doing bits of writing, especially for Eagle Media, who were now owing me for two scripts, which was three thousand quid I really needed! I was going up to London and doing the filming to go with their booklet. Rachel, the director and a friend of ours made sure I got paid for each of those. But I was already screwed, doing a line of 'Brown' before I did the 'Q & A' interview. Fucked with a capital 'K!'

Life was just falling beautifully apart. After Dave's funeral, I stood outside, hoping I had hit the right mark, between light and dark with the words and the bits I chose to read. It turned out I needn't have worried, it seemed everyone had really liked the way it had gone.

As I waited around a couple came up to me, who were relatives. They looked a bit tidy, well off, a real couple, arm in arm and much in love. They were obviously nice people, right and proper; I was just about to apologise when the woman smiled and told me how she and Sean, her husband, had really loved the Service. "It was exactly as Dave would have wanted it. Well done." As they walked away she turned round and said over her shoulder, "I'll get you to do mine one day."

Considering her age and mine, me being years older, I laughed a reply along those lines. It was while I was writing the last chapter that the call came through, from Jane again, would I do Lynn's Funeral; she had died unexpectedly. Apparently she had again stated her wish after I buried Luke, Jane's son, some years after Dave. What a tragic fate. Death seems to follow me around sometimes like a bad dog.

Things were building to a crisis, but I was having trouble seeing past the weekly dilemmas as I was trying to keep on top of a heroin habit that needed daily feeding, twice if not three times. It was like a monster tumour growing inside me; every day made it a bit worse, the longer I waited for the surgery to cut it out the bigger it would have become, until its mere removal could have finished me off.

As an addict gets older, the character of the 'Cold Turkey' changes. Quite simply, imagine the tender flesh of a young Turkey, the ease with which the blood flows through the muscles and the way the flesh and bone unite. Imagine an old, gnarly, pissed off Turkey, who has spent a life chewing on 'Peas n' Grits,' the blood trickles slowly through the aching limbs, the dawn call, once a fierce piercing cry is now a breathless croak.

The strength needed to perform the physical feat of withdrawal from any long term Opiate abuse is incremental with every passing year. As the addiction increases in strength, the body weakens with every passing year. Suddenly the years make up a decade and then the decades start to stack up. I was looking down the barrel of a thirty seven year old gun, that was getting reloaded every day.

I tried to work out how long the latest habit had been going; I realised it was about four or five years. Sometime after the last weeks at Swalcliffe it had turned from being an indulgence to a need. All those bottles of Gees Linctus had mounted up and back in those days I had fingers in many Opiate Pies.

I could have wept every time I walked down the back garden knowing I was driving into town to score. Maud could only look on helplessly as the man she loved destroyed himself. No doubt she wondered if her love was not enough, if she had failed me. But she had no blame in the affair. She tried so hard it only made it worse. The holiday she had booked in Corfu the previous autumn I had messed up by breaking my foot three days before we left. So I was on pain killers for that and spent the following winter rebuilding the old walls of a brook running through a property in Buckland. The other guys would hear me scream abuse every time the broken metatarsal stepped on a stone under the freezing water. The doctor had put a cast on my foot, but three days in the sea had meant it was starting to fall apart, so I sawed it off with a knife and left it on the balcony of our villa. The scream of the maid alerted us to the fact she had found it.

It was as if I was cursed at the time. Perhaps 'Dancing with the Devil' just brings its own chaos with it. The first morning of that holiday there was a shutter banging outside our window. Thinking it might disturb Maud's slumber I hobbled round to close it. As I returned a Bee of some kind got stuck between the cast and my toes. As I stepped forward it was squashed and bit me with all its vigour. Fuck.

She was still asleep so I decided the best thing was to stick some of the local mud on it at the beach.

I hobbled the mile or so to the beach and sat down. As I examined the bite I noticed my leg was covered in a rash. In fact my whole body was coming up in virulent weals and spots. Bugger, I must have had an allergic reaction to the Bee. So, knowing it could spread to my throat I hobbled off to the doctor.

I knew where he was as I had spent the previous year trying to blague a prescription for Codeine out of him. Hopeless, the Greeks don't do opiates it seems, unless facing imminent death.

I could hear someone inside. I rang the small bell and waited. It could take five or ten minutes before the doctor poked his head out of the door. Then another half hour or so before being seen. He took one look at me and pulled me through the door. In minutes I was hooked up to a drip, lying on my back in some ante room. Maud didn't even know where I was. I could imagine her thinking I had gone off for a swim, then not being able to find me. It was awful, the first day of our holiday.

Many of the best times of our life were when Maud and I were near the sea, home or abroad. We also spent many weekends away at the Gower and elsewhere. I was learning to Kite Surf. Hoping to inspire me she had booked me a four day course as a Christmas present.

It was in Perranporth, Cornwall. We had a nice hotel for four nights. Sometime towards the end of March we were getting ready to leave the next day. It was Sunday and not the best day of the week to score heroin. Scripts and most drug deals would have been done on Saturday. Even Dealers take the Sabbath off.

But somewhere in England, I knew, there had to be some heroin. 'Brassy,' my mate Rob, was the guy with the connections while I did the driving. About five o'clock we set out for Cheltenham. I told my young lady I would be back as soon as possible. We were both looking forward to the trip.

She knew where I was going. God it was awful. We could hardly afford the petrol down there and here I was about to blow a hundred quid just to get me through four days away and back again.

There was nothing in Cheltenham, so we drove over to Gloucester, where the opportunities were maybe better but the territory much harsher. Driving round those areas, parking up and waiting, waiting, waiting. Then driving somewhere else, a few streets away. Parking, waiting, waiting, waiting. It was obvious to any school kid walking by, let alone the Police that we were here for one reason only. To score drugs. On top of which I had a Vauxhall Cavalier at the time. Great for being inconspicuous but it had a habit of stalling whenever the revs dropped too low or I stopped at a junction.

Sitting in the car at the traffic lights with the engine revving was dodgy as hell too. Round and round we went, for hours. Nothing. Shit. So, eventually it's getting near to ten, maybe eleven o'clock. My poor lady is wondering where I am.

So we give in. God knows what I'm going to do. I will have to score in the morning, but there's no time. We need to be off by nine. Fuck, fuck, fuck.

I drove him home and dropped him off in Didbrook. Then I headed home. As I came round the bend in Toddington my phone blinked. I pulled over and read the text. It was Brassy, 'He's got 7.'

Fuck, fuck, fuck. 'Where?'

'Glos.' Fuck, fuck, fuck.

It was nearly midnight. But what could I do? I couldn't go Cold Turkey half way through my Kiting course...'Oh excuse me while I throw up and quietly die in your toilet for three days.' So I just had to turn the car round and drive back to Rob's. I picked him up and we drove back to Gloucester, where on some grubby corner he picked up the seven small packets. He knew the deal and didn't even ask for one. He had his Meth script in the morning. He'd be alright. He was a real friend in a landscape where friendships are often fraught with need and needle.

Another hour or so and I was back at the same bend with the tiny packets stashed in my fags. So I got a few hours sleep, snorted a bag and off we went. I had agreed after the episode when I nearly overdosed waiting for Skinny, to abandon syringes, at the request of my lady.

I knew it was a promise that would only last as long as I wanted it to. So I agreed. As it happened I stuck to it and began sniffing the heroin up my nose. I never took to 'Chasing the Dragon,' it seemed far too wasteful an operation. I liked to know every particle of the drug had been ingested. So I snorted it. I never figured it could be as bad as shooting it up. It left no 'Track Marks.' But I was wrong.

Needless to say, the seven bags hardly got me through the four days and I had to beg Brassy to leave me a swig of Meth, hidden outside the front door of the cottage he shared with his Mum, Mary. So there I was, on our late return, having to detour past his place to pick up the bottle. It was there. That was the kind of bond we had. One that was forged in a weekly battle of life and death on the streets of freaking Gloucestershire. Whatever next?

The Floods! I was sitting at home listening to the reports on the radio when I began to realise that the current spate of rains was going to bring the county to its knees. That morning my daughter had phoned to say she had just left her rented house in Tewkesbury before the ground floor was flooded. It was touch and go whether she could get her motorbike clear. She did. Then I heard the roads were flooding around me.

Every time I watch a natural disaster on the News I think of junkies. I know it sounds mad, sad and bad but nobody realises that for them, life is calculated in periods of six to eight hours, fix to fix. Three days submerged, snowed in, or under curfew, is just not survivable. I suddenly realised Maud would have trouble finding a route back from work in Cheltenham and also I need to score pretty damn quick because the supply chain was about to stop, dead, until the waters receded, whenever that might be.

I headed to the motorway, the M5 South. I had the radio on and was picking up the news flashes. I got on the the slip road and made it down. Spray was firing off with every passing truck and car. Then news came on they were closing some junctions.

I think I was the last car that exited at Junction 11 on that afternoon. Luckily 'Gray' my port of call for so many years down the Moors, was in and had gear. I bought six bags for sixty quid, snorted one and set off to rescue Maud. Knowing the Cotswold hills as well as I did I managed to cross over the highest points until we arrived eventually at Stanway Hill, above Toddington. We could swim from there. We didn't need to. We made it home, just.

She was so thrilled I had risked everything to get over to Cheltenham and bring her home safely. I had done it for her, I would have done it anyway, drugs or no drugs. But I knew in my heart of hearts, I had done it for the heroin, to score first and save her second.

It was an awful admission to myself. I would face a similar situation weeks later, but the consequences of that would last a lifetime.

Somewhere, in the middle of this maelstrom, came a phone call from a Social Worker. I can't remember her name. "Is that Geoffrey Smiles?"

I always paused before answering this question on the phone as it could be a 'Cold Caller' or worse still some Loan Company wondering where their dosh had gone and why their Direct Debit had not been paid for months. However, in the time it took me to draw breath she went on, "Are you the brother of Clare Moorhouse?"

This wasn't a bank. "Sure. Oh God." I said, before I could think, "Is Clare ok?" I suppose I knew the answer to that already. "How can I help?"

The woman's voice went on to explain that she was telephoning to discuss placing Clare in a Secure Psychiatric Unit for her own safety. Before I had visions of 'One Flew Over The Cuckoo's Nest,' she went on to say that it had its own garden and was really a lovely place. It was just a chance for her to be safe and get the counselling she needed, as well as to stabilise her on regular medication.

I should have realised, I should have remembered Chris and Sylvan, I should have known and I should have yelled, 'No, no, no!' But I didn't. I listened, as we all do to the 'Specialist' believing there is some higher power or knowledge they must have. She explained the obvious advantages that twenty four hour care could offer as regards keeping her safe from harm or self harm and that Clare's episodes of depression and her suicide attempts were getting more extreme.

I didn't know all the details then. I was of course very concerned for her welfare and for Jessica too, who was no doubt getting caught up in the crossfire between her father and Clare. Realising the error of her decision to leave her daughter, I think Clare was hoping that Mark might have let Jessica into her life again. But he wasn't helping that to happen at all. He played the 'I must keep my child away from any undue emotional stress' card. Personally I think it was him that was incapable of facing the situation or indeed any real emotion at all. Surely he knew what happened to Clare's mother? Surely he must have thought this is not going to turn out well? Surely, seeing Clare almost every week he must have seen the changes, seen the signs of danger? No.

Clare was getting desperate. The medication they had put her on only made things worse.

If a car is heading towards a cliff, it's a scary place to be. But if, at least if the driver is in the driving seat they can try to turn the wheel and avoid the disaster.

Anti Depressant drugs have the effect of moving the car driver to the passenger seat at first, then to the back seat or even the boot! Once the driver's hands come off the steering wheel, it's hopeless. It is, to be fair, as Pink Floyd so beautifully expressed a state of being 'Comfortably Numb.' Yet now, immobile in the back of the car there is no hope of avoiding the cliff drop, there is just the vaguest idea that the crash landing won't feel so bad wrapped up in cotton wool pills.

The Valium and Librium that was liberally handed out to people in the Sixties and Seventies had the same effect. Confusion. Loss of Self. Loss of sorrow, but at the expense of ever feeling joy again. It created a bland, purposeless, meandering mush of a meaningless life. A 'Less' life. All the Bass in the Blues is gone, but also the bright Treble melody is lost. All that's left is a toneless, emotionless tune.

However I listened to her voice extolling the benefit of this Unit. I should have sensed this was just the usual Mental Heath Care and Protection procedure. They were duty bound to offer to do this in case the patient became a danger to herself or others? I protested gently that my sister was a Free Spirit and unlikely to take well to being locked up on a ward.

The woman's voice went on, "Oh, it's not like that. She can go out into the garden any time, friends can come to visit and take her out if the staff agree." A slight pause, she continued, "I know Clare is a keen gardener, I'm sure Clare would enjoy the gardens there, perhaps she could do a bit..." The voice trailed off. A longer pause, waiting for my answer.

No answer.

The voice went on again, "We really need to keep Clare safe." Then the final ploy, "Also we need to protect those vulnerable people around her," with the coup de gras, "from any further harm..." I knew she was referring to Jessica.

That did it. There was nothing I could say to reject that argument. Any sane, caring relative would be forced morally to make the same decision. But this was Clare. I really didn't know how bad it was. I had to trust in the second hand reports from her friends.

I wasn't really sure I knew my sister's state of mind at all at that time. If only I had thought back to our mother I might have recognised the look in her eyes. As children we had gone to different schools and grown up with different lives. Our love as adults was built from the sorrow of our childhood.

Her forays into Ayahuasca had been a revelation for her. Perhaps too much! She had suggested I try it, as there was much evidence it might help addictive behaviour. She loved me so much. She worshipped me as a child. The Big Brother. The Head Boy. The prize winner. The race winner. The Poet. The tall blond boy with blue eyes. Her brother. The star that lit her night sky in the lonely school dormitory, where she was bullied and made to feel inadequate as she wore glasses.

Her poor eyesight would have made it difficult to do well in sports and enjoy the sense of status I had discovered at school. She told me the only time she was not bullied was after the news that our mother had committed suicide spread through school. Then of course, after the cease fire she was teased cruelly again, along the lines that Norma had killed herself, as Clare was her daughter. Children can be so cruel and apparently girl bullies have a reputation as being even worse than boys.

Clare was so innocent, so young, so desperate, so lost, she thought news of her mother's death had all been a ploy, by our father David, to trick the bullies. She believed that when she came home for the holidays Mummy would be there. It had all been a bad dream. How desperately the minds of children seek any escape to find solace from a cruel life.

God, I don't know if I can even write this...

...anyhow, I agreed.

A few weeks later I had a call from Doctor L at the Unit asking about our relationship and so on; also would I like to come up for a meeting to discuss her situation. I said I'd love to and maybe I could bring her back to my cottage in the Cotswolds for a short holiday.

He seemed to think that was a possibility. A couple of weeks later I set off to Brighton.

I was ushered into a Meeting Room after I had been given the tour of the Unit. Yes, there was a garden, but the door to it was always locked. My heart sank. The walls around it were high, but not so high they might seem imprisoning, yet high enough to state clearly, 'No chance of climbing over me.'

My heart sank deeper.

Dr L, who spoke primarily, was a balding, plump, comfortably attired African, who I reckoned to be in his thirties or forties. He introduced the team of staff and explained their roles. He began to give me a sketch of how they were helping Clare, what her current situation was and that today's meeting was to decide if she could come and spend a week with me in the Cotswolds.

He said they wanted to meet me in person as they also had to decide whether they felt I was going to be able to help and so on. Fair enough, I thought, they don't know me. Clare wasn't there at the time. I tried to get across how much I loved her and that being a teacher I was a responsible citizen. I didn't mention I was knee deep, or rather up to my nostrils in Heroin and about as emotionally stable as a three year old. But I seemed to reassure them.

Nonetheless any person with a medical background should have spotted the tell tale signs that I was clearly on Opiates and had probably been so for awhile, my eyes were 'pinned,' my skin grey and I certainly didn't suffer from being overweight. Maybe Clare had told them and they weren't concerned about it? She, like me, was always pretty honest about stuff like that.

Doctor L and his staff must have known about our mother's death, her history of depression and many suicide attempts. Here we were again, thirty two years later, staring at the same incomprehensible scenario; the deepest, darkest mystery, the black dog, the howl, the urge for self destruction.

The detuning of the spine.

Doctor L began to read through his Case Notes on Clare. One thing that surprised me was she stated she had never really known our mother and had few memories from her childhood. Although she was ten when Norma died, going to boarding school, around seven or eight had taken her away from home, just when she needed a mother the most.

Doctor L carried on his resume. Clare was a baby when we moved to Canada, then Bermuda and Uganda, as my parents sought their fortune, or at least an adventure. We finally settled in Kent.

Clare had poor eyesight and underwent operations as I had on my ears. At that time I must have been, at least for a few years, a paragon of virtue, the high achieving school boy. Yet, just three years later, I was expelled from Public School and ran away from to London.

Doctor L's voice softened a bit. A year later Norma committed suicide, after an argument with her son. It felt odd to hear him refer to me as 'Her son.'

We skated on the thin ice of these topics as the meeting went on. I could feel them checking me out, seeing if there was enough strength to carry this out. I wish I had failed.

Dr L rounded up the debate. He must have got the silent nod from his colleagues. They consented to the visit as long as I agreed to follow and administer the medication plan Clare was on, to the letter. I did think to myself that trusting a junkie to administer a medication plan was a bit squiffy.

One of the staff went to get Clare. I stared at the high garden wall through the window of the seminar room.

Clare, poor darling, was not really there. Well, she was, but under a sea of ice, staring up through the cold blue haze at the shimmering distorted face of her brother. Geoffrey. She loved me. She would go with me. Of course.

I told her how much I loved her. We both cried.

Dr L nodded, the meeting was over. He asked Clare to show me the garden while they prepared her list of medication. I was going to ask about the locked door to the garden but I didn't want to rock the boat. I just wanted to get Clare out of there and everything would begin to come back together.

We did, but it didn't.

It's so hard, even just to open the memory box that contains these events. I'd do anything else, other than write this now. But it has to be done.

This story must be told, with all its awful ugly truth as no doubt there are other Clares and Geoffreys.

It was strange, having her there in the car and yet she was not quite there. I felt I was reaching across and yet, not quite grasping her hand. A finger here, a thumb there, drifting past under the ice flow.

We arrived back at Windsong hours later. It's a long drive. During the journey Clare had told me of some harrowing moments. Nights of drinking to excess and taking whatever pills she had, hoping it would be enough. On one desperate occasion in Brighton, she had walked into the sea, late at night, which is treacherous enough during the day. But, unable to drown herself, she had scrambled up the beach to the main road where an Asian man in a car stopped to help her.

She was soaking wet, freezing, emotionally wrought and still under the influence of the pills and drink. He helped her into his car and then raped her.

'Suicide' and 'Rape' were banging gongs in my head, tolling bells across the frozen wasteland, but I still couldn't bear to think such a thing could ever happen again. We'd done that, we'd been through that, as children, surely not again. Surely?

I shrugged off that thought as I made coffee and a joint for us. Maud came home from work.

I was very aware of the light my Irish lass brought to the cottage and my life. Yet recently, it seemed to be just drugs, debts and unscheduled deaths knocking at our door. Now Clare was here too. Admittedly the band still played on, the open mic nights at The Royal Oak were great fun and the party scene was still out there, somewhere. But we had fallen off the trail, or rather I had fallen off.

She came back each evening that week to my blue, pin pricked eyes and Clare's vanishing stare. I felt to blame, culpable for bringing all this woe into her life. She was, after all, younger than us both. However, Maud had experienced family traumas too and she wasn't about to let either of us down in our hour, or week, of need. Sadly, despite her love we were both pretty hopeless cases. My heroin habit was raging with every new twist of the knife in life and Clare just seemed lost, not really 'Clare' anymore.

This wasn't leading me any nearer to detox.

I considered if it would be better to give Clare some heroin, rather than all the anti depressant drugs. At least she would feel great for a day. But no, I had my own monster to feed and I knew Dr L wouldn't let her visit again if they tested her positive for smack. So I easily convinced myself to just forget that idea.

Fuck, what does it matter what we did that week?

Tuesday.

Wednesday.

Thursday.

Then Friday.

It was the worst day of my life and probably Clare's.

As the days had crawled by on their knees I failed to get through the haze to Clare. The situation was stressful for Maud and I felt I needed to protect her from any further sorrow coming from my side of the family. This was my shit, my sister, my family crap.

Maud was more innocent in many ways than us and I felt really bad putting her through this, on top of my heroin habit, the debts and the daily chaos.

The plan, as set out by Doctor L, was for Clare to return with me to the Unit in Brighton, on Sunday.

That Friday night we had arranged to go out and see a Reggae Band in Cheltenham, something Clare loved, something she would have adored.

But, I changed my mind, that morning.

This wasn't going to work.

I couldn't put Maud through any more of this. It was her weekend too. She deserved a break from all this shit. I don't think she would have cared at all and if she had, she would never have said so. But I cared.

I told Clare we were going.

She didn't understand.

She didn't want to go.

She pleaded with me, "But Geoffrey, we're going to a Reggae Gig tonight. Please, let me stay."

I can't even hear the word Reggae now, without my heart sinking, momentarily, under the ice.

We argued.

It got worse.

She kept on saying, "But Geoffrey, we're going to a Reggae Gig tonight."

It was awful.

I wanted to leave and get her back to the Unit.

I opened the car door and said, "Come on Clare, we've got to go." She did not want to get in the car, so I shepherded her into the back seat, but she got out the other side.

I was getting pissed off now. "Come on. Now!" I shouted, "Stop fucking about Clare. We are going back." I pushed her back in the car, not roughly but firmly. I jumped in the front and started the engine. She got out.

"Oh, come on Clare, this is stupid! We've got to go. I've got to get back tonight."

She wasn't listening. She was crying. She just kept saying, "Geoffrey. The Reggae gig."

"Fuck the reggae. We're going." I shouted loudly at her. She cowered like a frightened child.

I'll never forget that look.

Oh god. Kill me now.

I pushed Clare back in the car and drove off quickly. She sobbed in the back. "Why? Geoffrey, why?"

Oh god. I wish I knew.

I slowed down at the roundabout in Toddinton to turn left and I heard the car door open. "Fuck! Clare! What are you doing?" I slowed down but didn't stop in case she jumped out and ran off.

I turned round and screamed at her, "Stop! Clare! Shut the car door! What the fuck are you doing?" My voice had reached a primeval scream. It would have turned the wind back. Something within her broke.

Oh god. I wish it hadn't.

The car door closed and I accelerated up Stanway Hill, a series of sharp curves, wondering if at any moment she would jump out. But my last outburst had quelled her. She slipped back under the ice. She stared into nowhere, sinking in the back seat, saying nothing now.

Oh god. I wish she had.

I drove faster, straight through the traffic lights at Stow On The Wold, heading towards Oxford. We passed by Adlestrop, where I had taught and a few miles further on we came up the hill to Chipping Norton. Clare suddenly became agitated again and started opening the door. Shouting was useless. I knew where the Police Station was in the village. I needed help, fast.

Oh god. I wish I hadn't.

It became a scene from Hell.

As soon as I stopped the car she reached for the door handle. I grabbed her arm. "Clare. Stop it! We need to get help. We need to take you back, to the Unit in Brighton."

"I don't want to go back." She begged me.

"But Clare, they will look after you there."

"I don't want to go, Geoffrey…the Reggae Gig?"

It was a scene from Hell.

Nobody would help me. I was shouting at people walking by, 'Get a Policeman!'

Nah, they didn't want to know. One couple shouted abuse at me. "Get off her." To them it looked as if I was dragging Clare back into my car. I was actually just trying to get her out and over to the station.

Somebody eventually went in and I think he must have said there was a guy trying to abduct some girl in the Police Station carpark.

That at least got a Policeman outside.

I tried to explain to him the situation and between us we got Clare over to the Station door and into a waiting room.

A very confused policeman then tried to work out what was going on. If he had trained with the Drugs Squad he might have realised I was on some sort of drugs and she was freaking out on something else.

Oh god. I wish he had.

He hadn't and opted to call his colleague.

The two policeman had a discussion and suggested we travel to Kidlington Police Station. I think they had better access to facilities and Doctors there.

They told me they would drive Clare over. I should follow behind in my car. They understood that I was trying to return her to hospital but it seemed nobody was sure who was responsible for her now; as she came from Brighton, I lived in Gloucestershire and here we were in Oxfordshire.

I saw the Police Van and before I could think, 'No' they had locked her in, behind the steel mesh of the cage inside. She looked at me. A van for drunks and runaway dogs. I followed the flashing lights, aware how ironic it was, as I spent most of my life avoiding them; which reminded me, I had to score the heroin I needed for the weekend at some point that day.

As any professional junkie will tell you, Friday is a problematic day for scoring, because anybody who works will have their wages to spend. If people bought four rather than two bags of smack, or ten rather than five, the supply was liable to run out. I had to get in there early. I rang Gray and placed an order. He would keep it for me, as long as he could; but that didn't mean forever. I had to get over to him before somebody else tried to score it.

At Kidlington the policemen unlocked the van door and let Clare out. I parked in a gap between a row of Police cars. How stupidly ironic, a car that had done more drug deals than trips to the shops was now jammed in a cop parking bay. They led us through a side door and took us to the Desk Sergeant, who began to take all the same particulars I had already given the other policemen. The two coppers smiled, "They'll get you sorted out mate. We just need to get a reply from Brighton about the transport." They left. They'd done their best.

Clare was taken away from me and put in another room or cell. I think they wanted to stop her running off and keep her safe.

Next came the Doctor. I recognised the kind of a woman she was the moment she walked in, well heeled, well educated, well upper middle class, the sort of woman who polished her own Brogues. She could almost have been a female version of our father. She asked about the medication Clare was on and kindly didn't ask me what I was on.

Her expression changed as we talked as if a sad memory had sprung up in her, she seemed truly concerned for a moment with these two 'Enfants Terribles.' But like most doctors she was already behind time on her schedule and having given Clare a dose of some more tranquillisers she was gone.

I waited.

I looked at the Sergeant who relayed what I already knew, while he studiously avoided looking at me. "The Doctor's given her something to calm her down. As soon as we get word from Brighton, we'll know what the plan is and who will be coming to get her."

I waited.

When the answer finally arrived it seemed Brighton didn't want to know, or at least felt they were not responsible for Clare as she wasn't in their county. They were not prepared to send an ambulance all the way to Oxfordshire.

"Don't worry," the Sergeant said, without moving his stare from his desk top, "Somebody will have to provide the transport." He cleared his throat, "Sooner or later."

I waited.

Clare was in a cell. They had taken me down there briefly before the Doctor's visit to reassure Clare I was still there.

They thought that might help.

Then the Doctor arrived.

They thought that might help. It didn't.

I could still hear her voice, from somewhere down the corridor, "Geoffrey. Geoffrey? Geoffrey!"

I waited.

I could also hear that little Monkey whispering in my ear. 'We need a fix soon.'

I waited.

I could hardy wander over to the Desk Sergeant and ask, 'Mind if I pop out and score some smack?'

I waited.

I must have waited there for hours. We had left Windsong early that morning and now it was nearly five o'clock. I was getting jumpy. The junkie in me was starting to 'kluk' like a hen staring at a fox.

But I waited.

The voice down the corridor became weaker.

I waited.

The voice in my head got louder.

I waited.

The voice down the corridor became silent.

I waited.

The voice in my head screamed.

I waited.

Then I couldn't wait anymore.

Fuck! Maud would be home soon. I'd completely forgotten about letting her know. She would be expecting to go to the Reggae Gig. My heart sank.

Deeper into the ice. Somewhere down there I passed Clare in frozen motion.

Fuck! I really needed to score.

I stood in front of the Desk Sergeant. There was no way he could avoid my stare now. "Er, has there been any news on an ambulance yet?" He shook his head as if to say, 'Do you think ambulances grow on trees?' But I went on, "I'm going to have to go at some point, soon. If there's no update I wanted to say goodbye to Clare first."

I waited as he looked away.

I don't know who he was.

I know it wasn't his fault.

He was just doing his job.

He was being sensible.

He said to me, "It's probably best if you don't. It will just set her off again. Best leave it."

Sixteen words to add to the twenty four already burnt in my soul.

I nodded. What could I say? 'Fuck you. Let me see my sister!'

Oh god, I wish I had.

I never saw Clare again.

OMEGA TO ALPHA

nEXt...

I had to score. I returned to my car, waiting in the row of Police vehicles. It looked incongruous and radiated a hopeless stare from its windows. Inside, no doubt there were bits left over from my joints and probably a wrap or a twist of tin foil from some brassy hitch hiker chasing the dragon over Bishops Cleeve Hill.

I turned left and followed the signs blindly. As soon as I was a safe distant from the 'Fuzz Shop' I found a side street and pulled up. I rolled a fat joint and let Gray know I was on my way, now he would definitely hold onto the gear for me. Old drug addicts like us looked after each other. If he needed a lift, anytime, anywhere, he knew I'd do it. As with Crispin and Rob, we helped each other out, like a couple of old soldiers stumbling across a battlefield, trying to get through another day, another week of chemical warfare, somehow.

I've tried in earnest to get across what it's like to be a Heroin addict. I appreciate it's hard to understand why someone would contemplate going through all the horrors just for that moment of release. But it's never as simple as that, in the same way that life is never that simple. Every junkie has their story to tell, I guess this is mine; past traumas may have healed to a degree, but the daily grind of getting a fix still goes on, scoring another bag and another bag and another bag. The nEXt one.

The chances of getting off after ten or so years of use are slimmer than sliced bread, after twenty years nonexistent, after thirty impossible, after thirty seven years...it just doesn't happen. For, as the addiction strengthens, the body and the centre of willpower weakens, until finally an invisible line is crossed; a Border Crossing that states clearly there is no going back from this point on. Sadly it's hard to know what hour of what day that line was passed. After that there is no hope of getting off as it's just too much of a battering for the body, the brain and the soul to take. It is truly the worst place on earth to be, like drifting towards Niagara Falls knowing it's too late and the current is too strong for any hope of rescue.

But I wasn't about to have that debate right then. I needed a hit, all that could wait for another day, any other day except today.

Of course it's always another day...the nEXt day.

Clare had busted my heart and I had broken hers.

Of course it still hadn't registered where this could all lead, I believed Clare would get back to the Unit once the hospital got their act together. Surely she would eventually get over this phase of depression and life would go on. Surely she could never repeat the circle of pain our mother began all those years ago. Even if she was angry or sad with me there was always Jess, always the children.

I didn't dare to imagine her despair when they told her I had gone. But of course I did, again and again in my head. I thought of how it must have echoed my parents from long ago. 'Your brother has gone.'

She was just a child then, now she was forty three and the story was the same. 'Geoffrey's gone.'

Poor girl, no chance.

I walked up the path to Graham's and knocked the window twice. We all had our special knocks. The door opened four inches.

His eyes glanced at me, "Alright Smiles?" I went in.

The room was as it always had been; the TV was on and 'Ginge' the cat lounged in front of the fire, which was off. Gray had guessed I was desperate from my call and got some supplies in. He counted me out five bags. I rolled up a tenner and snorted one.

It was my moment. For a few minutes the pain went out of my soul as I watched some meaningless crap on the TV, waiting for the buzz to hit. I was fucked. I told Gray what had happened, he was a good friend. He didn't say much. There was really nothing to say.

Once the fire in my eyes had lit, I rolled a joint and got my shit together. I stashed the other four bags and left.

Half an hour later I was home. Maud was already back from work. She asked, "Did I want to go to the Reggae Gig anyhow?"

"No. Sorry darling. My brain still chokes at the mere mention of a Reggae Gig.

The next morning I phoned up and discovered Clare had been returned to the Unit, eventually. The staff didn't seem unduly concerned. According to them Clare had settled down and seemed to be fine. I suppose they were trying to be positive. I figured they had probably given her some more 'meds.'

It was Saturday, I was with my belle and despite the heroin, the debts and everything else I had to try to make a life for her, make love for her.

Back in the Spring of that year we had finally changed my solo mortgage with sixty five thousand pounds owing on it, for a shared mortgage of a hundred and forty. I had always wanted to keep the house separate from my relationships as I hoped to pass it onto my children. But after ten years with me Maud didn't want to be just a 'Lodger' anymore. I could understand that.

The bank HSBC were throwing offers of loans at us and leapt at the chance to remortgage the cottage.

Her salary was twenty grand or so and I had a letter from a guy I was working for, saying I earned eighty pounds a day as a labourer for him. On the basis of that, only that, they gave us the mortgage.

The last thing I remember the man saying as we were leaving the manager's office was, "Are you sure you don't want another ten or twenty thousand?"

I looked at Julia who had managed both our bank accounts for years and replied firmly, "No thanks." I trusted her, I had painted her flat, I thought she was on our side. I was surprised we had got this far, with my track record of bank debts being 'consolidated' into other debts, while adding more debt, nEXt one!

In my mind I reconciled the situation by thinking along the lines that I now had a mortgage of seventy grand, my half to cover, that wasn't such a big increase. Maud had her half and we could pay off her student loans and our credit card debts. We could both start the race again. Everything seemed a bit brighter on the financial front.

But I was still spending two hundred a week on smack and fifty on dope and tobacco. A grand a month just to get me out of bed each day. I can't say I was ever really that stoned either. I was just ticking over, trying to keep that kluking monkey off my back. But every day, the little fat fucker was eating my bread and getting heavier to carry.

Summer was coming, I knew if ever I was going to get off the gear it had to be this time of year and not when the cold weather returned. I needed the sun, its light and warmth, to heal me.

One evening a few weeks later we were sitting on the couch. There was a knock at the front door. I got up and glanced through the window to see who it was. Two Police officers. Fuck! It was too late to stash anything. There were no curtains. They knew we were in. I opened the door and noticed one of them was a female Officer. "Can I help you?"

The man asked, "Geoffrey Smiles?" I nodded. "May we come in please?" I nodded.

I could tell from the look on his face that he wasn't here to bust me. My first thought was perhaps my daughter had been in an accident; she rode a motorbike at the time and it used to worry me. But in my heart of hearts I knew it could be another reason. I just didn't want to even think that thought.

"Would you like to sit down?" The officer asked me. I didn't really. But I did. With every word he said I could feel the nEXt coming. "I'm afraid I have some bad news for you Geoffrey, your sister, Clare..." he looked at me for a moment to confirm what he already knew, "has died today. I'm sorry."

There was a pause. I couldn't move or say anything. Tears glazed over my eyes. My lips moved silently, 'Oh God. No. Not Clare. Surely?'

Maud held my hand. I wiped my eyes. I stared for a moment at the officers. "How did she die? I thought she was in hospital. They said they'd look after her."

There was a pause. The Police Woman spoke. "I'm afraid Clare committed suicide. She was supposed to meet up with her daughter today. So Clare was staying for a few days with a friend." She mentioned his name. "I'm afraid she didn't turn up for the meeting." It was Jessica's eleventh birthday. "When her friend came home from work he found Clare."

There was a pause. The male policeman cleared his throat, "I'm sorry. Clare had hung herself."

There was a pause, which still goes on in my life, an echo, a voice, "Geoffrey. Geoffrey? Geoffrey!"

The two officers left. They informed me there would be an inquest in the coming weeks.

An Inquest? A court case? I would be expected to attend and state my bit, whatever that was.

I also had the funeral to arrange. There was nobody else in the family to help. The father of her daughter wanted no part of it.

He had been no help at all during Clare's periods of depression. He wanted to keep his daughter as far from the trauma as he could. Fair enough.

But the trauma was her Mother. Now it was too late. Forever was too late.

Hindsight is a cruel thing, of course we didn't know that Clare would finally succeed. I presume most of her close friends would have thought like me that it was a cry for help, to resolve the issues surrounding Clare leaving her daughter. I was sure she would get better. But that was the Clare I knew, not the person submerged under all those anti depressants. I had read the list of side effects on the leaflet that came with her meds. 'May cause suicidal tendencies. Disorientation.' What. What? What!

I would learn later that the deepest period of the depression is not always the most dangerous. It is as people get better that it becomes risky, as they suddenly find the strength to go through with it.

I was angry that Dr L had let her out. Why had the friend gone out to work? Hadn't Dr L specified clearly enough, 'Do not let Clare out of your sight.'

It seems she had been making progress. It seems she had been looking forward to the visit. It seemed something had gone dreadfully wrong that morning. It seemed a lot of things too late.

I managed to get Sheila to contribute to the funeral. She agreed but I had to pay back anything over a limit she set. Which I did in the end after she wrote to remind me. It was in that letter I discovered she had bought, 'Clare's little house,' for her.

I had been the Celebrant at a few funerals by then but this was going to be the hardest. It had to be me to do it. Nobody knew her as I did, as a child and our family history. I prepared the Order of Service.

A week or two later we gathered at the appointed hour. I watched the hall fill up with all the colourful characters she had known. At the back, in black, was Sheila with her two daughters. They stayed for the Service, then quickly left in some Hummer like tank with blacked out windows. Just about summed it up to me, seen and yet unseen. I expect they were quietly horrified by it all. The junkie brother burying the suicide sister.

I remembered David's funeral, the Order of Service which mentioned three daughters...No son.

Despite that dark cloud I felt only genuine sympathy and sorrow from Clare's friends and our cousins. We had all lost such a lovely person, a mother, a sister, a friend and a Gardener of Eden.

As I drove back after the Wake I felt only bleakness. I was hoping the funeral might salve my busted heart, however seeing all those beautiful people who loved her, or worked with her, only made it seem all the more awful.

The whole event also brought my mother's death back to me. This circle of time, this tragic flaw in the wheel that had rolled around for thirty three years, until it came to rest at the same place, on suicide.

At least I had Maud. She was, as always, just perfect. She bolstered me up from every angle and never was recriminating or spoke an ill word to me about my fucked family, my debts, my drug habits. Naturally, she desperately wanted me to get off. She could see my life falling apart, but she had always deferred to my right to do and to be as I wished, without any protest.

However, that didn't stop her worrying that Clare's death might precipitate my own demise; my drug habit at that time looked like it was going down a One Way road to Hell. She wasn't the only one who had considered that and when Saffron asked her to help she had the impetus.

They decided between them to do an 'Intervention.' These became popular with Detox Units as a way of getting friends and family to encourage a junkie to get through the door. Stage One.

I was in the back garden at Windsong when I heard a car pull up. As I walked round and saw Saff's face I knew something was going on. I also immediately thought for some strange reason, 'They've come to do an Intervention.' Nobody had ever done such a thing before with me, so how I knew it was coming I don't know.

We went in and Maud began, "We want you to try to come off the drugs Geoff. We're both worried."

Saffron added, "Look, I know it's hard, with Clare's death and everything but we don't want to lose you too. I've found a Detox place in Luton that will take you for twelve weeks. I've got a loan from the bank for nine thousand pounds to pay for it."

I didn't need to hear any more. I was floored, so touched that my daughter, who was struggling with money like us all had done that.

I agreed.

But, I wanted to do it my way. There was no chance I would accept my daughter paying to clear up a pile of crap I had created of my own volition.

They both insisted I call this place, at least to hear what they had to say. I did. I wasn't reassured. They wanted all the money up front. No refund. If I stayed for two days, it was still nine grand. Knowing the relapse rate I thought, 'Yeah, how many people pay all that for a shit weekend in Luton. Luton? Luton!'

The guy on the phone argued, "But come on Geoff, how much money do you spend on drugs a week, a month? How much will you spend over the next year?" He was good. There's no reply to that. How much money have I spent over thirty seven years on drugs? I'd guess a fair to middling small fortune.

I thanked him for trying to convince me and put the phone down. I looked at the two most important women in my life, I felt Clare and Norma there too. It was do or die time. "Ok. This is what I'll do…"

Unfortunately, before anything could happen the inquest was due and I had been asked to attend.

I was in a state. My habit, if anything had increased over recent weeks and I had a stack of Credit Cards paid off with the remortgage to use. Boy were they happy for me to be spending again. My credit limits were upped even more to five figure sums.

Temptation and desperation make one hell of a dynamic duo.

I thought about the Inquest. Another Court Case. I just couldn't get my head, or my heart, round it. I persuaded myself, 'What? Were we going to get a 'Not Guilty' verdict at the end? Will the Judge say 'Sorry it's all been a big mistake,' Clare is going to be waiting outside?'

What could I tell them anyhow. We came from a family with a mother who committed suicide when we were young. We never quite got over that or through it, or whatever one is supposed to do about it. Maybe write a book about it, so maybe it will mean something to somebody, or stop somebody else making the wrong decision. Game over. We had both done the best we could to piece it all together and then David had died. Then, we only had each other. We lived far apart and I am a junkie who can't leave for the weekend without towing a pharmacy round behind me. It was all just awful, dreadful, sorrowful. Shit. Shit? Shit!

It was as if we were both driven by that disaster. I kept running to stop from falling for years and Clare just went from one Port and Brandy in a storm to the next. Underneath everything was our mother. It took me years to get Clare to stop wearing only black. I bought her colourful scarves every birthday and Christmas until she found the light again. From then she was a patchwork of rainbows.

I love her.

I didn't go to the inquest.

It was hopeless. Hope less.

I was booked on a flight a day or so after for Corfu. I was going for four weeks, two alone and then my belle would join me and Saff for the final week.

I was taking one credit card, American Express. No money. The room was paid. The Taxi was paid. They took me to the airport. No going back.

I had about fifty Codeine to get me from home to Arillas. I had done half of them by the time I made the Departure Lounge. In the taxi I made him stop so I could get a Coke. I quietly munched the rest as we crossed the island, finally descending towards the seaside. It looked beautiful.

I was sweating. It was hot. However, inside I was starting to freeze. One day without any smack had already started the withdrawal. I was fighting it off until I got to my room. George, a Greek friend in the village had sorted me out a room. It was cheap and near the sea, but also on the road the mopeds took when they were hurrying home after the clubs and restaurants shut.

The noise didn't bother me. I wasn't going to be sleeping anyway. I told George the score and he was cool with that. He was pleased to see me as always. I had entertained the locals in the bars and on the beach with my guitar on several occasions and was affectionately known as, 'You crazee Englishman.'

I had a system, a basic plan for each day. Arillas, apart from its beautiful residents, has one advantage over any other resort I have come across as regards trying to detox, at one end of the beach it has cliffs made of grey, hard mud, when mixed with water it makes a soft paste which can be rubbed all over the body. As that part of the beach is also the 'Anything goes, nudist bit,' I could have a joint, cover every inch of my body and then bake in the hot sun for half an hour.

Lying there, covered in mud is very primeval; it also makes for some great holiday pics. However the main benefit is it sucks the toxins out of the body, through the skin and lymphatic drainage system. Diving into the sea a plume of grey ash explodes in the water. I knew the quicker I could get the heroin out of my system and all the accumulated by products the faster the journey across the ice would be. I just wondered how deep that crevasse was going to be. For it was out there, waiting for me. I knew that for certain. I'd seen the view from above so many times before.

So, twice each day I was going to stagger to the beach, do the mud, sunbathe, swim; get a coffee from George's Crepe Cafe, where Cosmic Smiles was often playing on his CD player. Later I would get back to my room. I had to cook spaghetti and red sauce each day and get it down me. Try to keep it down. I had just enough money for food.

That evening I began sneezing, eyes watering and feeling like my life just went down the toilet. Over the years I had felt the change in the detox process as my body became less able to rid itself of the drugs. It took longer and longer each time to reset. I had no idea how bad this one was going to be. Very few junkies ever snorted the stuff; generally smoking or injecting heroin were the most common ways. I had felt that snorting it couldn't be so bad. I was totally wrong about that.

The problem with the timescale was it drew out the sleepless nights into weeks. After a few weeks with no decent sleep a brain does start to go really mad. It desperately reaches out to find some idea, some hope to cling to, however mad it may be. It was the end of August. I didn't know then my first night of decent sleep wouldn't be until mid February. I had no idea the Monkey on my back had turned into an Elephant that summer.

I sat on the bed. I got up. I walked to the window. The street below began to light up with the evening, people were enjoying their holiday, going to eat, have drinks, dance, make love. A happy normal life.

I felt like I did the day in the plane with Alan, waiting to crash land, looking down at the boats on the sunny estuary, the glint of cars by the beaches and knowing I just could not get down there to join them.

I went to the table and rolled a fag. I stuck a bit of grass in. I opened the shutter. The noise from below hit me like a Marshall Stack. I shuddered. I lit the joint and puffed the smoke out through the small gap. It mingled with the smell of Greek Cuisine and danced off into the stars. I stuck the butt in a coke can. I sat down. I stood up. I walked to the window. I went to the desk. I sat down. I stood up. I walked slowly to the window. My hand looked old as it drew back the catch. The noise was loud. I breathed the smell. I closed the shutter. I went to the desk. I hid the baccy and grass in the drawer. I went back to the bed. I lay down. I got up. I lay down. I got up. I lay down. I turned to the wall. I turned to the door. The heat and the cold clammy sweat covered my back. I took off my vest, sling onto the floor and lay on the cold marble. For a second it felt good. But it was cold. I had to stand up. It felt like raising a marble monument to get up. I sat on the edge of the bed. I stood up. I lay down on the cool marble again. I crawled slowly to the toilet. I sat there, waiting to puke up or crap out my life.

Every cell in my body had one thought, one thought only, 'Where the fuck is the heroin?' Even the word as it ran through my thoughts clashed like twenty large cooking pots falling to the floor. I stared at the pattern on the floor. I thought about Clare. My heart went nuts. My hands were clenched. Tears that had been frozen underground burst through the surface, fresh springs unleashed.

I washed my face, it stared at me like a stranger. I went back to the bed, sheets damp and limp. I lay my hands against the wall, it sweated. I turned over and looked at nowhere. I got up. I lay on the floor. I got on the bed. It was still early, maybe nine o'clock. I hadn't even got to midnight. How bad could it be? How far down the ice wall? I rolled off the bed and lay on the marble floor. It busted against my bones.

Fuck. I was alone.

My flight home wasn't due for another four weeks. I couldn't escape. I was in solitary confinement in the middle of a beautiful holiday resort.

I waited until the cold began to burn. I used the bed leg to pull myself up. I lay back the other way. The white sheets were twisted into vines, snaking over the mattress. I let them strangle my limbs. I turned to the wall. I looked at the window. It was night now. The blue sky was black above and coloured with the shop lights below. I was marooned between the two.

The plan was to eat each day. I figured maybe best to start that tomorrow. I lay back down on the cold fists of the floor.

An expanse of ice below me and before me. How far it reached over the horizon I didn't know. I did know I had to start walking. If I stayed where I was I would die in my frozen footsteps. It may take years but I would die a junkie; my galleon trapped in pack ice, drifting with the currents north and south, to pointless west and meaningless east, a frenzied trapped shadow in shadow of the midnight sun.

I could feel the Pack Ice squeezing my hull, gripping the prow, my brow bolted down with ice picks. The sound of the ice wailing, the tears and cries of past voices, trapped like me in this vacant wasteland. In the distance the roar of rogue waves smashing into the cliffs of icebergs, diving beneath, pummelling the broken ice into walls of rolling white waves.

By midnight my stomach was crawling. The pain is like being winded. Staring at the toilet. It feels like I need to throw up. But there was nothing inside me, except misery, to chuck up or choke on.

There was no sleep, other than passing out from sheer exhaustion, somewhere between the bed and the floor. But then I would have the most vivd dream about scoring some gear. There it was in my hand, three, four, maybe five wraps, but as I tried to take it, I woke up.

Waves and rushes of sexual feeling flushed through me. Having been submerged for so long they soared like Icarus and burnt in the flames of flickering night. Again, again and again I ejaculated seconds of relief as the body clung to that emotion for a few seconds before it fell back, panting, breathless into the iced water. Then back to twisting, turning, smoke a fag, put it out, roll a joint, smoke it, stub it out next to the other dead one.

Lie on the floor, press the wall, get up, sink down, slip back between the ice floes like a Seal trying to escape ten Orcas, knowing I was firmly gripped in their uncaring teeth. It was about three o'clock now.

The last of the village mopeds were screaming up the hill on their way home to a normal life. Soon the blissful resort of Arillas would snore amongst the lull of Cicadas, with only me awake and dying with the aroma of Fig trees drifting across the stars.

The silence only made the noise of the Tempest in me louder, the unearthly cries from the buckling ice beyond, warning me that worse was to come. The weight of all those years of 'snow,' brown and white, was hammering against my spine with the screech of daemons possessed with the unpossessed.

Maybe five o'clock now. Light is beginning to break somewhere beyond the line of my sight. A Cockerel calls out and the first dog barks, then the next and then the next, as if some roll call is being carried out, dog by dog. The black between the shutters is now grey. I'm crawling over the bed, back to the floor. Stand up, sit down, roll a fag, smoke it, stub it, bin it, do it all again and again. nEXt. nEXt? nEXt!

Perhaps six o'clock now. The first moped returns down the hill. A little later a lorry. I hear a door open and shut. A cough. Somebody shouts at a dog. The bed looks exhausted, the floor is worn out, the table legs are scarred and weak at the knees. I have a fag. I lie down on the cold heat of the hard soft marble.

I stand up.

I sit.

I lie.

Past seven o'clock by now. A small shop must be opening, not too far away. I hear two Greek voices, an old man and a boy, their Flip Flops clatter across the sandy pavements of dawn.

Nine o'clock? The sun is up. The heat is squeezing in through the doors and windows, running sweaty palms over my body. I have a plan. I must stick to it. I have to go to the beach. Feeling half dead I want to avoid the living people. I wondered how I looked. I must have exuded an air of utter hopelessness.

That's how I felt.

I was broken.

I was busted.

I had a shower, put on clean shorts and filled my beach bag. I quietly walked down the hall and out. The white sun blinded me. I headed away from the road and took a track than ran down the side of the flats towards the beach. There was a man up ahead. I tried to follow him, keeping up his pace as I wasn't sure if I was walking too slow, too fast, too left, too much to the right, my legs were so exhausted, my brain was begging me, 'Give up. Give up? Give up!'

The beach was empty. I turned and walked slowly towards the grey cliffs, until I reached the part cut off by fallen lumps of clay and plants. I found a spot.

I unpacked my beach bag and spread out my towel trying to look like a normal tourist. I didn't.

I collected a few handfuls of mud. I found a broken plastic bottle and dissolved the lumps in seawater. I stirred it with a shard of bamboo. I waited for awhile as it began to settle and dissolve. Then I began to spread the mixture over my legs and chest. I lay down on the sand and cooked in the morning sun.

Inside myself the motionless, muddy body turned to the left, then the right, then I got up, then I lay down again. Eventually I threw myself in the sea. Fuck! It was so cold. I hadn't an endorphin left to my name and despite being mid summer every lick of the sea was like a Polar Bear's tongue.

I lay there all day, baking, occasionally rolling a joint and hoping it would knock me out. It didn't. I only felt worse. Dope is not the best thing for a detox, it almost intensifies some of the withdrawals, but then again, it provides a short interlude, a brief distraction of addiction in lieu of the greater addiction.

I had a plan. Before I left the beach I had a second mud wrap and dip in the frozen sea. I walked out up to my chest, then I sank below the blue surface. I opened my eyes, staring at the blurry haze around me.

Then I screamed aloud, "God! You fucking bastard! God! You fucking, fucking bastard! How could you do that? To Clare? God. God? God! You fucking, fucking, fucking bastard." I don't believe in a God as such, some bearded bloke sat on a cloud, but I believe in the concept and I know the Devil so well I can smell his After Shave coming up the road.

I screamed as loud as I could. Trying to get the pain out of me, until, gasping for air, I surfaced; praying nobody had heard me. God. God? God!

I looked across the undulating turquoise expanse at the beach. Nobody had moved, the browning bodies inert, oblivious to the drama drowning out to sea. I took a deeper breath and sank below the surface again. This time I screamed louder and louder, "Fuck you god! Fuck you! Fuck you! You fucking, fucking bastard." I watched little bubbles of 'Fuck' rise to the surface, until my breath expired again. I did this until all the little 'Fucks' dissolved into the sea and I had no voice to scream any more.

Then, slowly, I paddled my way back to the beach. The holiday makers, supine on their towels, didn't budge, nobody seemed to notice me.

I was invisible.

I carried on like this for two weeks. Every day I took the dusty track to avoid the happy crowds gathered in the cafes and bars. I marvelled at the scent of fig trees and the vibrant colours of flowers. These were things I usually missed when I was stoned, the eyes always looking inside, not outside. Each day I blindly followed the legs of some unsuspecting person, like an Arctic explorer in a blizzard to the sea. Every day lying there in the mud. Falling into the ocean. Drifting away from the beach and then sinking beneath the surface. Screaming. Screaming? Screaming!

Later on I would follow another pair of legs back to the room. It was like trying to catch up a sprinter in front of me, every surge of effort left me breathless. But I didn't want to appear broken, busted, beaten, in case somebody stopped to talk to me.

The only person I could cope with was George. He was such a strong, gentle man. His smile and his eyes forgave me everything. I would watch from across the road until the Creperie was fairly quiet and then wander over; ducking past the postcard stands and racks of scarves from the supermarket next door. He would push a coffee and some crepe at me, smiling. As I reached for my bag to pay he would shake his head and wink, "No no, Geeeff, my friend, my dear friend. It's ok."

George had once had a friend like me, a man from the village who sailed the world but brought home the same sickness. I had met him before, but now he was gone. George knew the score.

The coffee would help me get back to the flat for my spaghetti and sauce. Then the sleepless night, twisting like a cornered Cobra, turning, burning, freezing, sweating, lying, sitting, standing. On the bed. On the floor. At the desk. Back to bed. Back to the cold, brutal marble floor. Every morning scraping the nights's sweat off in the shower and then the walk to the beach.

By day ten I had lost any sense of reason.

I lay there for hours and hours trying to work out how I could get from Corfu to Gray in Cheltenham, on one crap Credit Card. Then return again, before anybody knew or Maud turned up. I went through every transaction, making sure it was all possible. Could I get the Tube with a Card? Could I pay the taxi with a Card? In those days, sadly no. I figured a way round that. I figured a way round everything. But in the end as I got up to get the card, I would fall back with sheer exhaustion. It was hopeless, I hardly had the strength to call a Cab, never mind catch a plane.

This is the crucial moment when most detox plans fail, when the man at the Luton Unit takes breakfast up to an empty room, smiles to himself, makes the unmade bed and organises a repair for the broken window catch, while pocketing seven grand for ten days accommodation. Lack of sleep twinned with withdrawals is just too much for any brain to deal with, when it knows the simple answer to all this shit is one little hit, one little fix, one little snort, one little wrap. Surely one won't hurt? If I could have walked fifty miles, barefoot on tarmac, I would have, to get that one hit. However, as much as I considered this, again and again and again, I just couldn't cross two seas as well.

Also the thought of letting Maud and Saffron down was one of the driving forces that kept me going when all I wanted to do was give up. "Kill me now! Fuck. Fuck? Fuck!"

At least Clare and my parents would be there waiting for me. It was simply awful.

Week three. Maud arrived. We moved to a hotel that was quieter, at the far end of Arillas. We did the walk to the beach together. She put up with my frantic moods and shifting desire for sex, then to be alone, then more sex. Alone. Alone? Alone!

Week four, Saffron came. The days were bearable but the nights continued the torture; as if my body could stave off the horror until exhaustion allowed the frozen pack ice back, to press against my hull and seep into my blood.

Somehow, somewhere, between the beach and the sleepless nights I crossed the unseen border. I got back to the safe side of that invisible line again.

We returned to England and I began work again. They were kind to me on the site. Rich and Paul let me wander round in a haze for the first month. Even putting my boots on was a monumental effort. I was so weak I couldn't lift my feet. It was an exhaustion that sucked the lifeblood from every cell.

Coming home I would just lie on the floor inside the kitchen door, like a man who had run a marathon, utterly busted.

Part of the deal with the girls was that on my return I attended Narcotics Anonymous. I had always shied away from doing meetings or seminars; I felt talking about drugs sometimes made the desire worse. Also such places were a haven for contacts to score.

I found the venue in Cheltenham and waited as the room filled up. I was surprised by the mix of people and how many were gathered around the table.

The guy in charge began the meeting with a brief chat and then we all introduced ourselves. My turn came. "Hi, my name is Geoff and I'm an addict...In recovery at the moment."

Such meetings usually have a Guest Speaker who recounts their experience of being an addict. This lasts awhile, then we say something or nothing.

Like anybody else who ever has ever attended such a meeting, I was touched, very touched.

To sit there listening to guys and girls who had been through similar frozen wastelands and made it back to Base Camp was truly humbling.

During the week Maud had arrived in Corfu we had wandered over to San Stefano to visit a lady who made fabulous jewellery from glass. Her name was Perdita and I had commissioned a ring from her. It would be ready in time to take home. It was going to be a reminder forever of that trip...Or perhaps more importantly the trip back. I wore it every time I went to Narcotics Anonymous.

Something else happened while we were in Corfu that was to seal my fate in another way and lead to a great change in my life. It was in San Stefano as we wandered round the usual little supermarkets in such villages we found ourselves standing next to a rack with all the usual foreign Newspapers in it. As I glanced at the headlines, I noticed photos of people queuing up outside some shop or other. I picked up the paper and read it.

Maud was looking at some postcards on the next stand. I called her over, "Hey babe, have you seen this? Looks like some Building Society is in trouble. Everybody is trying to get their money out. Weird?"

The firm was called Northern Rock and the rest is history. As well as the debt ridden oceans we had sailed and the ice that had crushed my crippled ship we now drifted up against the cliffs of Northern Rock and what was left of our pretty little cottage was battered to bits in the ensuing storm of financial recession.

It would take six years to crush the bow, but after three years I watched all the joy drain out my belle's eyes. Despite the temporary relief it had given, our remortgage now needed paying every month.

Maud was learning the hard lesson that property ownership can be a brutal weight to carry. We were sinking into the darkness of debt again.

On one of our camping trips to Wales I watched her return from the toilet block, walking up the field with the woes of the world on her back. This was never what I intended to bring into anybody's life, let alone the woman I loved.

The house had always been my deal, my problem, my responsibility. Now we shared it and she couldn't manage. It was still my problem.

I can imagine the concern of Maud's friends as she recounted what it was like living with an addict. I can only apologise that I brought this shadow into their lives; I never thought in the early days that Maud and I would last twelve months never mind that many years and in the early days my daemon was not so active. Perhaps watching 'Trainspotting,' on that first date was an omen. Perhaps a lot of things.

If I have any defence it is somewhere in the story line of this book. I never woke up one sunny day and thought, 'I know, today I'm going to fuck up my life,' or, 'My next best career move is becoming a smack addict.' Shit happens, those vicissitudes of fate that appear unannounced and break our hearts.

If I have any purpose in writing this book it is to prove that survival is possible, against all the odds; even after decades trapped in the shifting ice flows a frozen heart can be rescued to live and love again.

Despite the eternal temptation and financial woes I managed to stay clean, though I smoked dope like a Jamaican chimney on fire. However, as I finish this final, final edit of nEXt, I managed to knock that on the head, or perhaps out of my head at last. After fifty years of drug abuse I am now completely clean. Maybe somewhere inside my heart I feel I have paid my price, I have grieved all I could for those I have loved and lost. I have served my sentence. Perhaps writing this book also helped. I recommend it as therapy for the Past and as hope for the Future.

We had survived the 'Noughties,' but the decade to come demanded a new start. I didn't want Maud to be dragged down with me again; to sink this time under the ice shelf of ever increasing debts and ever decreasing credit facilities, as the banks tightened their reins on wild horses like me.

So, I let her go. We planned it like adults. She left at the beginning of February. With her departure, even my tenuous attempts to pay some of the debts their monthly quota was buggered. I was on a one way road to homelessness, again.

I spent thirty four months not paying the mortgage we had set up. Anybody who has had the misfortune to miss a month or two on their rent or mortgage knows what kind of shit was flying through my letter box and down my phone. In the end, because it never really stops, even after the house was gone, so I didn't answer a direct call for about ten years. That shut them up.

Meanwhile, every month I expected to be my last.

I purposely avoided any proper relationship during those years, knowing full well my ship was on the verge of breaking up at any moment. I wasn't about to enrol any new crew for that.

Then, standing on the broken ice flows one fine day, I watched as my ship eventually sank.

On May 18th, 2013, I left Windsong forever.

My new home was a turquoise Toyota Hiace, albeit, with a brass bedstead in the back, it was still a van.

I had decided there was only one thing which would recompense me for the loss of my castle, which was to return to the sea, the Great Mother, the one who always looked after me.

The beach at Llangennith was my haven, for I've always felt if I stayed long enough playing by the sea, under the grey scudding clouds of the late afternoon, that as I walked back up the beach I would find the place where my parents and now Clare waited for me, forever, always, watching over me.

I would stop and sit down by an empty towel on the deserted beach and feel for her fingers, pressed in the sand, into the palm of my hand.

The End.

Geoff Smiles.
Llangennith.

From Hither to Laugharne

On a day like this, you could walk,
 from Hither to Laugharne;
Across Dylan's salted marshes,
 where the Samphires swarm,
Their corduroy voices, recalling
 one, long, childish afternoon.
Yet, as skyfall brings the tide
 to buckle breaking full,
You would need to swim for your life,
 to cross that silken pall,
To land your feet in the Messiah's mud,
 beneath his vacant hut.

However, from hither my eyes
 study the serpent's glide,
Her silvered back, diamond black,
 cuts the underbelly of night,
Her flickering tongue,
 mercurial in the first starlight.

I burn in sunsets, with the words
 of forgotten verses, remembered.
Faces in silk silhouette, pressed
 like leaves into pages of regret,
Blind drunk horizons, dancing,
 towards Dylan's death.
Mourning nights are ushered
 towards the pew drop dawn,
As his silent desk, fattened with verbs
 and nouns, awaits the Poet's choice.

2014

Quilted Tides

The tall ships lie harbour side
Awaiting the call of Neptune,
From his bed of quilted tides.

The broken seas with their elephant snores
Chatter in suburban murmurs as they
Clock in and out upon the sandy shore.

Within the reeds and long grasses far beyond
The Gauguin dreams of a blue eyed prophet
Tumble on the leaded verses of pencil thought.

Such knowledge labours whale like
On the searching shoulders of youth
Until the lashes of time lighten his load.

This labour is divined in a universe
Of circles within the circle of circles,
Inside which he stalks the meaning.

Pausing onboard a wooden dream
As it drifts with a cargo of clues
Sinking into view on a blue blue sea...

As the tall ships lie harbour side
Awaiting the call of Neptune
From his bed of quilted tides.

1991

The Violet Hours

Sometimes it's hard to find
The words you want to say,
There's a thorn crushed deep inside your heart
Bears witness, to the day, the day you left, far behind.

Roses scattered on the fire
Smoulder incense on the violet hours,
The flames dance the devil's song
Through your heart, all night long, all night long.

Ashes of the dawn, coal black,
Simmer in the embers of our love,
The North wind begins to blow and
The candle burns, in the sorrow, of the dark.

Time alone keeps its course
It flickers in the pale lamplight,
Beckons forth our memories
As shadows mingle, in the quiet, of the night.

I've lived my life in scrapbooks
With the songs that I sing,
Caught by flights of fantasy they echo,
In my mind, in my heart, in my soul.

Sometimes it's hard to find
The words you want to say,
There's a thorn crushed deep inside your heart
Bears witness, to the day, the day you left, far behind.
  1990

The Last Rose

Sapling Spring thrust her green fingers
Through the earthen clay of Winter,
Fostered her children to the fields and forests
As Summer warmed the wombs of Mother Nature.

Our hearts gave succour to their growth
We raised our silken spirits to theirs
Growing with the climbing rose
We meandered through the seasons.

Now Autumn's hands, weatherbeaten and hardy,
Have culled the weaker petals from their buds,
Leaving their fleeting beauty to wither beneath
The frosty glaze of approaching Winter

Yet one Rose has sustained its heart
Against the anguish of Autumnal moods
Wrapped in blankets of pink and red petals
It holds the love we share throughout all.

1988

Wintermere

Beyond this lake of evensong
The hammer of rock lies black
A sullen corpse, grown cold
As fox's blood dashed upon the
Wasteland of winter's old age.

Crackling and snatching the bracken
Growls up at passing bootsteps,
Laced by flat thumb fingers
On bended autumn knees.
The errant whistle of man
Issued from broken dreams to
The northern winds, winds up the
Hillside at dusk, seeking adventure.

In retreat a boat mourns the dreaded hours,
Its wake entrusted to the moonshine of
Waves within the eyes of an old man.
Upon the barque of shadow
Three fingers ply their silver threads
Casting doubt to the reflections of worth,
Fishers of manna and sky.

The rock attends time in handfuls
Grasping centuries in its fisted knuckles
Crushing wrinkled decades in crinkled waves.
A man covets the grain of sand
That ebbs in the palm of his mind,
Until it slips gently from his hand
As the tideless lake flows into night.   1985

Tapestries

In satin hours of rosewood mystery
The owl call of midnight beckons me,
To an ebony womb of darkness
As the ivory tusk of moondusk rises.

In our bower of stolen hours
Clutched from the hands of time,
We tread a course of threaded discourse
Weaving our tapestries of life together.

Sharing secrets like antique trinkets
Plucked from inlaid boxes of memory,
We wander across each other's minds
Through the cobwebbed museum of yesterday.

In such moments of shared perception
With the palm of my mind held in yours,
I see my book of days open at a new page
And find your name already written there.

1989.

BV - #0010 - 280324 - C0 - 210/148/29 - PB - 9781399982504 - Gloss Lamination